BEYOND INDUSTRIALIZATION

BEYOND INDUSTRIALIZATION

Ascendancy of the Global Service Economy

Ronald Kent Shelp

PRAEGER SPECIAL STUDIES • PRAEGER SCIENTIFIC

Library of Congress Cataloging in Publication Data

Shelp, Ronald K.
    Beyond industrialization.

    Bibliography: p.
    Includes index.
    1. Service industries. 2. Industry and state.
I. Title.
HD9980.5.S45   338.4′7   81-4505
ISBN 0-03-059304-2   AACR2

Published in 1981 by Praeger Publishers
CBS Educational and Professional Publishing
A Division of CBS, Inc.

521 Fifth Avenue, New York, NY 10175 USA
© 1981 by Praeger Publishers
All rights reserved

123456789 145 987654321
Printed in the United States of America

ACKNOWLEDGMENTS

This book was originally commissioned as part of the 1980s Project of the Council on Foreign Relations. Thus, although it is being published independent of the council, its development was strongly influenced by the dedicated, untiring, and strong-minded views of those on the council staff involved in the 1980s project studies.

Not surprisingly, I consider the council's interest in undertaking a study on the implications of services for the world economy a wise one, consistent with the 1980s project belief that many of the assumptions, policies, and institutions that have characterized international relations during the past 30 years are inadequate for the demands of today, much less the next few decades. The subject of services, like many other 1980s project studies, will be an issue of major international concern for at least the next 10 to 20 years. Here, as elsewhere, there will need to be substantial adaptation of institutions and behavior to respond to changed circumstances.

This book grew out of my professional interest in international commerce in services. I have been fortunate to be closely involved with the development of services as an issue from its quiet inception beginning with the inclusion of service provisions in the U.S. Trade Act of 1974. By 1977, with little visible progress evident from this congressional initiative, it became obvious that the international consensus necessary to move this subject onto the international agenda would never occur until a conceptual framework was constructed.

This study is an attempt at helping to build this framework. The broad sweep of the book—and the resultant generalizations that inevitably follow from such an ambitious approach—has produced many weaknesses that are very obvious to the author. Hopefully, the benefits of drawing attention to the broad-ranging implications of services and stimulating further substantive research and analysis into the many subjects touched on in this book outweigh the disadvantages of this approach.

The lack of attention that has been given to services was both a handicap and an asset. While the lack of data and the absence of a theoretical foundation or general body of knowledge on services were a severe limitation, the very absence of preconceived notions had its advantages. To an unseasoned academic, the benefits of not being intimidated by what the experts think cannot be overstated. It is much easier to prepare oneself for criticism when that criticism must be directed solely to the merits of the work at hand—and not judged against the established dogma on the subject.

Any effort to recognize all who helped with this book is doomed from the beginning. I have taken full advantage of the wisdom of those I have been fortunate enough to encounter during the process of preparing this book. Many are not even aware they helped, since often the nature of our encounter did not directly relate to this subject matter. But the variety of individuals—from governments, businesses, academia, research institutions, and other interests—who have enriched my thinking is plentiful. Only those who have been more directly involved in the fostering of this issue will probably see reflections of their thinking and our discussions in this study.

Throughout this process the encouragement and guiding hand of Edward L. Morse, Executive Director of the 1980s Project of the Council on Foreign Relations at the time the study was commissioned, were constant. Even after departing the council for government service, he maintained an active interest until the study was finalized. His successor, Catherine Gwin, was equally supportive and helpful in shaping the development of the book. The other two council staff members intimately involved with critiquing and reviewing this study, William Diebold, Jr., and Helena Stalson, unfailingly offered important and incisive criticism as the book passed through several drafts. Council editors Tom Wallin and Robert Valkenier edited the manuscript. Besides putting it in excellent shape for publication, they achieved the more difficult task of helping make the subject matter manageable.

I received excellent research assistance from several sources. June Mueller Peno did a commendable job of uncovering and analyzing data on services in socialist countries. She also helped research the role service issues played in the founding of the International Trade Organization and abstracted the history of thinking on a General Agreement on Tariffs and Trade (GATT) for Investment and related ideas. Richard Lehmann was diligent in the difficult task of developing data on services in the developing countries and provided excellent advice on how to shape various concepts. Steven Samson was untiring in updating the data on services in industrial countries. Eva S. Cantwell provided invaluable research and editorial assistance from beginning to end. Finally, the late Dr. Joseph D. Peno helped guide me through the difficult realm of economic theory and services.

As already stated, many in government, or once in government, influenced my thinking, but a special tribute is due Geza Feketekuty, Assistant U.S. Trade Representative for Policy, for his conceptualization of this complex issue and his unique ability to develop a strategy to deal with services in the international arena.

I was fortunate to participate in a series of seminars and conferences relating to services. The enforced discipline that preparation for such sessions engenders and the beneficial interchange that often resulted were of immeasurable value. Of special benefit were the Ditchley Conference on services in May 1980 and the research seminars funded by the German Marshall Fund and the Rockefeller Foundation at the Aspen Institute at Wye Plantation, Maryland (March 1980), and the Trade Policy Research Centre in London (June 1980). The latter institution, under the direction of Hugh Corbet, has consistently been ahead of the game in anticipating international issues. Services is no exception.

The centre pinpointed services as a coming international issue in the early 1970s and has carried out a work program on services ever since.

I have had the rare opportunity shared by but a few who have prepared theoretical studies advocating policy prescriptions: the chance to help implement the policies proposed. In this regard, I am especially indebted to the U.S. Chamber of Commerce for establishing its International Service Industry Committee and designating me as chairman. This provided a unique opportunity for me to work closely with my fellow colleagues in other service industries, along with distinguished academics and former senior government officials, in developing and pushing for a broadly conceived work program on services.

I am grateful to my employer, American International Group, and especially its chief executive, M. R. Greenberg, for an abiding interest in this subject. Without such encouragement, I could not have participated in the wide range of activities that broadened my knowledge and influenced my thinking on this subject.

Nevertheless, out of admiration and respect for those who have helped, I alone accept responsibility for the final product. Although many deserve credit for what is right, they should not be held accountable for the result.

CONTENTS

LIST OF ACRONYMS

AIMU	American Institute of Marine Underwriters
APESC	Asia-Pacific Economic and Social Commission
ASEAN	Association of Southeast Asian Nations
CACM	Central American Common Market
CARECOM	Caribbean Common Market
COMECON	Council for Mutual Economic Assistance
DISC	Domestic International Sales Corporation
ECOSOC	Economic and Social Council (United Nations)
EEC	European Economic Community
FASC	Federation of ASEAN Shippers' Council
FCN	Friendship, Commerce, and Navigation (Treaties of)
FTO	foreign trading organization
GATT	General Agreement on Tariffs and Trade
IACA	International Air Carriers Association
IATA	International Air Transport Association
ICAO	International Civil Aviation Organization
ILO	International Labour Organisation
IMCO	International Maritime Consultant Organization
IMF	International Monetary Fund
ITO	International Trade Organization
ITU	International Telecommunications Union
LAFTA	Latin American Free Trade Association
MFN	most favored nation
MPS	Material Products System
NFTC	National Foreign Trade Council
OAU	Organization of African Unity
OECD	Organization for Economic Cooperation and Development
SDR	special drawing rights
SIC	Standard Industrial Classification
SPBEC	South Pacific Bureau for Economic Cooperation
TDF	transborder data flow
UNCTAD	United Nations Conference on Trade and Development
UNDP	United Nations Development Program

BEYOND
INDUSTRIALIZATION

1

THE POLITICAL ECONOMY
OF SERVICES

Political power in today's world no longer reflects economic reality. Although most of the dominant economic powers are service economies, neither national nor global political structures manifest this fact. This development is not unprecedented. History is replete with parallel situations.

The rise of a merchant class preceded the transformation from a feudal system to a nation-state configuration. The latter political development was hastened, partially, as a response to the demands of this new economic power—the merchants. A political construct had to be devised to meet their needs: a transportation network enabling travel from feudal center to feudal center, a juridical/police system to ensure safety, and a monetary framework to facilitate trade. Later, as societies changed from agricultural to industrial economies, the political power of the paramount economic interest—the landed gentry—was eventually weakened in order to accommodate the needs of the new economic power: the industrialist. For example, we recall the struggle in England over the use of land: grazing rights versus industrial sites. The capitalist class ultimately prevailed—a fact unmistakable in the legislative and administrative policies of this era. But the success of the new industrialists depended on a viable, productive working class. As in the past, however, the economic importance of the working class was not immediately translated into political clout. It required a potent and organized labor movement to bring this about. The union movement ultimately became a political force that commanded the enactment of a broad legislative program and left a legacy of influence that continues until the present day.[1]

Ultimately, in each of these instances, political reality caught up with economic reality. The dominant economic players of each period eventually became the political power brokers whose voices were heard in determining the themes that dominated national and international agendas. But in each instance, the time required for political consciousness to be sensitized to changing

1

economic circumstances directly bore on the ability to integrate new conditions into policy formulation with a minimum of disruptiveness. This is equally true today.

The predominant economic interest in many nations today—the service sector—has yet to translate its economic prevalence into political power. As a result, social, economic, and political frictions are beginning to surface because of divergences between the interests of the traditional political forces and the service sector. A growing array of issues that must ultimately become the concern of public policy is presently being ignored, although, admittedly, a clear statement of these issues is yet to be made.

The overriding reason service interest concerns have not yet surfaced in political consciousness parallels earlier historical experience: it has failed to organize itself as an effective political force able to compete with other well-entrenched economic interests. The United States is the only service economy where there are perceptible bare beginnings of a self-identity on the part of the service sector—an identity that transcends the parochial concerns of each individual industry and moves toward a more cohesive appreciation of mutual self-interest. But even in the United States, however, this movement is in its infancy. To succeed, it must unify with sufficient conviction to forcefully address the concerns arising out of the common threads its members share.

Even then, the obstacles will be formidable. Not only are competing interests well established, but their power is grounded in a philosophic standard that enjoys broad international acceptance. This can best be countered by putting forth a persuasive apology for this new economic activity—perhaps nothing less than a *Das Kapital*[2] for the service society. In this study I will explore in some detail the failure of those who would be expected to perform this gargantuan task, the theoreticians of political economy, to do so. I will suggest that traditional economic analysis has always ignored services—and continues to—even in light of the emergence of a number of major service economies. Perhaps theorists have habitually concentrated for so long on classical capitalism, and its preoccupation with industry and industrial economics, that the coming of political awareness of the service society will precede the establishment of its intellectual foundation. Without doubt, however, the theoretical underpinning eventually will be constructed. How soon that occurs will be a major determinant as to when rational policy formulation takes hold. The foregoing suggests that this book, while detailing the economic reality of the modern service economy, will be equally concerned with the political ramifications of this development.

One factor that frustrates reasoned discourse about services is the difficulty of defining what we are talking about. *Services* encompasses such an enormous and heterogeneous grouping of activities that there is a disposition to dismiss it as a generic concept of little practical meaning. This observation is worth heeding. Dissecting the plethora of activities that constitute this vast category of economic activity into something more meaningful is essential. I would be the last one to suggest that a new political compact will be molded from an amalgamation of the seemingly inexhaustible inventory of activities that fall under the rubric of services: bankers, retail proprietors of every kind, information suppliers, franchisers, insurers, traders, stockbrokers, the learned professions, and so on.

Instead, I am talking about those kinds of service activities that involve production and employment of consequential magnitudes. Further, as the title of this book suggests, these service producers are likely to extend their activities beyond national boundaries and become active competitors in the international marketplace. This characterization brings certain services immediately to mind: air and maritime transportation, financial services such as banking and insurance, construction and engineering, tourism, and motion pictures. But the dynamic changes occurring in services, described later, suggest the deficiency of the too obvious. The revolution underway in services will foster new forms, yield new sources, and produce new services.

It is here that the traditional international services will find allies to form a new constituency that will shape tomorrow's public policy debates. This constituency, once organized, will leave its mark on the policy process. Its concerns will compete with traditional interests for attention. The implications of this development are of such dimension that broad and extensive public discussions will be unavoidable. It will of necessity sweep across a broad range of policy areas. A change that imports such a fundamental alteration of economic and political power will result in intensive and acrimonious debate. But the shift to service economics, and how that is likely to be perceived by many powerful interest groups, may sharpen the inevitable conflicts even more than usual. The perception of many will be that they have more to lose than gain.

For example, to most labor union leaders, a society where the majority of workers are found in the service sector is bleak. Those in manufacturing will measure it in terms of job loss, caused in part by the relocation of national plants overseas. Others will despair because of their past failures in organizing services, with but one major exception—the public sector. The traditional power elites of the labor movement, the leaders of manufacturing unions, will find little to rejoice about in the success of their colleagues who succeed in organizing service activities. This can only mean a diminishing of traditional industrial union influence in labor circles.

To industrial, military, and political leaders, a service society connotes the decline of the industrial base, which directly undermines a nation's economic independence and its national security. It raises the specter of the dangers of too much internationalism and provides a persuasive mantle in which to wrap protectionist fears. It reinforces underlying apprehensions about the malevolence of multinational corporations with their alleged ability to relocate at will without consideration of national interest.

To the elected and the professional public servant, the fundamental changes suggested by the emergence of services go beyond the anxieties highlighted above. A confusion will be created that complicates a clear definition of constituent concerns. He will be buffeted between the old forces and the new voices. Those interests on the wane will be better organized, clearer, and more outspoken in their demands. The new service interest bloc will be less cohesive and certainly less articulate in expressing its preferences, partly because of the absence of historical experience in defining what it wants and partly because it lacks a theoretical basis on which to ground its concerns.

One can almost write the script that will be played out in this process. Below I have posed some of the issues that are inevitable—and should be.

Does a society really want to evolve into a service economy? Is this manifestation of the most advanced stage of progress really desirable? What are the implications for the national interest, the standard of living, and a way of life? The issues, despite their importance, have never really commanded public attention or captured the imagination of leaders. Attention and energies are easily diverted to more immediate problems, which, ironically, may be intricately related to the existence of a service economy.

There is one definite implication of a service economy that is only dimly perceived, or at least not well articulated publicly: it is inextricably linked to the international economy. If a society becomes service oriented, by definition it demands and produces proportionally more and more services. This does not mean a cessation of either its demands for or its production of goods. But since the consumption of goods continues to grow as an economy grows, then (barring extraordinary increases in productivity) as a service-oriented nation evolves, more of its needs for goods (especially goods with a high labor input) will be filled from abroad. In short, the evolution of industrial economies into service economies is inherently linked to the increased production of goods in other nations. With this development come increased specialization and changes in the sources of production. This is the one statement most observers would probably accept concerning the international impact of service economies. However, a recurring theme of this study is that there are many other inseparable linkages between service economies and the international economy—linkages that have significant impacts on nonservice economies as well as on service economies.

On its face this hypothesis seems to suggest that services themselves are produced almost exclusively in national markets. At first glance this seems logical, considering our basic assumptions about the nature of services. There would be no reason to obtain services abroad since the process and product can easily be duplicated in any market. Even if it were desirable to buy services overseas, they are by nature difficult to trade because they must be produced in the market where they are used and they cannot be stored. This view, like many other perceptions of service economies, may be fallacious. It must be examined more closely.

If it is indeed true that services only play an insignificant role in international trade, and if the nature of services is such that no nation is likely to obtain or exploit a comparative advantage in their production, then the Cassandras who say that nations that become service economies will go into decline ought to be heeded. A nation cannot possibly expect to buy ever larger shares of its nonservice needs abroad if it has nothing to sell in return. Only by owning overseas production facilities that supply those needs or by producing earnings from overseas investment that can be used for that purpose—something the United States has done most successfully—can a nation hope to afford to be a service economy. But as recent waves of nationalizations have indicated, this is a fragile base on which to build a country's prosperity.

What is doubly alarming about this thesis is that its implications go far beyond pure balance-of-trade considerations. It strikes at the very fiber of a nation, threatening its vitality, strength, and even its national character and way of life. If in the future most of the advanced nations are to center their economic activities around services, generally characterized as being labor intensive, devoid of technology, and lacking economies of scale, this is a bitter pill to swallow. Is this the reward to nations that have attained what is presumably the highest stage of economic development? Will real maturity not imply being "industrialized" but rather being "beyond industrialization"? Will we no longer blithely characterize nations as industrial and undeveloped? Instead, will there be at least three broad categories: service or postindustrial, industrial, and developing?

It is difficult to visualize the postindustrial economy as becoming the ultimate goal of those nations now striving for development. Indeed, will this or the Third United Nations Development Decade proclaim as its objective the achieving of service economies for some percent of the world's countries? Many developing nations, one suspects, will have second thoughts about this being the ultimate goal of their strivings. In fact, perhaps developing countries' perceptions are more incisive than is often perceived since industrialization—not postindustrialization—is their avowed goal. Perhaps postindustrial nations like the United States are too having second thoughts. Witness the current fervor to "reindustrialize America."

One shortcoming of the limited focus that has been given service economies is that it has considered the consequences only from the perspective of developed countries. The implications for others, primarily the developing nations, have been ignored. From that perspective, a multitude of questions immediately arise. Will those developing economies best positioned to take advantage of growth opportunities rapidly switch from debtor to creditor nations as the demand for their natural resources and industrial goods in developed countries accelerates? Will they themselves start evolving into service economies? Will they start investing abroad as industrial nations do? What will be the role of their service sectors? If international trade serves as the engine of development, logically they will have a growing indigenous service sector resulting from industrialization, economic diversification, and greater affluence. But if their primary emphasis is on industrialization, will the need for services be met from overseas, at least initially?

In theoretical terms such a development would complement the structure of the world economy. Service economies would import more goods from other economies than they export, but they would export their services to these developing economies. This, of course, is contrary to some of the traditional views of services and their limited international role. An additional problem with this simplified scheme is that the two leading actors in this drama do not behave as this theory indicates they should. Service economies often protect their industrial and agricultural sectors and are more open toward foreign competition in their service sectors. Developing economies tend to protect both their industrial and service sectors as infant industries. The implications here, however, are more complex than they seem. Service economies seem to find each other the least protective of their respective service sectors and thus more open to foreign penetration. Furthermore, since service economies are the major consumers of services, in both absolute and relative terms, they themselves actually provide the largest potential market for each others' exports of services.

This is a broad-brush treatment of a very complex issue. It fails to distinguish between nations falling within various stages of development, and it neglects socialist or non-market-economy nations whose view of services differs significantly from that of market-based countries. But it does indicate that there are some legitimate and troublesome questions relating to the evolution of the most advanced nations into service economies. We are far from ready to resolve these questions; in fact, it is even doubtful that the questions can be adequately framed at this point. Thus, well-intentioned policy makers attempting to address these issues are tackling a subject that is ripe for popular exploitation but is also entangled with implications which go well beyond what the subject appears to comprise at first glance.

SPECULATION ON THE NATURE OF SERVICE ECONOMIES

The implications of service economies are staggering, especially when the effects on nonservice economies are also kept in mind. A host of conjectures and questions arise. Will a service economy be built primarily on supplying personal services, which are highly consumer oriented and related to more affluence and higher standards of living; or will it be one in which the skills and talents required of most of the labor force are more sophisticated, similar to what is found only in the elite or managerial class in an industrial society? Does it complement the no-growth philosophy many see as a necessity for advanced societies in coming years? Or, on the contrary, does it signal the possibility for continued and even accelerated growth, but without a drain on limited resources? Perhaps a shift to a service economy will reduce the magnitude of cyclic economic fluctuations, since the service sector, generally, is less affected by business slowdowns than is the manufacturing sector.

Will environmental concerns be less pressing in a society where industry is on the wane? What will a world beyond industrialization mean to organized labor? If employment switches from manufacturing, where labor is highly organized, to white-collar service jobs, where the labor movement has been less successful, does this mean that unions will atrophy or will they succeed in organizing the service sector? In the past, when technological advances in industry displaced workers, they often moved into services. Where do workers go if such advances come about in services? Efficiency in manufacturing was an original cause of service sector growth. If services become increasingly efficient, where does that lead us?

Since service industries tend to be labor intensive, are there likely to be shifts in job opportunities with a virtual disappearance of unemployment and poverty? Could this actually lead to labor shortages, with the absorption of minorities, women, and even retired people into the work force? Could it stimulate new waves of immigration into advanced economies to meet these needs? Or will the opposite occur? Do the skills required in a highly complex society reduce the possibilities for unskilled workers? Demographically, do service societies imply a return to a simpler way of life that relies less on urban centers, or will the society be so complex that it involves large numbers of workers and the need for proximity to various factors of production?

Today government is the largest service sector, and many services (communications, transportation, and the like) tend to attract government involvement. Does the development of a service society necessarily mean a larger governmental role in the economy? Or could it entail a decline? As business opportunities in advanced countries move from industry to services, private enterprise might begin to compete effectively with the government in providing postal, health, and even welfare services. What is the consequence for regulation of government-oriented services?

Will technological breakthroughs shift to those societies primarily producing industrial goods so that centers of research and development will move to those countries entering industrialization? Or do services themselves spawn technological advances? There may be a continuing deemphasis on engineering and the physical sciences in advanced countries, with accelerated training in the social sciences and professional fields. In education will the nature of a service society cause a renewed demand for teachers and related professions; and how will the needs of a service society affect university studies? Will new professions and academic disciplines be created that have not yet been conceived?

If service economies are indeed labor intensive and have low capital requirements, will there be a capital surplus? If so, what does this mean for the service industries now associated with the placement of capital—investment banking, for example? Perhaps surplus nations will invest overseas even more than advanced nations do today, further internationalizing capital markets. It is possible that the growth of services will stimulate the emergence of a plethora of new enterprises, industrial conglomerates that might diversify into services in response to shifting tastes.

In short, a myriad of questions are to be considered, many of which are obviously beyond the scope of this book. These issues provide fertile ground for the efforts of researchers, philosophers, speculators, and corporate planners. The questions raised indicate just how little we know about services and the way they affect the societies in which they are dominant. The little we do know about service economies indicates that the entire concept is intimately linked to the international economy, and as a result, there are policy implications for all nations in the emergence of service-oriented economies.

This study of a world where service activities are increasing in significance is based on a thesis that is derived more from intuition than from tested observation and is hamstrung by the lack of empirical data and theoretical considerations of the subject. It is sixfold:

1. Services in many national economies and in the international economy are more important than is generally recognized and will become more so in the years ahead. Their impact potentially touches on many surprising areas not at all evident on first examination.

2. The nature, functioning, and role of services in national economies and the international economy are not well understood. How they are perceived is often without foundation, permeated with misconceptions and inaccuracies. Traditional theories of economic, political, and social development and of international trade and investment need to be reexamined in the light of their applicability and validity with regard to services.

3. Governments are not prepared to deal with service issues because their growing importance has not been recognized by policy makers. This has occurred because of the failure of the key service industries to present their concerns effectively. Thus the development of national service economies with international links is ahead of the perception of policy makers. Even as this changes, the lack of a theoretical understanding of services combined with data shortcomings will hamper the policy-making process.

4. National policies toward services, when they exist, reflect this general misunderstanding and lack of detailed knowledge of services. These policy shortcomings also are reflected in international policies toward services, when they occur.

5. The unreadiness of our national and international institutions to address the complex issues that will accompany the development of a global economy where service activities play a prominent role will inevitably lead to conflicts. Small skirmishes are already evident. Much larger ones are just over the horizon. Problems of the kind that severely disrupted international commerce in the past are at this point probably unavoidable.

6. Though policy making may not catch up with economic reality soon enough to adapt our institutions to changing circumstances, it is time we begin. Services will be high on national and international agendas for a long time to come whether we are ready to deal with them or not. It will be tragic if a reasoned response is impaired by a failure of preparation.

Throughout this study I will concentrate primarily on the international aspects of service industry issues, although, naturally, domestic issues are inevitably involved. First, I look at the meaning of services. This is followed by a look at the present and projected importance of services in both statistical and non-economic terms. This survey covers industrial, developing, and socialist economies, and considers in broad terms national policies toward services.

Next comes a review of theoretical perceptions of services. Comparisons will be made with the functioning of goods in international commerce, and the validity for services of traditional theories of economic development and international trade and investment will be considered. Following this, I will review the regulation of services, focusing for the most part on the treatment of foreign-supplied services.

In closing I will review past efforts to liberalize the flow of services internationally and then will suggest how liberalization might be undertaken more successfully in the 1980s. Not only will new approaches be prescribed, but the remedies suggested will be built on a conceptual analysis of services that is distinct from previous or even present views.

NOTES

1. For an analysis of evolving economic systems and changing political structure, see Robert Heilbroner, *The Making of Economic Society* (Englewood Cliffs, N.J.: Prentice-Hall, 1975).

2. Karl Marx, *Capital: A Critique of Political Economy*, ed. Frederick Engles, trans. Samuel Moore and Edward Aveling from third German edition, revised and amplified according to fourth German edition by Ernest Untermann (New York: The Modern Library, 1906).

2

THE MEANING AND
SIGNIFICANCE OF SERVICES

I began this study with a fairly clear idea of the meaning of *services*. However, as often happens when one examines a subject in greater depth, the increased awareness of its complexity created confusion where before there seemed to be clarity. The following discussion illustrates some of the difficulties.

In this chapter we look at the international role of services in general and specific terms, attempting to see both the forest and the trees at the same time. The task calls for a patient and detailed analysis of the basic elements of international services. The depth of the analysis is often limited by a lack of data, but, nevertheless, a sharper picture does emerge. This painstaking approach provides the necessary background for the analysis and proposals that are made later.

DEFINING *SERVICES*

Although I can offer no solid definition of *services*, I will attempt to explain some elements of the confusion.[1] There are two common theoretical approaches to defining *services*. The first is based on the output of the production process and emphasizes the intangible nature of service products. The second emphasizes the method of production and defines *services* residually as being those productive activities that are neither manufacturing, mining, nor agriculture. Both of these theoretical abstractions initially seem clear and precise, but problems arise when we try to apply them to reality. The first definition, which emphasizes the intangibleness of the product, is too narrow because some services, such as construction and publishing, do produce tangible goods. The residual definition, on the other hand, is too broad. It does not describe any special characteristic of services but, rather, is a negative classification in that it defines them by what they are not. It is not a true definition. An adequate one, it seems to me, if it were to be formulated, would lie somewhere between the two. The most that can be said at the general level is that *services* encompasses an extremely heterogeneous group of economic activities often having little in common other than that their principal outputs are for the most part intangible products.

Although this definition lacks the elegant precision of tight economic analysis, it is meaningful in that its very vagueness conveys the inherent complexity of the subject. It provides us with an appreciation of some of the problems we will confront. The definitional and related problems become particularly complex at the international level, as illustrated by a few of the most important ones described below.

In this study, I try to gauge the significance of services for national economies as well as their impact at the international level. In doing so, I am forced to rely on the national accounting methods used by these economies. Yet as the Appendix to Chapter 2 discusses in detail, at least three general accounting systems are used by individual nations and international organizations. How they define and classify services is far from consistent. As an example, transport activities would generally be classified simply as a service. However, the United Nations Economic Commission for Latin America treats them as part of basic services, which it includes with goods.

Another difficult problem area concerns how to separate the measurement of services from that of goods. Most goods and services have components of each other involved in their production processes. For example, the production of goods requires various business services and might include building, construction, engineering, employment, equipment leasing, and other services. Conversely, many services require manufacturing processes. For example, air and maritime transportation depend on the use of airplanes, ships, and the sophisticated technology associated with them. The motion picture industry, generally classified as a service, is based on a nonservice productive process.

In measuring the value of the goods ultimately rendered, the cost of the total product includes but does not isolate all service costs that have gone into its production. In the case of a service, valuation is much more difficult. Generally, it is determined by totaling the wages of those involved in producing the service. The associated costs of the goods or the nonservice activities involved in the process are not included. There are, of course, exceptions. For example, trade or retail services are often measured in terms of consumer outlays for goods.

Specific international services are dealt with in the next section in considerable detail. In selecting those to be studied, I chose from the classifications used by the United States in its Standard Industrial Classification (SIC) System and the U.S. National Income Accounts because they approximate those used by other nations. SIC numbers 40 through 90 cover the service sector. These include hotels and other lodging places; establishments providing personal, business, repair, and amusement services; health, legal, engineering, and other professional services; educational institutions; membership organizations; finance, insurance, and real estate (including rent and imputed rent for owner-occupied dwellings); wholesale and retail trade; and general government, transportation, communication, and public utilities. Although some of these services are not very significant internationally, there are very few that do not have some international involvement.

Obviously, there are various ways one might categorize these services. For example, one might create major groupings such as financial and related services; transportation, communications, and public utilities; community and government services; professional services; and personal services. No approach, however, would be totally adequate. For one thing, these approaches do not include service activities other than those provided by a service industry itself so that, for example, a service provided by a manufacturing or extractive firm to its affiliates or nonaffiliates tends to be overlooked. So do new services. However, as we identify the important international services and begin to understand service activities in general, a sense of how best to categorize or organize them to facilitate dealing effectively with service issues should begin to emerge.

There are the possibilities of confusion and honest differences of opinion as to what international services actually include. For example, there is a tendency in balance-of-payments accounting to treat all items falling under invisibles as services. Under invisibles are included (1) government services and transfers and (2) private services, including transportation (mainly shipping and aviation services), travel expenditures, income on investments (interest, dividends, and royalties), private transfers (immigrants' remittances and so forth), and miscellaneous or other services.

It may be appropriate to include some government transfers among services, such as foreign aid to develop public health programs, but food aid or arms transfers, both of which are considered invisibles, are not services. Many also maintain that because investment income is an invisible, it is a service. Although this makes the task of proving the importance of services in the international economy much simpler, it is misleading and erroneous. It in effect equates international investment with services, even if the investment is not in a service industry, or even if the income generated by the investment is not the result of a service activity. Only the revenue flows from a service industry investment or the income attributable to a service activity should be included. So while investment income may be treated as service income in balance-of-payments terms, it should not be treated as a service activity in itself.

My purpose is to examine service industries and service activities. Granted, this is easier said than done; it requires attention to the nuances. For example, many nonservice industries supply services, both domestically and internationally. Whether such services are properly reflected in data as international service transactions is questionable. Certain activities that might not seem to be services should perhaps be so treated. For example, if a manufacturer supplies engineering services to its overseas affiliates, it seems clearly involved in a service transaction. But is the same manufacturer also providing a service when licensing the production of its product and receiving royalty and trademark fees?

This is certainly a gray area, with room for legitimate disagreement. These fees are treated as invisibles or services in balance-of-payments accounting. But so are the earnings from nonservice firms on direct investment overseas. In this study, ideally, I would like to include such transactions if they are generated by what would generally be accepted as a service, while excluding those that are not. But no such clear definitional consensus exists, and the data available fail to make such distinctions. So all that is possible presently is to suggest this ideal, do the best one can with the data available, and hope the exercise helps clarify the problems if not shape solutions.

I now turn to review the significance of services in national economies and international commerce. Following this descriptive exercise, I will try to make sense out of the empirical evidence available on services. Taken alone, the evidence does not necessarily explain what services, especially international services, are all about. Without interpretation, those services on which this study is really meant to focus are lost in the aggregate.

SIGNIFICANCE OF SERVICES

Classical theory describes economies as passing through three stages—agricultural, manufacturing, and services—and often equates levels of development with the stage an economy is in. I have chosen to look at services in various economies by dividing these economies into those which seemingly are developed or developing or in transition between two stages. Obviously, economies seldom fall so neatly into any such classification; nevertheless, many industrial and developing nations superficially seem to fit one of these general patterns and will be treated accordingly.[2] The discussion also examines socialist or nonmarket economies, discussing them as a separate group. This is undertaken not because they are presumed to follow different development patterns but because these economies themselves treat services so differently.

Classical assumptions about the evolution of services lead us to expect services to be highly important in economically advanced economies while relatively insignificant in developing countries. The following analysis provides a test of this hypothesis.

ADVANCED ECONOMIES

United States

On the basis of the accepted definition that a nation becomes a service economy when more than half its work force is employed in producing intangibles,

FIGURE 2.1

U.S. Employment Growth in Services, 1925–75

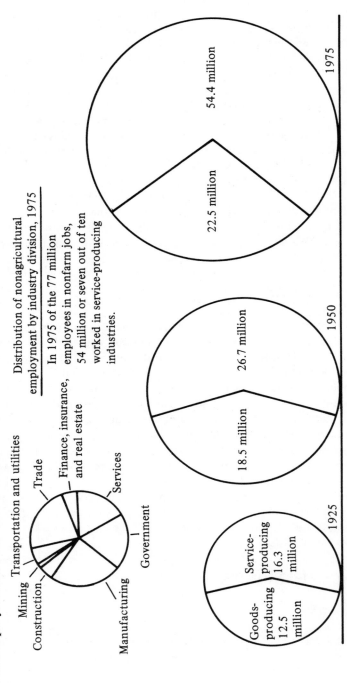

Distribution of nonagricultural employment by industry division, 1975

In 1975 of the 77 million employees in nonfarm jobs, 54 million or seven out of ten worked in service-producing industries.

Mining
Construction
Transportation and utilities
Trade
Finance, insurance, and real estate
Services
Government
Manufacturing

Service-producing 16.3 million
Goods-producing 12.5 million
1925

18.5 million
26.7 million
1950

22.5 million
54.4 million
1975

Source: U.S., Department of Labor, Bureau of Labor Statistics, *U.S. Workers and Their Jobs: The Changing Picture* (Bulletin 1919) (Washington, D.C.: Government Printing Office, 1976).

14

FIGURE 2.2

Nonfarm Jobs, 1979

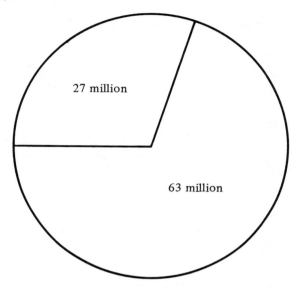

27 million

63 million

Note: In 1979 of the 90 million employees in nonfarm jobs, 63 million or seven out of ten worked in service-producing industries.

Source: Updated by author.

the United States not only was the first service economy but has been one for four decades. The United States crossed this threshold in 1940, and by 1975, two-thirds of the work force was so employed. The U.S. Bureau of Labor Statistics estimates that by 1990, 71 percent of the work force will be employed in services, that is, approximately 84 million out of a total employment of 118 million.[3] The bureau earlier calculated that even if one takes a much more restrictive view of services, dividing them into 14 major categories but excluding many services such as trucking, railroads, communication, utilities, insurance, banking, and trade, 6 million new jobs will be added in the service sector by 1985, whereas manufacturing will only add 4 million people.[4] The sector's growth accounted for the creation of almost 18 million new jobs during the past ten years as compared with the creation of less than 2.5 million jobs by the goods-producing sector of the economy.[5] In looking at this spectacular growth, however, we must also bear in mind the growing importance of government, which is expected to account for approximately 5 million of the 6 million new service employees. It should also be remembered that these data measure

FIGURE 2.3

U.S. Real Gross National Product: Services and Nonservices Components, 1947-75

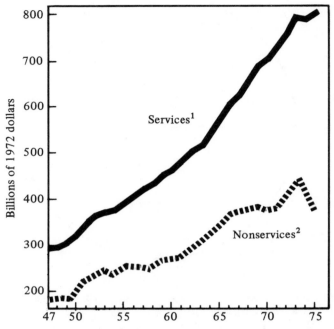

[1]Value added in transportation, communications, utilities, wholesale trade, retail trade, finance, insurance, real estate, miscellaneous services, and government.

[2]Value added in agriculture, forestry, fisheries, mining, construction, manufacturing, and "rest of world" sectors.

Source: U.S., Department of Commerce, *U.S. Service Industries in World Markets,* 709-720 (Washington, D.C.: Government Printing Office, December 1976), p. 10.

only those employed in service industries themselves, not those performing service functions but working in the nonservice sector.

The development of the United States's service economy, as defined by employment, during the past half century is illustrated in Figure 2.1. It shows that since 1925 service-producing industries have contributed almost 80 percent of the total growth in nonfarm employment. In 1979 of the 90 million employees in nonfarm jobs, 63 million or seven out of ten worked in service-producing industries (see Figure 2.2). Similar trends are demonstrable for the contribution of services to gross national product (GNP). As can be seen from Figure 2.3, services currently account for roughly two-thirds of U.S. economic output. Table 2.1 indicates the services and nonservices components in real GNP from

TABLE 2.1

U.S. Real Gross National Product: Service and Nonservice Components, 1975–78 (in billions of dollars)

Value Added in:	1975	1976	1977	1978
Service-Producing				
Transportation	47.0	48.6	51.0	54.6
Communication	36.4	39.5	42.5	47.4
Utilities	30.1	30.5	31.4	32.4
Wholesale and retail trade	206.2	218.9	228.0	239.1
Finance, insurance, and real estate	182.3	192.0	205.8	216.1
Miscellaneous services	145.2	151.9	159.5	169.1
Government	162.7	164.7	165.5	168.6
Nonservice-Producing				
Agriculture, forestry, and fisheries	37.0	36.2	38.3	38.7
Mining	19.0	19.2	19.9	20.8
Construction	49.8	53.8	56.6	59.2
Manufacturing	277.1	303.5	325.8	341.6
Rest of world	4.9	6.8	7.6	8.1

Source: U.S., Department of Commerce, Bureau of Economic Analysis, 1980.

1975 to 1978. By 1980 it was expected that almost 70 percent of GNP would be contributed by the service sector. This general expansion is also reflected by related economic indicators, such as disposable income. U.S. consumers spent about 31 percent of their income on services and 56 percent on nondurable goods 29 years ago.[6] By 1979 these percentages were approximately 37 and 43 percent, respectively.[7]

U.S. Services in International Markets

Since the United States is clearly the most advanced of service economies, a look at the U.S. service sector within the world economy should provide not only some indication of its impact internationally but also a general idea of the international importance of services. Table 2.2 would suggest that U.S. service sector exports by themselves are relatively small, especially if compared with the overall economy, the output of the service sector itself, and total U.S. trade.

TABLE 2.2

Estimated Foreign Sales of U.S. Services Industries, 1974

	Billions of U.S. Dollars
Total foreign sales	50.0[a]
Exports	7.0
Passenger fares	1.1
Air freight	0.4
Ocean freight	1.5
Other transportation	0.1
Film rental	0.3
Reinsurance	0.6
Contractors' fees[b]	0.5
Communication	0.5
Management fees and services to affiliates	1.3
Business services to nonaffiliates	0.7[c]
Overseas affiliates sales	43.0
Banking	12.0[c]
Insurance and other finance	2.1
Wholesale/retail trade (value added)	6.4[c]
Advertising	3.4
Franchising	1.5[c]
Transportation, communication, and utilities	2.7[c]
Other[d]	14.9
Services consumed in the United States by foreign nationals	8.7
Tourism in the United States	4.0
U.S. port and airport charges	3.5
Other	1.2

Note: Data in this table are derived principally from balance-of-payments and industry sources, but the data in this table measure flow of services rather than financial receipts. Some data, particularly for insurance, are weak.

[a]The comparable figure for total foreign sales of U.S. goods-producing industries in 1974 was $414 billion.

[b]Overseas construction contracts led to an estimated $2.5 billion in follow-on merchandise exports from the United States in 1974.

[c]Denotes estimates.

[d]Probably largely composed of sales in hotel/motel, equipment leasing, and construction/ engineering industries.

Source: U.S., Department of Commerce, *U.S. Service Industries in World Markets: Current Problems and Future Policy Development* (Washington, D.C.: Government Printing Office, December 1976).

TABLE 2.3

Estimated Foreign Services Industries Sales to the United States, 1974

	Billions of U.S. Dollars
Total sales to the United States	28.8[a]
U.S. imports	7.9
Passenger fares	2.1
Air freight	0.2
Ocean freight	3.3
Other transportation	0.7
Film rental	0.1
Reinsurance	0.7
Direct insurance	0.2[b]
Communications	0.5
Management fees and business services	0.1
Affiliate sales in the United States	20.9
Water transportation	0.4
Air transportation	0.6
Other transportation	0.8
Communications	—[c]
Utilities	—[c]
Banking	4.4
Insurance	4.5
Real estate	0.5
Other financial	1.9
Hotels and lodging	0.3
Advertising	0.1
Accounting and motion pictures	0.2
Engineering	0.2
Wholesale trade (value added only)	4.9[b]
Retail trade (value added only)	1.7[b]
Other	0.4
Services consumed abroad by U.S. nationals	8.3
U.S. tourism abroad	6.0
Foreign port and airport charges	1.8
Other	0.5

[a]The comparable figure for total foreign-company produced sales of goods in the United States in 1974 is $116 billion.

[b]Denotes estimates.

[c]Less than $10 million.

Source: U.S., Department of Commerce, *U.S. Service Industries in World Markets: Current Problems and Future Policy Development* (Washington, D.C.: Government Printing Office, December 1976).

Furthermore, these data indicate that service exports have been growing less rapidly than merchandise exports. On the import side, estimated service sector imports (Table 2.3) were $7.9 billion in 1974, resulting in a service sector trade deficit of about $1 billion. Like service exports, imports have been growing less rapidly than merchandise trade and are primarily concentrated in the transportation sector. According to this 1974 Department of Commerce projection, service sector trade is likely to remain relatively small in the future, although service exports are about 30 percent of the value of total exports.

These figures, like so much data in this field, are questionable. The Department of Commerce is completing a new study, expected to be released in early 1981, that will show a dramatic increase in U.S. service exports. A recent survey undertaken by *Business Week* suggests U.S. service exports in 1979 were nearly $36 billion and would be $45 billion in 1980.[8] Obviously, there are conflicts in the data. Even so, considering my supposition that substantial amounts of service exports are not calculated (the discussion in the Appendix to Chapter 2 explains the reasoning), I suspect that service exports, if anything, are considerably understated.

In contrast, service sector income associated with investment overseas is significant, as can be seen from Tables 2.2 and 2.3. More important, the sales of U.S. services affiliates overseas have been growing rapidly in recent years. Sales grew at an average annual rate of 15 percent during 1966–70 but accelerated to an average annual growth rate of 31 percent during 1970–74. In 1974 sales increased 47 percent, and this does not even include $7 billion in U.S. services sales overseas by nonservice companies.[9] As these figures only indicate sales, there is no meaningful breakdown on how these sales translate into earnings and income. So, although still relatively smaller than the sales of goods-producing affiliates overseas, services sales are growing remarkably—in fact, more rapidly than the sales of goods affiliates. Services accounted for about 12 percent of U.S. affiliate sales, other than petroleum, in 1966. In 1970 they accounted for roughly 13 percent; by 1974 they accounted for 17 percent. It is interesting to note that in 1970 about two-thirds ($30 billion) of U.S. affiliate sales were in the developed countries. This amounts to about 3 percent of the market for private services in Organization for Economic Cooperation and Development (OECD) countries other than the United States.[10]

Future growth estimates are favorable. The Department of Commerce sees the activities of service affiliates abroad as exhibiting some of the classic signs of the beginning of a growth boom. Rapid growth in the world demand for services should make it an ever more important factor in U.S. international commerce. The new commerce survey, when released, is expected to confirm these trends.

A comparison of the performance of service industries at home with those succeeding in international markets (compare Tables 2.2 and 2.4) reveals a correlation. Excluding government services, we find banking and financial services the leader in the international sector with a similar ranking domestically. The position

TABLE 2.4

Gross National Product Originating in the Services Sector, 1978 (in percent)

| | Proportion of U.S. GNP | |
Sector	1975	1978
Transportation	3.7	3.8
Communications	2.5	2.6
Utilities	2.4	2.5
Wholesale trade	7.9	7.2
Retail trade	10.4	9.8
Finance, insurance, and real estate	13.8	14.0
Miscellaneous services	12.0	12.6
Government	13.2	12.2
TOTAL	65.6	64.7
Total excluding government	52.4	52.5

Source: Compiled by author.

of transportation in both markets is similar if both trade and investment are linked. Although communications and utilities are of importance domestically, their participation in international markets is negligible.

Other Developed Countries

The United States is clearly the most advanced service economy. But other major industrial countries are not far behind, with employment rates in services analogous to those found in the United States. Such a trend was projected in a 1966 study, as indicated in Table 2.5, and by 1976 almost all of the advanced industrial countries had moved toward a service economy much more extensively than projected. Indeed, the Netherlands, Norway, and Germany surged dramatically and became service economies. For example, even excluding government services, in 1976 the Netherlands employed 42 percent in services; with government workers included the total was 69 percent. In Norway it was 39 percent without government, 65 percent in all; in Germany the corresponding figures were 34 and 55 percent, respectively.[11] By the late 1970s, Japan had become the number-two service economy in terms of employment.

Taking the OECD as a whole, throughout the first eight years of the 1970s the proportion of employment in agriculture declined in all OECD countries;

TABLE 2.5

Proportion of Total Civilian Employment in Commerce and Services (in percent)

	About 1960	Projections Made in 1966	
		About 1970	About 1980
Austria	13.8	15.4	17.3
Denmark	27.3	31.7	37.5
France	28.6	34.6	44.3
Germany (F.R.)	34.0	38.2	44.5
Ireland	29.5	29.3	35.8
Italy	20.6	24.9	32.2
Netherlands	31.3	32.3	33.6
Norway	27.5	31.4	36.8
Portugal	18.6	18.5	18.2
Spain	22.4	23.8	25.3
Sweden	35.5	40.9	46.8
Switzerland	29.8	30.2	30.6

Source: Organization for Economic Cooperation and Development, Social Affairs Division, Manpower and Social Affairs Directorate, *Manpower Problems in the Service Sector*, Papers for a Trade Union Seminar, Supplement to the Report (Paris: OECD, 1966).

after 1973 industrial employment fell except in southern Europe, but expansion in the service sector continued regularly over the period.[12]

There can be discontinuities over time and even declines in employment in the service sector. But the general trend is clearly upward in countries experiencing economic growth, and the projections are for a continued acceleration of service expansion.

As for service sector participation in GNP, the same general growth trend is evident. Excluding the United States, the services component of the other developed countries within the OECD accounted for over half of their combined gross domestic product (GDP) in 1974. By 1972, 12 OECD countries already had more than 50 percent of their GDP resulting from service output. In recent years, services have accounted for even larger shares of GDP in those countries (see Table 2.6). Similarly, OECD trends in the consumption of services parallel those in the United States: as incomes go up, the consumption of services increases.

One interesting contrast between the United States and other OECD countries is the proportional relationship between employment in services and GNP in services. In the United States over two-thirds of employment is in services, and approximately the same percentage of GNP results from services.[13] However, in most other developed countries, despite high percentages of GNP resulting from services, smaller percentages of the employment are provided by services. It could be, although it seems unlikely, that the rest of the OECD countries are far more productive in services than the United States. Another explanation might be that the services contributing to GNP in the United States are less capital intensive and more labor intensive than those in the other OECD countries. Most probably, the explanation lies in the inadequacy of data.

TABLE 2.6

Service Sector Proportion of Gross Domestic Product:
Selected OECD Countries, 1978
(in percent)

	Total Proportion	Proportion Excluding Government Services
United States	63.58	50.88
Australia	53.60[a]	41.17
Norway	56.40	41.59
Japan	56.80	48.25
Belgium	57.69	43.66
Canada	55.16	39.26
Netherlands	53.75[a]	39.62
Denmark	56.08[b]	39.29
Sweden	51.62	29.70
United Kingdom	53.24	40.75
France[c]	52.71[d]	41.00
Spain	50.36[d]	41.83
Italy	50.89	39.10
Austria	48.42[d]	35.97
Germany	28.92	17.24

Note: Data represent percentage of gross domestic product accounted for by gross product originating in services sectors.

[a]1976.

[b]1974.

[c]Estimated on the basis of other European Economic Community countries.

[d]1977.

Source: Organization for Economic Cooperation and Development, *National Accounts of OECD Countries, 1961-1978* (Paris: OECD, 1980).

TABLE 2.7

The United Kingdom's Share of World Invisible Trade (in millions of dollars)

	1977	Percentage of World Total	1978	Percentage of World Total
United States	55,818	19.5	70,375	19.7
France	23,433	8.2	32,272	9.1
United Kingdom	25,585	9.0	31,052	8.7
West Germany	24,436	8.6	30,649	8.6
Japan	15,458	5.4	18,567	5.2
Italy	13,983	4.9	17,851	5.0
Belgium-Luxembourg	14,112	4.9	17,199	4.8
Netherlands	12,672	4.4	15,199	4.3
Switzerland[a]	8,058	2.8	10,637	3.0
Spain	6,531	2.3	9,478	2.7
Austria	5,521	1.9	6,986	2.0
Canada	5,967	2.1	6,642	1.9
Saudi Arabia	6,070	2.1	_[b]	_[c]
Norway	5,347	1.9	5,928	1.7
Denmark	4,393	1.5	5,327	1.5
Yugoslavia[a]	4,205	1.5	4,960	1.4
Sweden	3,699	1.3	4,416	1.2
Mexico	3,563	1.2	4,349	1.2
Korea	2,786	1.0	4,084	1.2
Singapore	3,048	1.1	3,564	1.0
Iran	2,739	1.0	_[b]	_[c]
Egypt	2,469	0.9	3,343	0.9
Australia	2,285	0.8	2,662	0.8
Israel	2,237	0.8	2,549	0.7
Greece	2,030	0.7	2,514	0.7
Others	29,104	10.2	34,358	9.6
World Total	285,549	100.0	356,444	100.0

Exchange rates: 1977 1.1675$/SDR (special drawing rights)
1978 1.2520$/SDR

Note: Total invisible receipts (excluding miscellaneous government transactions).

[a]Including miscellaneous government transactions.

[b]Saudi Arabia and Iran combined; International Monetary Fund estimate of 11,483.

[c]Saudi Arabia and Iran combined total 3.2 percent.

Source: Committee on Invisible Exports, *World Invisible Trade* (London: Committee on Invisible Exports, August 1980).

Services in International Markets

Two major statistical problems inevitably arise. First, statistics dealing with invisibles are inadequate, as I have noted above, because items that do not solely result from service activities, such as investment income and certain government transfers, are included. Second, and much more important, is the absence of any study of the other developed countries that is comparable with the Department of Commerce's *U.S. Service Industries in World Markets*. There is no way to effectively compare the performance of the other developed countries with the United States. There are not enough data to test the findings for the United States that the role of services in the international economy is related more to investment than to trade and that domestic and international strengths parallel one another. All that can be attempted here is a rough sketch based on invisibles statistics.

A look at the importance of invisibles in the balance of payments in selected developed countries shows that the top ten invisibles earners in the world are all OECD members (see Tables 2.7 and 2.8). Tables 2.9, 2.10, and 2.11 provide us with a better picture of the role of services in trade because invisibles are

TABLE 2.8

**Top Ten Invisible Earners, 1973, 1977, 1978
(in millions of dollars)**

	Total Receipts			Percentage of World Total		
	1973	1977	1978	1973	1977	1978
United States	36,176	55,818	70,375	22.0	19.5	19.7
United Kingdom	18,705	25,585	31,052	11.4	9.0	8.7
West Germany	12,431	24,436	30,649	7.6	8.6	8.6
France	11,958	23,433	32,272	7.3	8.2	9.1
Japan	7,725	15,458	18,567	4.7	5.4	5.2
Italy	9,688	13,983	17,851	5.9	4.9	5.0
Netherlands	7,739	12,672	15,199	4.7	4.4	4.3
Belgium/Luxembourg	5,166	14,112	17,199	3.1	4.9	4.8
Switzerland[a]	4.939	8,058	10,637	3.0	2.8	3.0
Spain	5,049	6,531	9,478	3.1	2.3	2.7

[a]Includes miscellaneous government transactions.

Note: Excludes government receipts not included elsewhere.

Source: Committee on Invisible Exports, *World Invisible Trade* (London: Committee on Invisible Exports, June 1980).

TABLE 2.9

Composition of Invisible Receipts, 1978

SDR (special drawing rights) million

Country	Transport	Travel	Investment Income	Other Services	Total	Rank
United Kingdom	7,061	3,825	7,725	6,191	24,802	3
United States	7,730	5,820	34,590	8,070	56,210	1
European Economic Community						
Belgium/Luxembourg	2,095	1,091	5,493	5,058	13,737	7
Denmark	1,665	908	399	1,283	4,255	15
France	5,768	4,738	6,408	8,862	25,776	2
Italy	2,705	5,019	1,619	4,915	14,258	6
Netherlands	3,642	1,000	3,865	3,633	12,140	8
West Germany	5,560	3,860	6,830	8,230	24,480	4
Western Europe						
Austria	393	3,765	776	646	5,580	12
Finland	497	350	124	565	1,536	28
Greece	510	1,054	102	342	2,008	25
Norway	3,144	446	315	830	4,735	14
Portugal	193	468	50	169	880	34
Spain	1,329[a]	4,383	1,044[a]	814[a]	7,570[b]	10
Sweden	1,479	430	437	1,181	3,527	17
Switzerland	246	2,515	3,248	2,487	8,496[c]	9
Yugoslavia	n.a.	n.a.	n.a.	n.a.	3,962[a,c]	16
Other						
Australia	1,264	315	329	218	2,126	23
Canada	677	1,650	1,463	1,515	5,305	13

Japan	6,640	370	4,200	3,620	14,830	5
South Africa	579	291	249	682	1,801	26
Argentina	355	224	270	119	968	32
Brazil	453	54	514	540	1,561	27
Mexico	198	1,992	195	1,089	3,474	18
Panama	79	152	428	258	917	33
Venezuela	264	272	666	89	1,291	30
Egypt	509	560	115	1,486	2,670	22
Iran	n.a.	n.a.	n.a.	n.a.	n.a.[d]	21[a]
Israel	638	475	395	528	2,036	24
Jordan	101	272	41	466	880	35
Saudi Arabia	n.a.	n.a.	n.a.	n.a.	n.a.[d]	11[a]
Philippines	111	168	145	551	975	31
Republic of Korea	502	326	230	2,204	3,262	19
Singapore	1,086	418	308	1,035	2,847	20
Taiwan	343	500	326	332	1,501	29
Total of top 35	59,272[e]	49,211[e]	87,834[e]	69,289[e]	269,568	
Rest of World	4,645	5,098	2,073	3,333	15,149	
World	63,917[e]	54,309[e]	89,907[e]	72,622[e]	284,717	

n.a. = not available

[a]Economists Advisory Group estimate.

[b]Miscellaneous government receipts for 1978.

[c]Includes miscellaneous government receipts.

[d]International Monetary Fund estimate for Iran and Saudi Arabia combined, SDRm 9,172.

[e]Excludes Yugoslavia but includes International Monetary Fund combined estimates for Iran and Saudi Arabia.

Source: Committee on Invisible Exports, *World Invisible Trade* (London: Committee on Invisible Exports, June 1980).

TABLE 2.10

Composition of Invisible Payments, 1978

SDR (special drawing rights) million

Country	Transport	Travel	Investment Income	Other Services	Total	Rank
United Kingdom	6,791	2,365	6,446	2,936	18,538	5
United States	9,210	6,760	17,380	2,370	35,720	1
European Economic Community						
Belgium/Luxembourg	1,945	1,809	4,979	3,413	12,146	6
Denmark	1,213	960	1,025	662	3,860	20
France	5,857	3,430	5,267	5,812	20,366	4
Italy	3,432	963	2,499	3,341	10,235	9
Netherlands	2,169	2,711	3,781	3,021	11,682	7
West Germany	6,290	11,550	5,020	10,960	33,820	2
Western Europe						
Austria	407	1,959	1,165	941	4,472	17
Finland	580	319	679	389	1,967	26
Greece	387	179	217	198	981	32
Norway	1,865	1,011	1,808	966	5,650	12
Portugal	354	127	306	142	929	33
Spain	1,000[a]	453	1,787[a]	694[a]	3,934[b]	19
Sweden	1,917	1,121	1,058	1,330	5,426	13
Switzerland	405	1,666	491	1,791	4,353[c]	18
Yugoslavia	n.a.	n.a.	n.a.	n.a.	2,594[a,c]	24
Other						
Australia	2,037	550	1,705	443	4,735	15
Canada	1,004	2,880	5,285	2,300	11,469	8

Japan	8,650	2,950	3,510	6,250	21,360	3
South Africa	750	361	1,186	1,246	3,543	22
Argentina	348	247	838	243	1,676	28
Brazil	1,262	203	3,894	899	6,258	11
Mexico	525	1,055	2,424	486	4,490	16
Panama	92	29	471	28	620	34
Venezuela	1,002	1,293	954	397	3,646	21
Egypt	439	206	316	411	1,372	30
Iran	n.a.	n.a.	n.a.	n.a.	n.a.d	14a
Israel	718	276	797	591	2,382	25
Jordan	193	166	19	87	465	35
Saudi Arabia	n.a.	n.a.	n.a.	n.a.	n.a.d	10a
Philippines	401	41	468	277	1,187	31
Republic of Korea	944	165	818	1,366	3,293	23
Singapore	623	77	369	440	1,509	29
Taiwan	620	399	407	334	1,760	27
Total of top 35	67,881e	50,860e	82,072e	56,607e	260,014	
Rest of world	13,170	4,048	10,519	6,701	34,438	
World	81,051e	54,908e	92,591e	63,308e	294,452	

n.a. = not available

[a]Economists Advisory Group estimate.

[b]Miscellaneous government receipts for 1978.

[c]Includes miscellaneous government receipts.

[d]International Monetary Fund estimate for Iran and Saudi Arabia combined, SDRm, 9,172.

[e]Excludes Yugoslavia but includes International Monetary Fund combined estimates for Iran and Saudi Arabia.

Source: Committee on Invisible Exports, World Invisible Trade (London: Committee on Invisible Exports, June 1980).

TABLE 2.11

National Balances of Invisible Trade, 1969, 1977, and 1978

SDR (special drawing rights) million Country	Transport			Travel			Investment Income			Other Services			Total		
	1969	1977	1978	1969	1977	1978	1969	1977	1978	1969	1977	1978	1969	1977	1978
United Kingdom	19	336	270	84	1,744	1,460	1,197	300	1,279	1,083	2,511	3,255	2,383	4,891	6,264
United States	-433	-1,630	-1,480	-1,330	-1,110	-940	5,800	15,440	17,210	2,251	4,990	5,700	6,288	17,690	20,490
European Economic Community															
Belgium/ Luxembourg	26	158	150	-138	-624	-718	16	459	514	98	2,076	1,645	2	2,069	1,591
Denmark	153	412	452	12	-2	-52	-39	-469	-626	113	588	621	239	529	395
France	-70	-175	-89	128	395	1,308	312	566	1,141	66	1,868	3,050	436	2,654	5,410
Italy	-214	-597	-727	1,139	3,308	4,056	106	-923	-880	298	1,153	1,574	1,329	2,941	4,023
Netherlands	475	1,595	1,473	-192	-1,150	-1,711	217	297	84	12	311	612	512	1,053	458
West Germany	-202	-420	-730	-986	-6,010	-7,690	38	220	1,810	-1,118	-2,740	-2,730	-2,268	-8,950	-9,340
Western Europe															
Austria	-2	-41	-14	489	1,411	1,806	-44	-288	-389	-60	-301	-295	383	781	1,108
Finland	6	-99	-83	1	-2	31	-77	-516	-555	-5	54	176	-75	-563	-431
Greece	47	197	123	102	699	875	-34	-121	-115	18	66	144	133	841	1,027
Norway	877	1,241	1,279	-95	-492	-565	-74	-1,270	-1,493	84	75	-136	792	-446	-915
Portugal	-18	-138	-161	101	229	341	-11	-152	-256	40	-13	27	112	-74	-49
Spain	-22	210	329	1,195	2,962	3,930	-166	-651	-743	-38	-194	120	969	2,327	3,636
Sweden	-1	-672	-438	-238	-688	-691	6	-403	-621	-71	-156	-149	-304	-1,919	-1,899
Switzerland	-15	-124	-159	431	976	849	519	2,149	2,757	276	682	696	1,211	3,683	4,143
Yugoslavia	-5	n.a.	n.a.	168	n.a.	n.a.	-90	n.a.	n.a.	247	n.a.	n.a.	320	n.a.	n.a.

Other

Australia	-337	-732	-773	-62	-194	-235	-554	-1,349	-1,376	-102	-254	-225	-1,055	-2,529	-2,609
Canada	-187	-334	-327	-198	-1,341	-1,230	-1,149	-3,559	-3,822	-453	-834	-785	-1,987	-6,068	-6,164
Japan	-921	-2,050	-2,010	-93	-1,480	-2,580	-287	100	690	-720	-2,280	-2,630	-2,021	-5,710	-6,530
South Africa	-158	-166	-171	-24	-73	-70	-391	-966	-937	-109	-519	-564	-682	-1,724	-1,742
Argentina	-107	28	7	-64	20	-23	-219	-495	-568	-73	-28	-124	-463	-475	-708
Brazil	-139	-836	-809	-49	-149	-149	-344	-2,939	-3,380	-89	-311	-359	-621	-4,235	-4,697
Mexico	-95	-231	-327	528	802	937	-617	-1,899	-2,229	113	482	603	-71	-846	-1,016
Panama	-11	23	-13	48	116	123	-25	-48	-43	106	199	230	118	290	297
Venezuela	-176	-723	-738	-83	-660	-1,021	-801	-165	-288	-84	-252	-308	-1,144	-1,800	-2,355
Egypt	-91	66	70	-20[a]	477	354	-60	-164	-201	58[b]	438	1,075	-113	817	1,298
Iran	-189	-1,825	n.a.	-33	-729	n.a.	-774	24	n.a.	-52	199	n.a.	-1,048	-2,331	n.a.
Israel	-16	-38	-80	22	273	199	-78	-358	-402	-3	-149	-63	-75	-272	-346
Jordan	-19	-109	-92	-9	156	106	16	26	22	12	388	379	0	461	415
Saudi Arabia	-16	-1,337	n.a.	9	-97	n.a.	-673	-25	n.a.	-39	-656	n.a.	-719	-2,115	n.a.
Philippines	-94	-233	-290	-10	94	127	-78	-275	-323	-23	91	274	-205	-323	-212
Republic of Korea	-89	-274	-442	5	229	161	-4	-508	-588	11	633	838	-77	80	-31
Singapore	65	449	463	64	279	341	37	-93	-61	-22	644	595	144	1,279	1,338
Taiwan	-69	-215	-277	54	209	101	-21	-143	-81	-25	2	-2	-61	-147	-259
Total of top 35	-2,028	-8,284[c]	5,164[d]	956	-422[c]	-570[d]	1,654	1,802[c]	5,530[d]	1,800	8,763[c]	13,244[d]	2,382	1,859[c]	12,590[d]

n.a. = not available

[a] Payments only, as receipts are not published separately but are included in "other services."

[b] Includes travel payments.

[c] Excludes Yugoslavia.

[d] Excludes Yugoslavia, Iran, and Saudi Arabia.

Source: Committee on Invisible Exports, World Invisible Trade (London: Committee on Invisible Exports, June 1980).

disaggregated. By eliminating investment income, even though some of this investment income results from pure service sector activities, and concentrating on transport, travel, and other services, we can begin to get a rough idea of the significance of services.

As can be seen from Tables 2.9 and 2.10, transport, travel, and other services taken together are not very important when considered in isolation to the volume of exports and imports of commodities and manufactures. This generally compares with the position of the United States on trade in services, especially for the most advanced industrial countries. Those that have much more significant earnings from service trade are smaller, less industrialized countries with important shipping or tourism sectors, such as Norway, Austria, Denmark, Greece, Yugoslavia, and Spain.

Because of the statistical shortcomings indicated above, we can only surmise that the other OECD nations follow a pattern similar to the United States in their overseas investments in service industries. In support of the view that their activities parallel those of the United States, there are the results of the 1974 benchmark data survey on foreign investment in the United States, the last such survey publicly available. The affiliates of service industries from abroad operating in the United States had sales of $20.8 billion, more than double the value of U.S. service imports. In fact, if the transportation sector is excluded, 92 percent of all foreign service sales made to the United States were made through their affiliates in the United States.[14] This pattern, if it applies elsewhere, would lead one to conclude that it is through investment that services have their most significant impact on international markets.

A rough estimate of the comparative strength of services domestically and internationally for OECD members (excluding the United States) is possible. But it is handicapped by our limited knowledge about the performance of OECD service company affiliates abroad. Transportation has consistently been responsible for the largest gross flows in the invisibles account in many OECD countries, but the importance of the domestic transportation sector varies by country. It seems unlikely that there is much correlation between the two, since certain nations contribute proportionally much more to this sector internationally.

As to the "other services," such as banking, insurance, construction, payments for film and television, telecommunications, and international trade expenses such as commissions and agency fees, the OECD area as a whole has a persistent surplus with the rest of the world on this item, as can be seen in Table 2.11.

Correlations are difficult, but if we look at the invisible flows, there does seem to be a relationship between a country's international activities and its domestic sector. For example, the United Kingdom, a traditional provider of international financial services, also has important domestic banking and insurance industries. As for West Germany, it has had a persistent deficit in invisibles with major items being travel and other services. By 1978 the deficit was almost $11.7 billion, which indicates that Germany is still primarily an industrial economy. No comparison between its international service and domestic activities is possible. Italy has a structural surplus in invisibles that has grown over the last decade to more than $5 billion in 1978.[15] Since this surplus comes primarily from tourism and workers remittances from overseas, parallels with the domestic service sector are meaningless. As for Canada, all major service items are in deficit, which reflects its national strength in primary industries. Although Japan has become the second service economy in terms of employment, Japanese invisibles have been and continue to be in deficit. This reflects its dependence in shipping and the weakness of the domestic service sector. In 1978 it had an $8.6 billion deficit in its invisible account. Norway's invisible surplus has fallen over the last decade, but the transportation sector has grown substantially. Norway is a great shipping nation, and there are thus parallels in its domestic and international activities.[16]

There are some interesting anomalies. Invisibles exports are more important than goods exports for Spain, Greece, and Portugal, which one would not expect, given their lower level of development. In each the surplus results from tourism, which is a special factor making services very important in a nonservice economy.

DEVELOPING COUNTRY ECONOMIES

In a study prepared for the OECD Development Center in 1970 entitled *The Employment Problem in Less Developed Countries*, David Turnham concluded, "With regard to the general importance of service activities in less developed areas, the paucity of relevant studies, either empirical or theoretical, is little short of astonishing."[17] Because of the lack of data, it is not possible to examine the evolution of the service sector in developing countries over an extended period. Given these constraints, however, the available findings are nevertheless startling. According to economic theory, we should expect, for the most part, a relatively unimportant service sector in terms of employment, percentage of GNP, propensity to consume services, and international involvement. Instead, we find the exact opposite. The role of services in the domestic and international activities of the developing countries is surprisingly important.

Employment in services represents a substantial portion of total employment for most developing countries as can be seen in Table 2.12. In the OECD study *Service Activities in Developing Countries*, in 56 countries for which labor force data were available, an average of 28 percent of the economically active population is employed in services. For more than a third of these countries, service employment accounts for 30 percent or more of the total, and in three developing countries over half the labor force is in the service sector. Thus, ironically, there are developing countries that technically qualify as service economies, since more than half of the population is employed in services.

Obviously, there are special reasons for the high employment share of services for many of these countries. The six having the highest proportion of

TABLE 2.12

Frequency Distribution of Developing Countries by Share of
Total Allocated Employment Accounted for by Services

Employment in Services as Percentage of Total Allocated Employment	Country	Frequency	
		Number	Percentage
50 or more	Malta, Israel, Kuwait	3	5
45 to 49	Trinidad and Tobago, Surinam, Uruguay	3	5
40 to 44	Argentina, Chile, Venezuela, Taiwan, Barbados	5	9
35 to 39	Libya, Mauritius, Jamaica, Panama, Brazil	5	9
30 to 34	Greece, Spain, Costa Rica, Mexico, Colombia, Jordan, Ceylon, Malaysia	8	14
25 to 29	Paraguay, Peru, Iran, Korea, Philippines, Cyprus, Egypt, Tunisia	8	14
20 to 24	Ecuador, Indonesia, Ghana, Dominican Republic, El Salvador, Guatemala, Nicaragua	7	13
15 to 19	Syria, India, Pakistan, Khmer Republic, Fiji, Turkey, Yugoslavia, Algeria, Morocco, Honduras	10	18
10 to 14	Thailand, Ivory Coast, Liberia, Sierra Leone	4	7
9 or less	Nepal, Botswana, Gabon	3	5
Total*		56	100

*Total may not add due to rounding.

Source: Organization for Economic Cooperation and Development, *Service Activities in Developing Countries* (Paris: OECD, 1974).

employment in services have two common features: they are relatively small in both area and population and high in urbanization concentration. One would thus expect a heavy concentration in personal or domestic services, such as vendors, lottery salesmen, shoeshine boys, and the like.

It is true that these activities combined with others such as government and community services provide over half of total service sector employment in all the countries surveyed. But, commerce, which includes banking, insurance, real estate, and wholesale and retail trade, accounts for nearly 30 percent of

TABLE 2.13

Annual Growth of Allocated Employment by Sector for 14 Countries (in percent)

Country	Agriculture and the like	Industry	Services				Total Employment	Period Covered
			Commerce	Transport and the like	Other	Total Services		
Europe								
Greece	-3.7	1.9	4.9	3.3	-0.6	2.0	-0.7	1961-71
Spain	-2.7	3.0	4.8	2.1	3.7	3.8	1.0	1960-70
Africa								
Egypt	0.2	6.6	-0.7	4.8	-1.2	-0.3	1.1	1960-66
Tunisia	-2.5	4.9	1.5	4.1	9.6	6.4	-0.1	1956-66
Latin America								
Chile	-1.2	3.8	4.9	7.3	2.2	3.8	1.9	1960-71
Mexico	-1.7	3.3	1.1	0.3	5.3	3.4	1.3	1960-70
Nicaragua	-2.2	1.4	5.8	4.5	5.8	5.7	0.7	1963-71
Venezuela	-1.3	6.4	7.3	6.4	4.2	5.5	3.3	1961-71
Asia								
Indonesia	1.3	0.3	n.a.	n.a.	n.a.	9.1	2.5	1961-64
Israel	2.6	4.9	5.5	7.0	4.2	4.9	4.0	1961-67
Korea (South)	0.8	7.4	15.0	17.6	2.7	9.4	5.0	1966-71
Malaysia (West)	-0.1	3.4	2.6	1.1	2.5	2.3	1.0	1957-67
Pakistan	3.6	8.2	12.0	16.4	1.2	7.6	4.7	1961-68
Philippines	2.1	6.4	5.5	9.8	7.8	7.4	4.0	1960-70

n.a. = not available

Notes: The growth rates by sector refer to the total number of employees, self-employed, and family workers who can be allocated by sector; the rates for "total employment" refer, in addition, to persons who are gainfully employed but who could not be allocated by sector.

Source: International Labour Organisation, *Yearbook of Labour Statistics* (Geneva: ILO, 1968, 1972). (Extracted from Organization for Economic Cooperation and Development, *Service Activities in Developing Countries* [Paris: OECD, 1974].)

service employment, and transport, communications, and storage account for 15 percent.

So in assessing future growth in developing country service employment, it is necessary to depart from the traditional assumption that services are either insignificant or only important in sectors such as personal services. The foregoing figures support the conclusion that a wide variety of services play an important role in the economies of many developing countries. As for future development,

TABLE 2.14

Frequency Distribution of Developing Countries by Share of Gross Domestic Product (factor cost) Accounted for by Service Sector

Service Output as Percentage of Gross Domestic Product	Country	Frequency	
		Number	Percentage
60 or more	Jordan, Singapore	2	3
55 to 59	Malta, Israel, Vietnam (South)	3	5
50 to 54	Cyprus, Greece, Tunisia, Mauritius, Costa Rica, Dominican Republic, El Salvador, Guatemala, Jamaica, Panama, Brazil, Uruguay, Burma, Fiji	14	21
45 to 49	Spain, Algeria, Kenya, Malagasy Republic, Southern Rhodesia, Upper Volta, Nicaragua, Paraguay, Surinam, Syria, Ceylon (Sri Lanka), Taiwan	12	18
40 to 44	Turkey, Egypt, Botswana, Tanzania, Honduras, Trinidad and Tobago, Korea (South), Malaysia, Philippines, Thailand, Zaire	11	17
35 to 39	Yugoslavia, Gambia, Ghana, Liberia, Sierra Leone, Swaziland, Uganda, Zambia, Haiti, Iran, Pakistan	11	17
30 to 34	Malawi, Iraq, Kuwait, Saudi Arabia, India, Lesotho	6	9
25 to 29	Libya, Ethiopia, Niger, Nigeria, Togo	5	8
24 or less	Burundi, Nepal	2	3
Total		66	100

Source: Organization for Economic Cooperation and Development, *Service Activities in Developing Countries* (Paris: OECD, 1974).

TABLE 2.15

Frequency Distribution of Developing Countries by Gross Domestic Fixed Capital Formation in Service Activities

GDFCF in Services as Percentage of Total GDFCF*	Country	Frequency	
		Number	Percentage
70 or more	Israel, Greece, Cameroon, Fiji	4	15
65 to 69	Uruguay, Mauritius, Botswana	3	11
60 to 64	Ethiopia, Kenya, Tanzania, Togo, Zambia, Korea (South)	6	21
55 to 59	Tunisia, Iraq, Syria, Cyprus	4	14
50 to 54	Mexico, Bolivia	2	7
45 to 49	Spain, Gambia	2	7
40 to 44	Thailand, Egypt, Taiwan	3	12
39 or less	Lesotho, Rhodesia, Jamaica, Swaziland	4	15
Total		28	100†

*GDFCF stands for gross domestic fixed capital formation.

† Total may not add due to rounding.

Source: Organization for Economic Cooperation and Development, *Service Activities in Developing Countries* (Paris: OECD, 1974).

the best projection can probably be made by extrapolating the current growth rates of service employment into the next decade.

Table 2.13 shows that during the 1960–70 decade in almost every developing country the proportion of the labor force in services grew much more rapidly than either agriculture or industry. In fact, in Latin American and in most Asian countries the service sector absorbed most of the new entrants to the labor force during the 1960s. On the assumption that this trend continues, services will become even more significant in developing nations.

Developing economies where services constitute a major portion of economic output are much more numerous than those where services are a major provider of employment. As shown in Table 2.14, for 19 selected countries, more than a quarter of the sample, services provide over half of the total GDP. For over half of the countries the share of service output is in the range of 35 to 49 percent. In most countries, services make up a larger share of GDP than either agriculture or industry.

It is important to consider which elements of the service sector make contributions to GDP. As might be expected, there are significant differences between those services providing the largest percentages of GDP and those providing the largest shares of employment. The following discussion is based on averages, and there is a great deal of national variation from these averages because of structural differences in the various economies and the inaccuracy of statistics.

The most significant element of services production is provided by wholesale and retail trade, which, on the average, accounts for 30 percent of total service output and 30 percent of GNP. Public administration is the next most important activity, and, like wholesale and retail trade, its importance varies with the country being considered. This is followed by "other services" (here defined to exclude financial services), which provide 18 percent of total service output and 8 percent of total GNP. Transport, storage, and communication are next in importance and account for 6 percent of total GNP and 14 percent of service output. Banking, insurance, and real estate are least important and on average account for only 2 percent of GNP and 5 percent of the total output of services.[18]

As for the contribution of services to GNP in the future, recent trends are likely to continue. Services have grown rapidly throughout the last decade,

TABLE 2.16

Frequency Distribution of Developing Countries by Expenditure on Services of Total Private Consumption Expenditure in the Domestic Market

Expenditure on Services as Percentage of Total Private Consumption Expenditure	Country	Frequency Number	Frequency Percentage
40 or more	Fiji, Venezuela, Israel	3	10
35 to 39	Cyprus, Jamaica, Rhodesia, Jordan, Singapore, Taiwan	6	21
30 to 34	Thailand, Malaysia, Panama, Barbados, Zambia, Spain, Greece	7	24
25 to 29	Tanzania, Sierra Leone, South Vietnam, Korea (South), Malta	5	17
20 to 24	Khmer Republic, Sudan, Togo, Ceylon	4	14
19 or less	Lesotho, Malawi, Ghana, Niger	4	13
Total		29	100*

*Total may not add due to rounding.

Source: Organization for Economic Cooperation and Development, *Service Activities in Developing Countries* (Paris: OECD, 1974).

usually more slowly than industry but always well ahead of agriculture; there is no reason to expect this pattern to change. Capital formation is one possible measurement that might be used to predict the continuing importance of services. Table 2.15 shows that for 28 developing countries fixed capital formation in service activities averages a startling 56 percent of total capital formation. For a quarter of the countries the service share exceeds 65 percent. This consists primarily of building and construction work, with more than half of total capital formation in services occurring in the transport/storage/communications sector and the ownership of dwellings. One would not expect the bulk of capital formation in a developing country to be occurring in services. On the other hand, many would argue the above activities are on the boundary line between services and something else.

In trying to assess the propensity to consume services, there is an even more serious problem of data for the developing countries. For example, it is difficult to distinguish between expenditures on goods and on services. Table 2.16 examines the reported expenditures for services in a selected group of 29 countries. Services expenditures in these countries, taken together, average 31 percent of total private consumption. Comparisons among the countries indicate a correlative relationship between rising income and increased expenditure on services. Since all such studies tend to understate the true significance of the consumption of services because they often exclude such important service items as health and education, which are supplied free or below cost by governments, the consumption of services may be significantly higher.

Developing Nation Services in International Markets

I now turn to examine services in the international activities of developing countries. To get some sense of their importance, we will look at the invisibles transactions of 18 developing countries selected from Africa, Latin America, Asia, and the Middle East.* These countries span various levels of wealth and differing economic systems—capitalist, mixed capitalist, and centrally planned.

In 11 of the 18 countries considered, exports of goods have increased significantly more than have exports of services, rising an average of 80 percent more than services from 1967 to 1973. Only in four countries—Mexico, Nicaragua, Senegal, and Zaire—have exports of services increased more than exports of goods. In these four countries service export growth has been very significant: approximately 33 percent in Mexico, 55 percent in Nicaragua, nearly 300 percent in Zaire, and 800 percent in Senegal.

---

*The countries that the author examined include Algeria, Argentina, Brazil, Colombia, Egypt, India, Indonesia, Iran, Korea, Malaysia, Mauritania, Mexico, Nicaragua, Pakistan, Senegal, Thailand, Uruguay, and Zaire.

In 12 of the 18 countries, service imports have increased at a rate that matches or exceeds the increase in the import of goods. In 11 of the 18 countries, the relative share of services in the total imports of goods and services remained about the same or increased. Although the rates of growth differ markedly among countries, the average rate of growth in service imports for all the countries selected was 131 percent, compared with an average rate of 152 percent in goods imports. While most developing countries in the sample were significantly increasing their exports of goods relative to their total exports during the period, imports of services in the majority of countries tend to be increasing at a rate that matches or exceeds the import of goods. Although one would expect such a pattern for exports, the growth of service imports is somewhat surprising. In many of these countries, one would expect accelerated capital goods imports and not growing service imports.

Looking at the dependence on invisibles trade for all countries (not just developing nations) in the years 1960, 1969, and 1976, we find that the countries most dependent on service exports include the United States, various Western European countries, and several of the developing countries—Argentina, Korea, Egypt, and Iran. For these countries invisibles accounted for about 26 percent of their trade. Although invisibles' receipts were not overly significant—only about 10 percent of total receipts in trade—it is somewhat striking that by the 1970s, 15 developing countries had moved into the ranks of the 35 countries most dependent on invisibles trade.[19]

Because of the lack of data, it is difficult to determine for developing countries which individual service industries are most important internationally. However, by referring to the National Balances of Invisible Trade (Table 2.11), we get an indication in aggregate terms of the important service industries for those developing countries ranked among the "top 35" invisibles traders. Transportation is consistently a deficit item for all, except Greece, Panama, Israel, and Saudi Arabia. Travel for the great majority is their single positive contributor in the invisibles account. "Other services" also provide positive inflows for a few nations—Greece, Yugoslavia, Mexico, Panama, Egypt, Philippines, Thailand, and Singapore.[20]

Finally, the importance of the investment-related activities of the developing countries should be examined. Surprisingly, many developing countries do have overseas direct investments. Studies by the Committee on Invisible Exports show investment income receipts between 1964 and 1973 for a group of countries, including some developing countries.[21] The latter are in many ways more significant than might be expected. For example, among European countries, Greece experienced a 51.1 percent increase in such income between 1969 and 1973; Yugoslavia, 42.2 percent; and Spain, 83.6 percent. Among developing countries in Latin America: Brazil, 96.5 percent; Mexico, 19.9 percent; and Venezuela, 21.5 percent. In the Middle East the figures for Egypt are 41.4 percent; Iran, 22.8 percent; Libya, 18.9 percent; Saudi Arabia, 41.8 percent; and Turkey, 34.3 percent. In the Far East Singapore has increased its receipts 25.3

percent. Although these countries generally have a net deficit in the investment income account, and the increases generally start from a small base, it is nevertheless significant that they have growing overseas investments at all. Information is not available as to what percentage, if any, of these receipts come from service industry investments overseas. It is probably a safe assumption that the overseas investments of developing countries in services industries are negligible and not important to their economies. The data gaps for both the international investment and trading activities of developing countries make any attempted correlation between important domestic sectors and international activities impossible.

SOCIALIST COUNTRY ECONOMIES

This investigation of socialist countries is limited to the members of the Council for Mutual Economic Assistance (COMECON). As before, the discussion first focuses on growth trends and the composition of the service sector in the COMECON countries; then it analyzes the small size of service output in socialist countries compared with international trends and discusses prospects for service sector growth and international trends. The analysis in some cases does not include all service activities due to data limitations.

Treatment of Services in National Accounts

Unlike capitalist countries, the Soviet Union and Eastern European countries mainly use the Material Product System (MPS) instead of the GNP system for national income accounting. The MPS makes a distinction between productive services and nonmaterial nonproductive services. *Productive services* are defined as those directly connected with physical production and include trade in goods and transportation and communication services used in producing goods. Passenger transport, other communications, housing, health, education, finance, insurance, public administration, and repair and personal services are regarded as nonmaterial. Only productive services, goods production, and turnover taxes are included in "material product." Nonmaterial services, although they are calculated in most cases, are regarded as contributing to the redistribution of income rather than the creation of output. In addition, some activities regarded as service industries by countries using the United Nations System of National Accounts are classified as part of the productive sphere in socialist countries. These include utilities such as gas, water, and electricity.

The MPS concept also varies among the socialist countries. Currently, Czechoslovakia and the Soviet Union exclude passenger transportation and communications for nonmaterial purposes from the material product sector. Other Eastern European countries have at various times enlarged the material product sphere to include these activities. Naturally, these classification differ-

TABLE 2.13

Annual Growth of Allocated Employment by Sector for 14 Countries (in percent)

Country	Agriculture and the like	Industry	Services				Total Employment	Period Covered
			Commerce	Transport and the like	Other	Total Services		
Europe								
Greece	-3.7	1.9	4.9	3.3	-0.6	2.0	-0.7	1961-71
Spain	-2.7	3.0	4.8	2.1	3.7	3.8	1.0	1960-70
Africa								
Egypt	0.2	6.6	-0.7	4.8	-1.2	-0.3	1.1	1960-66
Tunisia	-2.5	4.9	1.5	4.1	9.6	6.4	-0.1	1955-66
Latin America								
Chile	-1.2	3.8	4.9	7.3	2.2	3.8	1.9	1960-71
Mexico	-1.7	3.3	1.1	0.3	5.3	3.4	1.3	1960-70
Nicaragua	-2.2	1.4	5.8	4.5	5.8	5.7	0.7	1963-71
Venezuela	-1.3	6.4	7.3	6.4	4.2	5.5	3.3	1961-71
Asia								
Indonesia	1.3	0.3	n.a.	n.a.	n.a.	9.1	2.5	1961-64
Israel	2.6	4.9	5.5	7.0	4.2	4.9	4.0	1961-67
Korea (South)	0.8	7.4	15.0	17.6	2.7	9.4	5.0	1966-71
Malaysia (West)	-0.1	3.4	2.6	1.1	2.5	2.3	1.0	1957-67
Pakistan	3.6	8.2	12.0	16.4	1.2	7.6	4.7	1961-68
Philippines	2.1	6.4	5.5	9.8	7.8	7.4	4.0	1960-70

n.a. = not available

Notes: The growth rates by sector refer to the total number of employees, self-employed, and family workers who can be allocated by sector; the rates for "total employment" refer, in addition, to persons who are gainfully employed but who could not be allocated by sector.

Source: International Labour Organisation, *Yearbook of Labour Statistics* (Geneva: ILO, 1968, 1972). (Extracted from Organization for Economic Cooperation and Development, *Service Activities in Developing Countries* [Paris: OECD, 1974].)

ences complicate the evaluation of data for individual countries and COMECON as a group.

Service Industry Employment

Labor input data indicate that services have been a major growth area in most Eastern European countries and the Soviet Union over the last few decades. In the Soviet Union, 22 percent of the economically active population was employed in nonmaterial services in 1974, compared with 15 percent in 1960. As can be seen in Table 2.17, the six Eastern European countries have also experienced increases in employment in nonmaterial services over the same period. This pattern holds true for the Soviet Union, even when *services* are defined more broadly, as can be seen in Table 2.18. The rising importance of services in the Soviet Union in the last 15 years is also reflected in wage gains, with nearly a 100 percent rise, compared with 35 percent for the rest of the economy. In the general economic reform begun by Aleksei Kosygin in 1965, large wage increases were given to the long-neglected service workers in the form of increased bonuses paid from incentive funds based on profits. By 1974 services employment

TABLE 2.18

Growth Rates of Average Annual Employment, Soviet Union, 1950–75 (in percent per year)

Average Annual Employment	1950–58	1959–65	1966–70	1971–75
Total civilian	1.9	2.0	1.9	1.7*
Nonagriculture	3.7	4.5	3.5	2.5
Industry	4.0	3.9	2.9	1.5
Services	3.0	5.5	4.3	3.3
Other	4.8	4.3	3.4	3.0
Agriculture	0.1	−1.3	−1.1	−0.4*

*1971–74.

Note: The services covered in this employment data include both nonmaterial and material services: trade, public dining, material-technical supply, sales, and procurement; housing-communal economy and personal services; education and culture; art; science and scientific services; credit and insurance organizations; and government administration.

Source: Murray Feshbach and Stephen Rapawy, "Soviet Population and Manpower Trends and Policies," in *Soviet Economy in a New Perspective: A Compendium of Papers*, U.S., Congress, Joint Economic Committee, 94th Cong., 2d sess., October 14, 1976, table 9, p. 133.

TABLE 2.19

Annual Average Employment for Selected Branches of the Economy, 1975 and Percentage Change, Soviet Union, 1950–75

	Employment, 1975 (in thousands)*	Annual Average Percentage Change			
		1950–58	1959–65	1966–70	1971–75
Total*	126,649	1.9	2.0	1.9	1.7
Industry	34,030	4.0	3.9	2.9	1.5
Services	45,545	3.2	5.0	3.8	3.2
Transportation	9,150	4.1	3.5	1.9	2.8
Communications	1,540	2.6	6.1	5.7	3.0
Trade, public dining, material supply and sales, and procurement	8,890	2.8	5.3	4.6	3.4
Housing, communal economy, and personal services	3,815	3.1	4.5	5.0	4.6
Health services	5,790	5.1	4.9	3.5	2.6
Education and culture	9,145	3.5	6.0	4.0	2.7
Art	445	5.6	4.1	2.2	1.6
Science and scientific services	4,010	8.2	10.1	4.3	4.4
Credit and insurance organizations	520	-0.2	2.1	5.3	6.0
Government administration	2,240	6.9	1.7	5.2	3.5

*1974 employment data for total; and percentage change for 1971 through 1974. Total includes agriculture, forestry, independent artisans, construction, and other miscellaneous categories not presented separately, which are not available at this time for 1975.

Source: Murray Feshbach and Stephen Rapawy, "Soviet Population and Manpower Trends and Policies," in Soviet Economy in a New Perspective: A Compendium of Papers, U.S., Congress, Joint Economic Committee, 94th Cong., 2d sess., October 14, 1976, tables 10 and 11, pp. 135, 136.

averaged 33.8 million or 27 percent of the total employment. If transportation and communications are included, as they are in most capitalist countries, the figure rises to 35 percent.

Among the individual services, science and scientific services had the fastest employment growth throughout the 1950–75 period, although growth has slowed substantially in the last ten-year period (see Table 2.19). Credit and insurance organizations have experienced large increases in employment since 1966, reflecting the government policy of capturing the liquid assets of the population through the sale of insurance. Increases in consumer services employment result from government efforts to bring the level of consumer services more in line with demand. Transportation, communications, trade and material supply, sales, and procurement are services that are in part productive, as they include services to the material production sector as well as final consumers. With the exception of transportation in the 1966–70 period, their employment has consistently grown two to three times the rate of the overall economy since 1959. The increase in these sectors, especially as far as they represent gains in productive services, reflect expansion of the service infrastructure as the economy develops.

Government administration employment rose at more than twice the rate of employment in the economy as a whole between 1966 and 1975, but even then it accounted for only about 2 percent of total employment. This is much smaller than one would expect for a country at the Soviet Union's level of development, and with a centrally planned economy. Analysts differ in opinion as to how to measure Soviet government activities. Thus it is unclear if the data accurately show the size of the government sector.

In other Eastern European countries, service industries also experienced rapid employment growth between 1965 and 1975 (see Table 2.20). Romania was the only exception to this trend, with employment growth in industry outpacing trade, transport and communication, and the "other" sector. The service sector's share of total employment in these countries rose from between 17 and 36 percent in 1965 to between 23 and 40 percent in 1975. In 1975 East Germany had the largest percentage of employment in services (40 percent) followed by Czechoslovakia (37 percent) and Hungary (35 percent). These employment data are not entirely comparable with the Soviet man-year equivalents data presented above, but it does give a rough idea of the significance of employment in services. Despite the growth in services, none of these economies can yet be defined as a service economy.

Service Share in GNP

In GNP terms, the impact of services on socialist economies has been relatively constant since 1950, an evaluation based on estimates made by Western analysts. As noted above, the net MPS is cumbersome for dealing with

TABLE 2.20

Structure and Growth of Employment by Major Sector, Eastern European Countries, 1965, 1970, 1975

	Structure (percentage of total)			Indexes: 1965 = 100		
	1965	1970	1975	1965	1970	1975
Bulgaria						
Industry (including handicrafts)	26.3	30.4	33.6	100	121.6	143.7
Agriculture and forestry	45.3	35.7	28.1	100	83.2	70.0
Construction	7.0	8.4	7.9	100	127.2	127.9
Transport and communications	5.1	6.0	6.4	100	116.0	132.7
Trade	5.2	6.1	7.8	100	124.8	170.7
Other	11.1	13.4	16.2	100	129.0	167.0
Total	100.0	100.0	100.0	100	105.3	112.6
Czechoslovakia						
Industry (including handicrafts)	38.3	38.0	38.5	100	107.7	115.3
Agriculture and forestry	21.1	18.3	15.2	100	94.2	82.6
Construction	8.0	8.6	9.3	100	116.1	132.2
Transport and communications	6.5	6.8	6.5	100	114.4	116.3
Trade	8.4	9.0	10.3	100	116.4	140.0
Other	17.7	19.3	20.2	100	118.4	131.5
Total	100.0	100.0	100.0	100	108.6	114.8
East Germany						
Industry (including handicrafts)	41.4	42.1	42.0	100	103.6	105.6
Agriculture and forestry	16.1	12.4	11.0	100	78.6	70.9
Construction	6.1	8.0	7.5	100	134.0	128.1
Transport and communications	7.1	7.2	7.6	100	103.4	111.2
Trade	11.5	10.9	10.6	100	96.7	96.2
Other	17.8	19.4	21.3	100	110.5	124.6
Total	100.0	100.0	100.0	100	101.8	104.1

46

Hungary

Industry (including handicrafts)	34.3	35.7	35.5	100	111.4	112.9
Agriculture and forestry	28.1	24.8	21.1	100	94.9	82.3
Construction	6.4	7.5	8.2	100	125.2	140.8
Transport and communications	6.9	7.3	7.8	100	113.7	123.8
Trade	7.3	8.2	9.1	100	120.5	135.9
Other	17.0	16.5	18.2	100	104.2	117.3
Total	100.0	100.0	100.0	100	107.2	109.3

Poland

Industry (including handicrafts)	28.6	30.3	30.8	100	119.0	136.2
Agriculture and forestry	39.4	34.6	30.6	100	98.8	98.2
Construction	6.8	7.3	8.9	100	121.2	165.3
Transport and communications	5.9	6.2	6.3	100	119.0	136.2
Trade	6.1	6.9	7.5	100	126.5	154.5
Other	13.2	14.7	15.9	100	124.3	151.4
Total	100.0	100.0	100.0	100	112.3	126.4

Romania

Industry (including handicrafts)	18.8	22.5	30.1	100	122.5	168.0
Agriculture and forestry	57.6	50.3	39.1	100	89.3	71.1
Construction	6.4	7.6	8.1	100	121.3	132.4
Transport and communications	3.5	4.1	4.7	100	117.6	140.4
Trade	3.9	4.3	5.5	100	112.4	145.5
Other	9.8	11.2	12.5	100	118.9	135.4
Total	100.0	100.0	100.0	100	102.4	104.9

Notes: "Other" includes personal services, health, education, and public administration. Services are transport and communications, trade, and other.

Source: Thad P. Alton, "Comparative Structure and Growth of Economic Activity in Eastern Europe," in *East European Economics, Post-Helsinki*, U.S., Congress, Joint Economic Committee, 95th Cong, 1st sess., 1977, table 7, p. 218.

services as they are understood in this study. The estimates include household and communal services such as housing, utilities, repair and personal care, education, health, and art. The service category also includes science and general administration, credit and state insurance, and military personnel costs.

Estimates of GNP for the Soviet Union provide a reconstruction of growth data for services, but there is no analysis available of the amount of GNP that is derived from services. Table 2.21 indicates that services other than construction, transportation, communications, and trade grew at less than half the rate of GNP in the 1950-60 decade and have come in line with the overall rate of increase in GNP in the 1960s and 1970s. These GNP estimates for the Soviet Union support the employment data in indicating that transportation, communications, and trade have continued to grow substantially faster than the overall economy throughout the 1950-75 period.

Growth trends for GNP by end use (see Table 2.22) indicate that in the early 1970s household services rose 3.9 percent in line with the overall increase of GNP of 3.8 percent. Administration and other services, after declining between 1950 and 1960, increased about the same as overall GNP in the 1960s and 1970s. This decline is possibly a result of Nikita Khrushchev's efforts to reduce the party apparatus and dismantle some of Joseph Stalin's security administration.

TABLE 2.21

Gross National Product by Sector of Origin Excluding Weapons (factor cost), Average Rates of Growth, Soviet Union, 1951-75 (in percent)

	1951-55	1956-60	1961-65	1966-70	1971-75
Industry	10.3	8.9	6.6	6.2	5.9
Construction	11.0	10.4	4.5	5.8	5.6
Agriculture	4.1	4.1	2.4	4.2	-2.0
Transportation	12.2	10.9	8.7	6.7	6.3
Communications	8.1	7.0	7.1	8.9	7.2
Trade	10.4	8.5	4.9	6.5	5.0
Services*	2.4	2.2	4.7	4.2	3.6
GNP	5.8	5.8	4.9	5.3	3.7

*Including military personnel costs.

Source: Rush V. Greenslade, "The Real Gross National Product of the U.S.S.R., 1950-1975," in *Soviet Economy in a New Perspective: A Compendium of Papers*, U.S., Congress, Joint Economic Committee, 94th Cong., 2d sess., October 14, 1976, table 2, p. 272.

TABLE 2.22

Gross National Product by End Use (factor cost), Average Annual Rates for Growth, Soviet Union, 1951-75 (in percent)

	1951-55	1956-60	1961-65	1966-70	1971-75
Consumption	5.9	5.4	4.0	5.1	3.8
Household consumption	6.0	5.6	3.8	5.3	3.9
Consumer goods	6.7	5.8	3.3	5.6	3.9
Food	6.0	4.5	3.0	4.7	2.8
Soft goods	8.2	10.1	3.8	7.2	4.5
Durables	19.4	13.3	5.9	10.8	10.8
Household services	4.3	5.3	5.1	4.6	3.9
Communal consumption	5.6	4.2	5.1	4.0	3.6
Health	7.7	5.9	3.1	3.9	2.9
Education	4.4	3.1	6.5	4.1	4.0
Fixed investment	12.2	10.3	7.1	6.3	5.4
New fixed investment	12.6	10.3	6.8	6.4	4.5
Machinery and equipment	11.3	12.6	10.8	7.6	8.4
Construction and other	11.4	10.4	4.3	6.5	5.0
Net addition to livestock	65.9	−1.8	23.1	−0.2	−14.7
Capital repair	9.8	10.3	8.9	6.0	9.4
Research and development	8.4	12.6	8.8	6.7	6.1
Administrative and other services	−4.1	0.3	3.4	4.7	3.9
Outlays (not included elsewhere)*	3.3	−0.3	6.3	3.2	−3.7
Gross national product	6.0	5.8	5.0	5.5	3.8

*Includes defense, net exports, change in inventories and reserves, unidentified outlays, and statistical discrepancy.

Note: Total gross national product (including weapons production).

Source: Rush V. Greenslade, "The Real Gross National Product of the U.S.S.R., 1950-1975," in *Soviet Economy in a New Perspective: A Compendium of Papers*, U.S., Congress, Joint Economic Committee, 94th Cong., 2d sess., October 14, 1976, table 6, p. 276.

In the Eastern European countries the service sector maintained its proportion of GNP between 1965 and 1975, as can be seen in Table 2.23. Bulgaria was the only exception, with increases from 29 to 33 percent of total GNP over the period, reflecting gains in transport and communications and

TABLE 2.23

Composition of Gross National Product by Industrial Origin, East European Countries, 1965–1975 (in constant prices)

	1965	1970	1975
Bulgaria			
Industry (including handicrafts)	29.1	34.0	35.7
Agriculture	35.7	28.3	25.1
Construction	6.4	6.8	6.4
Transport and communications	6.1	8.3	9.4
Trade	5.3	6.2	7.2
Housing	6.7	6.3	6.1
Government and other services	10.7	10.1	10.1
Total	100.0	100.0	100.0
Czechoslovakia			
Industry (including handicrafts)	40.0	41.5	42.4
Agriculture and forestry	18.7	18.3	17.5
Construction	5.3	5.3	5.4
Transport and communications	10.5	10.0	10.2
Trade	6.8	7.8	8.7
Housing	9.6	8.5	7.8
Government and other services	9.1	8.6	8.0
Total	100.0	100.0	100.0
East Germany			
Industry (including handicrafts)	41.0	42.5	42.5
Agriculture and forestry	15.8	13.8	13.5
Construction	4.7	5.9	6.2
Transport and communications	7.0	7.5	7.8
Trade	9.4	10.0	10.8
Housing	8.9	7.9	7.1
Government and other services	13.2	12.4	12.1
Total	100.0	100.0	100.0

(continued)

trade.* In the other five countries, although some service branches increased, declines in others left the service share of GNP essentially unchanged for the ten-year period.

---

*Services include transport and communications, trade, housing, and government and other services.

TABLE 2.23 (continued)

	1965	1970	1975
Hungary			
Industry (including handicrafts)	33.5	34.4	33.5
Agriculture and forestry	25.9	22.4	22.8
Construction	4.5	5.7	5.6
Transport and communications	9.7	9.9	9.7
Trade	5.6	7.2	8.1
Housing	10.0	9.0	8.4
Government and other services	10.8	11.4	11.9
Total	100.0	100.0	100.0
Poland			
Industry (including handicrafts)	32.0	35.8	37.5
Agriculture and forestry	30.0	24.5	19.1
Construction	7.0	8.4	10.4
Transport and communications	7.8	8.7	11.5
Trade	6.0	6.5	7.4
Housing	7.5	7.1	6.1
Government and other services	9.7	9.0	8.0
Total	100.0	100.0	100.0
Romania			
Industry (including handicrafts)	26.5	35.5	39.5
Agriculture and forestry	42.0	31.3	29.4
Construction	6.7	7.5	6.2
Transport and communications	5.5	7.0	8.0
Trade	5.5	6.5	7.0
Housing	5.4	4.7	3.9
Government and other services	8.4	7.5	6.0
Total	100.0	100.0	100.0

Source: Thad P. Alton, "Comparative Structure and Growth of Economic Activity in Eastern Europe," in *East European Economics, Post-Helsinki*, U.S., Congress, Joint Economic Committee, 95th Cong., 1st sess., 1977, table 2, p. 206.

Growth rates by sectors of the economy, shown in Table 2.24, indicate that trade, transport, and communications were strong sectors of growth in most of the countries from 1965 to 1975. Slow growth in other services, such as communal services, defense, and education, and the emphasis on material output overshadow these trends in the aggregate data. For example, in Poland and Romania service sector growth, except for science, was overshadowed by the large increases in industry. These trends are in sharp contrast to the employment

TABLE 2.24

Growth of Gross National Product by Sector of Origin, East European Countries, 1965–76
(average annual rates at constant prices; in percent)

	1965–70	1970–75	1965–75	1976
Bulgaria				
Gross national product	4.8	4.5	4.6	4.6
Industry (including handicrafts)	8.6	5.6	6.8	5.0
Agriculture and forestry	−0.8	1.7	0.7	1.4
Construction	6.2	3.3	4.2	4.9
Transport and communications	11.9	7.4	9.6	5.7
Trade	8.7	7.9	8.0	7.3
Housing	3.7	4.2	4.0	3.8
Government and other services	4.4	3.6	4.0	5.4
Czechoslovakia				
Gross national product	3.5	3.4	3.3	1.9
Industry (including handicrafts)	4.1	3.8	4.0	3.3
Agriculture and forestry	3.5	2.5	2.0	−3.1
Construction	2.7	3.7	3.5	3.4
Transport and communications	2.1	3.7	3.2	2.8
Trade	7.0	5.8	6.0	3.4
Housing	0.9	1.5	1.2	2.0
Government and other services	2.7	1.9	2.1	1.0
East Germany				
Gross national product	3.2	3.5	3.2	2.4
Industry (including handicrafts)	4.1	3.3	3.6	4.1
Agriculture and forestry	0.4	3.9	1.2	−7.7
Construction	8.1	4.5	6.1	5.3
Transport and communications	4.2	3.9	4.4	7.4
Trade	4.5	5.3	4.8	3.5
Housing	0.8	1.2	0.9	1.5
Government and other services	1.2	2.1	1.6	2.2

(continued)

growth in services in the socialist countries. On the GNP side, services more or less simply held their own with the exception of some increases in transportation, communications, and trade.

In consumption, as can be seen from Table 2.25, the rate of growth of per capita consumption of personal services was faster in the 1960s and 1970s than in the earlier decade. This coincides with the growth pattern that can be found

TABLE 2.24 (continued)

	1965-70	1970-75	1965-75	1976
Hungary				
Gross national product	3.1	3.6	3.1	1.2
Industry (including handicrafts)	3.4	3.1	3.0	2.5
Agriculture and forestry	0.7	3.8	1.1	-4.9
Construction	8.0	3.2	5.6	4.5
Transport and communications	3.2	3.6	3.4	0.3
Trade	8.3	6.0	7.4	6.6
Housing	0.9	2.0	1.3	2.2
Government and other services	2.1	4.8	3.6	3.8
Poland				
Gross national product	3.8	6.7	5.2	5.7
Industry (including handicrafts)	6.4	7.6	6.9	7.0
Agriculture and forestry	-1.1	1.7	0.8	-1.0
Construction	7.8	12.3	9.7	4.5
Transport and communications	6.3	12.5	9.1	12.6
Trade	5.8	9.7	7.4	9.8
Housing	2.8	3.3	3.2	3.3
Government and other services	2.7	4.1	3.3	4.7
Romania				
Gross national product	4.5	6.1	5.6	7.1
Industry (including handicrafts)	11.0	9.2	10.1	7.8
Agriculture and forestry	-1.8	3.8	1.9	8.6
Construction	7.7	2.7	6.0	4.2
Transport and communications	10.5	8.6	9.0	4.5
Trade	8.1	8.1	8.0	8.6
Housing	2.1	2.5	2.4	2.8
Government and other services	2.4	1.9	1.8	2.3

Note: Table constructed from least-squares fit of $l_n = l_0(1 + r)^n$.

Source: Thad P. Alton, "Comparative Structure and Growth of Economic Activity in Eastern Europe," in *East European Economics, Post-Helsinki*, U.S., Congress, Joint Economic Committee, 95th Cong., 1st sess., 1977, table 18, p. 237.

in employment data. The sharpest per capita increase between 1950 and 1975 was in personal transport and communications, which increased over fivefold. Per capita consumption of utilities rose steadily, and repair and personal care, after remaining almost unchanged in the 1950-56 period, increased rapidly in the later period. These gains followed the government emphasis on expanding service facilities in 1963/64. Per capita consumption of health and education

TABLE 2.25

Growth of per Capita Consumption in the Soviet Union, 1950–75

	Indexes (1950 = 100)					
	1950	1955	1960	1965	1970	1975
Total consumption	100.0	129.3	159.2	180.5	226.8	264.9
Household	100.0	130.3	161.8	182.4	231.5	270.8
Goods	100.0	131.4	163.8	181.4	229.4	266.1
Food	100.0	125.6	144.3	159.1	189.4	210.0
Soft goods	100.0	142.6	212.8	232.7	320.5	367.0
Durables and miscellaneous	100.0	223.3	382.7	473.7	751.9	1,196.2
Services	100.0	121.9	148.6	188.5	245.7	303.2
Communal	100.0	124.0	142.7	169.9	198.0	228.7
Education	100.0	115.6	125.2	160.9	188.2	222.4
Health	100.0	139.5	174.4	185.9	215.1	239.4

	Average Annual Rates of Growth					
	1951–75	1951–55	1956–60	1961–65	1966–70	1971–75
Total consumption	4.0	5.3	4.2	2.5	4.7	3.2
Household	4.1	5.4	4.4	2.4	4.9	3.2
Goods	4.0	5.6	4.5	2.1	4.8	3.0
Foods	3.0	4.7	2.8	2.0	3.5	2.1
Soft goods	5.3	7.4	8.3	1.8	6.6	2.7
Durables and miscellaneous	10.4	17.4	11.4	4.4	9.7	9.7
Services	4.5	4.0	4.0	4.9	5.4	4.3
Communal	3.4	4.4	2.8	3.6	3.1	2.9
Education	3.2	2.9	1.6	5.1	3.2	3.4
Health	3.6	6.9	4.6	1.3	3.0	2.2

Source: Gertrude E. Schroeder and Barbara S. Severin, "Soviet Consumption and Income Policies in Perspective," in *Soviet Economy in a New Perspective,* U.S., Congress, Joint Economic Committee, 94th Cong., 2d sess., October 14, 1976, table 1, p. 622.

54

have experienced a reduced rate of growth since 1965. After the substantial expansion of these services in earlier decades, the slowdown possibly reflects the success of government programs in earlier years.

Comparisons with Other Economies

The service sector in socialist countries plays a much smaller role than would be expected, given their relatively high level of industrialization. Services by and large have not grown dramatically in those countries despite their higher and higher levels of development. Despite the increases noted above in employment, the service sectors of the COMECON countries remain dwarfs when compared with their Western counterparts.

Two questions follow from this observation. Why is the service sector small in socialist countries? Is the smaller size adequate or desirable for providing the normal requirements of economic life and continued growth?

Studies of the Soviet and Hungarian economies have determined that the small size of the service sector is mostly caused by socialist policy toward economic growth.[22] Economic resources are diverted from present consumption to future use through investment in heavy manufacturing, which results in a small share of GNP devoted to private consumption (durable goods as well as services). Furthermore, Soviet production techniques are highly capital intensive in manufacturing and labor intensive in agriculture, which creates less urbanization and thus fewer services. Another factor is that private activities are generally forbidden; thus small independent retailers, craftsmen, or suppliers of services do not swell the size of cities as they do in market economies.

As the Soviet study points out, two aspects of the economic system contribute to the small size of the service sector: the organization of the economic system and ideology. In a centrally planned economy, service activities such as wholesale trade—a necessary link in the capitalist production process—are undeveloped. On the other hand, public administration, which would be expected to be large in a centrally planned system, is nevertheless very small in the Soviet Union. The Soviet explanation for this is based on ideological considerations. All services, including public administration, have a low social value and are considered nonproductive economic activities. With the exception of large investments in education and health services, which are recognized for their value in increasing the productivity of labor, the Soviets have remained ideologically biased against a large service sector.

The study of the Hungarian service sector focuses on the anticipated size of the sector in the near future and the question of whether it should be neglected at this stage of development. If 18 OECD countries are taken as a model, investment in services in Hungary should have amounted to almost 57 percent of all investments between 1961 and 1965 and exceeded 61 percent in the 1976–80 period. The actual proportion of investments going to services remained almost unchanged at roughly 45 percent throughout the period.[24] Thus the situation in Hungary is deteriorating relative to other countries in comparable stages of development. The lag in investment is seen as even more serious than the low proportion of labor in services because the effects are cumulative.

The small supply of labor and fixed assets in the service sector in Hungary translates into a larger-than-expected use of these productive factors in industry and, to a lesser degree, in agriculture. The study, however, points out that industry was not able to absorb the extra productive factors and turn them into proportionately higher output during this period. In short, the return on investment in industry is too small.

The study concludes that neglecting the service sector is not necessary for more rapid economic growth; further, that growth of production in the productive sector may in fact be hampered by holding back services. Without sufficient service infrastructure, production costs could rise; thus increases in output would call for larger and larger inputs of labor and fixed assets. In some socialist nations this fact, plus the general desirability of providing services, is beginning to be recognized. Romania, for one, recently held a national conference on services and has shown some interest in focusing on these activities.

Projections

The general consensus in the current literature is that the service sector will continue to grow in the socialist countries of Eastern Europe and the Soviet Union in the next decade. There is little indication, however, that the historical bias of socialist countries against services will change. Nevertheless, pressure from consumers for more personal services and from the productive sector for increased production-related services will necessitate continued growth of service output. This can be seen in the Soviet Union's Tenth Five-Year Plan for 1976–80. It does not indicate a substantial shift to accelerated service industry growth, although it emphasizes substantial efforts in improving the quality of services. Wholesale trade, in particular, is to be strengthened to improve ties between industries, producers, and final consumers. The plan calls for greater responsibility of trade enterprises in providing the necessary amounts and assortments of goods to stores. This represents a recognition of the importance of trade services in providing flexibility and feedback to the economic system.

Education is to be augmented, with emphasis on vocational education and on-the-job training. Research and development institutes will receive additional emphasis, particularly in the area of efficient delivery of knowledge to the productive sector. Although growth in health care will be slower, quality is expected to improve. Finally, the standards of communication services are to improve, with the number of telephones increasing 40 percent.

The current system of centralized control with its bias toward meeting output quotas discourages innovation and also hampers rapid adjustment to consumer demand. Fundamental measures to increase the system's flexibility would probably give a sharp boost to many service industries. This would entail not only a more efficient wholesale trade sector but also better management, communications, transportation, and government planning. It would surely require a more rapid increase in output of services because these activities in particular provide the infrastructure for flexibility in the economic system.

Services Traded Internationally

The importance of services in international trade is difficult to evaluate for socialist countries because of the lack of data. Information on hard currency trade, however, indicates that, at least in the Soviet Union, trade in invisibles is an increasingly important source of foreign exchange. In 1975 the Soviet Union incurred a large trade deficit because it needed to import large amounts of Western grain at a time when the recession in the West had depressed Soviet export earnings. Since 1976 Soviets have made efforts to reduce the size of the trade deficit by continuing to reduce nongrain imports, increase gold sales, and minimize cash outlays.

Transportation and tourism are the only services that seem to be significant earners of hard currency for the Soviet Union, although as Table 2.26 indicates, these invisibles still make a very small contribution, compared with merchandise exports, gold sales, credit, and arms sales. Receipts from transportation, mainly shipping, are expected to grow steadily[24] —the result of a definite Soviet policy

TABLE 2.26

Sources of Hard Currency, Soviet Union, 1977, 1978 (in millions of U.S. dollars)

	1977	1978
Total	20.6–19.0	23.4–21.3
Merchandise exports	12.5–12.0	15.0–14.0
Gold sales	1.3–1.2	1.5–1.4
Medium- and long-term credits	4.0–3.5	4.0–3.5
Arms sales	2.0–1.5	2.0–1.5
Tourism and transportation, net	0.8	0.9

Note: These figures were projected.

Source: U.S., Central Intelligence Agency, *Research Aid, USSR: Hard Currency Trade and Payments, 1977-78* (ER 77-10035 U), March 1977, table 2, p. 7.

to minimize the use of foreign bottoms in its foreign trade. In addition, Soviet luxury liners now operate in various regions on an uneconomic basis, which indicates the Soviet willingness to bear financial losses domestically in order to earn foreign exchange.

Net tourism receipts were projected to be about $180 million in 1977 and $220 million in 1978.[25] The Soviet state tourist agency, Intourist, and the state tourist agencies of most other COMECON members have opened offices throughout much of the world, indicating their policy of aggressively promoting tourism to earn foreign exchange. The Soviets also aggressively promote trade-related services, again with an emphasis on earning foreign exchange. For example, import/export contracts by foreign trading organizations (FTOs) are designed so as to ensure that the transport insurance is placed with the state insurance company. State trading companies try to export on a cargo insurance and freight (CIF) basis and import on a freight on board (f.o.b.) basis, thereby controlling the insurance on such transactions so as to place them with the state insurance company. U.S. insurance companies have objected to this, and negotiations have been underway for several years between the Soviet Union and the United States on a more equitable sharing of insurance in U.S.-Soviet trade. Other Eastern European countries have emulated this practice.

In addition to tourism and transportation, some socialist countries are also surprisingly active international investors in services. The Soviet state insurance company, Ingosstrakh, for example, has subsidiaries or branch offices overseas in Afghanistan, Austria, West Germany, Finland, Great Britain, Iran, Lebanon, and Mali. Ingosstrakh has also explored opening a branch in New York State. Poland's state insurance company, Warta Insurance and Reinsurance Company, Ltd., has offices in London and New York. The business aggressiveness of these socialist enterprises should not be underrated. Perhaps the most dramatic illustration was the past Soviet practice of reinsuring the U.S. Overseas Private Investment Corporation. Thereby, the Soviets were ensuring against the expropriation of U.S. property in developing countries, something U.S. insurance companies were unwilling to do at that time. Reportedly, the business was very profitable, with no losses incurred.

In the banking field, the Soviet Union and Eastern European countries also operate overseas. The Soviet Union has overseas affiliations in London, Singapore, Beirut, Frankfurt, Zurich, Paris, Teheran, Vienna, and Luxembourg. Other Eastern European countries have various smaller operations in Western Europe, Lebanon, and New York.

A striking example of the international activities of socialist countries is found in the construction industry. The COMECON countries have been aggressive and highly successful in winning bids on overseas projects. For example, the Soviet Union built a steel mill in Pakistan and a pipeline in Nigeria; Czechoslovakia has built a cement factory and a textile plant in the Middle East; and Poland and Romania also have had construction projects in the Middle East.

Finally, one other service area in which the Soviets are active, especially within the Eastern bloc, is in providing the management services of consultants, accountants, and engineers. Again, there are no hard data available, but developments in COMECON countries indicate that the Soviets are very active throughout Eastern Europe. This, however, does not earn convertible currency.

In conclusion, it seems that the Soviet Union and some of the Eastern European countries are aggressively expanding their international activities in services with the explicit intent of earning foreign exchange. In insurance, shipping, and perhaps construction, they are pursuing policies that violate recognized rules of international trade. Analogies can be drawn here to merchandise trade violations such as dumping, subsidies, and import restrictions. Like other commercial problems between the East and West, the nature of the socialist economic system makes their resolution exceedingly difficult. In short, although service activities in the COMECON countries are generally below international trends for their level of development, and virtually no correlation can be perceived between important domestic services and those that are active internationally, services, increasingly, are important earners of foreign exchange.

CONCLUSION

The foregoing pages have given us a sense of the aggregate importance of services today in national economies and the world economy. All signs indicate that services will be of greater importance in the future, a theme that will be expanded in the next chapter by drawing on Wassily Leontif et al.'s recent study, *The Future of the World Economy.*[26] However, services trends in the aggregate are meaningless in themselves; they fail to tell us what we need to know about services in international commerce. But data limitations make the task of interpreting what international services are really all about a tenuous proposition. A sound interpretation requires a totally restructured data-gathering base. My recommendations on the steps necessary to deal with the data problem are found in the Appendix to Chapter 2.

The limited data available give indications as to which services have the strongest international linkages. In the United States, if we consider both trade and investment in services, first in importance are banking, insurance, and other financial services, followed by wholesale/retail trade, transportation services, and passenger fares. In other industrial countries and among the top 35 countries where invisibles play an important role in trade, transportation is the most important, followed by "other services"—banking, insurance, construction, payment for films, commissions, and agency fees, and the like. Travel services rank third. Because data on investment in services are unavailable, this analysis is limited to services trade.

Among developing countries, which include many nations in the "top 35" list, travel is most important and transportation is second, but generally as a deficit item; and in some nations "other services" are significant. Again, overseas investment data are unavailable, but they should be insignificant. In the socialist countries important services internationally are transportation and tourism (in this case, involving more than passenger fares). Unimportant statistically but of special concern in terms of the working of the international commercial system are insurance and construction services.

At present, working within the constraints of limited data, these would seem to be the priority services to focus on in the context of international commerce, if priorities are to be determined solely by magnitudes of trade. However, this in itself is a faulty approach for determining what is important. As this analysis will suggest in subsequent chapters, other factors, such as the importance of a service to the international commercial framework, need be given equal if not priority consideration. An understanding of individual services activities, disaggregated from the broader, general framework suggested by balance-of-payments analysis, is required.

To do justice to service activities, we need to understand their role in the world economy: how they are regulated; what constraints they face; and broader issues such as their relationship to the transfer of technology, economic development, and facilitating trade. Subsequent chapters will address these questions. In addition, consideration will be given to the dynamics of services, including the evolution and development of new services that may already be more important than we realize or that may be important in the future. These are the elements that must be understood in order to fashion alternative regimes for international services commerce in the future.

APPENDIX TO CHAPTER 2

Service Sector Data Collection: Problems and Recommendations

In 1961 an article on world trade and invisibles written by Ely Devons was printed in *Lloyds Bank Review*. Devons commented, "Today's economists, both academic and journalistic, have an almost pathological and neurotic obsession with the state, actual or potential, of the balance of payments of the countries whose economic position is under their gaze. But they rarely, if ever, analyze the constituent items of the invisible account."[1] He suggested that the main reason for this was that appropriate data on invisibles were not available.

Devons's comments are even more relevant today. In the last 19 years, traders and investors in services have been increasingly active in international markets, making the role of services in the world economy even more important. Despite this growing interest, little is known about services, either in terms of data compilation or analysis.

There are six basic problem areas.

1. There exists a fundamental conceptual disagreement on the definition of *services*.

2. The utilization of different national accounting systems impedes both the compilation and analysis of services data. This is not a problem unique to services, but the situation is worse for services since national governments and international organizations have focused their investigative and analytical resources on goods rather than services. This lack of focus and coordination has aggravated the differences in the way these different accounting systems treat services.

The majority of industrial and developing countries follow some version of the United Nations System of National Accounts. Many of the former French dependencies use the Courcier System of National Accounts, while socialist states with centrally planned economies use the Material Products System (MPS). The latter two make severe distinctions in the way in which services are treated. For example, under the Courcier System in calculating gross domestic production, the value added of public administration, nonprofit institutions, financial intermediaries, and domestic services is excluded. The payments involved in these activities are recorded in these accounts but are treated as a form of transfer.

In the MPS, service activities are classified as productive (that is, those that are directly connected with physical production) and nonmaterial services. Thus distributive trade, goods transport, and communications services for productive enterprises are defined as productive services, while passenger transport, other communications, housing, health, education, and other social services, finance, insurance, public administration, and personal services are counted as nonmaterial services. As in the Courcier System, the payments for these service activities are calculated, but they are regarded as contributing to the redistribution of income rather than to the generation of output.

3. The third problem, closely related to the second, is that whatever system of accounts a country chooses to follow, it usually makes a number of changes in conceptualization, coverage, or classification. This is usually done to make the accounts more useful for internal purposes, to correct data gaps, or for other reasons. Numerous illustrations have been cited earlier in this chapter. Some countries classify an activity as a service, yet in other countries it is not treated as a service. Others classify in the aggregate certain kinds of services that would be treated separately or under different aggregate classifications elsewhere. This problem in classifying services results from the fundamental problem mentioned above—considerable confusion and disagreement on the definition of *services*. This will be clearly illustrated when I discuss some of the problems the United States encountered in its 1976 study.

4. There is inadequate compilation of relevant services data. This problem has persisted because of greater emphasis on goods, not services, in the international economy and lack of a statistical center or clearing house for information on service industry trade. A central point to collect service data is more

difficult to organize, because unlike the collection of trade data that occurs automatically through customs documentation, services trade does not pass through such channels.

5. Service data are so aggregated they are virtually meaningless. Examples have been cited in the text. Real estate services are often included with insurance and banking services. Statistics for wholesale and retail trade are frequently combined with hotel services. A large number of services are listed under other services, and this varies from country to country.

6. Many international service activities are more investment related than trade related, and these investment activities have been only superficially studied. Obviously, service industries are not the only kind of industries that have both trade- and investment-related activities. But the distinction is more difficult to make in services. While governments and international organizations have given international investment considerable attention, especially in the last few years, this has mainly focused on manufacturing and extractive industries.

Study by the United States of Its Service Industries in World Markets

A U.S. study of its service industries in world markets concluded that the methodology for compiling data on services is not well developed.[2] The available data that are so important for analyzing manufacturing and extractive industries, such as industry statistics, product detail, and country analysis, does not exist for services. Thus the authors of the U.S. study suggest that the service statistics used could be in error by several billion dollars. The description below of some of the problems encountered will illustrate the kinds of issues that must be addressed.

Service Industry Exports versus Exports of Services

The focus of the data gathered in the study is by industry, not by types of services. In other words, the effort was to quantify the overseas sales of service companies and their foreign affiliates rather than to measure the flow of services, regardless of the industry that produced them. This is a legitimate approach, but it can cause problems and lead to distortions. For example, if a nonservice industry is exporting services, it is not being accounted for in the data. So the consulting, banking, or insurance services provided by a manufacturing firm could be misread. New services being developed by nonservice industries are not likely to be included in a compilation of services data. In the long run, this is potentially significant because of the number of nonservice companies that are now diversifying and entering service markets.

Ownership of Services

The provision of government services is omitted in the U.S. study in order to focus on private service industry transactions. This is understandable for the United States because most international service industries are privately owned. In many other countries, however, the transportation, communications, and even the financial sector are government owned.

Where the Service Is Consumed

A problem that is not encountered in goods trade arises because the service exports may be consumed within the exporting country. A significant amount of services exports are receipts from foreign residents for services that were actually purchased and consumed entirely within U.S. borders. The most obvious example is tourism where receipts are collected for services wholly rendered and consumed within the borders of the United States. Educational fees paid by foreign students is a second example. U.S. port charges and airport landing fees paid for by foreign transportation firms are other examples. The U.S. study decided to treat services consumed by foreigners within the borders of the United States as nontraded services and not as service exports. Thus a separate accounting item in the balance-of-payments account was established.

There are probably numerous other less significant areas not considered by the authors of the U.S. study. For example, a foreigner may come to the United States to buy a life insurance policy and always pay the premium out of a U.S. bank account. Theoretically, the consumption of this service will never leave U.S. borders.

Measuring Exports of U.S. Services

There are many other problems in measuring the sales or exports of U.S. service industries. For example, management fees and services are considered a service industry export. Yet, the great majority of such fees are managerial, professional, and rental services provided by parent manufacturing and extractive industry firms to their affiliates. They are not transactions directly representing the export of services in the traditional sense and certainly not the export of services by service industries. The U.S. study included them because many of these services are similar to the outputs of service industry companies. This is complicated by the fact that service exports like these to nonaffiliated foreigners (foreign purchasers not affiliated with the parent firm) are not included because of lack of data. Yet such service sales are likely to become even more important in the future as these industries expand to find new customers for their services.

As for exports of service by service industries, oftentimes data on direct sales overseas are unknown. For example, the U.S. study noted there were no available data on the direct sales overseas of U.S.-based insurance firms. The study grappled with how to obtain data when, for example, a U.S. multinational buys one worldwide policy from an insurer in the United States in dollars to cover operations in various countries. A second example concerns how to measure the sales of those hundreds of U.S. insurance companies without overseas affiliates who insure the movement of goods in international commerce through purchases made directly from their U.S. offices. If the purchaser of the insurance is the foreign importer or exporter, presumably the purchase would be reflected through the trading transaction. On the other hand, the purchaser could be the U.S. exporter or importer who would purchase from a U.S.-based company. In that case, is it a U.S. export or import or a domestic transaction?

Measurement of Overseas Sales of U.S. Service Industry Affiliates

Various problems are also encountered in the collection of data for the sales of service industry affiliates overseas. The data on such affiliates are highly aggregated, divided into basically three categories—wholesale and retail, finance and insurance, and "other industries." In the U.S. system of data collection, "other industries" provides no disaggregation in the balance-of-payments statistics and includes a few industries that are not in the service sector, such as sales of agricultural affiliates. So for the U.S. study, to get any meaningful breakdown, industry and other sources had to be consulted; even then only rough estimates were made. Of the $25.9 billion in 1974 sales of "other industries," some $14.9 billion remain unidentified.[3] This includes important U.S. service industries such as construction.

Problems also arose in measuring finance and insurance. Sales figures for U.S. bank affiliates were not included in affiliate sales since the latest survey of U.S. investment overseas at the time the study was undertaken excluded them. Technically, *sales* is not a term applied to banking activities; instead, the concept of operating revenues is used. Therefore, bank exports had to be estimated through a complex formula that the authors of the report cautioned could be in error by $1 to $2 billion.

Another problem concerns separating goods from service transactions in certain industries—for example, both the products associated with such sales and the exports of construction/engineering services are lumped together. Similar problems were encountered in measuring the affiliate sales in wholesale and retail trade. The data do not distinguish between the value added by services and the cost of goods exported. Such data would make it possible to measure the actual services provided by wholesale/retail trade. Instead value added had to be estimated.

Steps toward Improving Service Industry Data

The difficulties encountered in the U.S. study graphically illustrate the general problems described in the beginning of this appendix. These are not easy problems to effectively deal with, but a meaningful understanding of services cannot be achieved unless a system is developed to produce a data base. Major industrial countries that have a large stake in services must come to terms with these issues, first, within their own country and, second, at the international level. One of the basic recommendations of the U.S. inter-agency Task Force on Services and the Multilateral Trade Negotiations was that a U.S. working group on international services data be formed to examine how international data are presently obtained, how unpublished data can be made more available, and how industry and geographic coverage of the data can be improved.[4]

Since industrial nations initially have the most to gain from adequate service data, a logical international forum in which to initiate discussions would be the Organization for Economic Cooperation and Development (OECD). This effort and experience could then be expanded to include other nations—industrial, developing, and socialist. The United Nations would probably be the best organization to coordinate this activity. It would not be a completely novel exercise, as the United Nations Commission on Transnational Corporations has already established a working group on international accounting standards; other UN agencies have undertaken similar work within their area of specialty. The United Nations Conference on Trade and Development (UNCTAD), for example, completed a study on an international system of reinsurance statistics. However, other international institutions with related functions and responsibilities will need to be involved. The International Monetary Fund (IMF), for one, recently sought to secure more comprehensive coverage of certain items of invisibles trade and also is attempting to improve the classification of transactions in the major areas of invisibles trade.

Such discussions should have four minimal objectives. First, an understanding must be reached on the definitions of *services* and other difficult issues such as categorization of services, treatment of royalties, the exports of nonservice firms, problems of nontraded services, and the like.

Second, one basic accounting approach should be adopted to measure services, with an agreement to minimize national modifications. Since there will be a resistance to changing national accounting systems, a minimal objective should be national commitments to maximize efforts to gather meaningful and comprehensive data on services on as disaggregated a basis as possible. In addition, attempts should be made to reach agreement on a system designed to translate different country approaches into a meaningful accepted international standard.

Third, data must be collected on the international investments of service industries. Industry-by-industry data on sales of overseas affiliates should be sought. Even more desirable would be disaggregated data on income—not sales—directly attributable to service industry investments overseas.

And fourth, a permanent mechanism should be established to regularly monitor and evaluate service data, including periodic adjustments in the collection system to take into account the experience in data collection and the need to measure new services.

NOTES

1. For a brief summary of other studies on international services and a more detailed treatment of the problems that arise in defining them, see the Bibliographic Appendix.

2. Maurice Lengelle, *The Growing Importance of the Service Sector in Member Countries* (Paris: Organization for Economic Cooperation and Development, 1966), p. 8. Lengelle has suggested an interesting way to look at this by dividing countries into four groups in relationship to employment growth in services.

> *Group 1:* Agricultural countries undergoing industrialization, where the growth of the tertiary sector appears to be slow.
>
> *Group 2:* Countries where the agricultural population has already declined substantially, but whose industrialization does not yet appear to be complete. The manpower released from the land swells the ranks of both the industrial sector and the service sector. The proportion of additional manpower entering the tertiary sector is higher than in the agricultural countries undergoing industrialization.
>
> *Group 3:* Countries where the industrialization process now appears complete and maximized. All manpower leaving the land seems to enter services.
>
> *Group 4:* Countries where the percentage of agricultural manpower is now extremely small . . . and employment in services continues to grow, at the expense of industry. In such countries, workers leaving industry seem to have superseded agricultural workers as a source of manpower for services.

3. U.S., Department of Labor, Bureau of Labor Statistics, *Occupational Projections and Training Data 1980*, Bulletin 2052 (Washington, D.C.: Government Printing Office, September 1980).

4. U.S., Department of Labor, Bureau of Labor Statistics, *U.S. Workers and Their Jobs: The Changing Picture*, Bulletin 1919 (Washington, D.C.: Government Printing Office, 1976).

5. U.S., Congressional Research Service, *U.S. International Service Trade*, prepared by David D. Driscoll, August 21, 1980.

6. U.S., Department of Commerce, Office of the Assistant Secretary for Policy, *U.S. Service Industries in World Markets: Current Problems and Future Policy Development* (Washington, D.C.: Government Printing Office, December 1976), p. 8 (hereafter cited as *U.S. Service Industries*).

7. U.S., Department of Commerce, Bureau of Economic Analysis, *National Income Accounts* (Washington, D.C.: Government Printing Office, 1980).

8. "The U.S. Lead in Service Exports Is Under Siege," *Business Week*, September 15, 1980, p. 70.

9. *U.S. Service Industries*, pp. 21-22.

10. Ibid., p. 21.

11. International Labour Office, *Year Book of Labour Statistics* (Geneva: ILO, 1976), pp. 331, 334.

12. Maurice Lengelle, "The Development of the Service Sector in OECD Countries and Its Implication for the Economy of the Western World" (Paper prepared for the Hudson Institute Conference on Outlook and Policy for Industrial Structure Change in OECD Countries, Washington, D.C., January 25-26, 1978), p. 9.

13. *U.S. Service Industries*, p. 7.

14. Ibid., p. 22.

15. Committee on Invisible Exports, *World Invisible Trade* (London: Committee on Invisible Exports, June 1980).

16. Ibid., p. 18.

17. Organization for Economic Cooperation and Development, *The Employment Problem in Less Developed Countries*, prepared for The OECD Development Center by David Turnham (Paris: OECD, 1970).

18. Derek W. Blades, Derek D. Johnston, and Witold Marczewski, *Service Activities in Developing Countries* (Paris: Development Centre of the Organization for Economic Cooperation and Development, 1974), p. 63.

19. Committee on Invisible Exports, *World Invisible Trade* (London: Committee on Invisible Exports, August 1977), p. 12.

20. Ibid., p. 18.

21. Ibid., p. 20.

22. Gur Ofer, *The Service Sector in Soviet Economic Growth* (Cambridge, Mass.: Harvard University Press, 1973).

23. B. Szabadi, "Relationship between the Level of Economic Development and the Services," *Acta Oeconomica* 15 (1975): 343–64.

24. U.S., Central Intelligence Agency, *Research Aid, USSR: Hard Currency Trade and Payments, 1977-78* (ER 77-10035 U), March 1977.

25. Ibid.

26. Wassily Leontief et al. *The Future of the World Economy*, A United Nations Study (New York: Oxford University Press, 1977).

NOTES TO APPENDIX TO CHAPTER 2

1. Ely Devons, "World Trade in Invisibles," *Lloyds Bank Review* (April 1961): 37–50.

2. U.S., Department of Commerce, Office of the Assistant Secretary for Policy, *U.S. Service Industries in World Markets: Current Problems and Future Policy Development* (Washington, D.C.: Government Printing Office, December 1976), p. 18.

3. Ibid.

4. Ibid. Since this report was published, there have been two such efforts. The U.S. Chamber's International Service Industry Committee released a report on data problems, including a series of recommendations for improvement. *Report on Selected International Service Industry Data*, International Service Industry Committee (Washington, D.C.: U.S. Chamber of Commerce, June 1980). In addition, the U.S. government has let two contracts to two private firms: (a) Economic Consulting Services and (b) Robert Sammons, Evelyn and Walter Lederer. One study will survey data resources and one will develop recommendations.

3

THE DYNAMICS OF SERVICES:
A CHALLENGE TO POLICY

Both economic history and empirical evidence suggest that services will become a more important component of the world economy. Yet any simple extrapolation of past growth rates obviously is meaningful only for the short-term future. A more sophisticated, long-range picture must be based on assumptions about the interaction of services with other economic, technological, and social developments. The best and most recent macroscopic analysis of this kind is a UN-sponsored study by Wassily Leontief et al. entitled *The Future of the World Economy.*[1]

PROJECTIONS

Leontief's study examines the future of the world economy to the year 2000, under alternative projections of the demographic, economic, and environmental state of the world in the benchmark years 1980, 1990, and 2000. The world is divided into 15 regions, each of which is described in terms of 45 economic sectors. The regions, although treated separately, are related to one another through a complex linkage mechanism, including exports and imports for some 40 classes of goods and services, capital flows, aid transfers, and foreign interest payments.

Although the study is clearly directed at manufacturing and primary products, it makes several perceptive assumptions about services during the rest of this century. Their projected role in the development process is especially noteworthy. Tertiary industries, which in the UN study include trade (wholesale and retail) and most other services except utilities and construction, are seen as a fast-growing sector of developing economies. The expansion of this sector in developing countries more or less parallels manufacturing, tending to exceed it at lower growth rates of gross domestic product (GDP) and falling short of

TABLE 3.1

Changes in Economic Structure—Scenario X
(percentage of total output originating in each sector)

Region	Agriculture and Mineral Resources	Manufacturing	Utilities and Construction	Services
Developing countries				
Latin America (medium-income)				
1970	21.0	31.5	10.2	37.3
2000	11.4	36.8	14.5	37.3
Latin America (low-income)				
1970	33.5	23.8	9.3	33.4
2000	16.1	28.5	16.2	39.2
Middle East				
1970	63.3	11.3	6.5	18.9
2000	15.0	31.0	17.5	35.6
Asia (low-income)				
1970	33.2	29.9	8.3	28.6
2000	19.4	32.3	11.0	37.3
Africa (arid)				
1970	28.1	33.6	7.1	31.2
2000	23.8	35.9	9.4	35.0
Africa (tropical)				
1970	46.9	17.8	7.9	27.4
2000	39.0	18.6	10.0	32.4
Developed market economies				
North America				
1970	6.6	39.3	11.6	42.5
2000	5.9	38.4	13.4	42.3
Western Europe (high-income)				
1970	8.2	42.5	10.7	38.6
2000	4.1	42.6	12.3	41.0
Japan				
1970	7.0	44.7	13.7	34.6
2000	3.0	46.1	12.7	38.2

Note: Data in this table relate to total output of sectors and are not directly comparable to sectoral shares based on value added.
Source: Wassily Leontief et al., *The Future of the World Economy*, A United Nations Study (New York: Oxford University Press, 1977).

TABLE 3.2

Regional Structure of Exports of Developing Regions
(percentage of total exports from each region, based on 1970 prices)

Region	Agriculture	Resources[a]	Light Industry	Machinery and Equipment	Materials[b]	Invisibles[c]	Subtotals	
							Agriculture and Resources	Manufacturing
Latin America (medium-income)								
1970	49.4	18.1	3.8	3.4	4.0	21.4	67.5	11.2
2000	21.6	34.9	9.0	11.1	8.6	14.7	56.5	28.7
Latin America (low-income)								
1970	31.6	52.0	2.3	0.7	2.4	10.9	83.6	5.4
2000	17.0	56.0	6.5	2.2	7.6	10.7	73.0	16.3
Middle East								
1970	8.6	84.7	1.2	0.5	0.7	4.3	93.8	2.4
2000	1.9	88.0	4.4	1.6	2.3	1.8	89.9	8.3
Asia (low-income)								
1970	40.3	11.2	26.9	6.5	5.3	9.9	51.5	38.7
2000	16.6	9.3	44.0	13.2	8.7	8.2	25.9	63.9
Africa (arid)								
1970	47.2	14.2	17.2	3.4	5.4	12.6	61.4	26.0
2000	36.3	9.8	23.2	4.0	8.8	17.9	46.1	36.0
Africa (tropical)								
1970	46.7	37.5	5.3	1.0	2.4	7.1	84.2	8.7
2000	23.2	62.8	3.7	0.7	2.3	7.3	86.0	6.7

[a]Resources include exports of petroleum, refining products, and primary metals.

[b]Materials (manufactured) exclude exports of petroleum-refining products and primary metals.

[c]Includes services and transportation.

Source: Wassily Leontief et al., *The Future of the World Economy*, A United Nations Study (New York: Oxford University Press, 1977).

manufacturing at higher rates. The study makes the important observation that the creation of a service infrastructure is essential as a basis for the development of the other sectors of the economy. So although under almost all the scenarios in Leontief's study—especially the higher-growth ones—manufacturing tends to lead development, services follow at slightly lower rates of growth and are an integral part of overall growth. In short, the growth of services affects the overall growth of an economy.

Table 3.1 shows that under scenario X, services grow in all regions, even when utilities and construction are excluded, but further service growth is relatively small in terms of total output in the developed market economies of North America, Western Europe, and Japan. In certain of the developing areas, however, services would grow remarkably over the 35-year period—so much so that they exceed manufacturing in each developing region. This growth is even more dramatic if utilities and construction are included as services. Thus the proportion of GDP contributed by services will increase in developing regions and approximate the levels that exist today in the most developed countries. The study finds the composition of the service sector in the developing countries quite different, however.

As to the study's projections of international trade, under most scenarios the share of manufactured products in total world trade has the edge, increasing from 65.4 percent in 1970 to 86.4 percent in 2000, while agricultural and mineral resources decline from 34.6 percent to 13.6 percent. The share of developed countries in most categories of exports is expected to fall, and conversely, the share of developing countries is expected to increase, with two main exceptions— agriculture and invisibles.

In general, the UN study's projected changes in the structure of international trade in invisibles indicate that developed market economies will increase their share of world exports of invisibles, although not significantly, while the developing market economies will reduce their share, and the position of the centrally planned economies will remain constant. (It is interesting to note that according to the UN study, the centrally planned economies have zero earnings from services in both 1970 and 2000. This seems to conflict with my earlier observations about the aggressive, but as yet relatively insignificant, international services promotion policies of these countries.)

As for imports, developed market economies are expected to significantly reduce their share, whereas the developing economies are expected to double their imports of invisibles. Under all scenarios the developed economies significantly reduce their imports of invisibles from 79 percent to 62 percent, while developing market economies significantly increase theirs from 13.9 percent to 27 percent. These trends are illustrated in Tables 3.2 and 3.3. Indicative of the anticipated future significance of trade in services is the projection that from 1970 to 2000 the developed world will move from a slight deficit ($1.9 billion) on services payments to a $23.8 billion surplus, while the developing regions will increase their currently insignificant deficit from $0.7 billion to $29.5 billion.

TABLE 3.3

Shares of Regions in World Imports (percentage in 1970 prices)

Region	Year	Scenario[a]	Agriculture	Mineral Resources	Light Industry	Machinery and Equipment	Materials	Invisibles[b]
Developed market economies[c]	1970		63.5	70.6	70.5	63.2	63.8	79.0
	2000	X	43.1	56.0	59.4	45.8	44.5	62.5
	2000	M	43.0	55.8	60.1	47.2	45.8	62.4
Developing market economies	1970		15.3	10.7	16.2	18.8	20.4	13.9
	2000	X	39.4	19.3	22.2	34.0	39.6	27.0
	2000	M	39.4	19.4	20.9	33.5	37.8	27.0
Latin America	1970		3.5	3.5	3.7	6.4	7.0	7.0
	2000	X	7.5	8.2	4.4	12.0	8.9	12.5
	2000	M	8.0	8.2	4.1	10.7	8.1	12.7
Asia and the Middle East	1970		9.3	5.7	9.4	9.3	10.0	5.0
	2000	X	28.6	10.3	15.1	22.0	28.4	12.7
	2000	M	28.3	10.3	14.3	21.3	27.6	12.6
Africa (nonoil)	1970		2.4	1.5	3.1	3.0	3.4	2.0
	2000	X	3.2	0.9	2.7	1.7	2.3	1.8
	2000	M	3.2	0.9	2.5	1.6	2.1	1.7

[a]X and M indicate names of two scenarios with different assumptions.

[b]Includes services and transportation.

[c]Does not include medium-income regions.

Source: Wassily Leontief et al., *The Future of the World Economy*, A United Nations Study (New York: Oxford University Press, 1977).

Thus, in the future the importance of trade in services seems likely to increase dramatically, particularly between North and South.[2]

DYNAMIC ASPECTS OF SERVICES

The foregoing projections, while impressive, fail to convey the true landscape of service activity in that they are based on past and present assumptions about services. They assume services are static and will remain so in the future. This view neglects dynamic elements of service sector development such as the emergence of new kinds, new forms, and new sources of services.

The entry of nonservice companies such as manufacturing firms into traditional service industries is one of these dynamic changes. We have seen many examples in recent years of manufacturers acquiring insurance companies, banks, brokerage houses, tourist concerns, and consulting firms—a trend that is likely to continue. Services are desirable because they often complement the nonservice aspects of a manufacturer's business and offer a means of diversifying corporate activities and earnings. This diversification is also sparked by the perception that many traditional industries are limited in their long-term growth potential, while services are seen as having continuing growth possibilities.

A second dynamic trend is the provision of managerial, professional, consulting, and rental services between nonservice firms and their affiliates. This too is a trend that is likely to continue. Perhaps the primary reason is the changing patterns of international investment resulting from nationalism. More and more, nations are demanding a larger and larger stake in the ownership of the overseas affiliates of international corporations. As a firm is forced into a minority position or denied any equity participation in its formerly wholly owned or majority-owned affiliates, it begins to export services to compensate for the lost earnings resulting from diminished equity. In essence, these firms are transforming themselves from manufacturing firms to service firms.

Beyond this, it seems likely that nonservice firms will provide services to nonaffiliates as well. This results in part from nationalistic moves which reduce the incentives to operate through direct investment. Thus, in lieu of a direct investment, a nonservice firm may sell its technology and management skills, which amounts to the export of services. Furthermore, as forced divestment decreases a firm's interest in providing services exclusively to its former affiliates, it may begin to export its services to nonaffiliated companies.

A third dynamic development is the creation of new services out of the traditional activities of nonservice firms. Usually this involves selling know-how to governments, health agencies, educational institutions, and other non-goods-producing industries. Another likely possibility, however, is directly competing with governments in providing such services instead of selling services to them. A good example is Westinghouse, which is designing, developing, constructing, and operating integrated systems that are in essence services. Through its subsidiary, the Public Systems Organization, it provides services in the justice, health care, tax, and revenue fields. While today such firms tend to concentrate primarily on their own national markets, it is likely that they will expand internationally, particularly in the developing world, given the needs of these nations for health care programs, communications facilities, and educational systems. In coming years we should witness nothing less than an explosion of international activity in what today is popularly described as the information or knowledge industries. In effect, what is often provided might be categorized as a new service in itself, in the form of technology transfer. This kind of technology cannot be transferred in the form of a packaged or "debundled" product, as it can in some fields. Most often, the transfer is an ongoing, dynamic process—a service—designed to contribute to the development of appropriate management expertise.

Another dynamic change will be the expansion abroad of services that have not been associated with international commerce. Franchising is perhaps the best example of where this trend can take us. The possibilities for expansion of this kind of activity appear unlimited. If auto leasing, hotels, and fast-food outlets can go abroad, why not virtually all retail services, from recreational and entertainment services to those mundane personal services that our preconceived notions tell us could never be marketed internationally? Why not dry cleaning, maintenance, home repair, and cleaning services? Franchising itself, of course, is not a separate service activity but a mode of operation that applies not only to services but also to nonservice activity. The very difficulty of characterizing this activity in itself suggests the complexity and diversity of service developments.

Finally, the opposite of my first observation of dynamic change is equally probable. As service firms expand, they are likely to move aggressively to acquire manufacturing and other nonservice activities in the same way manufacturing concerns have acquired service businesses. Such acquisitions could reflect various corporate strategies. One logical move would be to acquire manufacturing businesses that complement a particular service activity. For example, a bank might acquire a firm that produces travelers checks and prints currency. But the acquisition of nonrelated businesses, viewed as profitable opportunities, is also a likely possibility. Finally, we are likely to see a significant expansion of a trend already well under way—the entry of service firms into a variety of service fields, whether related to their primary businesses or not. In short, we will witness the emergence of the service conglomerate. Illustrative of this trend is the broad popular support for a legislative proposal that emerged in the United States at the beginning of this decade: the creation of export trading companies, modeled after the Japanese experience. This approach to international business, where in essence a package of goods and services is marketed, will in the long term hasten the emergence of international service organizations, providing a wide array of services, goods, and perhaps even commodities.

Business Week, in an article on the subject in 1974, said, perhaps dramatically overstating the case, "The next revolution in manufacturing will not be in the formation of new products, it will not be in the format of new production processes, it will be in the production of services."[3]

THE POLICY CHALLENGE

The foregoing presents political economy a formidable challenge. Comprehending the service role in national economies, much less the international economy, is something we are woefully unprepared for, even if we were in a static world. The dynamics of change already under way immensely complicate this task. This is demonstrated by a brief look at past and present practices in factoring service considerations into policy formulation in industrial, developing, and planned economies.

Industrial Nations

Although it is generally recognized among policy makers that the most advanced economies are services economies, this fact is not translated consistently into government policy, something not unexpected in light of my beginning observation on the lag of institutional response to economic change. The U.S. government provides an excellent example of national policies formulated with a bias toward manufacturing. If there is unemployment, officials suggest modifying the investment tax credit or accelerating depreciation rates as a stimulus to investment and job creation. Yet capital investment in plant and machinery is used almost exclusively by the manufacturing sector, since services are, for the most part, labor rather than capital intensive. If there is inflation, the focus is on structural defects: the cost of primary commodities and large wage settlements, both of which, while affecting services, are directed primarily at the manufacturing and/or agricultural sectors and do not come to grips with service industry-induced inflation. Government economic indicators of consumption, growth, inflation, and the like give primary emphasis to nonservice items—durable consumer goods, commodity prices, capital spending, and goods inventories. In short, there is a recurring inconsistency between the recognition that the United States is a service economy and the implicit assumption in most policies that the creation of jobs, economic growth, and price stability must come from the nonservice economy.

To pick only one little noticed but striking example, there are indications that service industries may be among the least productive of industries (although this is a subject that has not been adequately studied). It has been asserted that one reason for the spectacular growth in services is that they are less productive and more inflationary. If the difficulties in measuring service output or production could be overcome, it is argued, it would be evident that much of services growth reflects inflation induced by poor productivity. Yet although virtually all the literature available on services has tended to focus on the problem of productivity, this attention has failed to influence the formulation of national policies that would aim at improving productivity in services as a way of fighting inflation. The only U.S. government attention that I know of that addresses service problems is a series of studies done by the U.S. National Commission on Productivity.

Needless to say, a similar analysis applies to U.S. policies toward the international economy. The best illustration of this is in U.S. efforts to solve balance-of-payments problems by increasing exports of manufactured and agricultural goods. Hence, the U.S. thrust in the recent multilateral trade negotiations was to remove barriers on exports of industrial and agricultural products. Ironically, almost no attention was given to service exports, which are often the only positive component of the current account of the United States and several other nations. Similarly, U.S. export incentives and export promotion programs are tailored almost exclusively for manufacturing exports.

A second example of this limited focus in international economic policy making can be found in the dispute over the impact of U.S. multinational corporations on the U.S. economy. The liberal trading community argues that U.S. investment abroad contributes significantly to foreign exchange earnings and is the only way to penetrate highly protected foreign markets. They believe that such investment creates new jobs within the United States and in general protects U.S. technological and trading advantages in world markets. The other point of view, most forcefully put forth by the labor movement, is that U.S. foreign direct investment exports U.S. jobs, capital, and technology, which works against the well-being of the United States.

In all the studies that have been conducted on this subject by business organizations such as the U.S. Chamber of Commerce, the National Association of Manufacturers, and the American Committee for Emergency Trade, by labor organizations like the American Federation of Labor and Congress of Industrial Organizations (AFL-CIO), and government organizations like the Departments of Commerce and Labor, the focus has been exclusively on U.S. manufacturing investment abroad and not on investment in services. This reflects the bias of Americans against services and in favor of manufacturing in the formulation of international economic policy.

For the most part, policy makers have little perceived the importance, if any, of the role of services in the international economy. Intuitively, I think the bias comes from economic theory, which emphasizes the manufacturing firm at both the micro- and macrolevels. Another factor may be the empirical observation that services are less affected by economic fluctuations and thus need less policy emphasis. As a result there are virtually no coherent policies on services. In the past the only government policies that were directed toward services usually dealt with their regulation. They have tended, for example, to make such industries as shipping and aviation noncompetitive and oligopolistic in their international pricing. The effect of this governmental control of key international services is to isolate them from other economic activities and exclude them from the traditional international commercial institutions. This process has tended to reinforce an existing prejudice about services: they are a special case and are relatively insignificant in the bigger picture.

In general, then, there seems to be little awareness or action on the part of policy makers in the advanced industrial nations that responds to the growing importance of services both nationally and internationally. In fact, economic reality appears to be far ahead of the perceptions on which national policies are based. Furthermore, the bias of officials against services seems to aggravate this inconsistency.

Developing Nations

The principal goal of Third World countries is economic development, which is usually combined with a desire for economic and political independence from the industrial world. As a result, ironically, policy makers in the developing world often see a much closer linkage between national and international policies than do their counterparts in industrial countries. The goal of development necessarily links them to the international economy, yet the desire for independence involves lessening their dependence on the developed world.

Today the strategy of most developing countries is based on balanced development, recognizing the importance of both industry and agriculture, which differs from the exclusive focus of the 1950s and 1960s on industrialization. A key part of the strategy is export promotion to provide the earnings to pay for imports of capital goods, technology, and expertise needed for development. Exports are usually agricultural and mineral commodities, semiprocessed raw materials, and labor-intensive manufactured goods. Combined with this growth strategy is the welfare goal of alleviating the misery of massive poverty. Generally, huge amounts of public and private investment to stimulate job creation are seen as the best road toward this end. The goal of economic independence both complements and conflicts with these development objectives. It is complementary in that development, if achieved, over the long run should mean less dependence on foreign trade, aid, and investment; it is contradictory in that achieving development requires commercial interaction with the industrial world to obtain the necessary technology, capital, and investments.

As a result of the twin desire for development and independence, an awareness of services is more evident in the policies of developing countries than of industrial countries, even though services are much less significant in the developing nations. In their national development schemes services are an integral part of import-substitution policies. Various financial services such as banking and insurance and other sensitive areas such as communications, utilities, advertising, and shipping are all areas in which most developing nations seek to build up national industries. National control of these industries relates as much, if not more, to economic independence from the industrial world than it does to economic development. Governments prefer to control these services through direct ownership or indirectly through ownership by their nationals, because foreign participation in them does not seem to complement national objectives like earning foreign exchange, transferring technology, redistributing wealth, but ensures that sociopolitical, cultural, and national security goals are achieved. It should be noted, moreover, that such views are reinforced by developed countries that regulate and limit foreign participation in some of these sensitive industries. In the United States, for example, foreign investment in communications and advertising is restricted.

With regard to trade in services, while there is often but a limited awareness in developing nations of their potential for earning foreign exchange, with the primary focus being on tourism and, to a lesser extent, on shipping, there is a high level of consciousness of the need to limit service imports. Overall the primary limited objective for services is the development of a domestic economic infrastructure that is in national hands. These policies overlook the surprising significance of services to many developing economies, seldom consider their broader role in development, and hardly ever evaluate their potential for export earnings. These concepts will be treated more comprehensively in the subsequent chapter dealing with development and trade theory as related to services. In sum, these policy makers, too, are subject to the shortsightedness that has characterized their counterparts in the developed world. Since their thinking is so influenced by the latter, however, it is more understandable.

Socialist Countries

The attitudes of socialist countries toward services were discussed above in explaining why services constitute a relatively insignificant sector in these countries. The prevalent view is that many services do not contribute to national output but are merely transferors of wealth. Because of this conception, only services that relate to production, such as transportation, communications, utilities, and construction, receive any emphasis. So at the domestic level, services are neglected, much as they are in advanced market economies, but for different reasons. Socialist policy makers would share the view of developing nations that services activity should be an exclusive national function. But although this attitude permeates their entire political/economic philosophy, it has become common practice to make exceptions in the nonservice sector so as to attain the benefits of foreign investment and technology in modernizing their industry or agriculture. However, it is rare that a similar decision has been made for a service activity.

In international trade, the objectives of the socialist economies with regard to services in a sense parallels those of developing countries. The socialist economies need the products and sophisticated technology of the capitalist world, and this, in turn, requires foreign exchange. Among the industries that they see as potential earners of foreign exchange are such services as tourism, shipping, construction, and insurance. On the other hand, service imports are something to be minimized.

In general, the various services that have accompanied industrialization and increased wealth in the West lag behind in the socialist world. Instead, the focus is on manufacturing and modernization with an industrial orientation. It is difficult to say whether this neglect will eventually hamper economic growth, but experience elsewhere indicates it probably will. (As noted above, at least one Hungarian study has mentioned the possibility.) Barring a different policy orientation, the increasing service orientation of the West is likely to contrast more and more with the stagnation of services in the planned economies.

NOTES

1. See Wassily Leontief et al., *The Future of the World Economy*, A United Nations Study (New York: Oxford University Press, 1977). The findings of Ernst Lutz and Andre Sapir in their study, "Trade in Non-Factor Services; Past Trends and Current Issues" (Background Paper prepared for the World Development Report, World Bank, Washington, D.C., January 1980), generally bear out Leontief's findings.

2. Leontief et al., *The Future of the World Economy*, p. 60.

3. "Manufacturers Move Into the Services," *Business Week*, April 8, 1974, pp. 25-34.

4

ECONOMIC THEORY:
A HISTORY OF NEGLECT

Economic theory has little to say about services in general and virtually ignores international services. By and large, it has tended to treat services in international commerce by parallels with trade in goods and investment in manufacturing. Thus, by implication, theoretical economics assumes essentially that services are, in analytic terms, the same as goods and, therefore, that the same arguments apply to them.

The paucity of attention given to services in economic thought is a principal reason that the subject presents so many difficulties. The lack of a sound theoretical underpinning in economic theory applied to the service sector means that judgments on various policy questions are tenuous at best. Evaluations as to the costs and benefits that could result from liberalizing trade in a service activity, for example, are contestable. This study cannot remedy this deficiency; it would be presumptuous to even try. Instead it has a much more limited objective: illustrating the necessity for solid analysis of international service activity by suggesting how services might relate to economic theory.

In doing so, first, I will examine briefly the implications of services in the economic development process. This is followed by a look at how services relate to a few selected examples of international trade and investment theory. The preceding survey of the significance of services domestically and internationally provides us with an empirical background against which to examine these aspects of economic theory.

SERVICES IN THE DEVELOPMENT PROCESS

In development theory the most common assumption about the role of services is that their importance increases with economic development.[1] This growing importance is usually attributed to rising incomes, industrialization, urbanization, and other factors. Thus, in general, the expectation is that services should be insignificant in developing countries except perhaps where there has been extensive urbanization, as in some Latin American countries, when services are mostly personal and are in fact a form of disguised unemployment, or when a country enters advanced stages of industrialization. The inference, then, for international services is that they are necessarily insignificant in developing countries except perhaps for those in advanced stages of development.

These theoretical expectations contrast with evidence of the phenomenal importance of services in some developing countries. The foundation of such expectations, and one of their main drawbacks, is that their empirical validity rests on observation of the role of services in the economic development of the advanced countries. Yet circumstances today are often different for developing countries. For example, theory tells us that services will be important to a nation only when it has reached a relatively advanced stage of economic development. However, for many developing countries services play a large role in the national economy well before the local population demands them, simply because the country's service industry serves the international market.

As already noted, policy makers in developing countries see the development of national services as a critical form of import substitution in their efforts to be economically independent. Thus they seek to develop indigenous service industries to replace internationally supplied services. In addition, other intangible international linkages—such as the desire to imitate the consumption patterns of the developed world—also foster growth of the service sector. An important but often overlooked international inducement to service sector expansion in certain developing countries is its ability to provide a particular service that is desired by the industrial world. Usually this means a service activity has developed for international consumption even before a domestic market has been built up.

Clearly, tourism, the international service industry receiving the most attention by developing nations, is the prime example. This industry arises in response to the demand primarily generated by foreign consumers and is especially interesting because it cuts across a spectrum of economic activities. For instance, though one would tend to associate tourism with the hotel industry, studies have shown that nearly 70 percent of tourist expenditures are on expenditures other than those for services at hotels. This fact makes the impact of tourism difficult to quantify and suggests a relationship between the development of certain goods sectors and the tourism sector.[2]

Although tourism is the most striking example in terms of impact, there are others. For example, offshore lesser regulated, tax-haven banking facilities are usually provided in response to the needs of foreign interests from industrial countries. Captive insurance companies, again often in tax-haven developing countries, are created to serve foreign interests. Another example is the licensing of foreign ships under flags of convenience.

Other illustrations do not necessarily result from foreign demand but indicate that developing countries can successfully create international service industries that compete with those of advanced economies. Brazil, Korea, and other developing countries, for example, are winning major construction contracts in both developing and industrial countries around the world.

This discussion is meant to suggest that the world does not neatly divide into highly developed countries that are service economies, or fast becoming so; countries well along in their industrial development showing the beginnings of complementary services; and nations still comparatively undeveloped with most of their economic activity in agriculture and rudimentary industries and with almost all services being traditional ones.[3] We find, instead, a much more complex world economy. Economically advanced societies may have the larger part of their employment and GNP in the service sector but may also maintain mammoth industrial sectors and, in some cases, be major agricultural producers. A surprising number of developing countries qualify as service economies in terms of employment and output. These countries are producing new and complementary services—not just traditional ones. We also find relatively poor developing countries that are significant exporters of services. In short, there are developing nations that seem to have skipped a theoretical stage of economic development and others that are going through more than one stage simultaneously. And as discussed in the Bibliographic Appendix, for some developing countries, being primarily a service society is nothing new: it goes back to the turn of the century.

More important, however, than the assertion that theoretical perceptions of the stages of economic growth need to be reexamined, especially as applied to services, are the policy implications flowing from this observation.

Has our predisposition to relegate services to a status of lesser importance in the development process unnecessarily narrowed our perspective and perhaps deterred a meaningful examination of their role? Could there perhaps be alternative development schemes for certain economies where selected services are given major emphasis? Could not service exports or foreign investment in certain services drive the engine of development as do certain manufacturing or agricultural commodities in some development schemes? Surely, a balanced development plan would more fully integrate the service sector. Is it not conceivable that a faulty or at least insufficient analysis of development bottlenecks and problems often occurs because the service infrastructure that some would call the glue of development is not adequately provided for?

A practice of factoring services into development prescriptions would quite possibly lead to new approaches at the macro- and microlevels. Questions such as the following might be asked. Does the growing importance of the service sector in many developing countries offer unrecognized opportunities to redress some fundamental problems? Does the promotion of labor-intensive services offer possibilities for alleviating severe unemployment problems? Does the less cyclic nature of services provide a possible way to reduce the severe economic fluctuations plaguing many developing countries? And does the fact that many services are not capital intensive offer capital-short countries a way to maximize limited resources?

Finally, what are the political implications of a service economy? Small firms, high levels of self-employment, and the personalization of work—typical characteristics of many services, although not necessarily of international services—could enhance the development of a middle class, a societal characteristic often associated with political maturity. According to Russell Lewis, "The coming of the service society [is] . . . the opportunity to rehabilitate not only the philosophy of market freedom, but also the traditional belief in pluralist democracy." He argues that the growth of services favors the dispersion of power and that "the service economy [is] a sounder foundation for a liberal capitalist social order than the predominantly industrial economy . . . [and] is, paradoxically, also more compatible with ideas of social democracy than earlier stages of economic development."[4] Although this may be an extreme point of view and will not fit the objectives of many developing countries, at least it deserves to be considered.

SERVICES IN INTERNATIONAL COMMERCE

Before surveying several theories of international trade and investment to consider their relevance to services, a close look at the character of international services is in order. We know from previous chapters that international services can be both trade and investment oriented. The 1976 U.S. Department of Commerce study of services in international commerce, however, stressed that they were predominantly associated with investment rather than with trade. Statistically, the study pointed out that about 86 percent of estimated U.S. service sector sales overseas result from investment in foreign affiliates, while exports account for only 14 percent.[5] The explanation most frequently suggested for the investment predominance of services is that they cannot be shipped or stored. Thus they must be produced when and where they are consumed, which implies investment, not trade.

This generalization is questionable: it is called into question by the diversity of service sector activities. Further studies on services in the United States have suggested that the magnitude of service activity generated by trade is substantially more significant than previously realized. I would submit that as more comprehensive data are obtained and a better understanding of services trade and investment flows is developed, we will find service trade activity to be even more important.

Knowing the source of service sector revenue (that is, that it originates from the sales of overseas affiliates) does not necessarily tell us how international services function, even if it proves accurate. For example, simply because overseas affiliates of U.S. banks produce more dollars in revenue than do direct loans overseas of home offices, does that mean unquestionably that banking at the international level is primarily related to foreign investment? Further, do service activities appear to be investment related because there is no physical way to export them or because trade barriers force investment instead of exporting? To shed light on these questions, let us see, in general terms, how a few specific international service activities function.

There are surprising similarities among the international activities of financial services. Most banks undertaking international activities today obtain permission to establish representative offices but do not conduct commercial banking activities except in certain industrial countries, although historically banks operated through branches and subsidiaries overseas. In fact, many banks apparently eschew the direct investment route, even if it is available, preferring to do business from headquarters or through other arrangements. As a result, measuring international banking flows is not easy.

Accounting, brokerage services, and especially insurance are remarkably similar to banking. Though insurance appears to rely on investment and the establishment of branches, agencies, or subsidiaries abroad, many international insurance activities are carried out without overseas establishments. For example, transport insurance is provided by many insurance companies that have no offices outside their home countries. The same in true of other forms of coverage, such as products liability insurance on exports or bonding against default in overseas construction projects. Perhaps the least recognized example is reinsurance transactions. *Reinsurance*, simply put, is insurance on insurance, or the means by which insurance companies spread their risk through the purchase of insurance protection. International reinsurance is generally transacted by telegraphic or telephonic communications or on-the-spot visits of reinsurers to their clients overseas and need not involve the establishment of overseas offices. Thus reinsurance is a major export—not an investment activity—of several nations. One wonders whether other insurance activities or other financial services might not be more trade oriented if local regulations permitted. So, as with banking, the measurement of international insurance flows is obviously difficult.

Air and maritime transportation are generally thought of as trade related, providing nearly half of U.S. service industry exports. Yet though shipping is an important export and by nature would seem to fall in the trade category, there are investment activities associated with it. Most international shipping companies have in fact established themselves in one or more overseas jurisdictions. Thus revenue flows from shipping are hard to pinpoint. Construction and engineering services at the international level are difficult to characterize, in part because the final product is tangible. To provide the actual service, after winning a contract, the construction or engineering firm must be on the scene at least temporarily. Some firms—depending on the nature of their activities, the restrictions they face abroad, or the opportunities they perceive—establish themselves through affiliates in various markets, while others simply export their services.

Consulting would seem to be more export related than investment related, though consultants obviously have to be on the scene part of the time. Accordingly, leading international consulting firms have established offices abroad, although the investment involved is minimal. Advertising services are often provided at the international level, without local affiliation. Tourism is mixed because there are so many facets to it. Integrated companies, encompassing various elements of the tourist business, have both export activities and investment activities through ticketing and hotels, credit cards, and car rentals. Finally, new services such as those involving management or communications systems, which at present are mainly exported, will in time also probably establish affiliates that provide ongoing services and related products.

In sum, it is very difficult to characterize, without qualifications, the nature of international service activities. Almost all tend to be both investment and trade related. Yet many—banking, insurance, and advertising—could conduct more of their business through trade if regulation did not usually require the establishment of affiliates. (This point will be treated in more detail later.) Moreover, many international service companies that traditionally might have been only traders have invested abroad for a variety of reasons, including that of following their multinational clients overseas. Their behavior parallels that of goods-exporting firms, which over the long run invest overseas to overcome import barriers, broaden markets, and provide customer service.[6]

So although there is truth in the statement that services by their very nature are unique in that they must be consumed where they are produced, and the consumer plays a major role in production, it is also too simplistic. It implies that international services are necessarily investment oriented. It ignores the evidence that decisions to invest can be made for reasons similar to those governing such decisions in manufacturing—and not just because services, by their uniqueness, have no other alternative. In fact, theoretically, there is nothing to prevent certain services such as banking, insurance, advertising, construction, consulting, accounting, and others from being produced without direct investment occurring. As we have seen above, many of these services can be provided very successfully from the firm's home country.

DO CLASSICAL THEORIES OF INTERNATIONAL COMMERCE APPLY TO SERVICES?

The Theory of Comparative Advantage

Whether the theory of comparative advantage is applicable to international service trade is a striking illustration of the failure of economic theorists to come to grips with services. Where in the economic literature on comparative advantage can a discussion of the service sector be found? Can even one example using a service product to illustrate comparative advantage be recalled?

Recently, I participated in two research seminars on services, one in the United States and one in Europe, held to develop a research agenda for services.[7]

The discussions provided conspicuous evidence of the neglect of services in economic thought. Most striking was the realization by the distinguished group of participants from academia, government, and the service sector of the extent to which services have been ignored. This conclusion, while valid for the entire gamut of trade theory, is especially pronounced when applied to the heart of trade theory: comparative advantage.

While there was unanimous agreement on its universal acceptance as applied to goods trade, no such accord exists when it comes to service trade. Although almost all participants intuitively felt that comparative advantage was equally applicable to trade in services, not one felt this had been recognized theoretically or proved empirically. Clearly, the intellectual underpinning to justify the policy conclusions that might result from applying comparative advantage to services is not established. Nor is there a theoretical basis for applying a different conceptual framework to services trade. There is simply no accepted theoretical foundation on which to build.

Perhaps the traditional comparative advantage analysis will need modifying for services trade. Perhaps not. There are many challenging issues to be addressed. For example, because of the close linkages between trade and investment in service activity, should investment be factored into the analysis? Would the analysis of the relevance of comparative advantage to services be facilitated by measuring inputs that are necessary for service production instead of measuring output?

Even if the principle of comparative advantage were accepted as valid, many would argue that there are other transcending reasons that inveigh against the policy option its acceptance supports: liberalization. The sensitivity of many services, it is argued, makes regulation more desirable than competition, and effective regulation is disrupted by trade. Market stability is of overriding importance. Cartels in shipping and aviation, to cite but two examples, are in the national interest.

However, there are equally persuasive and often accepted reasons to justify transgression from allowing the benefits of comparative advantage to be realized in goods trade. In short, the reasons that might justify ignoring the policy consequences of accepting the validity of this economic principle for services do not invalidate the principle itself.

Below is a brief argumentation suggesting that the principle is indeed applicable to services. It is neither comprehensive nor flawless. It is meant only to suggest the kind of scrutiny that needs to be applied to trade in services.

Many observers believe that comparative advantage is not especially applicable to international trade in services because most services cannot be traded or are difficult to trade internationally. This would be correct if the characteristics of services were universally such that they could never be traded. Admittedly, a sharp distinction must be drawn between services and goods because the theory of comparative advantage is potentially applicable to all goods, whereas it is difficult to conceive of it ever applying to some services such as personal ones or some leisure ones. However, there is no basis to assume that the principles on which comparative advantage are based are any different for the services trade. The factors that give imported goods the edge in a market— natural endowment, technological superiority, and quality—also explain why imported services may be preferred.

Historically, the United Kingdom and, more recently, the United States have done well in international financial services because of their comparative advantage. The international political and economic environment enhanced the financial importance of London and New York, but there are also other causes. The costs of providing these services are reduced by centralization and the large volume of transactions that occur in London and New York. Furthermore, the U.S. and British roles in initiating and expanding these transactions gave them management experience that provided an edge. Despite the fact that other nations have developed their own insurance and banking industries, London is still the insurance center of the world, and New York and London are the international capital centers. This, in part, testifies to their enduring comparative advantage.

One perceptual barrier against understanding this as comparative advantage is the difficulty of conceiving of such transactions as imports or exports. Take, for example, a London insurance broker responsible for providing protection of a multimillion-dollar risk in Norway. In London he will walk the risk among the various Lloyds' syndicate members or other insurers and place percentages of the risk with each until it is fully subscribed. The end result is that the Norwegian concern is importing insurance protection from England and elsewhere through facilities in London. Thus the location of the production of the service, its movement in international commerce, and its consumption are very difficult to perceive. The fact that each of the exporters (insurers) is likely to reinsure (import) some portion of its risk share through various mechanisms and in several countries further complicates the transaction.

The regulation of services by governments complicates trade in services and obscures the application of the theory of comparative advantage. Often, regulation forces an exporter to invest if he wishes to compete; yet in many sensitive service sectors, the investment route today is precluded by limitations or outright prohibitions against foreign investment. The strict regulation of many service sectors is only a recent historical phenomenon in many nations, which explains why certain nations were able to establish and maintain comparative advantages in services, such as insurance, brokerage, and banking, that would be almost impossible to duplicate today. Ironically, regulation, or the lack of it, can occasionally create a comparative advantage, as can be seen from the success of countries that create tax-haven banking centers. Thus although the theory of comparative advantage does not apply as universally to services as to goods, a look behind the actual service transactions provides convincing evidence that it does apply in many cases.

The Infant Industry Argument

The infant industry argument is a familiar economic concept justifying protection, an accepted reason for deviation from the principle of comparative advantage. This concept frequently is put forth as a reason to protect a service activity. Yet its applicability to services, like comparative advantage, has not been subjected to economic scrutiny. Only occasionally are measures taken to protect a service industry described as being necessary to protect an infant industry from foreign competition. Instead, the concept is explained in different terms: every nation should develop its national shipping or insurance or banking industry; a secondary corollary is that every nation, if possible, should obtain its fair share of world trade in that sector. Then perhaps a more apt description of the reasons for such practices would be to describe them as an integral part of a general import-substitution policy, whether or not protection is needed.

So once again, a rigorous analysis of the merits of an economic concept— the infant industry argument—has not been undertaken for services in general nor on a case-by-case basis for specific services.

A yet unpublished study by Bernard Wasow and Raymond Hill of New York and Princeton universites, respectively, entitled "Public Sector Involvement in the Insurance Industry: The Implications for Economic Development," considers the merits of protection as applied to insurance.[8] Similar work should be undertaken across the spectrum of service sector activity. The Wasow-Hill study is illustrative of the kind of analysis that is sorely lacking. It focuses on a series of nationalized and restricted insurance industries around the world. Of special interest is its concentration on the indirect effects of protective insurance practices.

Traditional analyses of protective measures tend to consider only the direct effects. Thus if the petrochemical industry is protected or nationalized, the domestic growth of that industry is measured. It is no surprise that it does indeed grow. The same could be said of insurance. But the problem of such an approach, according to this study, is that it ignores the wider effects on an economy of measures to protect a specific industry.

Wasow and Hill find protectionist policies have an impact so widespread that they reach sectors of an economy not related to insurance. In their view, the best way to measure the cost of such protection is to assess it against the growth that would have occurred in other sectors of the economy if they had received the resources flowing to the protected sector. In the insurance case—and probably other industries—if skilled managers, actuaries, sales people, technicians, and clerks were employed elsewhere, what would have happened to the economy? The question they put forth is straightforward: not whether protection of the insurance sector results in growth of that sector, but, at what cost does this growth occur? Developing economies, like rich economies, are handicapped by a scarcity of factors of production, and although the insurance sector seems to demand little physical capital, it makes substantial demands on human capital.

The average educational level and the average skill needs in the insurance sector are much higher than in most other sectors in the economy, including the majority of manufacturing industries. Thus policy makers should ask themselves whether they would rather tie up skilled people and physical capital to provide the managers, buildings, and computers for the insurance industry or whether they would rather direct these resources into the nonelectrical metal sector, the fabricated-metal industry, or the furniture sector. Should, in other words, import substitution take place in insurance, or should it take place in other manufacturing sectors?

The study concludes that the development of insurance is likely to be very costly for a developing economy. Other sectors seem to offer alternatives in which the skill and capital requirements are lower or comparable to the insurance sector and where resources can be expected to generate a great deal more value added and many more jobs than in the insurance sector.

Like any such analysis, the findings are debatable. But it illustrates the kind of research required if a body of thought is to be developed that builds the kinds of understanding necessary to foster rational policies toward service activity.

The Product Cycle Theory

Let us now consider a modern component of trade theory—the product cycle theory. It is illustrative of a continuation of the historically acquired habit of forgetting services in theoretical conceptualization.

The product cycle theory asserts that stages of increasing standardization characterize the product cycle.[9] Initially, a new good is made in small quantities, manufacturing processes are highly experimental, and many different techniques are used. As markets grow, national and international specifications are agreed upon. Simultaneously, the number of processes and technologies decreases as inferior methods are weeded out. The surviving techniques become standardized and more familiar through established marketing channels. Thus in the early stages of the product's life, production and export advantages lie with sophisticated firms in advanced nations. As the product cycle unfolds, however, firms in developing nations begin making and exporting the product, with the help of the process of standardization. Longer production runs and proven technology bring production within the technical grasp of most nations, and standardized goods are more easily marketed, both because sales channels are established and product reliability is greater.

This underlies what Raymond Vernon calls the technological gap theory, which explains how the sequence of innovation and imitation vitally affects export patterns.[10] Early producers enjoy easy access to foreign markets, which is reinforced by technical and managerial expertise. Later, however, as the production process and technology are standardized, exporters must rely on some factor-cost advantage to secure a share of foreign sales. In certain nations, especially the United States, new products and processes are developed more readily in response to higher per capita incomes and the relative availability of productive factors. Initial export advantages are to be expected, but when that export position is threatened, producers must establish overseas subsidiaries to exploit what remains of their advantage. These leading countries retain their oligopolistic advantage for a period of time but then lose it as the basis for their original lead is completely eroded.

Clearly, the product cycle theory was devised with manufacturing products in mind. Whether or not the theory applies to services is briefly examined below; it could well offer a rudimentary understanding of the dynamics of service products and processes in international commerce. It is not intended to make an airtight case suggesting this theory does or does not apply to services. It does illustrate the price of neglect of services. By ignoring them, the implication is left again and again that services are an exception. They are left stranded without a theoretical foundation.

The core issue in this instance is obvious: Are service products and processes first developed in technologically advanced nations, then exported, and finally followed by direct foreign investment?

Although services, clearly, are composed of products with well-established production processes, these are not usually thought of as being subject to more than an occasional refinement or fine tuning, much less to innovation and technological change. It is difficult to see services as generating a stream of new products and processes, but this is a notion based more on ignorance than fact. The insurance, banking, and brokerage industries regularly develop new products and processes—recent examples being annuity-linked policies, automated fund withdrawal, and options trading. In shipping we have seen the introduction of containerization; in accounting, new methods of measuring foreign exchange exposure; in construction, prefabricated homes; and in communications, satellite transmission. In-depth research would confirm that virtually all service industries develop new products and processes.

To what extent does the development of new service products and processes go through phases that eventually lead to international standardization? Again, although in-depth research would be necessary, suffice it to say that many of the examples mentioned above are now used in countries other than where they were developed.

Vernon cites either of two reasons for the development of new products: high per capita income levels or the introduction of labor-saving technologies. Ironically, the former is one of the main reasons traditionally given in explaining why service economies develop. If this is a major reason for new products, then the product cycle theory would seem to be very applicable to services, perhaps even more so than to goods. As for the other reason, finding a substitute for high-cost labor, since most services tend not only to be labor intensive but more so than many goods, the theory would seem applicable here as well in that there is considerable incentive for developing new products and processes.

The aspect of the product cycle theory of concern to this study, how-ever, is its applicability to service sector penetration of international markets. Do service products and processes move abroad first through exports and then by investment, and is this caused by standardization? Put specifically, if an insur-ance company in the United States develops a liability policy to protect corpo-rate officers and directors, will it seek to market that product overseas? Or, if a bank develops a new savings/checking system, will it export that product?

The answer must be equivocal. It depends on whether the service is export-able if the product cycle theory is to be applicable; that is, can the service be provided through a trading mechanism or must it be associated with an on-the-scene or investment activity. Some services are clearly exportable: for example, a new concept developed by a consulting firm, a new form of transport insurance coverage, a new management system, or a motion picture refinement. However, as with a good, the uniqueness of these new services will in time become imitable when the service-exporting firm has lost its advantage. Then the firm's only chance of competing may be to become the service investor. Even if it maintains an export advantage, other factors such as government restrictions on service imports may force the same response. Some services (for example, automated fund withdrawal and new automobile rental services) would require a local oper-ating entity. Perhaps initially, but certainly over time, many others (for example, new insurance, banking and accounting products, construction technologies, and so on) would, while theoretically being exportable, need to be marketed from a local facility. However, one suspects a similar analysis would apply to different kinds of goods.

The product cycle theory basically assumes that new products originate exclusively in industrial countries. This is also generally true in services, but exceptions abound. For example, an international consulting firm advising a foreign, developing-country client often develops solutions that can be applied elsewhere. An advertising firm that develops new techniques for reaching those outside the money economy in developing countries will probably apply the same techniques in other developing nations or even in the poorer regions of industrial countries. Kidnap and ransom insurance, a popular insurance product in industrial countries, originated in developing countries such as Argentina in response to terrorism. But the spread of these new services to different countries is clearly dependent on the international orientation of service firms, although the transmitter to other countries may not be the originator of the service.

The final phase of Vernon's product cycle theory occurs when the overseas affiliate begins to export its products to third markets or back to its home base because of differences of labor or other factor costs. A study of this process in connection with services is long overdue; without it we can only surmise. I believe that this stage is much less likely to occur because the nature of services and especially the reasons service producers go abroad are often different from goods. A manufacturing concern often invests overseas for other reasons than simply holding, expanding, or securing markets. If production is no longer competitive at home, an overseas production site can be a way to sell at home as well as in other markets. Thus it may close down or at least reduce the home operation. Service firms usually establish themselves abroad to maintain markets or because this is the only way they can penetrate foreign markets. This does not mean that they close or cut back their home operations. Labor spokesmen who have criticized U.S. investment overseas as exporting jobs, capital, and technology will concede that it would be rare for a U.S. bank, insurer, construction firm, hotel, or accounting firm to invest abroad in order to substitute that investment for the firm's U.S. activity or to export the product of the affiliate back to the United States. I suspect shipping services might be an exception. Also, certain financial or other services sometimes establish themselves overseas to avoid taxes and regulation, which is a motivation quite different from the penetration of foreign markets, but this could lead to a substitute for the firm's activities at home or exports to third countries. For the most part, however, the likelihood of a service exporting back to the home market seems minimal.

For services that are easily traded, patterns in which affiliates export back to home markets are not easily discernible. The reasons for this seem to lie in the structural differences between goods trade and service trade and particularly what determines competitiveness in each. For example, it is difficult to visualize the overseas affiliate of a multinational bank or accounting firm competing with its parent or replacing the original facility in providing services to home clients. However, it is not inconceivable that affiliates could displace other firms by developing clients in neighboring third countries because of their proximity or the trade patterns between the host country and third countries.

In summary, there is considerable indication that much of the product cycle theory is equallly relevant to service commerce.

Reasons for Service Activities Abroad

An analysis of the applicability of the product cycle theory to services significantly expands the traditional view as to why service firms establish themselves overseas. The most common explanation is that services are "following the flag" and serving the interests of home country corporations overseas. How applicable is this tenet, both historically and today?

Service firms that have traditionally operated internationally, through trade and investment, became involved primarily to serve home country interests. Banking, insurance, transportation, and, to a lesser extent, accounting, advertising, tourism, and legal services are principal examples. In the U.S. case they went abroad principally to service their corporate clients or occasionally to serve government objectives. An example of the latter is Pan American Airways's establishing routes to advance certain U.S. foreign policy objectives. Once these services established themselves overseas, however, they naturally broadened their perspective and saw indigenous market opportunities.

Today the domestic competitors of the internationalized U.S. service industries are moving abroad as well in order to service their international clients and avoid losing out to the traditionally established firms. To a certain extent, this is a bandwagon phenomenon because it often results from imitation more than from perceived opportunity or necessity. Perhaps it also reflects a view of an increasingly intertwined world economy, which creates the need for firms to broaden their marketplace—one not necessarily limited to serving home country clients overseas.

A question with important future implications is the relationship between manufacturers and service producers in international commerce. Do goods producers sometimes export or establish themselves abroad because of the international activities of services instead of the reverse, as usually presumed? Past experience seems to indicate a positive relationship between the two kinds of activity, which is best illustrated by examples. The establishment of retailing and merchandising firms overseas may lead to trade and investment by goods producers to fill the demands created by these merchandisers. The entry of companies into international shipping may lead to the production of ships and other goods associated with that industry. The establishment of financial institutions abroad may lead to the export of computers and business machines to service their needs. The award of construction and engineering contracts overseas may lead to the sale of products used by the construction and engineering concerns. Providing communications services internationally may lead to the installation of communications-related equipment. The export of new services, such as health systems, may lead to a plethora of goods-related exports and investments. So neither historically nor presently is it fair to assert that service firms are simply following their goods clients. The relationship is more complex, but clearly it works both ways.

A final corollary to this discussion is that international service activities lead to trade and investments in related services. For example, the introduction of computer services induces imports of the associated software. The establishment of foreign insurance affiliates creates the need for risk management and independent claims services. The introduction of mass merchandising requires credit services.

Theories of Technology Transfer

The subject of technology transfer ranks near the top of most international economic agendas today. It is at the core of current thinking on the development process. Although there is not yet a comprehensive body of economic theory on the subject, we are well down the road to developing one. This would seem a subject especially relevant for services, since it cuts across both trade and investment activity.

Developing countries are concerned about the cost of technology purchases and the appropriateness of the technology being transferred, that is, whether the technologies devised for the needs of industrial countries are suitable for themselves. Industrial nations and their firms are worried about giving away their technology. Many, in fact, wonder if they should be in the technology export business. As a result of this furor over technology, an effort is under way to draft a code of conduct on technology transfer, and a major UN conference on the subject was held in 1979.

Yet, despite all this attention, there has been no focusing on the issue of technology transfer in service industries. Experts have concluded—more by default than design—that there is no significant technology in services, and, therefore, there is nothing to worry about or regulate. The implicit assumptions for this view are that services tend to be smaller, more labor intensive, less capital equipment-oriented, and lagging in productivity. In short, services are not technologically oriented. This conclusion reflects a bias as to what constitutes technology. It emphasizes the highly visible, capital-intensive, large-scale contributions to productivity that occur in agriculture, mining, and manufacturing.

I see, however, a distinct difference between this conventional view of technology and service technology, although this distinction is more one of perception than of actuality. The former consists primarily of high-technology installations, while service technology consists of something that might appropriately be dubbed invisible technology. But the most important elements of both technologies reside in the cerebrum and consist of technical knowledge and know-how, which seems to be acquired mostly through experience and training. In brief, both technologies are one and the same, only the manifestations of high technology or manufacturing technology are deceptively easier to perceive. Our main concern, however, is not with the definition of *service technology* but rather its relevance to international commerce and especially economic development.

The implications of service technology for economic development may be significant. A look at two service industries, insurance and mass merchandising, where in-depth research has been conducted, reveals interesting findings.[11] For example, large investment projects and complex industrial plants require sophisticated insurance-related technologies to reduce the economic disruptions and bottlenecks that can result from shutdowns or losses. This type of protection is based on what is generally termed *risk management*, involving risk analysis, loss-prevention programs, and the designing of insurance coverages involving a mixture of self-insurance, deductibles, and direct and reinsurance plans. Preliminary research suggests that the kinds of technologies involved in these services directly relate to the climate that encourages risk taking in a society and to economic planning and capital formation.

The core issue with respect to development then becomes how service technology is transferred. Again, this investigation of two service industries indicates some general conclusions. First, most of the technology cannot be debundled, to use the current jargon of the international technology debate— that is, an importer of service technology cannot simply buy it. It can only be transferred through experience and on-the-job training. This suggests that direct foreign investment is the most effective means of transferring it. A second conclusion is that the more commitment the investor or supplier has, the more technology is likely to be transferred. A supplier of service technology with a minority equity interest, or a technical service contract, is less likely to be as committed to the kind of local involvement that will ensure technology transfer than is the direct foreign investor who has a larger stake. If subsequent research supports this observation, the desirability of foreign participation in services becomes a less problematical question, especially since the advanced technology of services is developed in advanced nations, as are other kinds of technological advances.

These observations have important policy ramifications since developing and industrial nations wishing to control technology have not generally recognized the existence of service industry technology. It has not been consciously regulated. With services there has been no furor over licensing, patents, and the cost of the transfer. However, many nations are unconsciously regulating service technology transfer in that a majority of the Third World and much of the industrial world impose some form of control over foreign investment in service industries, especially in the financial sector, utilities, communications, advertising, and transportation. This often means nationalization, national ownership rules, or the outright prohibition of foreign participation in these sectors. In effect, therefore, many nations, including those that desperately need technology, are already regulating and restraining the flow of technology in services. If the fact that services do have technology is not recognized soon, the end result will be the emergence of new theories of international commerce—theories that once again ignore services.

The Oligopoly Theory of International Investment

Finally, I will examine the relevance to services of one well-recognized theory of international investment: oligopoly theory.

Direct foreign investment is generally associated in economic theory with oligopolistic industries. Studies have indicated that major foreign investors are usually the dominant firms in industries where a small number of companies account for a large proportion of total output.[12] The flaw in these studies is that they are based exclusively on manufacturing and extractive industries. This is another area where perceptions that guide policies regulating all international investment are based on research that excluded an entire class of international investment—services. Here again, we lack the empirical resources to examine the question in depth, but a detailed look at one industry and some observations about others suggest implications that should be considered by policy makers in both investor and recipient nations.

Paul L. Joskow, in an article in the *Bell Journal of Economics* in 1973, found that the general insurance industry is very competitive.[13] Basing his analysis on total U.S. property-liability premiums written, Joskow examined the premiums written by the largest firm, the 4 largest firms, the 8 largest firms, and the 20 largest firms for the United States as a whole. He grouped firms so that individual companies that have related ownership are considered in a group as one firm. He found, as of 1971, the top group had 6.2 percent of total net premiums; the top 4 groups, 19.8 percent; the top 8 groups, 32.8 percent; and the top 20 groups, 54.2 percent. Joskow further examined concentration ratios by individual lines of insurance and found the same approximate concentration. He went a step further and examined the bars to entry by new firms and found there were few, most clearly evidenced by the fact that 336 new firms entered the business between 1960 and 1971. Finally, he compared these concentration ratios with other industries (manufacturing) and concluded that the general insurance industry ratios are quite low.

As for the consequences of these findings at the international level, few U.S. insurers have established overseas affiliates. Generally, the insurance companies having important market share in the United States do not operate at all in international markets or, if so, only to a minor extent. We would expect that those that operate abroad have, for the most part, very small percentages of the market share in the countries in which they operate. This is unquestionably true in industrial countries and would probably be true in those developing countries that have developed their own insurance industries, which includes most of the Third World. In the poorest of countries where this might not be true, a surprising number have nationalized or imposed some form of national control pursuant to socialist or nationalist philosophies. So there would be no chance for market domination.

In short, the indications are that foreign insurance investors, at least those headquartered in the United States, are not oligopolistic.

Whether this finding is equally valid for other service industries requires research. Nevertheless, even a superficial look at the question may be helpful.

In banking the question of *oligopoly* appears to depend on how it is defined. Within the United States context, for example, there is little doubt that in terms of total loan volume or total assets, the industry is not dominated by a small number of banks. However, one could argue that in terms of volume of internationally oriented loans it is oligopolistic. Clearly, the banks that do international business are large ones, but whether their dominance of domestic banking activities matches their dominance of U.S. international banking activities is another question. As to their dominance in the countries where they operate, my impression is that while they dominate the internationally oriented business in many of these countries, they are relatively insignificant in the overall national market. I suspect the same would be true with legal and advertising services as well. Certain other services might be more likely to dominate both their national markets and the third country markets in which they operate; in particular, accounting, auto and truck rental services, communications, computer services, and motion pictures. A third category of services that would probably be oligopolistic in their national markets but not overseas are air transportation and, to a lesser extent, maritime transportation.

Obviously, one cannot generalize as to whether or not services are oligopolistic. The possibility that many are not, or, in fact, do not exhibit the same negative characteristics as oligopolistic firms in manufacturing or extractive industries, presents complex policy considerations for host countries, which often fear direct foreign investment because it is believed to dominate their economies. Those services without the traditional negative oligopolistic characteristics can probably make important and constructive contributions in foreign markets, other factors being equal. Such policy implications are even more persuasive if one accepts my earlier observations about the impact of services on technology transfer—their role in building the infrastructure for industrial development and encouraging the development of a middle class and pluralistic institutions.

In conclusion, it is clear that economic theory does a relatively poor job of helping us understand how services actually operate internationally. This poses problems when considering the ways services are regulated in the world economy and complicates policy prescriptions for how they should be dealt with in the future.

NOTES

1. See the Bibliographic Appendix for a more complete discussion of the service sector in economic development and a review of the literature on the subject.
2. Yves Sabolo, J. Gaude, and R. Wery, *The Service Industries* (Geneva: International Labour Office, 1975), p. 60.
3. This classification of services—complementary, traditional, and so on—is discussed in more detail in the Bibliographic Appendix.
4. Russell Lewis, *The New Service Society* (Harlow, England: Longman, 1973), p.155.
5. U.S., Department of Commerce, Office of the Assistant Secretary for Policy, *U.S. Service Industries in World Markets: Current Problems and Future Policy Development* (Washington, D.C.: Government Printing Office, December 1976), p. 17.
6. Studies of goods trade have demonstrated dramatic linkages between the home country firm and overseas affiliates in the purchases of each others' products. Similar studies of the relationship between service companies and their overseas affiliates would probably show the same interaction.
7. These sessions were held at the Aspen Institute in Wye Plantation, Maryland (March 1980) and the Trade Policy Research Centre in London (June 1980) under a grant from the German Marshall Fund of the United States and the Rockefeller Foundation.
8. Bernard Wasow and Raymond D. Hill, "Public Sector Involvement in the Insurance Industry: The Implications for Economic Development" (Study prepared for the Center for Applied Economics, New York University, New York, 1980).
9. Raymond Vernon, "International Investment and International Trade in the Product Cycle," *Quarterly Journal of Economics* 80 (May 1966): 191-207.
10. Ibid.
11. Joseph N. Peno, Bernard Wasow, Nancy Truitt, John Stephenson, and Ronald K. Shelp, "The Role of Service Technology in Economic Development" (Study being prepared

under the auspices of the Fund for Multinational Management Education, New York, forthcoming.

12. Stephen Hymer, "The International Operations of National Firms: A Study of Direct Investment" (Ph.D. diss., Massachusetts Institute of Technology, 1960). Hymer classifies major U.S. investors in manufacturing and petroleum industries by their level of concentration and finds that some 44 percent of these firms are in dominant industries where the concentration rate or ratio is greater than 75 percent, with another 15 percent dominant in industries where the concentration ratios were 50 to 75 percent. The 1966 U.S. Census of Foreign Direct Investment shows 50 giant firms account for over 55 percent of U.S. overseas investment, with the next 45 concerns accounting for another 11.7 percent and over 77 percent of the total value of all U.S. direct foreign investment accounted for by 170 firms out of several thousand reporting.

13. Paul L. Joskow, "Cartels, Competition and Regulation in the Property-Liability Insurance Industry," *Bell Journal of Economics* 4 (Autumn 1973): 375-427.

5

NATIONAL AND INTERNATIONAL REGULATION

The failure to integrate services into the body of economic theory that provides the intellectual foundation for international commerce directly bears on the regulation of international service flows. The vacuum it leaves provides an invitation to ignore the kinds of considerations that would be weighed in regulating other kinds of commercial activities. It encourages treating services as a special class of commerce apart from the norm. It undermines those who would try to integrate services into the existing institutions that establish standards for international commercial activities.

The abyss of analysis is fortified by the historical lack of organized political power in the service sector. If the heterogeneous, diffused service sector has failed to organize itself in most nations to strictly address domestic concerns, those services with international interests have been even more inattentive, much less effectual. With the exception of the transportation industry, services have seldom raised their voices in matters of national policy affecting international competition in their industry. This one exception is in most nations dominated by governments. Thus it is not surprising that this sector's interests have been heeded when others have not.

The transportation sector, interestingly, is the one sector where an international theory of regulation is well established. The bywords are familiar: cartelization is in the public interest; regulation is better than competition. Such principles, although simplistically overstated, have governed the international agreements negotiated to regulate transportation commerce. In essence, then, governments have taken their domestic transportation regulatory principles and elevated them to the international level.

Clearly, regulatory principles, or what might be termed *regulatory theory*, exist at the domestic level for the other service sectors that are subject to intense regulation. These have not been codified into internationally accepted principles to govern services commerce, however, although they clearly impact on the way foreign services are treated in national markets. Any effort to subject these services to international rules will have to contend with these principles. However, there are numerous other services that operate across national boundaries that are not subject to a coherent system of domestic regulation. The difficulties they encounter are subject to the whim of government policies and practices of each particular jurisdiction. Sometimes there are specific rules directed toward a service activity, sometimes only toward foreign involvement in that activity. Other times rules and standards of a general nature will impact. Often, specific principles that govern all or most foreign participation, especially foreign investment, will come into play in an economy.

Regretfully, or perhaps thankfully, an analysis of how each service industry is regulated nationally and internationally is far beyond the scope of this undertaking. My intention here is only to gauge the end result: what constraints the regulation of services places on international commerce in these services. Without doubt, the concerns manifested in domestic regulation will have to be understood and addressed on a sector-by-sector basis if meaningful regimes to govern international services commerce are to ever come into being. These will be considered in the concluding chapter of this study. The present discussion, however, is limited to examining the restrictions placed on international services by national regulations.

This will be followed by an examination of the regulation by international organizations, both regional and global. The discussion will look not only at those forums that have an actual voice in direct regulation but also at the outlook of those international organizations with considerable indirect influence on international movement of services. In conclusion, judgment will be offered on which restrictions have the most real economic significance, along with other generalizations about my findings.

I discussed on several occasions in this study the difficulty of unequivocally classifying a service as trade related or investment related and concluded that, contrary to conventional wisdom, many services have elements of both. Accepting this qualification, the analysis can nevertheless be made more meaningful by accepting a division along the lines of the Department of Commerce study *U.S. Service Industries in World Markets.*[1] Its review of 18 service industries divided them into three categories: those predominantly associated with investment—accounting, advertising, auto and truck leasing, banking, employment agencies, equipment leasing, hotels and motels, and legal services; those associated with both trade and investment—communications, computer services, construction or engineering services, educational services, franchising, health services, insurance, and motion pictures; and those that are primarily associated with export trade—air and maritime transportation. A review of the impediments raised in these 18 sectors does not comprehend all service problems. As the earlier discusssion on the dynamics of services indicates, the scope of service activity is much broader than usually recognized. Nevertheless, this approach provides a satisfactory overview from which to survey the nature of service problems.

THE REGULATION OF SERVICES IN NATIONAL ECONOMIES

National Regulation of Investment-Related Services

Turning first to national policies toward services and using the foregoing list of investment-oriented services, I will begin with the most regulated industries.

Banking

Many of the regulations that control international banks are also encountered by domestic banks—reserve requirements, liquidity ratios, credit ceilings, and the like. Since banks everywhere are subject to monetary and prudential regulation, these regulations can only be viewed as prejudicial against foreign banks if they are harsher than those governing domestic banks. Among the most common restrictions on foreign participation in national banking markets are:

Outright nationalization (although usually this will be directed against all banks, not just foreign banks).[2]

Prohibition against branch banking and a requirement of local incorporation, often accompanied by percentage limitations on foreign shareholding. In many countries banks must have boards made up exclusively or mostly of nationals of the host country.

The exclusion of foreign participation through administrative discretion, so that foreigners cannot obtain permission to participate through any corporate form—be it a branch, subsidiary, or representative office.

Limitations placed on those licenses granted to foreigners. These can take the form of prohibiting the acceptance of deposits, not allowing foreign banks access to Central Bank credit facilities, or applying stricter reserve requirements to them.

The imposition of higher capital requirements on foreign banks. Branches of nonnational banks must often be capitalized as if they were independent banks, thus excluding from consideration the capital of the parent bank.

Preferential treatment or quotas based on nationality for granting work permits: a requirement that "x" percent of all employees be host country nationals.

Foreign exchange controls, although not necessarily directed at the foreign banking community, that often require that transactions in a foreign currency be licensed by government and that interest payments on nonresident accounts and the repatriation of profits be restricted. There may be prohibitions on the financing of trade between third countries and restrictions on the use of residents' funds for lending abroad.

The last category fits into what can be classified as export controls, that is, restrictions on the overseas activities of domestic banks. For example, in the United States, the Federal Reserve System has tightened its regulation of overseas acquisitions by its members. Such regulation is unique in that it is a rare case of a restriction being placed against a domestic sector's expansion abroad, instead of the reverse.

Professional Services

The principal professional services used internationally are accounting and legal services, which are closely supervised in every country through standards of certification and professional affiliation. Thus a foreign firm wishing to operate in a country must generally establish a local affiliate. Although this might be possible, the basic constraint on the accounting and legal professions at the international level lies in the refusal to license nonnationals.

In accounting many nations have citizenship restrictions that make it virtually impossible for a foreign accountant to qualify to practice; often these are combined with discriminatory visa requirements. Some countries prohibit reciprocity for professionals of other nations under any circumstances. Others prohibit national accountants from making business associations with accountants from other countries. The activities of international firms are also thwarted in countries with legislation requiring that a firm's name also include the names of those associates who are titled accountants of that country.

Analogous restrictions are often applied to legal services. They include limitations on the licensing of nonnationals, prohibitions against soliciting local attorneys to associate with foreign law firms, and the absence of reciprocity for professionals from other nations.

One other restriction, which applies mainly to accounting, involves the regulation of payments for technology and services provided to affiliates by their parent firm. But this is more of a trade restriction than an investment one, again illustrating the difficulty in making clear-cut distinctions between the two.

Employment Services

Few nations permit foreign private employment agencies; and those that do closely regulate them, generally through requirements that they be licensed and post bond. For these reasons employment agencies operating at the international level are quite rare. The executive search firm, a related field, is permitted in some countries to operate, usually through their affiliation with consulting firms. Ironically, the International Labour Organisation plays a major part in limiting the international role of these firms. A resolution it sponsored outlaws all foreign private employment agencies or requires that, at a minimum, there be close government regulation. The only nations not subscribing to this resolution are the English-speaking countries and Spain.

Advertising

Advertising is primarily an investment-related service, with only a small fraction of overseas sales being exported from parent companies. Although the advertising itself is minimally regulated, the media in which it is placed are usually highly regulated. International advertisers encounter both investment and trade restrictions, such as national quotas and tariffs on training material imports needed to introduce new advertising technology. In some countries, requirements that foreign-controlled advertising firms divest themselves partially or totally have been imposed. As in many industries, difficulties in remitting funds overseas have been encountered.

Leasing

Automobile, truck, and equipment leasing services are subject to a minimum of regulation. However, the traditional international lessors (of autos and trucks) meet with two kinds of problems, depending on whether the overseas operation is carried on through a franchise arrangement or through a subsidiary. Franchisers encounter licensing regulations in countries where there is strict technology legislation. These include controls over royalties and the imposition of taxes and other fees. Operators of subsidiaries encounter fewer problems but face the possibilities of forced divestment, national ownership requirements, restriction on the repatriation of profits, and the lack of statutory protection for trademarks or company name identification. Here again, one finds an industry that though primarily conducted through overseas investment, encounters both investment and trade restrictions.

Equipment leasing is a complex industry that, although relatively new at the international level, is rapidly expanding. It cuts across a wide spectrum of industry and commerce. Lessors include manufacturing companies, independent leasing companies, lease brokers, and commercial banks. The bulk of overseas leasing activity consists of cross-border financing where the exporter in one country finances leased equipment from a client in another country for use in a third country. In many countries the concept is so novel that its regulation is often more accidental than intentional. Most of the restrictions arise in connection with establishing local affiliates and include national ownership requirements, profit repatriation problems, and controls on the extension of credit.

Hotel and Motel Services

The last category of investment-related service sector activity, hotel and motel services, is the least regulated. International activity in this industry has changed markedly in recent years. Originally, the firms operating internationally tended to develop and own their overseas properties, but today this is giving way to the marketing of management skills through management contracts. In part, the change has come about because of national policies limiting foreign ownership and, at times, decreeing expropriation of foreign-owned properties.

As a result of the movement toward management contracts, the more prevalent restrictions today are trade rather than investment related. Difficulties are encountered in maintaining quality because of restrictions on imports of the necessary equipment and spare parts. Foreign exchange controls and other constraints placed on travel severely affect the ability of hotels to attract tourists, although these are not necessarily always directed at the industry itself. Problems relating to standards arise because of national laws governing accounting and communications systems, product certification, and hotel regulations, some of which are established internationally through forums that govern the industry. They include rules on reservations, cancellations, overbooking, minimum liability insurance requirements, and the use of international credit cards.

National Regulation of Trade- and Investment-Related Services

This section on the national regulation of trade- and investment-related services, too, discusses services according to the severity of regulation, beginning with the most regulated.

Insurance

International insurers, like international bankers, must cope with a broad array of restrictions. The main differences in the regulation of the two industries result from technical and operational distinctions rather than from any variation in the intensity of the controls. As in banking, numerous countries have nationalized insurance.[3] Some have nationalized only part of the sector—life, general, or reinsurance. Many countries prohibit foreign insurers from establishing agencies or branches and only allow local subsidiaries, often owned primarily by nationals and, in some cases, with majority government ownership. Those countries that grant licenses (in whatever corporate form) often use administrative discretion to deny market access.

A related set of restrictions is the placing of limitations on licensed foreign firms. The limitations may include limits on the lines of insurance products a firm can provide, strictures against servicing certain buyers of insurance (for example, preferential government procurement policies that favor national insurance firms), and levy of higher capital and deposit requirements or discriminatory taxes on foreign enterprises.

A different kind of restriction denies foreign insurers without a local establishment from providing services that are normally traded on an export basis. Examples would be a requirement that transport insurance only be placed with firms established within a country, or controls over the import of reinsurance, or limitations on brokerage services.

Communications

The communications sector encompasses a wide range of industries, including telephone, telegraph, radio, and television. Generally these industries are closely regulated. In fact, foreign participation in radio and television through investment is nonexistent because foreign ownership of broadcasting stations is prohibited even in those countries that permit private ownership of these media. Thus the focus of international communications services is on investment and trade in telephone and telegraph services.

Investments in high-technology equipment provide on-site service facilities abroad. Exports consist of foreign phone calls and telex, the use of communications satellites, and the export of consulting and managerial know-how. In the telephone industry direct investors must generally operate through subsidiary companies, which are usually majority owned by the host government. There remain a few developing countries, however, where foreign investors have independent subsidiaries. As for telegraph services, many countries have nationalized telegraph networks that restrict outside competition. Certain countries allow wholly or partially foreign-owned local subsidiaries.

Other practices in this industry create hindrances to international competition. A serious constraint results from government-sponsored-and-financed consortia, which make competition difficult, along with various other marketing practices that prevent free access. Many countries also severely restrict foreign consulting engineers from providing their services.

The major international organization responsible for these industries is the International Telecommunications Union (ITU), under the auspices of the United Nations. Although it has been successful in creating international standards for communications, it is not organized to resolve the international trade and investment issues that arise.

Computer Services

Like the computer equipment industry, computer services is very technical and relatively new. Its products primarily involve management ideas and organizational systems, including the development of software packages, data processing services, the management of computer facilities, and computer-related services such as leasing and rental, as well as consultant and maintenance services.

Current restrictions on international commerce in computer services cut across both investment and trade lines, and new constraints are on the horizon. Some countries allow independent subsidiaries, but in many cases, only minority partnership is permitted. Restrictions on data transmission are becoming recognized as a matter of major international concern. There is a growing trend of requiring that data files remain in the country of origin rather than be transmitted across national boundaries to computer banks located within the country of the parent company. In 1973 the Canadian government issued the first software patent, which, if upheld in patent courts, could form the basis for tariffs on the content of computer software. The United Kingdom and Canada are attempting to develop a workable formula that would allow tariffs to be levied on the value of the data stored in punch cards and magnetic tapes.

Computer service firms often require leased communications lines to transmit their data. In many countries these lines are under the jurisdiction of government agencies, which themselves often offer data processing services. As a result, foreign firms can find it difficult to lease lines, and in some countries foreign firms are discriminated against by a surcharge that is added to their leasing rates. The competition from nationalized and subsidized companies is likely to become more problematic in the future.

Some effort is being made at the international level to create international standards. For example, the European Economic Community (EEC) is working on standardizing selected computer languages. The creation of data computer network standards would no doubt have a significant impact on exporters of computer services.

Problems confronting the communications, data processing, and information industry are proliferating at a rapid rate and are viewed by many as the major service industry problem. The dependence of numerous other industries, both service and nonservice, on this kind of service activity provides a striking exemplar of the symbiotic relationship of many services to the functioning of the modern global economy.

This description of the problems in communications/computer services does not do justice to the complexity of this issue and only lightly touches the kinds of problems that are beginning to surface. For example, the information industry, which provides a wide range of data based services, is in its infancy—yet it is already encountering problems like those suggested above and some unique ones of its own.

The major problems arise out of the regulatory response of governments to major technological changes that have taken place in these industries. Whereas some governments have encouraged innovation and increased competition by encouraging the application of new technology, other governments have acted to limit the internationalization of these services. Taken as a whole, we see the prohibition of certain transborder data flows, often in the name of protection of privacy, restrictions on the use of foreign data processing or information services, discriminatory taxation of international data transmissions, and numerous other impediments.

Education and Health Services

The leading providers of health and educational services within national markets are governments. There is, however, some international involvement through private firms. In education, we find that activity centers around exports of vocational training materials to technical schools. These are often run by noneducational institutions such as business corporations, equipment manufacturers, and government agencies. The thin line between the export of educational services and the export of educational materials such as textbooks with audiovisual supplements is illustrative of the way services and goods can be so closely intertwined.

The primary constraint on international suppliers of educational services is the appropriation of teaching materials or software by governments and nationals in violation of copyright agreements. Among these pirated educational materials are industry film and course materials. The lack of protection limits international expansion in the growing educational services field.

The health care industry both exports consulting services and invests in hospital facilities overseas. It is a growing service industry, sparked by the demand from foreign governments for new hospitals and health care technology. Its activities include management contracts with existing hospitals and the replacement of outdated facilities with modern facilities containing the latest equipment.

The restrictions facing international health service firms arise because of the extensiveness of government involvement in health care and are similar to those that confront communications services. The restraints include requirements that nations or the government own the majority of a facility, unfair competition from government-sponsored-and-financed concerns, and problems with importing medical technology and equipment.

Motion Pictures

In this industry are firms that produce motion pictures and exhibit them as well as those that produce for television or other media using film or tape. Investments are principally in marketing and distribution facilities, and exports usually take the form of film rentals. International activity in the industry is highly regulated. Restrictions are, in the main, trade related and involve screen quotas, which require theaters to devote a specific amount of time to showing domestic films; import quotas, which limit the number of films that can be imported for viewing; discriminatory admission and other taxes levied on foreign films; film rental price controls that discriminate against foreign firms; and the requirement that dubbing be done in local laboratories or the prohibition against any dubbing of foreign films. In addition, some nations grant domestic producers production subsidies. Sometimes there are investment restrictions, such as bans against subsidiaries of foreign distributors and laws that favor national import and distribution monopolies.

Construction and Engineering

Construction and engineering services perform functions ranging from the design and construction of large-scale industrial facilities, including turnkey operations, to the installation, maintenance, and operation of equipment, as well as consulting work in construction, engineering, architecture, and land surveying.

Construction companies service foreign markets by exporting construction/ engineering services and operating permanent construction affiliates abroad, entering into joint venture, or forming temporary affiliates. This sector is encumbered by formidable obstacles. On the investment side, the requirement of joint ventures is becoming common. Other restrictions include licensing procedures, quotas and other customs practices that govern capital goods imports (such as construction equipment), and stringent rules on the proportion of foreign to domestic goods used on a project. These restrictions are often used by the country importing the service as a lever to bargain with exporting nations for an improved financial position, as for example, forcing the exporting country to preferentially import its raw materials.

Technical standards can be applied in a discriminatory manner, and discriminatory government purchase practices are not uncommon. The ability to compete can also be affected by work permit and visa practices. Some countries require guarantees of contract performance that go beyond normally accepted international procedures. For example, Middle Eastern countries will accept only bank guarantees, not surety bonds,[4] and the former can only be obtained in certain countries like the United States at a prohibitive price. Many nations have policies aimed at assisting national industries in exporting to third countries. For example, governments form partnership relationships with their national firms to ensure them competitive advantages in their bidding on overseas projects. Government support can also include export subsidies, favorable export financing, tax rebates, and other forms of assistance. Perhaps the major trade impediment centers around the subsidization of projects in developing countries, which puts the companies of nonsubsidizing countries at a disadvantage.

Franchising

A *franchise* is a contract to distribute and sell goods and services within a specified area. Franchising itself is not a separate service industry but a mode of operation for overseas activities. It is common in many industries such as auto and truck leasing and hotels/motels. Other obvious examples are fast-food outlets and soft drink bottlers. Franchising is likely to grow rapidly in the future through the introduction of many new services, especially in construction, home improvement, maintenance and cleaning services, recreation, entertainment and travel services, automobile products and services, and retailing services.

As in many sectors, on the investment side local participation is often required. A constraint especially important to franchising is the prohibition of foreigners owning real estate and, in some cases, owning retail businesses. Trade restraints include limitations on royalty payments for licensing and trademark contracts (and the absence of trademark protection) and import restrictions on equipment that is essential to providing the service.

National Regulation of Trade-Related Services

Air Transportation

Air transportation is primarily trade, with overseas investments principally limited to small marketing and ground support facilities. It is a highly regulated industry, and almost every country reserves to its national airline all flights wholly within national borders. As a result of government dominance, the industry is permeated with restrictions and complex international treaties that significantly affect it. These practices translate into a variety of restrictions against foreign carriers. They include excessive and discriminatory charges for the use of airport facilities; discriminatory taxes on income, fuel, and other essentials; illegal ticket discounting and rebating; and ground-handling monopolies by foreign governments and their carriers for services such as catering, ticketing, reservations systems, and cargo/luggage handling. Thus, for example, a ground monopoly operating a national reservation system may only list the flights of domestic carriers.

The excess profits earned by monopolies are frequently used to subsidize the operation of national carriers. There are also preferential government procurement practices and limitations on the ability of foreign carriers to seek charter packages or limits on using certain airports. Currency regulations play a major role. In many nations local currency cannot be accepted for transportation sales unless approved by government authorities, and there are exchange controls that interfere with profit remittances.

These issues do not include the problems related to reciprocal access to air routes, which are negotiated through bilateral aviation agreements.

Three international organizations seek to resolve air transport issues. The International Civil Aviation Organization (ICAO) was created in 1943 "to develop the principles and techniques of international air navigation and to foster the planning and development of international air transport."[5] Among its objectives are preventing economic waste caused by unreasonable competition, ensuring that the rights of member states are fully respected, and avoiding discrimination between contracting states. Second, there is the International Air Transport Association (IATA), created in 1945, which is a voluntary organization open for membership to any air transport company that is licensed by a government eligible for membership in ICAO. Its original purpose was to study the problems of air commerce and provide a means for collaboration among airline companies. Over the years it has evolved into a forum for setting tariffs. Finally, the International Air Carriers Association (IACA), formed in 1971 to represent airlines that operate charters, seeks to ease restrictions that hamper the growth of low-cost international charter travel.

Maritime Transportation

The maritime transportation industry is highly regulated and characterized by a plethora of cartels, subsidies, and other market-distorting arrangements. Like air transportation, a high level of government participation in the maritime industry is a prominent factor. Governments provide subsidies, special tax and depreciation regulations, preferential treatment for the ship-building industry such as materials imported duty free, and cargo preference schemes limiting all or part of the country's exports or imports to national carriers. Governments often operate their merchant marine on a basis other than economic efficiency. Like airlines, merchant fleets are a visible expression of national economic power and considered vital to national security.

The complex collection of regulations governing shipping can be grouped into three categories: flag discrimination, cabotage laws, and operating subsidies. Flag discrimination, although difficult to define precisely, is easy to identify. It consists of a wide variety of governmental acts that direct cargo to national ships regardless of commercial considerations. This can be done through legislation, regulation, or other administrative measures stipulating or guaranteeing that a certain percentage of all cargoes, or certain types, such as government-owned or -sponsored cargoes, be reserved to national ships. There are a host of direct and indirect measures that can accomplish the same results through the discriminatory treatment of foreign shippers.

Cabotage laws reserve either a portion or all of a country's coastal trade to ships flying the national flag. It is a widespread practice. In fact, taking Western Europe as an example, only Belgium, the United Kingdom, Denmark, Holland, and Norway do not protect their coastal trade. The one main exception to the general tenor of cabotage laws is the transport of oil and oil products.

The third category comprises the operating subsidies that are paid by various governments to shipping companies. The United Nations Conference on Trade and Development (UNCTAD) defines nine different types of subsidies:

Direct subsidies for the construction, purchase, and improvement of ships;
Scrap-and-build schemes to renovate fleets;
Loans at low rates of interest;
Accelerated depreciation provisions on investment allowance or grants;
Exemption from income tax and other tax privileges;
Reimbursement of harbor dues, pilotage expenses, and canal fees;
Financing out of tax revenue the deficits of state-owned fleets or shipyards;
Contracts for the carriage of mail on favorable terms; and
Payment of freight at rates above world charter rates for government cargoes carried in national ships.

Surprisingly, there is no international organization that has effectively sought to resolve the major international shipping issues. One group that has dealt with them is the transport committee of the Maritime Organization for Economic Cooperation and Development (OECD), but its activities have been limited to discussions and information gathering. It can contribute to the resolution of shipping issues by urging individual countries to compromise on specific problems or by seeking a multilateral approach among OECD members, but as we will see, the OECD has difficulty in pressuring nations to avoid restrictive practices.

THE NATURE OF TRADE AND INVESTMENT RESTRICTIONS

With this broad-brush description of the constraints placed on services in international trade and investment, some general conclusions can be drawn and comparisons made with the regulations and restrictions imposed on nonservice industries. Naturally, however, the limits of such a discussion must be kept in mind, for some services, like other industries, have characteristics that make generalizations specious. Among these characteristics are an uncommon degree of government control and intricate and complex technical considerations. Clearly, many of the obstacles to international trade and investment in particular services arise from their close involvement with government. This is the obvious consequence of the fact that many highly sensitive services are closely regulated, banking and insurance, for example. There are also other services that most governments believe they should provide, such as health, education, transportation, and employment services. So the problems of some service industries are clearly different from those of most goods industries because of this strict regulatory climate and intensive public sector involvement.

The Department of Commerce study found that about half of the obstacles are investment oriented, that is, they generally relate to the operation of overseas affiliates.[6] Other obstacles and problems can be classified as having both trade and investment elements, depending on the particular situation. This convenient categorization is used with some modifications for the following discussion.

Investment Problems

Restrictions on remittances and repatriation of profits, fees, and royalties;[7]

Ownership restrictions that require full or partial local ownership or control of establishments and that may prevent market access to a foreign firm or allow only limited access;

Personnel restrictions such as local labor law requirements, licensing of professionals (generally based on nationality), visas, and work permits;

Discriminatory taxes placed solely or inequitably on foreign concerns;

Discriminatory practices of various other kinds levied against particular foreign service industries (for example, in banking the requirement that reserve ratios be higher for foreign banks; in insurance, higher capital requirements); and

Inadequate protection of intellectual property, trademarks, copyrights, and the theft of technology.[8]

Trade and Investment Problems

Government subsidies to locally owned firms to help them compete at home or in third-country markets;

Government-controlled facilities that are given unfair competitive advantages such as subsidies, preferential treatment, and so on, or that are operated on uneconomic grounds;

Discriminatory licensing regulations, fees, and taxes;

Restrictions on the importation of goods essential to the performance of services such as excessively high duties on imports of necessary materials or outright quantitative restrictions of imports;

Restrictive or discriminatory government procurement practices; and

The absence of internationally accepted standards and procedures for services with the result that national standards, even if not applied on a discriminatory basis, can create restraints on service activities.

The trade and investment problems of service industries are by no means unique to them. Such problems are of equal concern to other sectors.[9] However, in the service industries these problems may differ in degree or emphasis from those experienced by other industries. For example, the U.S. study[10] postulated that the treatment of royalties, work permits, and intellectual property is probably of greater importance to service industries than questions pertaining to expropriation or to imports of components and raw materials, which are presumably related only to goods trade. This is highly debatable. It is difficult to perceive of royalty and intellectual protection problems being of more importance to services. In fact, the opposite would seem to be true. Manufacturing processes are more subject to licensing for royalty payments than are services. On the other hand, the process itself might best be termed a *service transaction*.

Yet because so many services are highly sensitive industries, the possibility of expropriation is of special concern. A U.S. State Department study a few years ago indicated that the financial sector, especially banking and insurance, was second only to extractive industries in the number of expropriatory actions it has encountered.[11] Again, although imports of components and raw materials would seem to be of more importance to goods industries, one must conclude, after reviewing the various trade and investment problems of services, that goods imports are important and sometimes essential to the functioning of certain services. In fact, many of the obstacles to trade in services are actually problems pertaining to merchandise trade rather than services per se. For example, duties on advertising materials and educational equipment are problems of this type, as are mixing regulations stipulating that a certain portion of the goods used in construction projects must be of local origin. Though these are technically trade-in-goods problems, it is clear they also affect services trade.

All six problems listed under the trade and investment category are similar to the trading problems of merchandise, which were given much attention in the

Tokyo Round of trade negotiations. Whatever the extent of these problems for other service industries, they are especially prevalent in motion pictures, insurance, construction/engineering, and air and maritime transportation.[12]

The Department of Commerce study concluded that the obstacles to international trade and investment in services industries are general problems that affect both goods and service industries or industry-specific problems, unique to a particular service industry and not shared by other service industries. Thus, no such thing as general service industry issues can be isolated from other trade and investment issues. Some issues are unique to individual industries and will probably need to be addressed within a sectoral context. Others have a more generic character and are shared by a number of different industries, service and otherwise.

This leaves us with a difficult ambivalence about international services. The problems of services in international commerce are not unique, something separate unto themselves that cannot be dealt with in conjunction with the problems of other sectors. They are part and parcel of other issues of world commerce. But, within this general context, there is no denying that services, or at least some services, are unquestionably distinct and that dealing with their specific problems will require sensitivity to their differences. Instinctively, I suspect the same can be said about other industry sectors.

THE REGULATION OF SERVICES AT REGIONAL AND INTERNATIONAL LEVELS

I turn now to the regulation of services regionally and globally through various international organizations. I dealt with the industry-specific forums (where they exist) in preceding sections; and in the next chapter dealing with previous efforts at liberalization, I will examine two of the most significant international organizations, the OECD and the EEC. For these reasons, I concentrate here on the other regulatory and internationally influential bodies that deal with services, first looking at specific regional and UN organizations and then, more generally, examining how they have influenced the treatment of services.

Regional Organizations

Since the OECD and EEC will be treated later, I focus here almost exclusively on organizations of the developing countries.

Latin America

The Andean Pact was created in 1968 with the signing of the Agreement of Cartagena by Chile, Colombia, Peru, Ecuador, and Bolivia. Chile has since resigned from the pact and Venezuela has joined. The concern of the pact has been primarily with creating a common market for trade in goods. Unlike the EEC, it has not focused on the free movement of capital, labor, and services. In addition, it has taken on an antiforeign tone through the fade-out rules, which require multinational firms to divest over a period of time. The pact has also imposed severe restrictions that determine who may invest within selected economic sectors.

The service sector stands out as an area where limitations have been placed on foreign investment. The pact prohibits further foreign investment in the following service industries: commercial banking and other financial institutions, insurance, internal transportation, advertising, communications, and publications such as newspapers and magazines. Except for insurance, banking, and other financial institutions, those foreign firms already operating in the specified service areas must convert themselves into national firms. Although not mandated by the pact, some member countries have imposed similar requirements in the excepted industries, and some have imposed divestment requirements. Also, some members have made exceptions to the stringent pact rules. Nationals of the pact countries are allowed to invest in these service industries in other member nations, but that opportunity has rarely been pursued. When there has been intrapact cooperation, as in a regional reinsurance arrangement or a regional shipping company, the impact has been marginal.

The two regional integration groupings that have been in existence the longest, the Latin American Free Trade Association (LAFTA) (now called the Latin American Integration Association) and the Central American Common Market (CACM), have not imposed investment restrictions as has the Andean bloc. However, the CACM has for some years been preparing a new treaty that includes a common investment code, which might impose limitations on foreign participation in services similar to those in the Andean Pact.

In other aspects both the CACM and LAFTA are similar to the pact. Within the CACM the only regional agreement has been in shipping. There have also been some efforts in both organizations to form regionally based reinsurance companies and, in the case of LAFTA, regional banks. The reinsurance institutions are not seen as helping the area to become a reinsurance exporter or assisting in integrating insurance operations within the region but as helping it retain more insurance premiums within the area—that is, reducing its imports, thereby reducing foreign exchange outflows. Generally, regional banks are formed to finance development and occasionally to provide export financing. In LAFTA complementation agreements allocate industrial production to designated member nations, but none involve the service sector. LAFTA has put forth a proposal to study the feasibility of an integrated railroad system, but no action has been taken.

Caribbean

The Caribbean Common Market (CARECOM), a relative newcomer to the ranks of regional economic groupings, has not considered an investment code regulating foreign participation, but it has shown more inclination than might be expected at this stage to develop regional policies on services. A formal agreement on shipping has been established to help members attain a greater portion of North-South shipping traffic. There have also been periodic ministerial meetings on regional insurance policy. A goal of creating regional insurance companies headquartered in one country and with branches throughout the area has not been achieved because most of the CARECOM members wish to house the headquarters of such companies. The role of foreign insurers in this scheme is also a sensitive issue.

Asia-Pacific

In the Asia-Pacific region the major service sector regional activities have been in shipping and to a much lesser extent in banking. For shipping UNCTAD has provided support to the Asia-Pacific Economic and Social Commission (APESC), which has helped establish a formal regional agreement for cargo and container shipping arrangements. The South Pacific Bureau for Economic Cooperation (SPBEC) at present is exploring regional shipping arrangements.. The Association of Southeast Asian Nations (ASEAN) has created the Federation of ASEAN Shippers' Council (FASC). The Asian Reinsurance Company (formed through governmental initiative at the encouragement of the Committee on Trade of the UN Economic and Social Commission for Asia and the Pacific) requires Asian insurers to import a percentage of their reinsurance from it.

Through the ASEAN Banker's Association, in coordination with an Asian monetary group that includes non-ASEAN Asian nations, research has been conducted in banking, but no agreements have emerged. A committee has also been established to draft a common platform for providing regional incentives to external investment. Although only in its early stages, this could eventually lead to a more formalized approach governing foreign investment in the region. Cooperative arrangements also exist among ASEAN countries for providing medical and family health care services.

Africa

No substantive service arrangements have emerged from the Organization of African Unity (OAU) or from other African regional groups. Recently, an African reinsurance institution was established paralleling those in Asia and other areas. It requires all insurance companies operating in the area to purchase a specified percentage of their reinsurance from it.

International Organizations

UNCTAD

UNCTAD has gained unchallenged recognition as the principal advocate for the Third World in economic matters. Implementation of this mandate has led UNCTAD to seek to redress what it perceives as the economic imbalance between the developing and industrial worlds. The organization has carved out a major role for itself in the invisibles field and, to a lesser extent, in services themselves. The main focus of the UNCTAD work in services has been on insurance and transportation. Its activities in these two service sectors illustrate what one can presume to be its basic philosophy toward other services, even though they have not been the focus of study.

Insurance. With regard to insurance, in general terms UNCTAD recommends that the developed countries help and encourage the developing countries in the establishment and strengthening of their own insurance and reinsurance markets. One recommendation is that the right of developing nations to require insurance to be placed in their own national markets not be prescribed as a requirement for trade or aid. Also technical reserves and guarantee deposits of insurance companies should be invested in the country where the premium income arises, and developing countries should be encouraged to form regional reinsurance institutions.

UNCTAD has actively pursued the implementation of the many specific recommendations that have resulted from these broad outlines. It has looked to the United Nations Development Program (UNDP) to provide funds in response to requests for technical assistance in insurance.[13] These include the financing and organization of training courses and seminars for the staff of insurance supervisory services and meetings of insurance supervisors for the purpose of exchanging information and experience regarding insurance legislation and supervision. In carrying out such programs, the regional commissions of the United Nations have played a major role.

In sum, the UNCTAD view is that every developing country should build its own national insurance industry to the fullest extent possible. The principal implicit, and sometimes explicit, rationale behind this approach is that every nation should control its insurance industry because it is so essential to national well-being. For example, one consideration is that large sums of money are involved and the use of these funds should be channeled in the national interest. A second reason for national control is to consolidate the industry, presumably in the interest of efficiency but also to minimize "unhealthy" competition. Third, direct foreign participation in the insurance sector is not essential except in certain unique and large risks; in fact, foreign participation is often detrimental. Finally, the most often-cited reason for developing national insurance markets is to minimize the balance-of-payments costs associated with foreign participation in insurance and reinsurance. But the dominant reasoning behind the policy prescription seems to be directed at national independence and self-reliance—not economic efficiency.

This policy prescription for insurance is formulated without consideration of other economic factors. Many important questions are not addressed. Should every nation really develop an insurance industry? Does the concept of comparative advantage apply? And does the efficient allocation of scarce resources in some cases warrant developing other sectors instead of insurance? The UNCTAD plan envisions an import-substitution policy for the insurance industry in every developing country. The implementation of this philosophy can be seen in restrictions placed on foreign participation in national markets, constraints on reinsurance transactions, and the implementation of policies favoring the national industry over foreign insurers.

Shipping. The UNCTAD philosophy on shipping seeks preferential policies and other practices that guarantee developing countries a share of the world market. The centerpiece of this effort is the Code of Conduct for Liner Conferences, which seeks to allocate cargo sharing on a basis to ensure substantial revenue to developing countries. The convention, first drafted in 1974, is the first major convention ever prepared by UNCTAD. Although the United States has resisted the code, France and Germany were early proponents. Most European nations and Japan are expected to accede to the code along with many developing nations; so it is expected to be ratified. Developing nations, however, reportedly are unhappy with the European proposal to apply the rules to European-developing country shipping but not to trade with OECD nations.

UNCTAD has also sponsored conventions on multimodal transport, ocean container standards, and bulk shipping, each complementary to the goal of securing an adequate share of world commerce in shipping for developing countries. The first would seek to establish bills-of-lading priorities that ensure cargo placement with developing nation carriers. The standard convention has the intent of ensuring that the ability of developing nations to compete is not impaired by the development of new technology. There have also been proposals for establishing a common fund to guarantee parity in all shipping rates. Finally, more recently, UNCTAD has put forth proposals to eliminate flags of convenience or open-registry shipping. An UNCTAD Working Group has concluded that the expansion of open-registry fleets, accounting for a third of global deadweight tonnage, adversely affects the orderly regulation of world shipping as well as the development and competitiveness of fleets from developing nations that do not offer such facilities.

A struggle exists between UNCTAD and another UN organ, the London-based International Maritime Consultant Organization (IMCO). There is fear in UNCTAD circles that IMCO leans too much toward the developed countries and that UNCTAD initiatives might be hampered by IMCO. IMCO is more technically oriented than UNCTAD, with special interest in maritime safety, technical regulation, life at sea, and oil pollution liability.

Aviation. Attempts to structure common agreements in aviation appear also in the Convention on International Intermodal Transport, mentioned above. One proposal is for a single uniform bill of lading for all types of transportation, including air carriers. The goal is to achieve a separate regime governing liability, which will ultimately translate into restrictions on insurance placement. The UNCTAD objective here is to divert economic benefits to the developing countries by requiring that both cargo and carrier insurance be placed with developing country insurers.

United Nations Commission on Transnational Corporations

The recently launched forum of the United Nations Commission on Transnational Corporations is focusing surprising attention on services. The commission was created on the recommendation of the United Nations Expert Group on Transnational Corporations, appointed in July 1972. At the first organizational meeting of the commission, held in Lima, Peru, in March 1976, a comprehensive and ambitious work program was approved, which included undertaking a series of in-depth studies of selected industries in which multinational corporations play a major role. Many of the industries chosen are service industries, including banking, insurance, shipping, consulting, and tourism.[14]

This indicates that service industries are clearly on the minds of at least some of the developing nations. They believe that the high profile of certain multinationals—the oil companies, for example—has been examined ad nauseam. There is nothing more to learn about them and certainly little left to be legislated. But services, an unknown quantity, was a natural choice, especially since many services are highly regulated domestically, and multinational corporations appear to be important in certain of them. Besides, some Third World spokesmen argue that it is imprudent and unfair to treat all multinationals alike. If indeed services are different, they should be regulated accordingly.

The latter explanation may well be the reason why the UN Center on Transnational Corporations, the commission's secretariat, has embarked on a series of sectoral service studies. For my purposes, however, the important consideration is the probable thrust of this undertaking. Even the most sympathetic supporters of developing country aspirations would admit that they harbor strong suspicions of multinationals. Thus although multinationals may bring needed benefits to developing economies, they must be closely watched and regulated. For some, this bias is tempered in the case of services by a lack of information about them; for others, the lack of knowledge increases their prejudice.

The commission's activities with regard to services will inevitably complement the general goal of the commission's work. This is to gather information on multinational corporations in various sectors so as to assist developing countries in assessing them and negotiating with them. Accordingly, the commission has embarked on a threefold effort in support of its basic objective. The one that has generated the most publicity has been the formulation of a code of conduct guiding the relationships among multinational corporations and host and home governments, with primary focus on the conduct of the corporation. A second effort has been to gather information on multinational corporations through the establishment of a data bank. Finally, there are the sectoral studies that obviously relate to the first two projects. Findings of these studies will not only provide valuable information on multinational corporations for the data bank but are expected to influence the drafting of the code of conduct. It seems inevitable that the studies will reflect some of the philosophical biases that permeate other organizations such as UNCTAD. Findings on multinational corporation participation in a particular service sector are likely to be dramatized as highly significant and in need of redress. On the other hand, if a fair and objective attempt at understanding the international functioning of particular service sectors and addressing a broad range of economic issues is undertaken, productive and worthwhile recommendations could result.

The studies that are now complete, in banking and insurance, unfortunately, do not offer much encouragement toward that end. The banking study has been embroiled in controversy from the beginning. International bankers have argued with some vehemence that it is an inaccurate and biased description of international banking. As a result of their criticism, the study was withdrawn and recast. The first draft of a study dealing with reinsurance, while acceptable to international reinsurers, was found objectionable by developing country officials. In the view of most, the final version, while not controversial, is not particularly relevant. It can best be described as a throwaway. It suffered the fate that regretfully might be expected from the climate in which it was created: the necessity of being a document palatable to all interests involved but weighted toward the majority that dominates the UN center.

Given the current interest in the transborder data flow (TDF) issue, it is not surprising the UN center is undertaking work in this area also. A report due in mid-1981 has the objective of assessing the relevance of control over, and access to, information germane to developing nation development; analyzing the factors responsible for this growth of TDF, including technology, trade, and the global spread of transnational corporations; assessing its impact on factors such as centralization of decision making and possible increase in market concentration, national sovereignty, and the international system as it relates to the international division of labor, the North-South disparities, and bargaining; and reviewing regulatory efforts and considering the need for further action.

The objectives for this area of service activity parallel the thrust of the center's general work and resonate with the general UNCTAD philosophy on services.

The Influence of International Organizations on National Policies

There appears to be a causal link between the recommendations of international and regional organizations and the regulations put into effect by member countries. In insurance, for example, the UNCTAD recommendations that developing nations should develop regional reinsurance institutions is being implemented in several regions. In this case, an international organization, while itself unable to impose rules, has a pervasive influence. The regional groupings can have a more direct impact, as can be seen in the Andean Pact, where rules prohibiting further foreign investment in various sectors such as banking and communications have been adopted in the legislation of its member countries. Often regionally agreed to rules lead to even stricter regulation on a national basis than that called for by the region. To illustrate, although the insurance rules of the Andean Pact prohibit further foreign investment in insurance, they do not require divestment. Yet two pact members, Peru and Venezuela, have forced foreigners owning existing insurance firms to divest.

Those regional groups that have regulated services have done so more on a trade than on an investment basis. The best example, duplicated numerous times in different regions, is the establishment of regional reinsurance institutions and, to a lesser extent, the creation of regional shipping arrangements. Both are transactions that in effect establish a preferential policy favoring national and regional service sectors.

Although there clearly is at times a synergism between the policies and rules adopted at national, regional, and international levels, the case can easily be overstated. In fact, with the exception of the Andean Pact, international and regional organizations have not been very successful in affecting the regulation of services. And even within the pact a surprising number of exceptions have been taken to the generally agreed upon rules regulating services. Furthermore, many service industries have not been regulated at all. Only the more sensitive services—financial, communications, and advertising—have been subjected to rules.

Even when common policies are agreed upon in international organizations, their implementation depends entirely on member countries. This is not to say that the organizations are unimportant in their effect on the development of the regulation of service industries. Quite to the contrary, their influence, especially in the last two decades, has been enormous. They can claim a great deal of credit for the prevalent trend toward restricting services, but they have done this more through influence than through an actual ability to impose their recommendations.

Many of these restrictive tendencies were already well developed before international organizations provided a forum in which to confirm, advocate, and spread these views. Thus, the restrictions imposed by countries have had as much influence on international organizations as the organizations have had on the formulation of national policy. An examination of the time sequence of many of the restrictions, especially investment restrictions in sensitive services like banking, insurance, communications, and trade restrictions in shipping, reveals that strict regulations existed long before international organizations themselves took up the cause. In fact, many of the restrictive trends originated in industrial countries. Thus the relation between the international organizations and their members is symbiotic, and the policies prescribed are derived from the examples provided by both developed and developing countries.

By contrast, the thrust of the OECD and the EEC has been toward liberalization of international commerce in services. Although their success has been limited, their efforts are in direct opposition to the prevalent trend among developing countries.

JUSTIFICATIONS FOR RESTRICTIONS ON SERVICES

What reasons are given for policies that restrict the flow of services? Do they differ among countries or according to the stage of development? Perhaps the most striking observation is that whatever the sector—be they sensitive ones like banking, insurance, transportation, or communications or even less sensitive ones like construction, accounting, or consulting—the reasons for protection are remarkably similar. A second interesting observation is that similar arguments may be used to justify both trade and investment restrictions.

Justifications of Developing Nations

The classic justification is Alexander Hamilton's infant industry argument.[15] It is particularly popular in developing countries and is extended to the protection of banking, insurance, shipping, and other services. In short, it claims that small industries do not have the economies of scale to compete with large established firms. Thus if they are to expand enough to become competitive, they must be protected in their home markets through high tariffs or some other form of protection that restricts foreign competition. To illustrate the argument, an UNCTAD Secretariat report, the "Establishment or Expansion of Merchant Marines in Developing Countries," states:

> The infant industry argument ... is a relevant one because of 1) the high capital cost in setting up the industry which would mean that they would have to start on a small scale, 2) the significant economies of scale which can reasonably be expected to be reaped in the course of time, 3) advantages in the form of trade connections and customary goodwill which established owners enjoy, and which would take a new owner some time to acquire during which he will be at a disadvantage.[16]

This argument, however, like some of the other arguments used by developing nations to justify their restrictions, is sometimes shaded somewhat differently when applied to services. For example, although the infant industry argument for services is generally advocated as necessary to encourage the development of a vital national sector, it is not as generally argued, as in nonservices, that in the absence of protection from foreign competition, the industry will not develop. There is no evidence to support the argument that banking, accounting, consulting, insurance, or construction cannot develop because of overwhelming foreign competition. In fact, the existence in most developing countries of dominant national firms that developed without protection and compete alongside foreign firms in most of these sectors belies this supposition.

A second argument commonly used to justify restrictions, especially in developing countries, is that certain industries should be domestically owned and controlled. In other words, foreign competition should not be allowed to dominate vital national industries. This reasoning is used to support the prohibition of foreign investment in communications or the exclusion of foreign airlines, to defend cabotage laws restricting coastal shipping to national vessels, and to justify nationalizing or severely controlling foreign investment in the financial sector. It should be noted that this argument is often used in industrial countries but described more often in terms of national security or ensuring domestic employment. For example, in the United States coastal trade is restricted to ships under the U.S. flag; and limitations on foreign participation in communications exist in many industrial countries. Such restrictions are generally justified on national security grounds.

Closely related to the two main arguments are further justifications that relate to specific sectors. For example, it is argued that banks and insurance companies must be closely controlled in order to ensure that their credit and investment policies are in harmony with national objectives. It is also argued that balanced economic growth requires governments, especially in developing countries, to develop their own national industries in a variety of areas, including services such as airlines, banking, insurance, merchant marine, transportation, and communications.

One recurring economic justification for restricting both trade and investment in services comes directly from the realities of international economic life rather than from a philosophic or theoretical perspective. It is the balance-of-payments argument. The assertion is that expenditures on service imports are a waste of valuable foreign exchange. The same statement could be made about any number of imports, service or otherwise. This is an accepted justification under the General Agreement on Tariffs and Trade (GATT) rules for taking temporary protective measures in goods trade. Considering the doubts harbored about the value of service activities discussed earlier, judgments on service imports are likely to have the same perspective as judgments about luxury items or other consumer imports.

What is surprising is that the balance-of-payments argument is also used to justify the prohibition of foreign investment. In insurance, for example, it is argued that foreign companies reinsure a higher percentage of their business abroad than do national companies, thus utilizing valuable foreign exchange, and they further exacerbate balance-of-payments problems through their remittances of earnings. Analogous arguments are made for banking and other services, such as construction/engineering, computers, and communications. It is often argued that these services import too much merchandise, which hurts the balance of payments. These and other services are also criticized for unnecessarily using foreign exchange to purchase technical, managerial, and other services from their parent firms.

The criteria that developing countries currently use for attracting and admitting new foreign investment reflect the primary benefits they see resulting from such investment—increased exports and the transfer of technology and, to a lesser extent, job creation. In deciding to permit foreign investment, a determination is made by the developing country as to whether a particular investment will contribute to the exports of the country or technology vital to modernization will be transferred. I noted earlier that the transfer-of-technology question is often neglected when services are considered, even though in certain cases they have much technology to offer, both directly and indirectly. A similar argument can be made for the direct and indirect contribution of services to the balance of payments. Service exports themselves, the relationship of services to the production of nonservice exports, and the saving of foreign exchange they yield through import-substitution policies in service sectors all have a positive impact on the balance of payments. However, except for import-substitution policies, the impact of services on the balance of payments is seldom considered in making policies toward foreign participation in services. And even though most services are labor intensive, foreign investment in these sectors is not perceived as yielding anywhere near the employment magnitudes thought to result from manufacturing investment.

Justifications of Developed Nations

Industrial countries defend their restrictions of services in different ways than does the developing world because of their different economic circumstances. Nevertheless, there are similarities. For example, although the infant industry argument is not used to defend protection against foreign penetration in well-established traditional service industries, it is used to limit foreign penetration of new service sectors such as computers and communications. A second argument, shared with developing countries, but more often cited by the industrial world, is the national security argument, which asserts that a nation must control a specific industry in the interest of national security. In the industrial countries as well as the more advanced developing countries, this rationale is usually applied to utilities, communications, and transportation. Perhaps it is just a mature nation's way of saying it must act to protect what a developing nation might call a vital national sector. So the only distinction is using a justification shaded slightly differently to achieve the same end.

For the most part, however, the arguments of the industrial countries for protecting their services sound distinct from those of the developing world. Although if we look behind these rationales, they more likely are a reflection of similar concerns arising at different stages of development. The reasons advanced by industrial nations to protect services are often very similar to the environmental and consumer protection concerns we associate with manufacturing industries. For example, foreign bankers and insurers are told that the financial sector must be highly regulated to protect consumers and the general public, a criterion that can easily be used as an excuse to establish prohibitive admission standards. Similar arguments also are used to control franchising or leasing facilities and the activities of professionals such as doctors, lawyers, accountants, and engineers.

Some service industries are also restricted because of environmental concerns. Environmentalists might object to certain franchising operations, communications facilities, construction and engineering activities, and conceivably even hotels and motels on the grounds of environmental impact. A final defense that is used more by developed than developing countries argues that barriers are justifiable as a response to the constraints of other countries. In other words, retaliation is necessary, either to persuade other countries to remove their barriers or to protect one's own markets. For example, banking or shipping industries may oppose foreign competition on the ground that there is a lack of reciprocity in the countries of their competitors.

ARE SERVICE RESTRICTIONS PRIMARILY A THIRD WORLD PHENOMENON?

The foregoing discussion leads naturally to the question of whether service restrictions are mainly a Third World phenomenon. Since restrictions exist in both developed and developing countries, the important question is the relative magnitude of the problems in the two worlds. Magnitude should be measured not only by the numbers and kinds of restrictions but also by their economic significance.[17]

Studies show that although there are numerous restrictions in both developed and developing countries, in terms of number and diversity of restrictions, developing countries are clearly the most protectionist. But sheer numbers of regulations do not measure the impact of the restrictions on international trade and investment.[18]

Chapter 2 indicates the industrial countries are by far the most important markets for trade and investment in services. One can conclude that because of the amount of commerce involved, the barriers by industrial countries, and by the more advanced developing countries, have a much more significant economic impact on international trade and investment in services than do those imposed by the rest of the developing world. The assumption that barriers to services originate almost exclusively in developing countries is misguided, and a broader perspective on the problem is needed. On the other hand, as the latter markets grow, such restrictions, in the aggregate, will become more and more important; so the problem of protectionism in service commerce cannot be limited solely to countries in any particular stage of development.

APPENDIX TO CHAPTER 5

Regulation of Service Industries Compared with Other Sectors

Manufacturing (commerce in goods) is distinct from services—and from other sectors such as extractive and agribusiness—in that at least in theory it almost always has the option of serving foreign markets through exports rather than through investment. Its ability to export is affected by the imposition of both tariff and nontariff measures. Service exports are seldom dutied (although goods associated with the providing of services may be) but are subject to a wide variety of nontariff measures. In general, goods exports are more likely to be subject to trade restrictions because they are more likely to be traded. Yet many measures affecting trade in goods and commodities—subsidies and preferential government procurement policies—also affect services.

On the investment side, regulations depend on the particular industry. Nonservice industries confront the same kind of investment barriers that services do. For example, the steel industry is largely prevented from exporting to many developing countries, and it is also prevented from investing there. The best it can hope to do is to license its technology. Many light or nonessential industries such as cosmetics find themselves in the same situation. Other industries—capital equipment, electronics, pharmaceuticals, and textiles—must either license their production or invest because of restrictions. Agribusiness and extractive industries will often have to do the same but for a different reason: the resources they develop require on-the-spot participation.

So other sectors, like services, have their peculiar sensitivities and are submitted to various trade and investment restrictions. An important difference, however, is that although they are subject to the same government supervision any business enterprise must undergo, their actual business operations, if they are able to carry them on, are not generally regulated as closely as the more sensitive service industries, such as communications, utilities, banking, insurance, health, education, and professional services.

NOTES

1. U.S., Department of Commerce, Office of the Assistant Secretary for Policy, *U.S. Service Industries in World Markets: Current Problems and Future Policy Development* (Washington, D.C.: Government Printing Office, December 1976) (hereafter cited as *U.S. Service Industries*).

2. Ibid., pp. A39–A41.

3. Ronald K. Shelp, "The Proliferation of Foreign Insurance Laws: Reform or Regression?" *Law and Policy in International Business* 8 (1976).

4. *Surety bonds* are agreements providing monetary compensation for failure to perform specified acts within a stated time. Such obligations cover a broad field and include payment of debts and responsibility for default.

5. *U.S. Service Industries*, p. A228.

6. Ibid., p. 31.

7. Elements of this could, of course, also be considered a trading problem.

8. Elements of this could also be considered a trading problem.

9. See the brief Appendix to Chapter 5 for an expanded discussion comparing regulation of services and nonservices.

10. *U.S. Service Industries*, pp. 31, 32.

11. Shelp, "The Proliferation of Foreign Insurance Laws," p. 703.

12. *U.S. Service Industries*, p. 35.

13. This information was obtained from interviews with the U.S. delegation to UNCTAD meetings of the Committee on Invisibles and Financing Related to Trade (CIFT) following meetings held in Geneva in July 1973, March 1976, and December 1977, including private sector insurance adviser, James McLane Tompkins.

14. United Nations, Office of Public Information, United Nations Press Section, *Second Session of Commission on Transnational Corporations*, Lima, Peru, March 1-12, 1976 (Press Release TNC/10), March 16, 1976, p. 4.

15. Alexander Hamilton, Report on Manufactures, submitted to U.S. House of Representatives, 1791.

16. United Nations, Conference on Trade and Development, *Establishment or Expansion of Merchant Marines in Developing Countries*, Report of the UNCTAD Secretariat, 1968, pars. 229, 261.

17. The book *Invisible Barriers to Invisible Trade*, the Department of Commerce study, *U.S. Service Industries*, and especially the supplementary study contracted by the department to Wolf & Company all provide a general index of restrictions facing service industries around the world. In addition, there are numerous industy-by-industry surveys that show the same thing. These surveys confirm that restrictions are a universal phenomenon not limited by region, stage of development, or economic philosophy. See Brian Griffiths, *Invisible Barriers to Invisible Trade* (London: Macmillan, 1975).

18. The study by Ernst Lutz and Andre Sapir mentioned earlier sought to quantify restrictions. It found that in analyzing exchange restrictions in the 137 IMF-member countries, comprising 23 OECD and 114 developing countries, the purchase of foreign exchange for current transactions in services was controlled in 101 of the countries, including 9 OECD members. In addition, 9 OECD and 83 developing countries restricted the outflow of foreign exchange for international travel by residents. Payments for private services such as royalties and license fees were restricted in 6 OECD and 63 developing countries. Ernst Lutz and Andre Sapir, "Trade in Non-Factor Services: Past Trends and Current Issues," Background Paper prepared for the *World Development Report*, World Bank, Washington, D.C., January 1980.

6

PAST EFFORTS AT
LIBERALIZATION

Service activities in the world economy confront a wide array of hindrances. Although many—such as those confronting the communications, data processing, and information industries—are of recent derivation, others have existed for a long time. And although certain kinds of impediments are long standing, the instances in which services are subject to them have multiplied in recent years.

The above statement is, in itself, a testimonial either to the past lack of effort in addressing these problems or to the failure of those efforts that have been tried. This chapter examines past attempts to liberalize international commerce in services.

Primary emphasis is placed on the more successful multilateral approaches to liberalization that have occurred in the Organization for Economic Cooperation and Development (OECD) and the European Economic Community (EEC). This is followed by a discussion of the treatment of services in the unsuccessful effort to establish the International Trade Organization (ITO) in 1947/48, as well as a look at how services have been dealt with in its successor, the General Agreement on Tariffs and Trade (GATT). Last, there is a review of bilateral approaches to liberalization where the United States serves as the main example because of the inclusion of services in its Trade Act of 1974.

MULTILATERAL APPROACHES
TO LIBERALIZATION

OECD

Services are primarily dealt with through two codes of conduct that have been adopted by the OECD: the Code of Liberalization of Current Invisible Operations and the Code of Liberalization of Capital Movements. The OECD's

Committee for Invisible Transactions has primary responsibility for overseeing the codes through a review mechanism that seeks to remove reservations and derogations and to promote the general liberalization of invisible transactions and capital movements. Recommendations and comments of the Committee for Invisible Transactions are reviewed by the OECD Payments Committee prior to their submission to the Council of Ministers (the highest executive body composed of ambassadors of the member states to the OECD). Among the other important committees in the large and diverse committee structure of the OECD that deal with services are the insurance, shipping, and capital market committees.

Both the Code of Liberalization of Current Invisible Operations and the related Code of Liberalization of Capital Movements are based on the principle of complete *liberalization*—as they define it. The former code provides that the 24 OECD members shall eliminate restrictions among themselves on "current invisible operations." It is envisioned that members will also try to extend this liberalization to all members of the International Monetary Fund (IMF), which means that their efforts should be nondiscriminatory. Countries that cannot accept these principles entirely can, under the code, register their reservations. Furthermore, countries that agree to the principles of liberalization but wish to impose restrictions temporarily may do so.

Three main reasons for reservations are permitted: if liberalization conflicts with a country's internal legislation; if countries desire to protect particular industries (transport, insurance, and films are protected most heavily under the code); or if a country, like Greece or Turkey, believes that it is not economically developed enough to accept the principle of complete liberalization. A country may take temporary exception (derogations) to the code if its "economic and financial situation justifies such a course,"[1] for example, when liberalization measures cause serious economic disturbances or the country's overall balance of payments deteriorates to such an extent that drastic measures are required.

There are specific provisions under the code for reviewing the exceptions of member countries, and also general guidelines for seeking the removal of derogations, hopefully within 12 to 18 months of the time of their application. In this and the capital movements code countries are cautioned to be careful in invoking restrictions so as to avoid unnecessary damage to the financial or economic interests of any other member and to avoid discrimination between members. (The Appendix to Chapter 6 lists what are considered current invisibles operations.)

The coverage of the Code of Liberalization of Current Invisible Operations makes it strikingly clear that services cannot be equated with invisibles. Although it specifically includes many service industries (insurance, construction, professional services, advertising, and transportation), it excludes other major services (communications, utilities, banking, computer services, education, employment services, and health and hotel services) except indirectly where those services are involved in invisible transactions. It focuses on invisible transactions arising in international commerce, in general, and includes such divergent transactions as pensions, taxes, and court expenses. It seeks to facilitate the free movement of such transactions whether their source is industry, government, or personal affairs.

The Code of Liberalization of Capital Movements was adopted simultaneously with the one regulating invisible operations, which it closely parallels in procedures, including the system of reservations and derogations. The code requires the progressive abolition of restrictions to movements of capital to the extent necessary for effective economic cooperation. In particular, members are asked to treat all nonresident-owned assets in the same way, irrespective of the date of their formation and to permit liquidation of all nonresident-owned assets and allow the transfer of them or of their liquidation proceeds. Members are urged to avoid introducing new exchange restrictions that impede capital flows or strengthening existing regulations. As in the invisible operations code, however, a long list of reservations and derogations has been compiled. Similarly, members are asked to apply measures of liberalization to their overseas territories and to all members of the IMF. (See the Appendix to Chapter 6 for a list of what is covered by the code.)

The code treats much more than services and aims at liberalization of capital movements of all kinds, be they in nonservices, services, individual transactions, or government transfers. While it might seem to liberalize trade and investment in many areas, it only guarantees freedom of the transactions accompanying trade and investment. For example, the life insurance provisions may seem to permit free trade in life insurance, but they really provide nothing more than the free transfer of capital and annuities due to beneficiaries.

The first section of the code governing direct investment seems to be a far-reaching provision, even with its reservations and derogations, since it allows members to invest in other member countries. This is especially important for services with their high propensity to be investment related. However, closer scrutiny reveals that it does not say that direct foreign investment and other foreign-owned assets are to be treated the same as resident-owned assets; instead, it says members shall treat all nonresident-owned assets in the same way. Although it provides for the free transactions and transfers of funds for direct investments, it does not guarantee foreign investors access to restricted sectors or ensure equal treatment.

While the OECD capital movements code can be viewed as conferring the right of entry in the sense of transfer and investment rights, the operational rights commonly associated with the right of establishing operations are not included in the text. This anomaly lies in the historical reasons for the code, which was intended essentially to "liberalize restrictions on movements of capital to the extent necessary for effective economic cooperation." The right of establishing foreign operations and what that right confers have been dealt with at length in discussions in the Committee for Invisible Transactions of the OECD. The Committee for Invisible Transactions concluded in 1974 that "the text of the capital codes contains no suggestions that a general right of establishment, in the sense of operational rights in addition to the right of entry, was also to be created."[2]

However, if we review the operation of the code during the past 19 years, certain operational elements beyond the transfer of funds and initial investment do seem to have been accepted. For example, the parent company continues, after establishing a subsidiary or branch, to enjoy the right of extending a wholly owned enterprise to other investment activities. It also is entitled to issue securities in capital markets of the country of investment, as well as a few other minor points relating to establishment. But illustrative of just how far the codes fall short of guaranteeing full establishment rights is what they do not provide: freedom from expulsion; free access to the various legal forms of enterprise (company, partnership, and so on); freedom for foreigners to control all or part of capital and management; complete access to local financial markets; freedom to move and select a location; freedom to associate with national or foreign enterprises through joint ventures, parnerships, and the like; freedom in the internal organization and management of the enterprise; freedom to contract (including freedom to hire personnel, rent property, and hire services); freedom to manufacture, sell, lease, rent, transfer products, and acquire raw materials for use in manufacture; freedom to import and export materials and products; access to courts and administrative bodies; nondiscriminatory treatment in matters of taxation, customs, and social security; and freedom to practice regulated professional activities, such as engineering, architecture, and access to membership in chambers of commerce and other economic and professional organizations.

In its 1974 discussions, the Committee for Invisible Transactions concluded that both codes taken in conjunction, although providing support for certain elements of direct foreign investment under particular conditions, do not guarantee a general right of establishment. In fact, the committee admitted that many obstacles to establishment, which are of great concern to foreign investors, either are not covered or have only modest support under the codes.

The OECD codes are deficient in four important respects suggests Brian Griffiths in *Invisible Barriers to Invisible Trade*.

1. The membership of the OECD is too limited a body within which to seek comprehensive solutions to the problems of international commerce in services. As has been noted, many of the greatest obstacles are in less developed countries.

2. Even within the OECD, certain countries, such as Canada, Greece, Turkey, Portugal, and Iceland, do not adhere to one or both codes. The United States does not accept the premise of liberalization as applied to maritime rates; and virtually every member has reservations on insurance, road transport, and films.

3. Although the codes appear sound, certain OECD countries evade them through such devices as "voluntary" restraints and "guidelines."

4. The OECD codes tend to treat the symptoms rather than the malady. They focus on transactions and, thus, often miss the root of the problem. Australia, for instances, does not restrict its citizens from conducting business with foreign banks, which, under the OECD code, means complete liberalization with respect to banking has been achieved. But, in fact, Australia is highly protectionist in that foreign banks are prohibited from establishing branches there. The invisibles code is also inadequate in that it excludes transactions between governments. It thus neglects transactions in many sensitive sectors that governments own or regulate closely.[3]

The Example of Insurance

Besides the Committee for Invisible Transactions and the Payments Committee, another substantive committee in the OECD structure that deals with a particular service is the Insurance Committee. The report *Policy Perspectives for International Trade and Economic Relations*, prepared under OECD auspices by the High Level Group on Trade and Related Problems in 1972, cited insurance as the service that probably deserved first attention because of its economic significance and its complex technical difficulties.[4] This is also the only industry under the code whereby freedom of establishment is ensured. Thus, it is instructive to review the work of the Insurance Committee over nearly two decades to see how the code works and how difficult liberalization can be.

The code divides insurance into five items: social security and social insurance, insurance relating to goods in international trade, life insurance, all other insurance (direct), and reinsurance. The latter four are the heart of our concern. Transactions and transfers of these items are free only within the limits described in the insurance annex to the code. Insurance relating to goods in international trade is fully liberalized in principle (except reservations and derogations), but liberalization under life insurance and all other insurance is limited. The basic limitations under these two headings, which refers to insurance transacted between a primary insurer and a buyer, is that residents may take out insurance abroad only if all the main elements of the operation are foreign to the resident's national market. Specifically, as long as the insurance firm is not established in the customer's country of residence, the following types of insurance are permitted:

Life insurance other than group insurance;

Group life insurance, provided that the beneficiary resides outside of the country of the buyer and the commitments of the insurance firm are to be performed outside the country;

All other insurance except group insurance and compulsory insurance as long as the persons, property, or liabilities are outside the country of the purchaser; and

Group and compulsory insurance, provided the risks are situated outside the insurance customer's country.

In short, these insurance provisions say that direct insurance between residents and overseas insurers is allowed when the risks being insured do not cover any person resident in the same country as the purchaser, any property situated or registered in that country, and any liability incurred by such persons or in respect to such property. It also permits transactions and transfers when it is not possible to cover a risk in the member country in which the risk exists. In other words, the transactions are free only if the persons, property, or liabilities being insured are not located in the country where the person wanting to insure them is located.

In addition, there are numerous other exceptions to the principle of liberalization. All insurance transactions relating to air transport are excluded from liberalization because of a specific agreement that designates governments as the principal parties to an air transport transaction. Such transactions are not covered by the code. Second, all transactions relating to cabotage are excluded because the political and economic interests of certain maritime member states would be adversely affected.

A provision of the code unique to insurance concerns establishment. The code specifically states, "Where the establishment of insurers in a Member State is made subject to prior authorisation: a. that Members shall award insurers from other Member States treatment equivalent to that applied to national insurers."[5] So the Code of Liberalization of Current Invisible Operations does nothing less than guarantee freedom of establishment, although seven countries have lodged reservations. The litmus test these provisions must withstand is how they translate in practice into meaningful liberalization.

Finally, transactions and transfers in connection with reinsurance (transactions between insurers themselves) are liberalized under the code. Yet even the incomplete liberalization that does exist for insurance under the code has attracted no less than 42 reservations from 18 member countries.

From the beginning the Insurance Committee had as its primary goal the harmonization of insurance regulations in member countries so that the liberalizing principles of the Code of Liberalization of Current Invisible Operations could be effective. The idea is that with harmonization of their national legislation, nations are more likely to accept the principle of liberalization. Further, with harmonized legislation, liberalization is likely to be more meaningful.

A report entitled *Supervision of Private Insurance in Europe*, completed in 1963 by the Insurance Committee, contains detailed country studies, with analyses, comparisons, and syntheses of the insurance supervision laws of the European countries.[6] On the basis of the information collected, the committee was able to propose a common classification system for insurance. This system was recommended to the Council of Ministers for adoption in June 1964 and represented the first concrete effort to harmonize insurance supervision measures. However, the continuing slow progress in insurance harmonization is illustrated by the fact that although 14 member countries had indicated by 1967 their intention to conform to the recommendation, only 2 had taken effective action by the end of 1969.

Although the code says that reservations should be examined periodically with the intent of "making suitable proposals designed to assist members to withdraw their reservations,"[7] the last examination of insurance reservations took place in 1963. This illustrates one of the shortcomings of the code. This review process is the vehicle intended to encourage the lifting of restrictions. But if the process never occurs, the reservations and derogations are likely to remain in place. At the time of the 1963 review, the Committee for Invisible Transactions noted with regret that prior to that exercise insurance reservations had been examined only twice within a seven-year period (since the first invisible operations code was drafted in 1950) and that, in general, the recommendations of the Council of Ministers had gone unheeded. The committee concluded that an impasse had been reached and proposed that the periodic examination of insurance reservations be suspended until the Insurance Committee completed a report "containing proposals for coordination of the conditions under which insurance concerns are admitted and operated in member states and of their methods of supervision."[8]

Until 1975 the Insurance Committee conducted its work according to a harmonization program it had submitted to the Council of Ministers in 1964. It submitted a proposal to the Council of Ministers for "The Adoption of a Minimum Level of Solvency for Non-Life Insurance Concerns," but this proposal was never adopted by the council. As for life insurance, a concrete proposal was also submitted but has never been approved. In addition, the committee took up various other harmonization measures, but those proposals that reached the council were never approved, much less implemented by member countries.

Without question, a task involving such complex technical considerations takes time. This was reflected by the chairman of the Insurance Committee in his remarks to the council in February 1967 when he noted that he was struck "by the innumerable complications which even modest efforts toward harmonization raised" and that it should not be forgotten that discussions on harmonization had been going on for years among Common Market members.[9]

This touches on one crucial aspect of the problem. On those few occasions when the Insurance Committee has reached agreement on an aspect of harmonization and forwarded a proposal through the Committee for Invisible Transactions and the Payments Committee to the Council of Ministers, the council rejected the proposal principally because of the recalcitrance of EEC members. Their resistance is based on their belief that while the EEC itself is considering liberalization and harmonization of insurance, it should not commit itself to liberalization within the broader OECD framework. Only after agreement has been reached within the EEC itself is broader liberalization possible. This decision, taken by EEC representatives at the ambassadorial level of the Council of Ministers, is in direct conflict with the action of their national representatives on the Insurance Committee itself.

This stalemate was addressed by the Committee for Invisible Transactions in 1970 when it noted that the organization had dealt with the question of harmonization on many occasions since the first Code of Liberalization of Current Invisible Operations was adopted but that little progress had been made. So the Committee for Invisible Transactions took a series of specific actions aimed at completing the liberalization provisions of the invisible operations code. The committee proposed essentially that the code be made more comprehensive and complete by replacing the present items on "insurance related to goods in international trade," "life insurance," and "all other insurance" by a single item, "direct insurance," and liberalizing this new category. The committee further suggested that, due to the preoccupations of authorities in many member countries, it might be best if compulsory and group insurance were excluded from liberalization.

In making these recommendations, the committee summarily rejected the argument that direct insurance deserves a special position in the invisibles operations code because of various obstacles to liberalization, such as the need to protect the insured, third parties, and the domestic insurance industry; the requirements of domestic capital markets; fiscal considerations; and balance-of-payments considerations. Instead, the committee asserted that these points do not affect the legal judgment that the same procedural rules should apply to direct insurance as apply to almost all other invisibles. In short, the committee came down on the side of liberalization in principle, with members having the right to lodge reservations where necessary and derogations in special circumstances.

The committee recognized that if liberalization obligations are increased by strengthening the code, member countries have the right to lodge additional reservations and extend the scope of existing ones. As a result, all of the present restrictions might be maintained and the number of reservations increased correspondingly. Nevertheless, the committee felt that a more comprehensive approach to liberalization had the advantage of revealing restrictions in greater detail than the existing code permitted and would encourage liberalization. Under the partial liberalization there were, in effect, areas without obligations for member countries, but with a more complete liberalization of direct insurance, these obscure areas would be reduced, more restrictions would have to be covered by reservations, and the code would automatically present a fuller picture of the policy of each member country in the insurance field.

The Committee for Invisible Transactions also argued that since the last examination of insurance reservations was in 1963, it was time to review the reservations once again. The committee suggested that these examinations could be made more effective by asking each member country to state unequivocally and in detail the conditions that would enable it to withdraw each of its reservations, instead of merely stating in a general way its reasons for maintaining them.

Finally, the Committee for Invisible Transactions focused on the heart of the problem: the difficulties encountered with the harmonization of the various national supervisory regulations and the likelihood that this effort would continue for a long time to come. The committee felt that harmonization and liberalization should not be considered as alternative means of achieving the same objective. Although it recognized that harmonization is likely to facilitate the removal of restrictions, it is not an indispensable prerequisite of liberalization. There are member countries with efficient and prosperous insurance industries that have already liberalized; and there is no evidence that even if harmonization is achieved, it would inevitably lead to liberalization. Thus the committee recommended that there is no reason to suspend work on liberalization until there is harmonization.

The Council of Ministers, on receiving this report from the Committee for Invisible Transactions, asked the Insurance Committee for its views before acting. The latter responded negatively to the proposals, and the matter was dropped. The next blow to the Insurance Committee came in 1974 and 1975 when the council, apparently influenced by the OECD Secretariat, gave serious consideration to abolishing the Insurance Committee altogether because of its consistent failure to achieve results. Although the committee was saved by a special appearance of its chairman before the Council of Ministers, its focus was severely limited. The budget was reduced, Secretariat support was severely curtailed, and the committee's function was relegated to that of holding infrequent meetings to exchange information.

Until recently, therefore, meetings of the Insurance Committee consisted for the most part of lectures by EEC officials, who have only observer status, on EEC insurance developments. The committee also serves the function of providing a vehicle for non-EEC members to keep abreast of and try to influence EEC decisions on insurance. This state of affairs reflects the attitude of EEC members that liberalization cannot be advanced within the OECD until the EEC itself agrees on each and every phase of its own liberalization.

In 1977 an effort was made during a meeting of the Insurance Committee to reactivate it by reconsidering the 1970 proposals of the Committee for Invisible Transactions. During these discussions some members of the committee felt that since substantial liberalization had been achieved within the EEC, its members would now be in a position to approach liberalization within the OECD. The committee members adjourned with the understanding that they would consult with their governments about proceeding with liberalizations. A meeting scheduled for November 1977 to determine the outcome of these consultations was canceled because most members apparently had not contacted their governments. The next meeting was not scheduled until December 1978, and this was not an agenda item. Finally, during two meetings held in 1979, the committee began to focus with apparent seriousness on achieving liberalization in the two fields of insurance most directly related to international trade—marine cargo insurance and reinsurance. And in 1980, as will be discussed in the next chapter, initiatives in other OECD committees forced the Insurance Committee to again grapple with liberalization. Only time will tell if these efforts will be more successful than past performance has been.

Although the record of the OECD in achieving liberalization of capital flows and invisibles transactions has been, in general, commendable, its goal has not been to liberalize trade and investment in service industries themselves, although this result has been partially achieved. In those few cases, like insurance, where this was tried as part of the liberalization of invisibles and investment flows intended in the codes, progress has been minimal. Reservations and derogations abound.

EEC

With the signing of the Treaty of Rome in 1956, a group of European nations set about to establish an economic community. Included among its objectives was the liberalization of services, and considerable attention has been devoted to liberalizing certain service sectors within the EEC.

Articles 52 and 59 of the Treaty of Rome stipulated that there should be, first, the elimination of all restrictions on the free establishment of the citizens of any member country in the territory of another member and, second, the elimination of all restrictions on the freedom to offer services inside the EEC without establishing oneself in each member country. The treaty gave until December 31, 1969, as the period of transition during which all restrictions should be eliminated. Until 1974 the official EEC doctrine was that these two articles were not immediately operative but required specific implementation procedures.

In 1974, however, two rulings were handed down by the EEC Court of Justice that resulted in a fundamental change. The Reyners case concluded that under the treaty all discrimination based on nationality ceased at the end of the transition period, and thus freedom of establishment for citizens must take effect. The van Binsbergen case proclaimed the same thing for services.

This review of steps taken by the EEC to liberalize services will be conducted as follows: first, an examination of what has been done to provide freedom of establishment for service industries and, second, a look at EEC efforts to provide freedom of trade in services.

Liberalization of Insurance

Once again the main topic will of necessity be insurance, the reason being that it is the one service industry where considerable efforts have been made toward liberalization. A former director of the Invisibles Division of the EEC Commission noted that the EEC has spent some 20 years trying to liberalize the insurance sector and that this effort is expected to provide the prototype for other services, especially financial services such as banking. The process, long and arduous, illustrates some of the difficulties confronting any meaningful attempt at liberalization.

The thrust of the EEC work on insurance has been twofold. For some 17 years the EEC worked out rules to govern freedom of establishment in nonlife insurance. Simply stated, these rules spell out the terms under which an insurer headquartered in one EEC country may establish an affiliate in another EEC country. They also provide terms under which non-EEC insurers can establish themselves within the EEC. This directive, issued in 1973, with members having until 1976 to comply, is for all practical purposes unanimous.

The second phase of the liberalization process is aimed at providing freedom of insurance trade within the EEC. This means allowing an insurance firm based in one country to provide its services in other member countries without establishing itself in these countries. Although there have been many long and arduous discussions on freedom of service in insurance, it is a long way from being achieved, and even agreement on a draft directive is not likely to occur for years.

Perhaps the most interesting and somewhat ironic observation I can make about the EEC's approach on insurance liberalization is the fact that it has chosen to deal with investment issues first, leaving until later the question of freedom of trade in insurance. This is certainly a reversal of the approach usually followed in liberalizing trade and investment, but it is the approach that makes most sense in this case. It suggests that for at least some services the investment issues are easier than the trade issues.

Freedom of Establishment for Insurance Firms

The focus of EEC freedom of establishment is analogous to OECD efforts. Much of the OECD debate has revolved around the question of how much liberalization can occur in the absence of harmonization of national legislation. The same issue was central to the EEC debate, and the point of view favoring harmonization as a prerequisite for liberalization carried the day.

On July 24, 1973, following years of preparatory work, the Council of the European Communities issued the *First Council Directive on the Coordination of Laws, Regulations and Administrative Provisions Relating to the Taking-Up and Pursuit of the Business of Direct Insurance Other Than Life Insurance* and the *Directive Abolishing Restrictions on Freedom of Establishment in the Business of Direct Insurance Other Than Life Insurance.*[10] These directives allowed 18 months for member states to revise their national legislation and 30 months—until January 1, 1976—for the new regulations to come into effect.

The directive basically lays down a set of rules and regulations applicable to undertakings whose head offices are situated within the EEC. Through these provisions the EEC seeks to establish uniform rules governing the admission, operation, and closing of insurance firms that have their headquarters in the EEC and operate or wish to operate in EEC countries other than where they are headquartered. This does not mean that identical insurance legislation is now operative throughout the EEC but, rather, that the principles that govern the key elements of regulation are now uniform.

Of special importance is the treatment of foreign insurance interests. EEC officials have repeatedly stated that there is no nationality test governing this and other directives. In other words, if a company is incorporated and headquartered in the EEC, even if that company's capital is wholly or partially owned by interests outside the EEC, it is nevertheless an EEC company with the same rights and privileges as a company owned by the nationals of EEC member countries. Despite accusations that some national regulatory authorities have deviated from this principle, especially in permitting the establishment of foreign-owned EEC companies, there have been no specific challenges brought in the EEC Court of Justice asserting the principle has been violated.

Companies not headquartered in the EEC are subject to different treatment. Title III of the directive deals with agencies or branches established within the EEC that are headquartered outside. In many ways, it provides non-EEC firms with similar treatment in regulation, conditions of admission, and withdrawal as that for EEC companies. But there are very important distinctions, the most important being that the treatment of agencies and branches from third countries is left to the discretion of local supervisory authorities. Thus authorities are not prevented from applying more stringent financial requirements to non-EEC companies, nor do they automatically have to issue licenses to applicants headquartered outside the EEC, as they are obligated to do for qualified companies from EEC countries.

In addition, certain provisions in the directive could put non-EEC insurers at a disadvantage even if supervisory authorities do not discriminate against them. In estimating the solvency margins that must be maintained to operate within the EEC, an EEC company is allowed to make its calculations on an EEC-wide basis, whereas non-EEC companies must make their calculations on a country-by-country basis. In meeting this solvency margin, the EEC insurer may maintain the funds anywhere in the EEC. The non-EEC firm must maintain a part of the margin (the guarantee fund) in each country in which it operates. Another advantage EEC insurers have over non-EEC firms is that the deposits and other financial requirements they must have to qualify for operation can be maintained within their home country—that is, their home office assets can be applied to meeting financial requirements EEC-wide.

The directive provides two ways for non-EEC firms to overcome these disadvantages. Article 26 of Title III states that any company with a branch or agency within the EEC and operating in several member states may apply for one or more of the following advantages: the right to have the solvency margin calculated on the basis of the entire business it undertakes within the EEC, a dispensation from lodging the deposit required in each state in which it operates, and the right to maintain the assets representing the guarantee fund of the solvency requirement in any one of the member states in which it carries out business. To receive these benefits, however, every member state affected must approve; and as yet, these benefits have not been granted, perhaps because no firm has sought to obtain them.

The second alternative is in article 29 of the directive, which authorizes the EEC to negotiate bilateral treaties with non-EEC countries to allow mutually beneficial access to the EEC for their insurance companies and vice versa. The negotiation of an EEC-Swiss agreement was authorized by the EEC several years ago, and it is the only negotiation of this kind that has been undertaken. Negotiations have been ongoing since the mid-1970s, and an agreement was submitted to EEC authorities for approval in late 1979. It is rumored that Sweden is considering requesting a similar arrangement. Preliminary exploratory discussions concerning a bilateral agreement have been held between the U.S. insurance community, the U.S. government, and the EEC. One of the most obvious difficulties in this case would be the fact that insurance regulation is decentralized in the United States, with the states regulating it.

There have been many problems with the directive in the EEC itself. Not only have there been differences over what the directive means and whether governments have indeed implemented it, but there have also been serious problems for some European insurers in complying with the solvency requirement margins. Further, the Reyners and van Binsbergen decisions have complicated an already complex problem and planted in the minds of many the idea that there would no longer be an effort to coordinate legislation, but, instead, the restrictions would simply be abolished by an EEC-wide directive. Thereafter, the freedoms of establishment and services in insurance would be in effect.

Other directives complement this first establishment directive. There are, for example, directives that allow for the freedom of establishment of insurance brokers and agents (adopted by the Council in December 1976), that harmonize tax provisions within the EEC, and that determine EEC rules on products liability. The latter two directives are not yet in effect.

Life insurance is separate from general insurance in EEC regulations because it is regulated differently. Financial and solvency determinations are made on a basis different from nonlife insurance, and in most European countries life and general insurance must be conducted by separate entities. In December 1973 the Commission of the European Communities submitted to the Council of Ministers a proposal for a council directive on the freedom of establishment in life insurance; a few weeks later this was followed by a proposed directive that would abolish all restrictions inhibiting their freedom. In late 1978 these directives were approved by the Council of the European Communities. They follow the same basic format as the general insurance, nonlife directive. Title III contains rules governing agencies or branches that are established within the EEC by firms whose headquarters are outside it and provides for the negotiation of bilateral agreements.

The principal point of dispute that delayed these directives concerned specialization. The question here is whether one company can operate in both general and life insurance, that is, as composite companies, or whether two different entities are required. What complicates the issue is that a few member countries allow composite companies, while most do not. The EEC resolved the impasse through a compromise proposal, which allows existing composite companies to continue operating but requires them to separate life and general funds and management functions and prohibits the formation of new composite companies. To establish an entity elsewhere in the EEC, an existing composite firm would have to establish a separate general or life operation.

Although this directive clearly aims at liberalizing the provision of life insurance services throughout the EEC, discrimination against non-EEC companies is inherent in it. The advantages for member country companies are very similar to those found in the nonlife directive. There are different rules governing solvency for companies that are foreign to the EEC. And as with general insurance, supervisory authorities have the discretion to impose stricter financial requirements or refuse licenses to non-EEC insurance firms.

Freedom of Service (Trade) in Insurance

The concept of freedom of service or trade in the case of insurance is simple but dramatic. It allows for direct insurance dealings between customers and firms across the national borders of EEC members. In essence, it allows free trade in insurance, something quite revolutionary for financial services. Such a development is especially dramatic in insurance since, due to its characteristics, technical complexities, and sensitive role in national economies, it is often cited as the perfect example of why services are by necessity investment related. If the Common Market can achieve freedom of trade in the service of insurance pursuant to the goal of the free provision of services laid down in the Treaty of Rome, the realization of similar arrangements in other services becomes a realistic goal.

Discussions on liberalizing insurance trade first began in the EEC in 1967; since then the focus has been solely on general or nonlife insurance. Only when the EEC reaches agreement here are there likely to be discussions on similar arrangements for life insurance. By far the hardest question centers around which legislative or regulatory provisions an insurance company must observe in order to freely offer its services across national borders within the EEC. Should it observe the legal and regulatory provisions in force in the country where it is headquartered or those in the country where the risk is situated? This has remained a controversial question from the outset of the discussions, and only very gradually has there been an evolution toward a solution.

In the first stage of discussions, a draft directive was drawn up based on the principle that the insurance firm providing its services in other EEC countries must abide by the legislative, regulatory, and administrative provisions imposed by the country in which the risk or the insured is located. Since, for all practical purposes, this amounts to virtually the same principle embodied in the establishment directive, freedom of services would not really be realized.

But this approach was rejected in 1969 by the EEC Commission. The EEC's legal department argued that the solution contemplated failed to comply with the principles contained in Article 59 of the Treaty of Rome providing for removal of all restrictions on the free establishment of the citizens of any member country in the territory of another member and removing all restrictions on the freedom to offer services inside the EEC. A new approach emerged, based on the concept that a company offering its insurance services could do so solely by submitting itself to the regulations of its home country. Because of discrepancies among national laws and the likelihood of this leading to a serious distortion of competition, as well as the need to provide for adequate consumer protection, EEC officials accepted the necessity of some coordination. They concluded that it was best to approach freedom of service trade through a three-stage liberalization process: liberalization of transport insurance and industrial and commercial risks, liberalization of other types of nonlife insurance (except compulsory or required insurance), and, finally, the liberalization of compulsory insurance.

To implement this approach, coordination was seen as necessary in nine areas: control of overall policy conditions, elimination or exclusion from guarantees laid down by certain national laws, control of rates, measures to ensure that competition is not distorted, rules for the evaluation of technical reserves, balancing reserves, rules for investment of assets that represent technical reserves, coordination of essential provisions of the laws on insurance contracts, and unification of the rates of taxation on insurance contracts.

Agreeing upon such coordination measures, especially those on fiscal coordination, raised serious difficulties with some governmental representatives. Recognizing that these measures would require a very long time to negotiate, the EEC sought a provisional solution by preparing a new draft directive that is still under consideration.

The new directive departs from past efforts in that it seeks to provide freedom of services for all lines of general insurance—instead of liberalization by stages. This is a direct response to the rulings of the EEC Court of Justice, which have raised serious uncertainty over how the relevant Treaty of Rome articles should be interpreted. The negotiators remain convinced that a coordinating directive is needed, if for no other reason than to spell out which country's laws apply. In the new directive, however, the elements of coordination have been narrowed to three areas: coordination of rules for evaluation of technical reserves, coordination of balancing reserves, and measures to prevent distortion of competition (antidumping measures).

This does not, however, mean the abandonment of coordination in other fields. For example, on the difficult question of the unification of taxes on insurance contracts, the EEC has decided that this should be brought about at a later time. Until that time the legislation of the country where the risk is situated will apply.

With regard to legislation governing insurance contracts, parties may freely choose the applicable law—that is, they can choose among the various national legislations of member countries, and in certain cases, they can choose legislation from outside the EEC. However, they are obliged to abide by any imperative provisions of the laws of the country where the risk is located. Because of the practical difficulties of subjecting a contract to differing legislation simultaneously, the laws of the country where the risk is located are expected to apply in most instances.

As for rate control, the directive distinguishes between transport and aviation, difficult industrial and commercial risks, and other risks. The first category provides for coordination through the abandonment of all regulations on general conditions and rates. The second applies the legislation of the country where the risk is located.

In sum, this translates into a draft directive that applies some of the national legislation of the country where the insurer is headquartered and some of the laws of the country where the risk is located. This undoubtedly will cause difficulties. It means that the operations conducted under such a regime will be subject simultaneously to a certain amount of supervision from authorities in two or more countries.

Thus, although some progress has been made in liberalizing trade in insurance services, there is yet a long way to go. The gist of the difficulty is that true freedom of trade requires an extensive surrender of national supervisory control to regulators from other states—something that is only done minimally in the directives on freedom of establishment in insurance. Yet there will not be true freedom of service trade within the EEC until the principle that the law of the headquarters country applies is accepted. Only then will an insurer be able to supply his services across national borders without having to adjust to each and every jurisdiction.

One final important aspect of freedom of service in insurance is the question of how the benefits of that directive can be extended to insurance companies in non-EEC countries. This issue has caused quite a stir within the EEC. The first directive prepared by the commission gave non-EEC country branches and agencies the same privileges as EEC-based companies without the necessity of negotiating bilateral agreements. Not surprisingly, many member states were not happy with this approach, desiring instead to curtail the activities of firms that are foreign to the EEC. They argue not only that outsiders should be denied these benefits but also that the authorization for bilateral agreements between the EEC and non-EEC countries included in the establishment directives should not be permitted in this case. Thus the second draft directive denies foreign firms freedom of service privileges and does not provide for bilateral agreements. Since the commission seems inclined to fight for a more liberal directive, a likely compromise would be similar to the directives on general and nonlife insurance whereby a mechanism for bilateral agreements is provided.

This discussion illustrates that the services trade often has little to do with its unique nature but, rather, relates to whether governmental regulations allow trade. In the insurance case, regulation forces much activity to be associated with investment rather than with trade. It would be overstating the case to assume from this observation that all insurance activities could be just as easily traded or that this is the case with all services. This experience does indicate that some sectors we associate with investment might lend themselves to trade.

Liberalization in Other Service Sectors

Although insurance has dominated EEC initiatives to liberalize services, there has been activity in other areas. Considerable emphasis has been placed on banking and the liberal professions.

I mentioned earlier that the insurance directive is seen as a prototype for a similar directive in banking. A brief review of EEC progress in the banking sector should provide insight into the similarities and differences between banking and insurance, two of the most highly regulated service industries. This should also indicate some of the difficulties and opportunities for liberalization of services, at least in the financial field.

In December 1974, the Brussels Commission introduced a directive on the coordination of banking laws within the EEC. This simple directive replaced the original draft prepared by the six original members of the EEC, which was a more comprehensive directive containing 41 articles. It dealt with such matters as harmonizing the minimum capitalization requirements for banks, fixing liquidity and solvency ratios, creating guidelines for bank mergers, and designating the maximum shareholdings allowed by banks in industrial concerns. In contrast, the more limited 1974 directive contains only 14 articles. It is based upon the principle that supervision comes from the authorities in the country where the bank is headquartered. Under the directive, banks with branches in several member states of the EEC no longer have to meet solvency and liquidity requirements in each country nor subscribe capital in those countries. It is analogous to, but much more limited than, the insurance establishment directive.

Banks operating in other member states would be required to provide information regularly to the local supervisory authority. This information concerns four specific banking ratios described as "not a mandatory control mechanism but a common measure for discussion and comparison between countries."[11] These are the ratio of owned funds to deposits, the ratio of funds to assets, the ratio of owned funds to fixed assets, and the ratio between liabilities and liquid assets. For the time being, each country would specify ratios that would be observed in order to ensure liquidity and solvency. Over time, in order to avoid distortions in competition, these ratios would be harmonized.

Herein lies a distinct difference between the banking and insurance directives. The insurance directive establishes an EEC-wide solvency standard to govern insurance activities in all member countries, whereas the banking directive leaves this up to each member state with the hope that later coordination will resolve the differences. So, ironically, while this directive facilitates expansion through making it easier to operate on an EEC-wide basis through branch offices—by not establishing common financial standards for all member countries—it may place at a competitive disadvantage those companies that are headquartered in countries with the most rigorous supervisory standards. It is not surprising this approach faces considerable opposition from supervisory authorities and banks in countries that will be put in a disadvantageous competitive position by the absence of harmonization.

Along with the draft directive to the Council of Ministers the commission also submitted proposals to create a contact committee, composed of representatives of the commission and representatives of the banking authorities in each member state. This provides a forum to agree on methods, priorities, and timetables for future action. It received a cool reception within the EEC and was subsequently shelved.

As to the treatment of banks headquartered outside the EEC but operating through branches within it, the general terms of the directive are that they would be subject to the same rules in each member state and would be treated no more favorably than national banks of member states. The long-term intention seems to be analogous to the insurance directives in that "reciprocal agreements concerning the rules applicable to foreign branches will be negotiated between the Community and other countries."[12]

The monetary function of banking complicates the establishment of community-wide rules governing it. For example, if one country's central bank has reserve requirements for its banks that differ from another's, the absence of EEC-wide harmonization could well distort the monetary objectives of other countries where branches of that nation's bank are operating. The same observation applies to other aspects of bank regulation relating to monetary policy such as the discount rate—that is, the interest rate at which the central bank lends money to private banks.

Although at first glance these considerations seem to be completely distinct from insurance, on closer examination one finds analogies. Insurance, especially life insurance, a major provider of mortgages and other kinds of loans, also can be related to monetary policies. The credit policies of insurance companies are often seen as an instrument of national policy that should be compatible with national investment priorities. These issues were neatly avoided in the insurance directive, although surely they were discussed. In insurance each country was allowed to set policies in this area as it saw fit.

In conjunction with the banking directive, the EEC is considering other proposals that relate to the overall coordination of EEC banking. One is a deposit insurance scheme that would guarantee deposits up to a certain limit. Another would establish a bureau to facilitate an exchange of information on large borrowers. No serious consideration has been given as yet to a directive that would enable the provision of banking services without establishment.

The Liberal Professions

During the past several years, the EEC has made a concerted effort to enhance the freedom of self-employed people to establish themselves and to offer their services across EEC borders.

The Medical Profession

In June 1975 the Council of Ministers of the EEC adopted two directives governing doctors. One provided for the mutual recognition of doctors' diplomas, certificates, or other degrees and included measures designed to help them establish themselves in other EEC countries more freely. The second coordinated laws, regulations, and administrative practices affecting doctors. More or less analogous rules are in effect for nurses and health care technicians.

The EEC encountered considerable difficulties in reaching agreement on these directives, which contrasts with the rapid progress it made regarding free trade of goods. In 1968 the EEC approved the free movement of workers, but that applied mainly to wage earners. Providing the same benefits to the liberal professions is considerably more complex because practitioners must have a university degree and usually are required to be a national of the country in which they practice. The liberal professions are also closely linked with the social and cultural environment, which tends to make their practitioners much less interchangeable. Further, the laws and regulations that govern them are generally very national in character.

For these reasons, creating freedom of establishment and service in the medical profession is not an easy task. For example, before the directive on doctors was issued, a German could study medicine at an Italian university, but upon graduating he could not practice in Italy because of his German nationality and he could not practice in Germany because of his foreign diploma.

Although all such restrictions were to have been cleared away by the end of 1969, nothing really happened until 1974 because the official EEC doctrine was that the provisions for freedom of establishment and services in the Treaty of Rome were not immediately operative but required specific implementing texts. The Reyners and van Binsbergen decisions by the EEC court changed all this. They led to an acceleration of the liberalization process and to a new approach based on the judicial declaration that the Treaty of Rome must be effective immediately, even in the absence of specific implementing directives.

As a result, it is now possible for any doctor in the EEC who holds a diploma or degree awarded in any country of the EEC by a medical school that is included on a list given in the directive to practice his profession throughout the EEC.

The second directive coordinates the training in all EEC medical schools, requiring minimum standards for all types of doctors, nurses, and health care technicians. To supplement this effort, the Council of Ministers set up two bodies. One is a consultative committee for medical training, consisting of three experts from each EEC country—representing the appropriate professional body, the university medical faculties, and the competent government department. The second is a committee of senior civil servants from public health departments, charged with making a joint examination of any difficulties that may arise in the application of the directive.

This directive applies only to doctors trained in the member states and not to those holding diplomas from non-EEC countries. Member countries may employ doctors trained outside the EEC, but these are not entitled to the right of free movement in the EEC except on a short-term, temporary basis. Once the directives have been in effect for a time, amendments extending these benefits to non-EEC countries might be possible.

Legal Services

After eight years of deliberations, in March 1977 the Council of Ministers adopted a directive to facilitate the exercise by lawyers of their freedom to provide services within the EEC. Unlike the directives dealing with doctors, this one relates only to the freedom to provide services—not to the right of establishment. The latter objective is dependent on the mutual recognition of diplomas and appropriate coordination measures, something that has not yet been agreed upon. In view of the fact that this profession is closely connected with the social and cultural environment, mutual recognition of qualifications scarcely seems possible at this introductory stage.

The directive is based on the mutual recognition of a lawyer's status as it is defined in each member state of the EEC. It also covers all activities that are legally exercised by lawyers in the country where they are established, but member states can reserve certain acts for specific categories of lawyers.

In providing services across EEC frontiers, lawyers are exempt from any conditions requiring residence or registration with a professional organization. In representing and defending a client before the courts or public authorities in another state, lawyers practice under the same conditions as lawyers established in that state. They are subject to two codes of professional conduct, that of the host state and that of their home state. Member states can also require foreign lawyers from within the EEC to observe local rules of courtesy and to work in conjunction with a colleague practicing at the court in question who would, if necessary, be responsible to that court. The directive does not apply to lawyers from outside the EEC.

Other Professions

The council has prepared two directives for "fixing the means for achieving freedom of establishment and freedom to supply services for self-employed activities in the financial, economic and accounting sector."[13] Because of the technical nature of the engineering and architectural professions, directives have not yet been agreed upon in these fields, but they are under active consideration.

Other Services

A directive is in effect covering commercial agents. Another allows freedom of services and establishment in all press activities. Unlike other directives, this one also applies to press personnel from third countries. Others provide for the freedom of establishment for self-employed activities in road haulage, passenger transport by road, and goods and passenger transport by inland waterway. There is also a directive liberalizing itinerant sales and other service activities and others providing freedom of establishment for the following sectors: hairdressing and beauty salons, laundry services, photography, shipbuilding, and auxiliary transport services. In almost all cases, the benefits of these directives do not extend to third country nationals.

General Directives

To complement their work on the liberal professions, the commission has developed other proposals, guidelines, and directives. For example, the commission's proposal to accelerate freedom of establishment for self-employed persons, which gives particular reference to the mutual recognition of professional qualifications, emphasizes that there exists a broad comparability of professional standards within the EEC. For that reason, specific provisions about the training required for various professions should be avoided.

More than any other regional or international body, the EEC has earnestly sought to secure liberalization in services—a goal envisioned at its inception as inherent in establishing an economic community. The problems encountered and the years required to achieve progress testify to the difficulties of the task. The liberalization that has been achieved in large part results from the persistence of the civil service of the EEC, which demonstrates the positive contribution that an effective international bureaucracy can make. The commission of the EEC has untiringly followed this course, even when the political will of its members dictated otherwise.

The different problems that arose and the solutions developed for different services indicate that each has its own unique characteristics. Thus an independent approach to liberalization may be required for each. Even though the policies that result are not always consistent with work in other sectors, much less as liberal as might be intended in the Treaty of Rome, a pragmatic approach at least yields some progress toward liberalization.

In insurance the process involved first grappling with the issues of investment in one branch of insurance, then taking on freedom of trade in the same branch. This is a reversal of the traditional pattern of liberalization in international commerce; in the past, rules governing liberalization in trade have tended to precede efforts to establish similar rules governing international investment.

A similar pragmatism has been necessary for the achievement of some liberalization in the liberal professions. Doctors were simultaneously provided with freedom of establishment and freedom of services. But lawyers were granted freedom of services without freedom of establishment because of a lack of agreement on training and other procedural matters. In essence, the EEC simply did the best it could under the circumstances.

Liberalization within the EEC itself has in some cases placed those outside it at a competitive disadvantage.[14] In some sectors the EEC has adopted specific provisions encouraging the negotiation of bilateral agreements with outsiders. This at least recognizes the desirability of removing the disadvantages the directives place on non-EEC firms. Such bilateral agreements would not only extend the benefits of EEC liberalization to third countries but would also open these activities in those countries to EEC members. However, the directives regulating the liberal professions do not include such provisions even though there are non-EEC countries, at least within Europe, that have very similar systems. But since no additional constraints have been placed on non-EEC practitioners in the medical and legal professions, we must conclude that liberalization within the EEC has been a plus.

Through the mechanism of bilateral agreements provided in the insurance and banking directives, the EEC suggests the desirability of extending liberalization beyond its borders. The success of such bilateral agreements clearly depends on the political will of the negotiators. In the first bilateral negotiation, the EEC-Swiss negotiations on insurance, there was a tendency for some EEC authorities to insist that the basis for an agreement had to be Switzerland's acceptance of EEC regulations governing insurance. Other EEC officials argue that instead of identity of legislation, the goal should be agreement on principles. If the EEC insists on identical regulations as the basis for liberalization, negotiations between it and other countries, especially the United States, the world's largest insurance market in terms of premiums, would be virtually impossible because of the lack of centralization of U.S. insurance legislation.[15]

Services in the Original Discussions on the ITO and in the GATT

The origins of GATT can be found in the ITO, which was envisioned as the principal international trade institution to be established after World War II. At the first session of the Preparatory Committee of the United Nations Conference on Trade and Employment, held under ITO auspices, some delegates expressed the view that questions relating to services should be discussed. One delegate stated that the section on restrictive business practices would have no meaning if it failed to include services such as shipping, insurance, and banking. Others felt that this went beyond the scope of the committee.

The drafting committee of the Preparatory Committee met in the winter of 1947; and at this stage several delegates still felt that services should not be excluded from the section on restrictive business practices. In the summer session of the Preparatory Committee, Article 50 in Chapter V (Restrictive Business Practices) was drafted. It specifically addressed services.

> 1. The Members recognize that certain services, such as transportation, telecommunications, insurance and banking, are substantial

elements of international trade, and that any restrictive business practices in relation to them may have harmful effects similar to those described in paragraph I of Article 44. Such practices shall be dealt with in accordance with the following paragraphs of this Article.

2. If any Member considers that there exist restrictive business practices in relation to a service referred to in paragraph 1 of this Article which have or are about to have such harmful effects, and that its interests are thereby seriously prejudiced, the Member may submit a written statement explaining the situation to the Member or Members the private or public enterprises of which are engaged in the services in question. The Member or Members concerned shall give sympathetic consideration to the statement and to such proposals as may be made with a view to affording adequate opportunities for consultation, with a view to effecting a satisfactory adjustment.

3. If no adjustment can be effected in accordance with the provisions of paragraph 2 of this Article, and if the matter is referred to the Organization, it shall be transferred to the appropriate inter-governmental organization if one exists, with such observations as the Organization may wish to make. If no such inter-governmental organization exists, members may ask the Organization, under Article 69(c), to make recommendations for, and promote international agreement on, measures designed to remedy the particular situation as far as it comes within the scope of this Charter.

4. The Organization shall, in accordance with paragraph 2 of Article 84, cooperate with inter-governmental organizations in connection with restrictive business practices affecting any field coming within the scope of this Charter and those organizations shall be entitled to consult the Organization, to seek advice, and to ask that a study of a particular problem be made.[16]

Article 50 represents a compromise in that services within the jurisdiction of other international organizations were excluded. At the Havana Conference in March 1948, where the final draft of the ITO Charter was prepared, these special provisions with respect to restrictive business practices in services remained in the charter.

Clair Wilcox, chairman of the U.S. delegation in London and vice-chairman at Geneva and Havana, states that the proposed article to extend the charter to services was supported by the developing countries and opposed by the major maritime powers.[17] Today, by contrast, one would find few developing countries interested in including services in such discussions.

At the U.S. Congressional Hearings in 1950 on the ITO, the provisions on services received the same criticism as many other sections of the charter—they were too narrow in scope. The National Foreign Trade Council (NFTC) objected to the fact that the article in question only refers to restrictive business practices. The NFTC believed that transportation, telecommunications, insurance, banking, and other services essential to international trade are more subject to discrimination and control by government. As an example, the NFTC noted that governments sometimes require that insurance on goods trade be restricted to national firms. The council felt that to be effective the provisions for services should eliminate restrictive practices of all kinds.

The ITO Charter, at the insistence of the U.S. business community, also included general investment provisions. These amounted to no more than a statement of principles on foreign investment, falling short of the desire of U.S. firms at the time or the ambitious schemes now being suggested. But these investment provisions in the ITO Charter, for what they were worth, would nevertheless have included service investments.

These efforts to liberalize services were in vain because the effort to establish the ITO failed. Only the section of the ITO Charter dealing with commercial policy survived and became the basis for GATT. Later rounds of tariff negotiations amended GATT so that now it includes most of the commercial policy provisions of the final ITO Charter drafted in Havana. GATT, however, even in its present form lacks the broad scope and the organizational and procedural provisions of its progenitor.

GATT and Services

Until recently, the only real focus of GATT on services—other than rare discussions on motion pictures, which are specifically included in the GATT articles—was transport insurance.

In April 1953 the United Nations Economic and Social Council (ECOSOC) adopted a resolution concerning discrimination in transport insurance, which was referred to both GATT and the IMF. In response, the IMF made a study based on data gathered on 40 countries by the GATT Secretariat and reported back to the United Nations. It found that only a few countries use their exchange control machinery to restrict payments to foreign insurers for transport insurance. The IMF promised that

> in discussing with a member country the application of its exchange control system, the Fund will consider with the member how restriction and discrimination are applied in its territory to various categories of transactions involving commodities and services. Moreover, the Fund ... wherever it deems the situation appropriate, urges individual member countries to avoid exchange restrictions, including those placed on making payments abroad in respect of transport insurance.[18]

GATT, in response to the ECOSOC request, questioned its members on discrimination in transport insurance. From the 36 governments that responded to this query, GATT found that the discriminating practices engaged in by some countries affected the interests of others and clearly produced harmful effects on international trade. Nevertheless, GATT concluded that the evidence, though sufficient to justify that the contracting parties of GATT pursue the matter, was not sufficiently conclusive to warrant an international convention or an amendment of its charter. Instead, it decided to keep this item for the agenda of the next GATT session, and governments were urged to form an opinion on the kind of international action that might be required.

In August 1955 governments were again requested by GATT to submit views and recommendations on the question of discrimination in transport insurance. Germany and Pakistan sent statements, Sweden sent a memorandum, and the United States proposed a resolution. This resolution suggested that governments should avoid measures that would interfere with the freedom of buyers and sellers in the purchase of transport insurance, that they should submit information relevant to this matter, and that there should be a review of the situation again in 1958. In addition, the International Chamber of Commerce proposed a resolution, and the International Union of Marine Insurance also supplied a memorandum. As a result of the documents submitted, a special GATT Group on Transport Insurance held discussions in November 1955 but managed to produce little more than some supplementary information on the problem.

The United States argued that its resolution imposed no obligations but, rather, set a standard for limiting discriminatory practices relating to transport insurance. Debate among GATT members revealed a considerable divergence of opinion. The Scandinavian countries, Germany, the Netherlands, the United Kingdom, Italy, Belgium, and France supported it, while Austria, Brazil, Ceylon, Chile, Haiti, Czechoslovakia, India, Indonesia, and Pakistan stated they were opposed for various reasons. These ranged widely with such assertions as this topic is not really a GATT concern; sufficiently definitive information is unavailable; the insurance industry, like other new industries, needs protection; and such restrictions are necessary for saving foreign exchange. The end result was the establishment of a working party to study the problem.

The working party recomommended that governments should avoid measures that would have a more restrictive effect on international trade than those already in effect. Further, they should move as rapidly as circumstances permit to reduce any restrictive measures currently in force, with a view to their eventual elimination. The chairman, from France, in presenting the recommendation to GATT, called attention to its limited scope, noting that it did not concern itself directly with national insurance policies. Representatives from Australia, Brazil, Ceylon, Cuba, and Indonesia suggested that its adoption be deferred until the eleventh session of GATT. At the eleventh session the International Chamber of Commerce submitted a resolution pointing out examples of the damage to trade from measures restricting the freedom of transport insurance.

However, it was not until the thirteenth session of GATT in November 1958 that the two documents were submitted for discussion. During the interim the U.S. delegation stated in a memorandum that the discriminatory restrictions in transport insurance were contrary to the aims of GATT and argued that in the interest of encouraging trade the exporter should be permitted to protect himself by insuring against loss in a manner satisfactory to him at the lowest possible cost. Opposition came from developing countries, which felt that this would prevent them from developing local insurance industries. The Norwegian delegation proposed another examination of the issue and presented a resolution recognizing the desire of countries to take measures they considered necessary to develop a national insurance industry. It also differed from the U.S. resolution in that it proposed that governments should simply bear in mind the need to avoid harming trade and to complement the objectives and principles of GATT. It was finally agreed that the two proposals should be considered at the fourteenth session of GATT.

At the next session of the GATT, a majority of delegates supported the Norwegian recommendation, with opposition coming mostly from developed countries. The arguments of several developing countries sounded very similar to those heard today. They noted that restrictions on payments for transport insurance were recognized by the IMF as necessary for balance-of-payments reasons. Since GATT permitted the application of exchange restrictions for balance-of-payments reasons, the regulations in question were not contrary to GATT. More important, it must be recognized that developing countries want to encourage national insurance industries and thus were justified in requiring importers to insure with national firms.

The Norwegian recommendation only requested governments to report information on transport insurance to the GATT. Even this rudimentary surveillance function has never been achieved.

Motion Pictures

Motion pictures are the only service specifically included in the GATT articles. The treatment of them is quite exceptional in that restrictions are allowed in the form of quotas. The article dealing with films prescribes the form such quotas should take and seeks to prevent the screen time reserved for domestic films from being increased after 1947. The last provision weakly asserts that quotas are "subject to negotiations for their limitation, liberalization or elimination."[19]

For all practical purposes, the subject has never been dealt with in GATT. In fact, it has not been discussed for more than 25 years. There were, however, motion picture restrictions in the list of nontariff measures prepared for the Tokyo Round of negotiations.

The most striking aspect of the treatment of services in GATT over the last 30 years, other than the fact that basically they have been ignored, is the persistence of the reasons in opposition to liberalization. The strain on the balance of payments and the need to develop national markets are the same justifications we hear today in the United Nations Conference on Trade and Development (UNCTAD). Yet the argument that GATT per se excludes services, which has been put forth frequently in the United States in recent years since the U.S. Trade Act of 1974 mandated negotiations within GATT, does not surface in the history of GATT discussions on services.

Services and Nontariff Barriers

A few service issues were raised in the preparations for the Tokyo Round of negotiations when countries were asked to name the nontariff barriers they encounter. The resulting inventory of these barriers included several instances of constraints on services—mostly shipping, and one case of patents and trademarks. In the early negotiations, the only discussions of services occurred during the drafting of the Standards Code, which regulates standards such as environmental measures that affect trade. In these discussions, a definition dealing with services as well as products was referenced; but services were not really dealt with in the code that emerged.

In November 1977, after several years of discussions, the U.S. government, in compliance with the mandate of the U.S. Trade Act of 1974, raised some preliminary service industry issues in GATT. The U.S. initiative was twofold. First, it tabled several bilateral service industry problems to be discussed under the GATT umbrella and offered concessions to contracting parties in return for foreign concessions to its service industries. The EEC and one non-EEC nation also raised some country-specific service industry problems in Geneva. Second, the United States also tried to introduce services into the Non-Tariff Barrier codes, primarily the government procurement code. The procurement code, which establishes international rules for government purchase of goods, now covers "services incidental to the trading transaction," and the subsidies code also touches on services.[20] The United States has notified other nations participating in the multilateral trade negotiations that in the post-Tokyo Round period it intends to pursue broadening the government procurement code to cover services more comprehensively and has indicated its interest in exploring this concept in other areas as well.

This approach is treated in greater depth in the next chapter when the liberalization of services in the 1980s is considered.

U.S. Trade Act of 1974 and the Tokyo Round

The U.S. Trade Act of 1974 departed dramatically from earlier U.S. legislation governing trade. It begins by defining *trade* or *international commerce* as including services as well as goods and commodities and then proceeds to extend most of the provisions of the trade law to services. Covered therein is a wide spectrum of authorities, including the negotiation of trade agreements and the ability of the president to respond to unfair trade practices.

In essence, the act reflected the concern of a few important U.S. service industries with the restrictions confronting them in international markets. However, it would ascribe unwarranted prescience to those involved to suggest that underlying this legislative effort was a sense that U.S. services were rapidly becoming a crucial element in U.S. international commerce and that remedial efforts were needed to protect and assist them. The legislation was conceived for the most part by the aviation industry and was broadened and adopted primarily through the impetus of the insurance industry. These industries persuaded a few influential congressional leaders of the desirability of including provisions in the U.S. Trade Act of 1974 that gave authority to the executive branch to respond effectively to restrictions faced by service industries overseas. From its inception and even after its adoption, the inclusion of services in the legislation was resisted vigorously by the Nixon and Ford administrations.

Since its enactment a controversy has swirled around whether the legislation should be viewed as limited to providing a means for a case-by-case response to the unfair trade practices of other nations or whether it also mandates the introduction of services into GATT trade negotiations. As the concluding chapter will indicate, the more all-inclusive definition seems to have prevailed.

The Nixon and Ford administrations strongly resisted introducing services into the Tokyo Round of multilateral trade negotiations because services were not traditionally included in GATT. They felt that the preparatory work necessary had not been undertaken at home or abroad and that given the complexities of the Tokyo Round, in a period when protectionism was a recurring threat, the introduction of service industry issues would be unproductive and could retard the progress of the negotiations.

By contrast, the service industries—spearheaded primarily by the insurance industry, with support from the construction and transportation industries—felt that the Tokyo Round, with its emphasis on nontariff barriers, clearly meshed with the kinds of barriers faced by service industries abroad. Thus the negotiations provided a unique opportunity to deal with services. Those representing the U.S. service industries knew that little progress could be expected in the current round because the subject was raised in the postpreparatory stage without adequate preparation. Nevertheless, they felt that beginning such a discussion could pave the way for progress in a later round of trade negotiations. To their surprise, they encountered resistance in the response of private sector organizations like the International Chamber of Commerce and among specific service industry sectors in key industrial countries similar to that of the U.S. executive branch. The latter would have been expected to be sympathetic because of the importance of services to them.

The Ford administration finally responded to continuing service industry pressure by creating a high-level governmental interagency task force to study service industries at the international level with special reference to GATT negotiations. This study, nearly a year in the making, contrary to expectations, recommended, among other things, the inclusion of service industry issues in GATT negotiations on a selective basis. Shortly after the report's release, the Carter administration came to power and, after considering the recommendations of the task force, decided to try to introduce services into the Tokyo Round.

BILATERAL APPROACHES TO LIBERALIZATION: THE U.S. EXAMPLE

U.S. Bilateral Treaties: Their Relationship to Service Liberalization

The U.S. government has placed great emphasis on the negotiation of bilateral agreements with other countries. As the basis for U.S. bilateral commercial relationships, these treaties stress fair treatment for U.S. exporters and investors and equal access to markets. Here I address three aspects of bilateral treaties: whether service industries are covered, in both trade and investment terms; how successful the treaties have been in providing market access for U.S. services; and whether services are treated differently in nations that have bilateral agreements with the United States.

Treaties with Industrial Countries

I review here treaties between the United States and France, Germany, the Netherlands, Japan, and the United Kingdom. Most of these treaties, negotiated many years ago, have traditionally been called Treaties of Friendship, Commerce, and Navigation, or FCN treaties. Similar treaties negotiated today are usually referred to as Treaties of Amity and Economic Relations.

In general, the treaties provide two types of economic benefits. The first is called national treatment and means that nationals and companies of the other contracting party will be treated no less favorably than are nationals and companies of the host country in like situations. The other type of benefit, most favored nation treatment (MFN), refers to the treatment of treaty partners in trade matters in a manner no less favorable than that accorded to nationals or companies of third countries in like situations. The specific activities that receive these benefits are described in detail in the treaties.

Any specific mention of service industries tends to focus on financial services such as banking, utilities, transportation, and communications. Each of the treaties, except the one negotiated with the United Kingdom in 1850, specifically refers to these areas. All the agreements reserve the right to limit foreign participation in banking involving "depository or fiduciary functions," and most maintain similar reservations for communications and air or water transportation. Only the French treaty has broader limitations, including the production of electricity. Most of the agreements commit each of the signatories to avoid intensifying any existing limitations and to permit transportation, communications, and banking companies to maintain branches and agencies that are necessary for international operations.

None of the treaties places limits on insurance operations, but all treaties, except that with Japan and the original U.K. treaty, have an article permitting the placing of special requirements on alien insurance companies so that they furnish guarantees equivalent to those required of companies in the host country. Less sensitive areas such as tourism and professional services are not mentioned but presumably are covered by the general terms of the treaties.

With regard to investment opportunities and the repatriation of investment and earnings, all the treaties, including the U.K. treaty, contain provisions providing for national and MFN treatment for payments, remittances, and transfers of funds or financial instruments between the parties to the agreements. These clauses generally specify that exchange restrictions shall not be imposed in an unnecessarily detrimental or discriminatory way to the claims, investments, transport, trade, and other interests of the companies involved. These provisions apply to all investment, including services.

Treaties with Developing Countries

Below is a brief review of U.S. bilateral treaties with a selected group of developing countries: Argentina, Bolivia, Chile, Costa Rica, Egypt, Korea, and Liberia. The most recent is the Korean treaty, which was signed in 1956. The others were negotiated in the 1930s, and those with Latin America date back to the middle of the nineteenth century. There are many developing countries, including very important ones, that have no such bilateral treaties with the United States.

The earlier treaties negotiated with Latin American nations have a completely different format. The only comprehensive treaty is that with Argentina. The others cover, in broad terms, reciprocal freedom of commerce and navigation, and one mentions unlimited MFN treatment. Generally the focus is on trade—not investment—and when these treaties were concluded, commerce was more narrowly conceived to exclude services. Three treaties specifically mention financial entities or other services. The Argentine treaty is comprehensive in both specific and general terms, including everything from renting warehouses to a national treatment section, which by implication seems to extend to investment.

The more recent FCNs were concluded with Egypt, Korea, and Liberia. The Egyptian treaty is a provisional commercial agreement that is limited to MFN treatment and customs matters. The other two have provisions similar to those negotiated with industrial countries. Specific activities that are to receive national treatment are named, and provisions governing remittances and transfers of funds are included. The Liberian treaty is brief but very broad, providing freedom of investment, MFN treatment, and the like. It makes no specific references to sensitive service industries, whereas the Korean treaty, which provides for national treatment in all types of commercial, industrial, financial, and other activities, mentions banking, noting that each party reserves the right to limit the extent to which aliens may establish or acquire interests or carry on enterprises engaged in banking and depository or fiduciary functions. There is also an insurance reference in the treaty that liberalizes the freedom of marine insurance on trade between the two nations.

Effectiveness of Bilateral Treaties

Those sensitive services specifically included in the U.S. agreements with the five industrial countries examined here are usually treated in accord with the agreements. The only specific reference to insurance affirms the right of contracting parties to regulate it. In principle it seems to be entitled to national treatment. In Japan the insurance sector has been highly restricted, and only recently has there been meaningful liberalization. For example, U.S. firms requested permission to sell life insurance denominated in Japanese currency for nearly two decades before permission was granted recently to a few firms. In France, although foreigners can participate in the insurance market, it can be very difficult to obtain a license. In Japan new foreign banks are prohibited from entering retail banking, and it is often difficult to obtain licenses for new branches of existing banks. The U.S.-Japan treaty does, however, permit such limitations. In all the countries examined, there are various restrictions in the communications and transportation fields, but, in general, these are allowed in the treaties.

As for other service activities in which national treatment is implicitly provided for by the treaties, there are restrictions. France, for example, restricts accounting practice to its own citizens and requires accounting firms to be more than 50 percent owned by French citizens. In the United Kingdom, there are discriminatory visa requirements for foreign professionals and other limitations on foreigners practicing these professions, although EEC members are treated more favorably because of EEC rules. Restrictions place foreign film producers at distinct disadvantages in France, Germany, Japan, the Netherlands, and the United Kingdom. In short, the general national treatment clauses certainly have not prevented discrimination from arising in various service industries.

In developing countries there is a plethora of restrictions covering a broad spectrum of service industries. But most of the treaties I reviewed do not specifically provide for national treatment, except those with Liberia and Korea. Usually, they do provide for MFN treatment in trade, although service trade is clearly not the thrust of the provisions.

The Korean treaty exemplifies a broad national treatment treaty with few specific references to services. Korea has been fairly liberal in granting licenses to U.S. banks but has been restrictive toward insurance. U.S. or other foreign firms are denied life insurance licenses, and until recently in general insurance, foreign companies were only allowed to insure joint ventures from their home countries in dollar-denominated policies. Those foreign general insurance firms that do operate now do not receive national treatment. Korea also restricts various other services, including accounting, advertising, and motion pictures.

Those bilateral treaties that provide for MFN treatment provide little help in overcoming restrictions against services trade, although it cannot be argued that the MFN provisions are being violated since it appears all nations are equally discriminated against. Examples abound. In advertising Argentina prohibits commercials produced outside the country; Costa Rica requires those produced outside of Central America to pay a special tax. In insurance Argentina has a national reinsurance monopoly, restricts the purchase of reinsurance from international markets, and pursues a restrictive government procurement policy; Costa Rica has a nationalized insurance industry that controls all external reinsurance placements. In motion pictures Argentine films are protected. In transportation many nations have restrictions in both aviation and maritime transport.

In summary, bilateral agreements have not provided much in the way of liberalization in services, at least with the developing countries. Of the two treaties examined that provide for national treatment, one nation, Korea, has not acceded to the spirit of the treaty while the other, Liberia, has. The MFN provisions, while adhered to, have not prevented the imposition of a variety of restrictions on services trade primarily because there has not been a sustained international effort to reduce such service restrictions that would make MFN treatment meaningful. Agreements with developed countries do seem to offer more hope for liberalization of services because these countries take their obligations under the treaties more seriously and apply them with fewer transgressions.

But here, too, there are violations. And the treaties themselves limit national treatment in certain sensitive sectors. The MFN guarantees are not effective for the same reasons: they mean little in removing restrictions in services trade with the developing nations.

This limited survey suggests that the likelihood of service commerce being submitted to fewer restrictions between nations where there are bilateral agreements is marginal. On the other hand, the inclusion of services in such treaties at least provides a standard on which bilateral negotiations can be based. Although such agreements are described as a major linchpin of U.S. foreign economic policy, it is unrealistic to view them as a vehicle for really significant progress in services.

Bilateral Approaches through the U.S. Trade Act

I concentrate here on the effectiveness of the U.S. Trade Act of 1974 in promoting service liberalization on a bilateral basis.[21] The most important provisions for bilateral action are Section 301, which gives the president broad discretionary authority to respond to unfair trade practices affecting U.S. services, and Sections 102, 163, and 405, governing trade agreements. There have been several instances when U.S. service interests have petitioned for relief under Section 301 of the act, and at least one other where the threat of presidential action seemed to have played a contributory role in convincing a foreign government to cease its practices.

In one case, on September 10, 1975, Delta Steamship Company charged flag discrimination against the government of Guatemala. The Guatemalan government responded by satisfying the complainant, but it did not remove its general shipping restrictions. While the company in question withdrew its petition, the Office of Special Trade representative solicited further comments through the *Federal Register* but received none.

A second instance involves a charge on November 10, 1977, by the American Institute of Marine Underwriters (AIMU) that the Soviet Union discriminated against U.S. insurers through restrictions on transport insurance transactions between the United States and the Soviet Union. This complaint was filed after several years of unsuccessful negotiations between the U.S. government and the Soviet Union. On June 9, 1978, President Jimmy Carter found that the practices of the Soviet Union with respect "to Marine Insurance on bilateral U.S.-U.S.S.R. cargoes constituted an unreasonable burden and restriction on U.S. commerce."[22] On October 26, 1978, the United States and the Soviet Union signed in Vienna a memorandum of understanding providing guidelines for resolving the issue. At this writing an evaluation of the efficacy of the agreement reached is hindered by the current difficulties in U.S.-Soviet relations.

An informal use of these provisions in 1977 involved a foreign government's consistent refusal to fully license U.S. and other foreign insurers. A Section 301 petition was prepared by a U.S. insurer and reviewed by the trade negotiation office but was never formally submitted because an agreement was reached at almost the identical time the petition was to be formally presented. So the threat of a Section 301 petition, in some cases, may be as effective as a formal action, although in this instance the complaining company, American Home Assurance Company, in November of 1979 formalized its complaint in a Section 301 action because it concluded the government in question, Korea, failed to honor the 1977 understanding.* There may well be other instances where similar cases have occurred.

Another insurance case, again brought by the AIMU, attacked Argentine practices in the placement of marine insurance. This case was temporarily resolved through Argentina's agreement to negotiate at the time multilateral negotiations on this issue occur. A recent case involved a broadcasting dispute between Canada and the United States. President Carter made a positive finding for the complainants in this case and responded by recommending tax legislation to the U.S. Congress that would in effect subject Canadian broadcasters to the same treatment U.S. broadcasters receive.

A second area offering possibilities for bilateral action is found in Section 405 of the act. Its principal thrust is directed toward bilateral accords with Communist countries and seeks to ensure that bilateral agreements secure a fair share of the services trade for U.S. service concerns.

In two agreements that have come up for negotiation since the passage of

---

*In December 1980, the governments of Korea and the United States concluded an agreement which led to the withdrawal of the American Home petition.

the act in 1974—one with Romania and the other with Hungary—there were discussions between U.S. officials and representatives of the U.S. insurance industry who alleged that Eastern European countries follow a pattern similar to that of the Soviets in transport insurance on trade with the United States. U.S. officials were not persuaded of the merits of the case, primarily because of a lack of evidence, but they did raise the issue with the Romanians and Hungarians.

Finally, the general thrust of the act in Sections 102 and 163, which direct the president to take steps to remove restrictions affecting U.S. services and to report to Congress on his progress, provides an ongoing mandate to address restrictions affecting U.S. services wherever possible. The bilateral services requests made by the United States in the Tokyo Round, the U.S. push for service coverage in some of the multilateral trade negotiation codes, and the inclusion of specific service issues in other bilateral discussions and trade agreements are instances of the utility of these provisions in the act. Not surprisingly, this bilateral approach, especially the authorities provided in Section 301 of the trade law, have proved much more effective tools to address service restrictions than have bilateral treaties.

CONCLUSION

Only the EEC has undertaken a concerted program to liberalize trade and investment in services. This effort, an integral part of its drive to establish an economic community, contrasts sharply with other multilateral forums where service liberalization has been incidental, if not counter, to other objectives. In the OECD, the purpose of the liberalization envisioned in the Code of Liberalization of Current Invisible Operations and the Code of Liberalization of Capital Movements is to provide maximum freedom for such transactions. The codes benefit services to the extent that services or service transactions are covered. But they are directed at all invisible transactions and capital movements arising in international commerce. More important, such transactions are not equatable with service industries themselves and do not come to grips with many of their principal problems. The codes' coverage of specific services such as insurance and transportation are limited in scope and vitiated by lack of adherence. The issue of establishment (investment) is addressed in but one service, insurance; and even there, it does not come to grips with some fundamental issues. Besides, there are numerous reservations and derogations to the codes.

Until recently, the only services ever dealt with in GATT were motion pictures and transport insurance. Not even a modicum of trade liberalization has been achieved in these two sectors in GATT. The Tokyo Round of multilateral trade negotiations cracked the door to further service negotiations through their inclusion in the government procurement and subsidies codes and the bilateral requests made by various countries. But the covering of services in these codes is very narrow, and to date, none of the bilateral concessions requested have been granted.

The removal of barriers to service trade and investment achievable through bilateral means, while encouraging, can only scratch the surface of the multitude of restrictions. Only those nations having a large stake in service liberalization are likely to consider meaningful bilateral remedies. Their will to do so will be tempered by the efficacy of remedies available and the likely adverse impact such steps would have on other national concerns, economic and otherwise.

So the field is fertile for a broadly conceived initiative aimed at removing barriers to international commerce in services. The means available for undertaking such a program will be explored in the concluding chapter.

APPENDIX TO CHAPTER 6

Code of Liberalization of Current Invisible Operations

The annexes to the Code of Liberalization of Current Invisible Operations, especially Annex A and Annexes 1 through 4 of Annex A, list what are considered current invisibles operations. The list breaks down into ten categories.

1. Business and industry, including repair and assembly, technical assistance relating to the production and distribution of goods and services, contracting, authors' royalties, patents, design trademarks and inventions, salaries, and wages to nonresidents;

2. Foreign trade, including business travel, commission and brokerage, warehousing and storage, transit charges, customs duties, and fees;

3. Transport, including all kinds of transport, inland and external, and services connected with such transport including repair;

4. Insurance, including all life and general insurance, insurance related to goods in international trade, social security and social insurance, reinsurance, and insurance business operations abroad;

5. Films, including export, import, distribution, and use of printed films and other recordings for private or cinema exhibition or for television broadcasts;

6. Income from capital, including profits from business activity, dividends, and shares and profits, interest, and rent;

7. Private travel and immigrants' remittances, including tourism, travel for private reasons such as education, health, and family, and immigrants' remittances;

8. Personal income and expenditures, including pensions and other income, maintenance payments from legal cases, maintenance and repair of private property abroad, subscription to newspapers, periodicals, sports prices, and racing earnings;

9. Public income and expenditures, including taxes, government expenditures, and consular receipts; and

10. General, which covers advertising, court expenses, damages, fines, memberships in associations, clubs, and other organizations, professional services including services of accountants, artists, consultants, doctors, engineers, experts, lawyers, and so on, refunds in the case of cancellations of contracts and refunds of uncalled-for payments, and registration of patents and trademarks.

Annexes 1 through 4 to Annex A elaborate on certain categories such as insurance, which is given several pages of treatment due to its complexity. Concentration is on free trade in insurance, such as the transactions of insurance on goods relating to trade, the purchase or receipt of life insurance from abroad, the coverage of risk located in one country by an insurer based in another, or the handling of reinsurance. This annex does have a section on insurance operations abroad, which in broad terms seeks to guarantee national treatment to foreign insurers who establish themselves in other member countries of the OECD. Annex 3 to Annex A treats the "international movement of banknotes and exchange by means of payments by travellers." Also, international banking transactions connected with trade are partially included under foreign trade where banking commissions and charges under commissions and brokerage are covered. Banking is not otherwise specifically included in the code.

Code of Liberalization of Capital Movements

Annex A to the Code of Liberalization of Capital Movements outlines the areas the liberalization is intended to cover. They include the following.

1. Direct investment through creating a wholly owned enterprise, subsidiary, or branch or acquiring full ownership of existing enterprises and granting long-term loans (five years or longer); such transactions and transfers shall be free except when the investment is of a purely financial character designed only to gain for the investor indirect access to the money or financial market of another country, or when the amount involved would have an exceptionally detrimental effect on the interest of the member concerned (be it the investor or the investee);
2. Liquidation of direct investment;
3. Admission of securities to capital markets, including admission of domestic securities on a foreign capital market and vice versa;
4. Buying and selling of securities;
5. Buying and selling of collective investment securities;
6. Real estate operations;
7. Credits directly linked with international commercial transactions;
8. Personal capital movements such as family loans, gifts, and endowments. dowries, inheritances and legacies, and settlements of debts in the countries of origin;

9. Life insurance, primarily the capital transfers arising under life insurance contracts;

10. Securities and guarantees by nonresidents in favor of residents and vice versa;

11. Physical movement of capital assets such as securities and other documents of title to capital assets; and

12. Disposal of nonresident-owned blocked funds.

NOTES

1. Organization for Economic Cooperation and Development, *Code of Liberalization of Current Invisible Operations*, January 1975, pp. 6, 13.

2. Organization for Economic Cooperation and Development, Committee for Invisible Transactions, *The Right of Establishment under the Code of Liberalization of Capital Movements* (DAF/INV/74.15), Paris, February 25, 1974.

3. Brian Griffiths, *Invisible Barriers to Invisible Trade* (London: Macmillan Press, 1975), pp. 87–90.

4. Organization for Economic Cooperation and Development, *Policy Perspectives for International Trade and Economic Relations*, Report by the High Level Group on Trade and Related Problems to the Secretary General of the OECD (Paris: OECD, September 1972).

5. Organization for Economic Cooperation and Development, *Code of Liberalization of Current Invisible Operations*, Annex 1 to Annex A, Part III, March 1973, p. 38.

6. Organization for Economic Cooperation and Development, *Supervision of Private Insurance in Europe*, OECD Document 15/283 (Paris: OECD Secretariat, 1963).

7. Organization for Economic Cooperation and Development, *Code of Liberalization of Current Invisible Operations*, Article 20(a)(ii), January 1975, p. 20.

8. Organization for Economic Cooperation and Development, Committee for Invisible Transactions, *Liberalization of Direct Insurance* (C[70]15), Paris, January 26, 1970, pp. 3, 4.

9. Ibid., p. 5.

10. *Official Journal of the European Communities*, No. L228/3–No. L228/22, August 16, 1973.

11. Anne Howarth, "Restrictions on International Banking," Study for a Research Programme on International Investment and Trade in Services for the Trade Policy Research Centre, London, 1979.

12. Ibid.

13. "Proposal for a Directive Laying Down Detailed Provisions Concerning Transitional Measures in Respect of Certain Activities of Self-Employed Persons in the Financial, Economic and Accounting Sectors," *Official Journal of the European Community*, No. 115, September 1970, pp. 5–9.

14. At the same time, however, liberalization has on occasion removed obstacles previously confronting non-EEC members. For example, Ireland, on acceding to the EEC, had to adjust its insurance regulations to EEC rules. In doing so, it removed prohibition against third country insurers establishing themselves in Ireland. The intention of Portugal to join the EEC is even more propitious since the financial sector is nationalized and it will also have to adjust its legislation.

15. Clearly, the obstacles confronting a U.S.-EEC agreement are formidable. There are constitutional questions involving the authority of the federal government to negotiate such an agreement and supersede state authority in this area. The purely practical problem of

reconciling the complexities of the U.S. legal system regulating insurance with that of the EEC and its member nations would seem insuperable. Yet preliminary work has been initiated by U.S. international insurers working through the International Insurance Advisory Council of the U.S. Chamber of Commerce through a study comparing the two systems. There also have been very preliminary discussions between U.S. industry and the U.S. government as well as between the EEC Commission and U.S. authorities. The one factor that could provide the determination to overcome all these obstacles is the vital stake that the insurance industries of each have in the other.

16. United Nations Conference on Trade and Employment, Final Act *(Havana Charter)*, November 21, 1947 to March 24, 1948, Chap. 5, p. 36.

17. Clair Wilcox, *A Charter for World Trade* (New York: Macmillan, 1949), p. 108.

18. Raymond J. Krommenacker, "The Liberalization of Invisible Trade and the Inclusion of Services in GATT Negotiations: The Case of Transport Insurance," *The Journal of World Trade Law*, 13 (November 1979): 510-22.

19. General Agreement on Tariffs and Trade, *Special Provisions Relating to Cinematograph Films*, Article 4, October 30, 1947.

20. Trade Agreements Act of 1979, Statement of Administrative Action, Title III, Sections 301-309, June 19, 1979, 96th Cong., 1st sess., House Document No. 96-153, Part II.

21. The Trade Agreements Act of 1979 reaffirmed and strengthened the service provisions first adopted in 1974.

22. 43 *Federal Register* 25212.

7

THE FRAMEWORK FOR LIBERALIZATION

The thesis of this study, restated simply, is that the significance and functioning of services, especially internationally, are misunderstood, that even a cursory examination of them turns up startling findings with crucial policy implications, but that for a variety of reasons policy makers are unprepared to deal with this fact. As a result, policies, where they exist, are often ill conceived and have us on a collision course so that the kinds of difficulties that already are perceptible on occasion will reach serious proportions.

The study, unfortunately, does not indisputably support the thesis. The extraordinary lack of empirical data on services and the absence of a theoretical underpinning on which to base investigation have been recurring themes and obstacles to rigous analysis. However, although conclusive findings are unattainable, certain tentative conclusions are possible.

First, in purely statistical terms, even with all the data gaps, services are very important and will become more so—not just in industrial economies but in developing and socialist economies as well.

Second, international commerce in services is of growing importance, again not only for industrial nations as would be expected but surprisingly for many developing and even socialist countries.

Third, the changing nature of the world economy will foster the emergence of many new services as well as new suppliers of services in international commerce.

Fourth, the role and functioning of services in the international economy are consistently ill perceived, be it in the nature of their trade and investment patterns or their role in the development process. Yet there are indications that this role is a positive one.

Fifth, the relationship of services to a wide spectrum of noneconomic considerations—cultural, social, political, and demographic—is dramatically important and merits careful appraisal.

165

Sixth, the many positive roles services can play in the world economy are minimized by the considerable constraints under which they are placed.

Finally, this pattern adds up to a sum total of poor or nonexistent policy making. The time to begin to redress this unfortunate state of affairs is long overdue.

As a general proposition, services are like goods in their role in the world economy. Throughout this study I have suggested that many of the basic theories of international commerce are probably as equally applicable to services as goods. This means the same kind of benefits would arise from the liberalization of commerce in services that we associate with goods. In addition, there seem to be some very unique benefits associated with services. Wassily Leontief's conclusion that the development of the service sector is essential to overall national economic growth is worth remembering.[1]

On the other hand, many services are quite distinct from goods in that they are intricately connected to the culture and customs of nations. Professional services are a case in point. Other services are viewed as more closely intertwined with individual and national welfare than are many industries in the manufacturing sector. Examples are banking and insurance. Others, such as communications and shipping, are linked to national security concerns. Finally, all of these services, along with numerous others, are at the forefront of industries in which many nations wish to be self-sufficient. So it is not surprising that services tend to be more subject to government control. This adds up to a series of legitimate national concerns that must be considered in any program intended to remove constraints on international commerce in services.

This review of services in the world economy leads to three general types of policy responses. One response sees the increasing importance of services internationally as a positive development that is hindered by constraints. Thus a program of liberalization is desirable. The second policy option relegates the constraints imposed on international service activities to secondary importance, justifiable by other overriding considerations and the lack of conclusive evidence that illustrates the benefits of liberalization. Third, there is a middle ground between these two responses that appreciates the benefits of liberalization but recognizes the necessity to balance other legitimate concerns. Although I would favor the first option, I am forced to support the third because of the limited evidence available about services and recognition that other national concerns lead to constraints on services.

This option requires establishing a framework within which international commerce in services can be conducted and progress toward reducing barriers can be achieved. The framework should be viewed as a broad conceptualization of the principles that ideally should govern international trade and investment in services. Self-evidently, such principles will never be totally adhered to any more than that the generally accepted principles guiding trade in goods are inviolable. Nor will they necessarily apply to all services. As this study has illustrated repeatedly, services are too heterogeneous to hope that all-encompassing rules can be established. But the framework is meant to suggest the kinds of principles that efforts to establish rules to guide international commerce in services must be based upon.

THE GOVERNING PRINCIPLES

Since international commerce in services involves both trade and investment, principles governing each must be established. Let us first consider principles governing trade.

This study has concluded that trade in services is very much like trade in goods; the survey found close similarities in the impediments imposed on both. In fact, the six general categories of service problems I classified as trade/investment in Chapter 5 were all discussed in one form or another in the Tokyo Round of trade negotiations. Hence, many, if not most, of the principles governing goods trade should be applicable to services trade. A logical approach, then, would be to build a set of principles for service trade on the General Agreement on Tariffs and Trade (GATT) principles that govern merchandise trade.

The most important principle is that services trade should be conducted on the basis of something approximating the nondiscriminatory principle of GATT. This is the most-favored-nation (MFN) clause of GATT that states that all GATT members are committed to grant each other treatment as favorable as they give to any other country in the application and administration of import and export duties and charges. Stated another way, it means that all nonnational suppliers of traded services will be treated the same as all other adherents to the GATT rules. A subsidiary GATT principle is that protection, for the most part, should be given to domestic industry in the form of tariffs and not through other measures. The aim of that rule is to make the extent of protection clear and to encourage as much competition as possible.

This subsidiary principle will take a different shape when applied to services since restraints placed on services are not generally in the form of tariffs but are nontariff measures, the very kind of constraints GATT tries to avoid. GATT originally dealt with nontariff measures in its Articles 5 through 10, the so-called technical articles designed to prevent nontariff measures from being substituted for tariffs. The Tokyo Round of negotiations, the first wide-ranging negotiations on nontariff measures, established a series of codes of conduct to govern the application of nontariff measures. The primary purpose of these codes is to bring nontariff measures under more effective international discipline. The hoped-for result is the kind of principle that should govern trade in services: nondiscrimination in the application of nontariff measures (like MFN treatment for tariffs) but much more than that—the establishment of fair and equitable rules governing the utilization of nontariff measures. For example, the new GATT government procurement code goes far beyond ensuring equal treatment to foreign suppliers of goods—it seeks to put them on an equal footing with national suppliers.

The second principle, again analogous to GATT, would be to construct acceptable exceptions to the rule of nondiscrimination and fair and equitable treatment. For example, one situation that might justify exceptions would be the special circumstances found in regional trade arrangements. This is again analogous to GATT but makes sense in the context of trade in services as well. For example, if a regional bloc like the Andean Pact developed a regional policy in a service such as shipping, whereby the members of the pact grant one another cargo-sharing preferences, this might be a permissible exception to the general nondiscrimination principle if it were confined to intraregional trade.

A second likely exception to the principle would be special treatment for developing countries. GATT provides a dispensation whereby countries in the developing world are granted exemption from GATT rules and agreements under certain circumstances. Similarly, nontariff measures utilized to restrict service imports or enhance a nation's service sector(s) that would be prohibited or discouraged under the general principle could be allowed for developing countries under specific, carefully defined circumstances. Because of developmental needs or in recognition of infant industry status, a developing country might deviate from the principle of nondiscrimination and give special treatment to one or more of its service industries.

In addition, industrialized countries might consider the application of preferential measures for developing nations that are analogous to the generalized system of tariff preferences granted developing country goods and commodity exports. Also the imposition of nondiscriminatory nontariff measures acceptable for services trade might be eased for developing countries. As an example, in the supplying of construction services, some rules on subsidies might be waived for developing country suppliers of these services.

The third general principle, again analogous to GATT, would permit countries to derogate from the rules because of specified economic, trade, or other circumstances. Deviation might be allowed for balance-of-payments difficulties, for safeguard of an industry threatened by import competition, for national security considerations, or for reasons of public health. For instance, a nation in balance-of-payments difficulties might be permitted to restrict its insurance imports, or a nation might restrict foreign participation in its communications or computer industries for national security reasons.

Obviously, various other less central principles would be necessary—principles aimed at minimizing damage to the trading interests of other nations when derogations are involved or exceptions requested. These subsidiary measures would include consultation and complaint procedures, but they would derive from the three guiding principles governing trade in services.

With the foregoing principles as a guide, a framework of international trade in services could be constructed. It is equally necessary to have an analogous framework for international investment in services. As we have seen in Chapters 4 and 5, the nature of investment in services parallels trade in services in that service investments are very much like other kinds of investments, and the problems confronted are similar. Thus, the principles governing international investment in services should vary little from those for investment in general. But there is one difference in the rough parallelism to trade: consensus on the principles that should govern international investment of any kind is nonexistent. Although some noticeable headway has been made on certain principles such as incentives/disincentives that unduly skew investment, there is no meaningful existing framework governing international investment activities to draw upon. Later in this chapter, I shall suggest some of the elements for a regime governing international investment.

Simplistic as it may sound, the three principles suggested above to govern services trade are equally sound for investments in services. Regulation of such activities should be conducted on the basis of nondiscriminatory, fair, and equitable treatment between foreign and national investors. There should be acceptable exceptions to this rule, as well as special circumstances permitting derogation from the rule. In thinking about current international investment problems in services, no more than this need be said. The problems all relate to these principles.

Each and every service sector will have to be considered in light of the general principles. There will need to be an understanding as to what reasonable rules governing trade or investment in each sector would look like. Conceptually, in simplest terms, this means stripping a service industry to its bare bones by considering what commerce in it would amount to in the absence of accumulated incentives or disincentives. However arduous this may be, the failure to do so will make it very difficult to apply the principles and devise rules governing commerce in a particular service. Submitting commerce in selected services to international rules and procedures does not necessarily liberalize trade and investment in those sectors; it merely aims at developing internationally accepted standards of regulation. That is the kind of structure I am talking about.

This book has made patently clear that *services* subsume a large, heterogeneous category of economic activity whose most common characteristic may be nothing more than its inclusion within the classification. Even if discussion is limited to those services involved in international commercial activity, the differences among them and the way they are regulated are enormous. Thus a determination as to which services should be addressed within the framework suggested above—which is handicapped by the lack of previous experience—must be based on supposition at best.

The actual process of establishing rules and procedures governing services will in itself sort out the service activities to be included, just as addressing individual service problems will help devise the rules and procedures. The process is immensely complex and by its nature very long term; it will involve many different mechanisms and institutions. Some services will be addressed within one mechanism or one institution; some in another. Some may be dealt with in the relative short term; others only over the long haul.

Below I suggest various approaches, institutional and otherwise, as parts of a process aimed at establishing a framework to govern international commerce in services. That discussion will shed some light on the serivces meant to be included within our framework. But there is no way at this juncture to make it definitive, except in those few situations where the process is already well under way.

The "new" services—those that may exist but are not yet perceived as such and those yet to be created—also will have to be melded into the process at some point. At present, the only guidance we have as to which services we are talking about is that those services internationally traded, invested, or both should logically fall within this framework. But are all services so defined to be included? And where and how will they be addressed? The best that can be offered now is some initial guidance in general terms as to the services that I believe should be dealt with. Though not all-inclusive, it is meant to give some idea of where we are headed.

The selections are made on the basis of an amalgam of criteria: services that currently, in purely statistical terms, play a major role in the world economy, or those projected to do so; those whose importance to the smooth functioning of international commerce, directly or indirectly, is essential; and those included for very special or unique reasons.

I previously determined that those services at present playing a significant role in international commerce as measured statistically are transportation, tourism, and several that are categorized in balance-of-payments analyses as other services, specifically, insurance and financial services, construction, and engineering. In general, these services are the most important in statistical terms in each of the three kinds of countries I examined—industrial, developing, and socialist. Considering their importance to all types of economies, it is not surprising that most but not all of these services are highly regulated and confront an array of restrictions. This is especially true of transportation, financial services, and, to a lesser extent, the construction/engineering sector.

Ideally one would expect all these services to be included in any program developed to govern commerce in services. Yet some are difficult to deal with by their very nature, while others are very sensitive and governments will be most reluctant to consider submitting them to new rules and principles. Thus there is a temptation to exclude certain services from the process at the outset, in the interest of making the process workable. This is especially true of air and maritime transportation, professional services, communications, even tourism, and perhaps others. Let us review each.

Of all services, there is the greatest temptation to rule out transportation services. They are already subject to a morass of complex international rules and are overseen by well-established international organizations. Progress in dealing with them seems impossible. Yet they are not only the most important services traded internationally in aggregate statistical terms but in virtually every individual nation's trade in services as well. Further, they play an integral role in the entire trading process. To exclude them from the framework governing services would, therefore, mean limiting the work in the services to those of less conse-quence. Besides, there is a glimmer of hope in that, largely due to the impetus of the United States, a few beginning steps have been taken toward opening up competition in aviation and perhaps even in shipping.

There is a strong case for including the other services of current impor-tance—financial services and construction/engineering. They are statistically important, involve both trade and investment, and face an array of restrictions, especially financial services. Though financial services, especially insurance, are technically complex, the progress that has been made in liberalizing trade and investment in insurance in the European Economic Community (EEC) and, to a lesser extent, in the Organization for Economic Cooperation and Development (OECD) indicates dealing with them is not impossible.

Tourism is an especially difficult decision. Definition of this sector is elusive because it includes a heterogeneous composite of industries. Yet it is the one service industry of most direct interest to a significant number of developing countries—countries that, in the absence of other factors, perceive they have much less to gain from participating in a program involving services. Although there definitely are constraints on some aspects of the tourism industry (for example, hotel/motel, automobile rentals, and franchising), these restraints are not of great importance and are most often imposed by those very nations wishing to develop their tourist industries. For the most part the real determi-nants affecting the development of tourism are not restraints on particular tour-ism trade but involve other factors, such as limitations placed on the avail-ability of foreign exchange for touristic purposes. This is an issue that is at best tangential to any regime governing international commerce in services. So, al-though the general principles guiding commerce in services might apply to tour-ist services, tourism cannot be singled out as an industry unto itself, nor should it command priority attention. While establishing rules for those service sectors comprising the tourist industry may be a lesser priority, the building of a general framework should, over the long haul, be applicable to these activities.

Communications, computers, the information industries, and utilities are rather special services. (The latter has been ignored throughout this study. Its problems do not seem very relevant to a general set of rules governing services, since most problems that arise are best dealt with on a bilateral basis, for ex-ample, the U.S.-Canada power grid.) But the communications, computer, and information industries recently have become dramatically important because of the transborder data flow issue. Restricting the transmission of data across national borders is a nontariff measure that has impact far beyond the industry itself: it touches on spectra of service and nonservice industries dependent on such data. In fact, the spectra of industries and issues touched by this gen-eral area of service activity are limitless. It is strikingly illustrative of how a service function can so directly link to the functioning of international com-merce. Constructing rules governing this activity is vital.

As for films, though their economic impact is not particularly significant and it is difficult to make a strong case for the increased welfare that would result from liberalization of this sector, it would be foolish to eliminate the one service that is clearly included in the articles of GATT. Besides, the kind of value judgment made above should be avoided in the same way that such judgments do not enter into liberalization involving trade in luxury items.

Problems in professional services, while considered by many as purely investment related, come down to questions involving recognition of professional qualifications across national boundaries. It can be argued that these are the purest of service industries. So while their problems may seem minor relative to other services, a services framework should be applicable to these sectors. Principles along the lines of those established in the EEC might encourage governments to accept more internationalization of professional services.

As for the various other service activities in international commerce, including new and emerging services, there is no reason to exclude them from the framework unless the way they function internationally or their role as perceived by governments dictate otherwise. Clearly, many of these services are not very important (for example, employment services), or the nature of their activities is so encompassing (for example, francising or leasing), or they are so intertwined with the public sector (for example, health and education services) that the relevance of rules governing commerce in these services will be problematical. Yet if we do not begin now to accumulate the experience to deal with today's less conventional services, we will be unprepared for tomorrow's task. In short, most services having international involvement should be considered for this framework. This does not mean they all have to be dealt with the same way, but they should be addressed in one way or another.

POSSIBLE APPROACHES FOR ESTABLISHING PRINCIPLES

The logical jumping-off point in formulating a specific program for services is to learn the lessons of the past. What stands out most in reviewing the history of efforts to govern services commerce is its startling lack of success. Why has the postwar period, which can be characterized, at least until recently, as following a fairly straight and narrow path toward liberalization of world trade in goods, failed to produce a similar result in services? I would suggest the following reasons.

The existence of severe constraints on merchandise and agricultural trade was universally recognized and given first priority.

Most service barriers are nontariff measures that were imposed in the postwar period at the same time nontariff measures also were being imposed on goods and agricultural trade (while tariff barriers were being dismantled). So if we have only just begun to attack nontariff measures on goods trade, services naturally took a back seat.

The lack of attention given to services has been reinforced by the prevalent notions about the nature and functioning of services in international commerce. There is no analytic underpinning to justify service liberalization.

The notion that services and their regulation are mainly investment related has pushed reform efforts into the background. There has been scant progress in dealing with international investment questions.

The lack of data has made it difficult to define what was at stake.

Only in the EEC—and to a lesser extent, in the OECD—have there been any efforts at liberalization. The latter has focused neither on services nor on what liberalization of services really means; the former, besides being painstakingly slow, is geographically confined to its membership. All this adds up to the observation that there has never been a comprehensive, sustained effort to liberalize commerce in services. Thus the primary lesson to learn from the past is that there are no past mistakes—just a history of neglect. That in itself is encouraging because it relieves us of the burden of trying to overcome a discouraging series of past failures. But at the same time, it provides us with only limited experience to draw upon in designing a program. Our principal resource is the recent Tokyo Round experience in seeking to control nontariff measures. And yet with every indication that services will loom larger in the future, thought must be given to the kind of trading/investment regime that will be desirable. A beginning effort now to establish principles governing services should help establish the rules for international commerce in services that will help reduce the future conflicts that are inevitable as the sector becomes more important.

The following sections examine various avenues that might be pursued to establish international standards to guide commerce in services. It will soon become obvious that I believe the principal burden for pursuing these alternatives will depend primarily on U.S. initiatives. As will become evident during the discussion, there is no easy path to follow; the alternatives are numerous and none is likely to provide an all-encompassing route. The possibilities do not seem to be mutually exclusive; in fact, it is quite conceivable that various initiatives can be pursued simultaneously in more than one place or by more than one means. Sometimes they may be complementary, other times not. Clearly, compromises will be required. For example, although the United States might gain more through bilateral approaches, it may have to forego such benefits in order to reach agreement on principles and procedures.

At the conclusion of this review of alternatives, I will suggest the way such a program addressing services is likely to develop—and in fact seems to be developing. This discussion will be organized sequentially as much as possible. Clearly, however, an effort of this magnitude, by its very nature complex, multifaceted, and long term, will be somewhat unchanneled. Many different avenues will be traversed at one time or another. There will be developments that do not obviously relate to this process but that, in retrospect, will be seen as integral to its development.

This discussion will give emphasis to how I see it developing within the major multilateral institutions, since therein, it seems to me, is where inevitably the core of the process must take place. However, the intent of this approach is to describe the process itself—the gathering of information, the formulation of concepts, the definition of issues, the determination of goals, the mobilization of public opinion, and the building of political consensus—not to predict a scenario that I expect to be confirmed when the historians examine this development with the benefit of hindsight.

Possible institutional avenues to establish understandings governing services that will be explored below include the existing multilateral institutions such as the OECD and GATT, and possible new multilateral institutions such as a GATT for Investment and a GATT for Services. Also, I will examine a combination of other possibilities ranging from bilateral and regional approaches to industry-specific mechanisms.

SERVICES IN THE OECD

Historically, the OECD has had the most experience in dealing with services. It is appealing as a forum for discussions of services in that the two codes it has adopted affecting them have elements of both trade and investment. Further, since its members are the countries that have the most at stake in services, it is a natural place to initiate such discussions. This is not to say that negotiations on services undertaken in the OECD necessarily must be ultimately limited to its membership. Instead, one can envision a process similar to the development of the GATT government procurement code. Laying the groundwork for that code originally began in the OECD, and it was transferred to GATT during the Tokyo Round. Something analogous could conceivably occur with at least some of the results of an OECD service exercise.

A seeming shortcoming of the OECD is that by its nature it has not proved to be a forum for effective negotiations leading to meaningful results. However, that might not be the serious drawback it seems. The OECD, especially in recent years, has shown itself a viable place to address difficult international concerns and develop a consensus on a developed country approach to them. Building such a consensus in services requires research, analysis, and policy development—functions for which the OECD is ideally suited. This bears on our primary goal of developing a set of principles governing international commerce in services—principles to be subsequently used by whatever institution in devising rules and procedures guiding such commerce. It was a similar process that gave us the principles that are the basis of the OECD codes on invisible transactions and capital movements.

In the fall of 1978, the United States launched a discussion on services in the Trade Committee of the OECD. This initiative, which encountered considerable reluctance from other OECD members, had the purpose of beginning a low-key discussion so as to build an understanding of services and develop a consensus to deal with them within the OECD framework as a first step. At its meeting in October 1978, the committee asked the OECD Secretariat to prepare an initial discussion paper. It was agreed that the aim would be to increase understanding of the impediments to the expansion of international trade in services and to develop alternative ways for reducing them.

The resulting paper[2] on trade in services, prepared by the Secretariat for the Trade Committee, addressed some of the conceptual problems that we have encountered in this study, such as whether work should be based on the notion of service industries themselves or on transactions in services. It noted the difficult data problems and discussed leading services such as transportation, insurance, films, construction/engineering, "other technological services," and miscellaneous services. Finally, it reviewed what has happened and is happening within the OECD with regard to services.

It found that the Committee for Invisible Transactions has made virtually no progress under the Code of Liberalization of Current Invisible Operations in removing the remaining hard-core restrictions in transportation, films, and insurance. As to the Code of Liberalization of Capital Movements, the report noted that a recent survey on direct investment found extensive restrictions, especially in banking, communications, and maritime transport. Further, it suggested that the restrictions, if anything, probably are understated because sectors reserved to public monopolies or sectors where there are restrictions on the right of establishment are not covered by the code at all.

The Trade Committee survey reviewed the work of the Committee on International Investment and Multinational Enterprises, which, pursuant to the OECD declaration on international investment, calls for treatment of foreign enterprises in a manner equivalent to domestic enterprises. While exceptions relating to the services sector have been reported in banking, insurance, shipping, and communications, the study concludes that a closer look at the service sector will probably reveal further restrictions. But it cautions that restrictions falling under the "right of establishment" are excluded and that the differing views on the scope of this exclusion may account for some countries not reporting service measures that were noted by others.

Finally, the Trade Committee report described the work of specific sectoral subcommittees—insurance, maritime transport, financial markets, and tourism—and concluded their present work would not make much of a contribution to a study of impediments to the expansion of international trade in services, primarily because of their orientation. The direction the Insurance Committee has followed since its founding, described earlier, illustrates the kinds of concerns that probably influenced the Trade Committee's thinking. The committee did not focus on the OECD work that has resulting in the voluntary "Guidelines on Privacy Protection and Transborder Data Flows."[3] But then, it is only very recently that this issue of "telematique" has begun to be recognized as a service issue as such. In essence, these guidelines, which apply to automated and manually stored personal data in both the public and private sectors, attempt to strike a balance between safeguarding the individual and discouraging national protectionism.

The Trade Committee had a somewhat preliminary discussion of the paper at its meeting on April 5, 1979, and a more thorough review at its October 1979 meeting. The discussion on April 5 pointed to the need for more detailed information about problems faced by service industries. It became obvious that in the absence of such hard data, discussions could well get sidetracked into tangential issues of no practical consequence. Therefore, following a U.S. suggestion, the committee invited member governments to supply the Secretariat with examples of problem areas as input for the October discussion.

The U.S. government began working with its service industries immediately to prepare such a study. Although it builds on earlier surveys such as the 1976 Department of Commerce study, the final product will be quite different from previous work simply because of the experience of the past few years. Service industries that were asked about their problems for the 1976 study responded with a spectrum of comments ranging from nationalization to fiscal problems. What the new survey attempts to do, in a limited sense, is focus more on the kinds of issues that would be addressed in trade negotiations on services. For example, service industries are asked to consider whether the kind of impediments they face constitute subsidies or whether they encounter restrictive government procurement practices. The United States is proceeding on the presumption that by submitting an inventory of impediments to U.S. services overseas, a similar response will be provoked from other member countries, if for no other reason than in self-defense.

This exercise in the Trade Committee is best viewed as a tool to build a foundation for future negotiations. At a minimum, it should help create a common pool of information, concepts, and terminology with respect to international commerce in services. Beyond that, it can provide a catalog of impediments to services trade and an outline of potential negotiable issues.

But strong and clear-thinking leadership will be essential to keep the exercise on track. The preliminary document put together by the OECD Secretariat for the Trade Committee's consideration recognizes this. Noting the complexity of services and the potential for confusion and disagreement in just defining what the Trade Committee should be dealing with, the Secretariat suggested consideration of an alternative "pragmatic" approach that would avoid the conceptual and data questions. A pragmatic approach should start from an analysis of the different characteristics of each service industry, look at the nature of impediments to international trade in these services along with other aspects calling for intergovernmental attention, and review the work already underway in the OECD and elsewhere. Reportedly, it is because the dangers recognized by the Secretariat manifested themselves to such an extent that alarmed U.S. delegates tried to discourage the committee from undertaking the kind of work that could delay progress for years to come and instead asked member governments to provide examples of problem areas for committee consideration.

However, the undercurrent clash of views on how best to proceed remained evident. A compromise eventually accepted involves, in addition to the survey of restrictions, the undertaking of case studies in four sectors—construction/engineering/consulting, banking, insurance, and maritime transport. The first is being conducted by the Trade Committee itself through the distribution of a survey questionnaire to the countries that participate in the Trade Committee. The other three sectors are being handled by the appropriate sectoral committees in OECD with emphasis on the compilation and review of existing studies. As an example, the Committee for Invisible Transactions and the Insurance Committee have established a joint working party to review the invisible operations code provisions dealing with insurance. Its basic mandate is to determine the relevance of the code to current practices. Does the code adequately reflect the range of problems confronting international insurance transactions today? What conditions would be necessary to persuade governments to remove reservations and derogations they have invoked under the code as currently written? This exercise is one of symbolic significance that bears directly on past criticism of the code as it relates to services, for it suggests nothing less than overhauling the code to attune it to the real problems of services. This is a dramatic turnabout from what the code now does—or was originally intended to do.

At this point it is premature to predict where the OECD exercise on services is headed—and certainly there is as yet no indication of what will be the key issues and most feasible approaches. The more important consideration is that an attempt to deal with services, however preliminary, has gotten under way.

SERVICE INDUSTRY ISSUES IN GATT NEGOTIATIONS

The following discussion of service industry issues treated in the GATT context is based on my perception of how their inclusion in GATT could actually develop. In essence, this means cautiously and slowly beginning to build on the work on services started in the Tokyo Round, and especially on the structure established therein to deal with nontariff measures. Embodied in this idea is a conviction that the exercise of grappling with services within the existing and evolving GATT structure, as well as in other institutions, will serve an essential educational purpose: it will familiarize both policy makers and technicians as to what services are all about, how they function, and how little understanding of them exists. This will help activate a public awareness and interest in the subject, which, over time, should engender a political willingness to tackle the issues.

In considering how services might be included in GATT, first, I examine how services could be included among the various means developed to deal with nontariff measures in the Tokyo Round, with special emphasis on areas where services were dealt with during the negotiations. This is followed by an examination of other areas in the GATT discussions where services might be discussed. In other words, discussions could be pursued simultaneously in several ways and no avenues should be viewed as mutually exclusive.

Nontariff Measure Codes

Service restrictions can almost always be categorized as nontariff measures, and many of them seem to fit neatly into several of the codes of conduct developed in the Tokyo Round. In fact, some preliminary steps involving services were taken in the Tokyo Round. The Non-Tariff Barriers codes most appropriate to services are those dealing with government procurement and subsidies and, to a lesser extent, standards and the quantitative restrictions/import licensing procedures.

Government Procurement

The government procurement code is the most suitable starting point for introducing services into GATT because the code, drafted in the Tokyo Round, already includes those services that are "incidental to the supply of products." Specifically, the code covers incidental services if their value does not exceed that of the products themselves. But it excludes service contracts per se.[4] However, the United States served notice near the conclusion of the negotiations that it planned to initiate a discussion in the post-Tokyo Round period directed at broadening the coverage of services. The final agreement states that not later than January 1, 1984 (three years after the code becomes effective), and preferably at an earlier stage, signatories will explore the possibilities of expanding the coverage of the agreement to include service contracts.

One aspect of the code that encourages participation is its nonbinding, voluntary nature. Thus a minimal number of countries can accept the code initially, with the expectation that others will adhere to it later. Given the past resistance to dealing with services in GATT (or anywhere else), the inclusion of incidental services in the government procurement code is a low-key approach likely to encounter the least resistance (although U.S. negotiators, who pushed for its inclusion in the Tokyo Round, did not find it easy going).

The objective of the code is to establish something close to national treatment of foreign supplies and suppliers in government purchasing. As with goods transactions, "buy national" objectives of governments in service purchases can be achieved both transparently through legislative enactments and through less transparent administrative practices and procedures. Again, as in goods trade, discrimination against foreign service suppliers can occur at various stages in the procurement process.

Let us use insurance to illustrate how government procurement policies affect foreign suppliers, keeping in mind that analogous practices often apply to other services like construction/engineering. A government may mandate that its purchases of insurance be made only from state or national insurance companies; some governments require that its purchases of insurance be only from national suppliers with some percentage, usually majority, of local ownership. These requirements effectively eliminate foreign firms from competing.

Government procurement restrictions in insurance can be applied indirectly to such an extent that virtually all insurance purchases by business, not just direct government purchases, are covered. For example, Argentina requires that all enterprises receiving any government benefits (such as tax forgiveness, import duty relief, or government contracts) insure with a national company that is 70 percent owned by nationals.

The starting point in including services in a meaningful way in the government procurement code is to reach a clear understanding on what is meant in the code by *services incidental to the supply of product*. The extent of coverage under the term is ambiguous, apparently by intent. Considerable effort was made by U.S. service industries during the congressional hearings considering the multilateral trade negotiation package in the spring and summer of 1979 to ensure that this definition covers as broadly as possible the services associated with trade in products. Encouragement for this viewpoint was forthcoming from Congress, and assurances were given by those in the administration who will implement the multilateral trade negotiation results that they will push for this definition.

It will be a challenging task because the apparent interpretation by the technicians who drafted the code is very narrow and would exclude most service transactions. Yet a broad interpretation will facilitate the mandate to broaden the code's coverage to include services per se. In essence, under such an interpretation, the same principles for guaranteeing foreign suppliers of goods a competitive opportunity would apply to suppliers of services associated with goods purchases. Thus in any such transactions—banking, insurance, shipping, engineering, construction, legal, or other—foreign suppliers of services would have the opportunity to compete. This means that the rules and procedures in the code governing notification of government intent to purchase, bidding procedures, specifications, and the like would apply to foreign service suppliers in the same way as they apply to national suppliers.

This is the first step. Within three years, work is to begin on applying the code to services in general—not just those connected with the supply of products. It will be a complex, drawn-out process. A determination will have to be made as to what kinds of services are affected by government purchasing policies so as to work toward agreement on applying part or all of the government procurement code to some or all services. Depending on the findings, other alternatives may have to be considered such as developing an annex to the code covering special considerations that might apply exclusively to services.

Subsidies

The subsidy code developed in the Tokyo Round seeks to ensure that all aids to industry be covered through new international rules on subsidies. While the code recognizes that there are distinctions between a subsidy for trade purposes and a subsidy for other purposes such as regional development industrial policy, employment incentives, and technological assistance, it establishes new rules and strengthens and refines existing international rules governing subsidies.

Again, as in the government procurement code, services are covered when they relate to goods trade. The main body of the subsidies code text contains no reference to services. But the annex to the code, the *Illustrative List of Export Subsidies*, includes subsidized services in Annex items (c), (d), (h), (j), and (k).[5] Thus services provided at preferential rates to benefit merchandise exports would be subject to the code's provisions. Subsidized service exports per se, however, are not covered by the code.

There are many examples of governmental aids to the service sector that distort international trade. One of the most obvious occurs in transportation. In shipping, apart from cabotage and flag discrimination, there is extensive use of construction purchase and ship improvement subsidies, scrap-and-build schemes, low-interest loans, and special tax exemptions. All these are in effect a form of subsidy, although some might not be defined as subsidies (especially export subsidies) under the GATT terminology.

As in the procurement code, a beginning step is to work within the framework of the new code and define and test the rules laid down therein. For example, in the services area, the illustrated list of export subsidies includes government supplies of mandated transport and freight charges related to export shipments on terms more favorable than those given domestic shipments, the provision of export credit and export credit guarantee (insurance) programs at subsidized rates, and the provision by governments or their agencies of imported or domestic services for use in producing exported goods on terms or conditions more favorable than provision of such services for use in goods production for domestic consumption.

The post-Tokyo Round period will involve the establishment of a structure to deal with the reforms resulting from the Geneva negotiations. For the nontariff measure codes, this probably will involve special committees regulating each code. It is in this context that opportunities to deal with the refinement of these general provisions governing service subsidies (and other service matters involved in the codes) can best be accomplished. The building of experience in dealing with the new subsidy rules on services will come from case instances that will arise as governments raise specific complaints concerning violations of the code. More than likely, complaints about subsidized services will not come from service exporters but from product exporters, placed at a competitive disadvantage because of subsidized services received by their competitors.

It is on this structure that, over time, a framework can develop to regulate service subsidies per se. Like the other codes, the subsidies code calls for periodic reviews—in this case, annually. This will offer the possibility of negotiating improvements in the code related to services. Again, during the U.S. congressional hearings on this subject, service industry sources recommended that efforts be undertaken to expand the code to cover service exports themselves.

To initiate a broadening of the rules to apply to services themselves, it will be necessary to decide what kinds of problems in services arise from subsidies. Thereafter, a determination of how the subsidy rules can be extended to services can be considered. This would entail deciding which of the permitted and which of the prohibited subsidies under the GATT rules relate to some or all services and which would apply. Logically, the new rules for consultation and dispute settlement developed in the Tokyo Round should apply to those services. It could be that some services should be subject to additional provisions annexed to the subsidies code or that some services will have to be dealt with solely in an ad hoc manner apart from the code.

Agreement on Technical Barriers to Trade (Standards)

The standards agreement aims to discourage the use of standards and certification systems to manipulate trade flows. It seeks to avoid this by encouraging the use of open and transparent procedures in the development of standards and certification systems. It seeks to ensure that standards are based on existing international standards, if they exist. Where they do not, the agreement seeks to encourage the development of such agreements.

The only service item touched on in the Tokyo Round was a reference to the services of testing laboratories in providing international recognition. But the standards agreement provides interesting possibilities for services. One of the major problems for most services is the absence of internationally accepted standards governing them. For example, many—such as health, educational, or financial services—are subject to regulation intended to meet general welfare objectives. This can easily be abused in the interest of preventing foreign competition. The consultative process wherein the standards code will be tested and administered could be utilized to begin explorations on a case-by-case basis in selected service sectors or to develop an understanding of the kinds of general standards that might be developed for services. Such a process will be essential over the long run if meaningful rules to govern services trade are to be developed.

Agreement on Import Licensing Procedures

During the Tokyo Round, a working group on quantitative restrictions and import licensing procedures put together a code on the administration of import licenses. It is intended to minimize the use of import licenses to block foreign competition. Although not envisioned as applying to services, it is another area for investigation since there are instances where foreign suppliers of services connected with the importation of goods are restricted through the administration of import licenses in competing to supply their services. For example, in the case of insurance, an import license can be used to deny the purchase of coverage from a foreign insurance supplier on the shipment of goods. Similar restrictions exist in shipping through controlling who will carry the goods and in construction/engineering services when the import license determines who constructs, engineers, or installs imported goods. As complaints are raised under this agreement, those countries whose services are denied access through such licenses, especially when the services are linked to goods trade, should use this mechanism to begin to broaden the code to apply to services.

Over the long term, the code might be one place to explore limitations on the licensing of services to compete in a domestic market. This admittedly transcends the code as it was conceived, since it touches on what are seen as establishment/investment questions. Banking, communications, accounting, and insurance are examples of sectors where a country can deny foreign suppliers access to its market through its procedures for licensing or authorizing entry. Through denial of licenses or specifying strict limits on the licenses granted, foreign service suppliers are effectively prohibited from competing to sell their services. Eventually, the code might be broadened to cover services encountering these difficulties; alternatively, subsidiary or new codes might be developed. If nothing else, experience with this kind of problem would be developed, which could eventually help in establishing rules elsewhere.

Bilateral Negotiations under the GATT Umbrella

Throughout the Tokyo Round, bilateral negotiations were conducted among the various participants. Basically, in these discussions nations sought concessions in return for the concessions they offered. Similar negotiations are under way continuously, even in the absence of multilateral discussions, but subject to GATT rules if the discussants are GATT members. Such talks can as well deal with services as with goods and commodities and are another means within the GATT context to build understanding of services commerce. For example, if the United States has made a concession to a developing country on tropical products, it might, in turn, seek a concession in services. In the U.S. context, this is compatible with the objectives of the Trade Act of 1974 and the requirement that the president periodically evaluate U.S. concessions to ensure that equivalent concessions beneficial to all sectors, including services, have been made.

As noted in the last chapter, the United States and other nations made a series of bilateral requests on services both during the Tokyo Round and in bilateral trade talks conducted independently of that forum. The United States approached 17 countries on service trade problems but received concessions in only a few instances. Requests made under this approach do not necessarily have to be limited to trade issues. Although focus should be on trade barriers in the interest of building consensus within the GATT context, there is nothing to prevent investment barriers from being addressed, especially if we keep in mind the difficulties in separating service trade issues from investment issues.

A good example of this occurred in recent U.S.-Taiwan trade negotiations under GATT auspices. In return for U.S. concessions, the Taiwanese agreed that one U.S. insurance company could be licensed in Taiwan where at present there are no foreign companies. Some would argue this is an investment question. It is debatable and probably involves elements of both trade and establishment. This particular issue is one where the reciprocal granting of MFN to all GATT members would not be required, since it is not viewed as a trade concession. On the other hand, other bilateral negotiations could lead to that kind of result. For instance, if the U.S. request to Canada in the multilateral trade negotiations to eliminate restrictions on imported radio commercials were granted under multilateral trade negotiation rules, all GATT members should benefit.

The bilateral approach also offers the most effective means, if not the only means, to negotiate with socialist or nonmarket economies on their barriers to service industries. Traditional trade negotiations with socialist GATT members have achieved fewer results because of the nonmarket nature of their economies. The market economies generally give more than they receive through their tariff concessions on a MFN basis and, more recently, through adherence to codes of conduct governing nontariff measures. Similar concessions by nonmarket economies are made virtually meaningless by the differing nature of their economic systems. Bilateral trade-offs on services would serve the dual purpose of addressing service problems while providing a way to balance the trade concessions more fairly. For example, negotiations with an Eastern European country to determine on whose ships grains shipments will be carried or where the insurance on such shipments will be placed can translate into measurable results and might compensate for failure to fully achieve merchandise trade goals.

Safeguards

The Tokyo Round discussions aimed at reforming the balance-of-payments provisions of GATT and Article 19, which covers emergency action on imports of particular products. Because agreement could not be reached, discussions have continued following the conclusion of the negotiations. There will be a continuing effort to address such issues within the new GATT consultative framework. This is, again, an area where, in time, as service problems are more firmly planted in the GATT consciousness, proposals for safeguard rules applicable to services should be studied.

As in goods trade, governments take safeguard actions against services for balance-of-payments purposes or general currency controls or to protect against import competition. For example, in regulating marine insurance on trade in goods, some countries impose currency and other restrictions to prevent purchases from foreign suppliers. Similar restrictions exist in shipping and numerous other services.

The accumulation of experience will help determine how applicable the principles concerning safeguards in goods trade might be for services. For example, in the case of safeguards to help services adjust to competition, guidelines that might be used in goods trade, such as the peril point at which imports threaten the national industry, may be inappropriate. In some services the real threat from foreign competition is negligible. For example, when countries restrict the import of advertising services from foreign suppliers, it is generally unlikely that this is done because the survival of the domestic advertising industry is threatened. Other reasons associated with the objective of developing a national industry more likely are the motivating force. But the basic principles permitting safeguard measures covering services should be similar to those in goods trade. Such actions should be taken only on a temporary basis and within a generally accepted international framework.

GATT Reform

During the Tokyo Round, discussions in the Framework Improvement Working Group ranged widely. They included discussions on balance-of-payments questions, dispute-settlement safeguards, and special treatment for developing countries. The impetus for this work came primarily from the developing countries and the United States, and it is expected to continue in the post-Tokyo Round period. It offers an opportunity to conduct a broader-based discussion on service questions as the work on services develops within GATT.

Over time the framework of the reform group might be extended to include a commitment to developing general principles, rules, and procedures governing services trade. Such an approach could deal with broadening the services provisions in the new GATT codes as well as amending or adding rules and procedures to the GATT articles for dealing with services. The thrust such changes might take is described later.

A FRAMEWORK FOR FUTURE GATT NEGOTIATIONS IN SERVICES

Once the various consultative committees created to implement the Tokyo Round decisions begin to deal with services, they will quickly discover the lack of comprehensive, consolidated information on obstacles to trade in services. This inevitably should spark what must be the first order of business before services can be dealt with seriously: the preparation of an inventory of service industry barriers like that prepared on nontariff measures following the Kennedy Round. Although some service industry barriers were included in the list prepared for negotiation in the Tokyo Round, a meaningful list of nontariff measures to services trade does not yet exist. The surveys cited earlier are inadequate (for example, the American survey under the auspices of the Inter-Agency Task Force is unsatisfactory despite its virtues).[6]

The more recent survey conducted by the International Service Industry Committee of the U.S. Chamber of Commerce in cooperation with the U.S. trade representative's office indicates the sum increase in sophistication on this subject in the past few years. This survey catalogs service problems in eight different generic categories. This cataloging, shown in the Bibliographic Appendix (entitled "Framework of Impediments for Use in Compilation of Impediments to Trade in Services"), has been widely accepted in international circles. For example, the International Chamber of Commerce, in its work on this subject, has adopted this model. It is this kind of approach that is required if services are to be dealt with in a multilateral context. Without an understanding of where their problems have common threads, we will be relegated to addressing services on an industry-by-industry basis.

But all these efforts lack the necessary international standing. Legitimacy can only come from a survey conducted under GATT auspices with the participation of GATT signatories (although the survey of problems under way in the OECD Trade Committee can be the initial block on which a comprehensive GATT inventory could be built). The U.S. government study and other such efforts lack the essential ingredient of directly relating them to what the GATT rules are all about. The U.S. survey, based on questionnaires and interviews with service industries, lists service problems but fails to relate them to subsidies, government procurement rules, safeguards, and import licensing restrictions. It also fails to clarify where they do not relate to GATT at all. Such a sorting-out process must occur in any inventory if it is to be a useful tool Only thereby will governments be able to determine the important problems and sort out those common to all services and those that are peculiar to individual ones. In short, an inventory will not only provide an agenda—it will serve as a diagnostic tool.

Brian Griffiths noted the difficulties encountered in preparing the inventory for the Tokyo Round.[7] GATT found that the total number of complaints amounted to about 800. These were later classified into 30 categories, 3 of which GATT originally chose to negotiate prior to the Tokyo Round. A similar categorization, however prolonged, must be done for services.

Counting the Tokyo Round, there have been seven major trade negotiations since the inception of GATT. It was widely believed at the conclusion of the Tokyo Round that it would be the last negotiation of this type. Former U.S. Deputy Trade Representative Alonzo L. McDonald and others argued that with its conclusion the progress achieved in trade negotiations in the past quarter century will have eliminated the great majority of hindrances to trade. Institutional reform and the new trading rules will have so considerably modified GATT that another prolonged, highly visible trade negotiating session would not be likely to produce substantial results and thus would not be worth the effort.[8]

Instead, negotiating should be a daily consultative process removed from the public eye, allowing the tough issues to be studied, analyzed, and resolved by the experts. Thus, the argument goes. Although Tokyo may be the last major round of trade negotiations, emerging out of it is an ongoing commitment to effective liberalization realized through the establishment of a permanent GATT negotiating mechanism.

This does not bode well for service negotiations. A strong case can be made that the dramatic factor that edged the Tokyo Round toward some meaningful trade liberalization was the high visibility of the political process surrounding the negotiations. In 1976, after three years of fruitless talks, the negotiations were recognized as being in serious trouble. The lack of political will on the part of the leading protagonists and the danger of a resurgence of protectionism were constantly in the public eye and led to the kind of attention by political leaders that produced the resulting agreements.

Let us suppose that what follows the Tokyo Round is the process predicted for future trade discussions. Such talks would be quiet, scarcely mentioned in the press, without the cacophony of international attention. There would be a continuous process wherein professional negotiators would sit down in the tranquility of Lake Geneva and focus on the difficult and tough trading issues. It is a most appealing idea and indeed might be workable if limited to the context of a postmortem of the issues dealt with in the Tokyo Round—assuming that these issues aroused no grave domestic problems in various national constituencies. But the likelihood of a process of quiet, daily negotiations establishing rules of the game to govern services trade is dubious. A more productive approach, at the proper time, would be the grandiose approach epitomized by the Kennedy and Tokyo rounds. At least one such negotiating round or something analogous to it is essential to galvanize an ongoing and permanent commitment to liberalization in services. Otherwise the political will and the momentum for negotiations will not be achieved.

Some indications that this philosophic outlook is taking hold became evident as those in senior trade policy positions began to benefit from the perspective allowed by time and distance from the exhausting experience of the Tokyo Round. Governor Askew, the immediate successor to Ambassador Robert Strauss as U.S. trade representative, stated: "So in time I think we'll have another round of trade negotiations to lower tariffs further and to make some adjustments in the Codes, based on what we might learn after a few years experience with them, and to deal with barriers to trade in services."[9]

On September 7, 1980, U. K. Minister of State for Trade Cecil Parkinson, speaking at Lloyds of London, suggested trade liberalization in services should be pursued, first within the EEC market and then throughout the GATT. And the month before, GATT Director General Olivier Long told the Geneva Association (Association Internationale pour l'Etude de l'Economie de l'Assurance) that GATT favored extension of its principles into services trade, but it would take a great deal of work and a long time to achieve results. On April 20, 1981,

U.S. Trade Representative Bill Brock announced a U.S. government work plan approved by the cabinet-level Trade Policy Committee. An essential element of the program announced by Ambassador Brock was the beginning of "domestic and international preparedness for future multinational trade negotiations on services."[10]

But the other side of that coin is that such a process can never occur until the groundwork is well prepared. First must come the accumulation of data and thoughtful analysis that enables the formulation of concepts—the kind of process that drawing up an inventory of barriers and dealing with services within the various GATT consultative groups engenders. That exercise and analogous undertakings in the OECD and other institutions can be instrumental in this process. Next must come a general agreement on principles—something that ultimately must be ordained at the highest political levels. These steps are all integral to the kinds of broad educational effort necessary for a successful launching of trade negotiations in services. Without this the necessary consensus will never be achieved to launch a major effort on the scale of the Tokyo or Kennedy rounds.

When the groundwork has been laid and the time is ripe for a more dramatic approach, one can envision a process paralleling the beginning of GATT. First, a temporary "cease-fire" would be imposed on all new regulatory actions, incentives, or disincentives to service trade. This could be followed, especially in the area of incentives/disincentives, by an in-depth continuation of the preparatory process begun earlier: information gathering, studies on how domestic policies affect trade, and movement toward harmonization of policies as a means of lowering barriers.

Finally, again following the GATT example, actual negotiation on the removal of constraints would begin. In short, the framework to govern trade in services could involve a parallel process to the development of the structure governing trade in goods: first, a cease-fire; second, a determination of the why and how of service regulation; and third, a major negotiating round to minimize restraints. Such a process, as in GATT, would be one of continuous development and refinement.

This approach in the case of services would, as in the case of GATT, not be inviolate. It would in no way prevent governments from taking additional measures to regulate their service sectors. But it would facilitate the establishment of rules to govern these steps.

One issue that will have to be addressed preparatory to such an undertaking is, Is the modification of the basic instruments of GATT necessary to firmly establish services in GATT? From the practical point of view of one who favors utilizing GATT to liberalize international trade in services, this approach seems fraught with dangers. To accept the argument that modification of the GATT articles is necessary to specifically include services implicitly justifies the position of those who believe that services are outside the domain of GATT. It also lends credence to the argument that the United States and other countries that seek to deal with services in GATT are consciously violating the GATT articles.

On the other hand, those who fervently proclaim that services are absolutely excluded from GATT are not facing the facts. Their claim does not square with the inclusion of motion pictures in GATT, the nearly ten years of GATT discussions on transport insurance restrictions, or those parts of the government procurement and subsidies codes that include services.

However, in all fairness it seems that some modification of GATT must be considered as part of a comprehensive approach to establishing services rules within its framework. A sustained discussion on services within GATT would probably necessitate this kind of modification. Several possible reforms come to mind. To begin with, the preamble of GATT, which includes among its objectives expansion in the production and exchange of goods, envisions these objectives as being advanced by "arrangements directed to the substantial reduction of tariffs and other barriers to trade and to the elimination of discriminatory treatment in international commerce."[11] Including services along with goods in the preamble, and making the definition of *international commerce* analogous to that in the U.S. Trade Act of 1974 whereby *services* are defined as being an inherent part of international commerce, would clearly place services within GATT. For the sake of consistency, similar minor modifications would probably need to be made in other relevant articles of the agreement.

A second logical place for amendment is Article 3 of Part II, dealing with "National Treatment of Internal Taxation and Regulation." The national treatment provisions seek to ensure that foreign products will not be placed at a disadvantage compared with nationally produced products. Services should be included here. Complementing this addition would be other adjustments throughout Part II to include services. This would include, for example, the articles dealing with restrictions to safeguard the balance of payments and those governing subsidies.

Although the changes above would clearly delineate the inclusion of services within GATT, a more comprehensive modification would be the addition of a Part V to the GATT as a chapter specifically dealing with services. A new chapter would have several advantages. It would confirm in unequivocal terms that services are part of GATT and would encourage the drafting of specific provisions that would address whatever special treatment services might require within GATT. These might include provisions exempting certain services such as utilities or internal communications from the GATT articles and special provisions governing services like health or educational services. Another provision might create a schedule of concessions for services similar to those that exist under Article 2 of Part I, which basically outline MFN treatment. Others might spell out national security exceptions and guidelines on government assistance for economic development.

WHY AN OECD–GATT–TYPE APPROACH

The necessity of this exercise being managed by a group such as the Trade Committee of the OECD cannot be overstated. A long gestation period will be required to prepare for serious multilateral discussions on services. Reaching that stage will depend on how well this preparatory phase is handled. The virtue of the Trade Committee or a similar group such as the GATT Consultative Group of 18 is that it centers the international exercise around a small cluster of basically like-minded people with the same general attitudes on international commerce. They are trade people and that is what is required if this issue is to be framed in the kind of context necessary for successful negotiations within institutions like GATT.

Surveying a few of the difficult issues that must be grappled with will dramatize why trade officials—and not sectoral experts—must guide and dominate the process. Our earlier look at the never-ending, fruitless negotiations within the OECD Insurance Committee perfectly capsulate the pitfalls that must be avoided.

For about a quarter of a century, the committee, composed of insurance regulators and their industry advisers (in other words, the technical experts) wrestled with the complexities of harmonization of insurance regulation, which in their view, is a prerequisite for achieving the liberalization intended in the invisible operations code. Their failure points to the principal reason technicians should not be at the center of the process: a parochialism, understandable but unavoidable, pervades their perspective. Regulators and those being regulated, naturally, are vitally concerned about any modification in the rules that are at the very center of their livelihood. To expect them to see beyond this narrow horizon is probably an unreasonable expectation. Yet somehow resolving the differences in various domestic regulatory systems so as to agree on reasonable international principles will be one of the most awesome tasks facing negotiators on services. The regulatory conflict will arise in a number of service industries besides insurance—banking, aviation, shipping, communications, and professional services. If the negotiation over regulated sectors is captive to the technical experts who lack a broad view of national policy, we will see nothing more than a rehash of the results of the past: emulation of each other's regulatory practices and imposition of similar restrictions.

This is not to suggest that the technical experts do not have an important role. They understand their sectors better than anyone. Their appraisal of what is workable will be essential. The legitimate national concerns they represent will indeed have to be weighed. After all, the regulatory standards that exist are nothing more than a reflection of an amalgam of national concerns. Agreeing upon international regulatory standards that balance these concerns while minimizing distortions of commerce in services will be the task.

Even if the experts overcome the parochial views that quite naturally permeate their perspectives, they are the wrong ones to be involved in the process because they are not plugged in properly at home. In the OECD insurance example, the decisions taken by the experts in the Insurance Committee apparently bore no relationship to official policy as determined at higher echelons of government. Again and again, decisions reached at the technical level, when brought to the political level, the Council of Ministers, were cast aside. In some sectors there apparently is no communication among different officials who represent the same government before the same organization.

Further, even if the technical experts have a substantial power base at home, it is unlikely to be integrated within the proper policy framework. The policy apparatus in the United States provides a salient example. Although the United States is the spearhead of the drive to have international service negotiations, it, too, has its domestic regulatory conflicts that must be sorted out. Even though the trade policy apparatus was recently reorganized, primary responsibility for individual services still remains with different government agencies. As examples, in the shipping field, negotiations are handled by the Maritime Administration in the Department of Commerce and by the Department of State. The Department of the Treasury, the Comptroller of the Currency, and the Federal Reserve Board all have responsibilities in the banking area.

Under the reorganization, the U.S. trade representative will coordinate the development of U.S. service policies and try to provide a broader forum for resolving agency conflicts through its Trade Policy Committee structure. It is hoped the participation of all relevant agencies in this process and the recent creation of a high-level Services Policy Advisory Committee, composed primarily of private sector service interests, and a lower-level Industry Services Advisory Committee, involving the industry experts, will provide the kind of apparatus necessary to achieve a consensus on national policy toward services. It will at least ensure that the issues are considered in a broad context instead of on a sector-by-sector basis.

A problem area termed by many as the service issue of first priority, the sine qua non of a service agenda, illustrates the absolute necessity of framing this agenda within the kind of structure I have suggested. The issue is in the data transmission area, often characterized more broadly as *telematique*. Fortunately, it has been addressed on a somewhat broader basis in the OECD International Communication and Computer Policy Committee, which developed the "Guidelines on Privacy Protection and Transborder Data Flows" mentioned earlier. Otherwise, the issue probably would not have been cast with a perspective nearly so broad. The negotiations would be expert to expert—limited to computers and communications specialists. We probably would have not heard even a passing reference to the possibility that data transmission restrictions might have trade implications. But even though the OECD has provided a forum offering a greater breadth of perspective to consider this issue, the discussions remain in the hands of a committee of highly specialized experts.

To ensure that the extraordinary ramifications of this issue are weighed, it must be broken out of even this broader but still-limited forum and discussed in a setting offering ample perspective. There are several reasons. First, it must be brought to the forefront of the international agenda. A forum that enhances that likelihood must be chosen. Second, it needs to be considered from a vantage point that supersedes the concerns of the various sectoral interests involved. Finally, it should be framed in a trade policy context. However, the outcry of alarm over this issue has yet to produce one of these results.

The long-run objective is to prepare the way for a meaningful negotiation that will yield concrete results for services in general. This can only occur if the framework is not limited to intrasectoral negotiations. Experts from within the same sector talking to each other will not yield liberalized regimes. Bilateral discussions are limiting enough, but when they are limited to a specific sector, the likelihood of reaching reciprocally beneficial arrangements is even less likely. What is required is a package with something for everybody. Only then will the political support be engendered to ensure that the outcome of a negotiation is accepted. This is best achieved by a multilateral approach involving enough different interests that there is the possibility of gains on all sides.

POSSIBLE APPROACHES

Now I will suggest some notions of the range of possibilities that could be an outgrowth of the work of the OECD Trade Committee and the preliminary initiatives underway in GATT. If sustained, the OECD Trade Committee exercise offers the opportunity to begin to build the documentation and knowledge necessary to deal with services in a meaningful way. At some point the committee may attempt to grapple with the data problem—a problem that will eventually require the kind of approach I suggested in the Appendix to Chapter 2. Some of the conceptual issues, such as problems of definition, also may begin to be understood. These are all necessary elements for putting the tertiary sector in proper perspective. But over the shorter term, a more immediate contribution to the process of building a framework for conducting international commerce in services can result from a proper channeling and utilization of the indications by governments as to the major problems their service sectors face internationally.

The OECD has taken the first steps toward developing the inventory of barriers I previously suggested as one of the early tasks to be undertaken by GATT. This should only be viewed as a positive development. It would be shortsighted to view the project as belonging to the exclusive purview of any particular institution. Efforts in both the OECD and GATT are probably as necessary as the parallel initiatives now under way in several private sector institutions. Although duplication may occur, every effort is surely worthwhile when there is such a paucity of data.

The current timetables for work on services in GATT and OECD suggest that the latter organization will be first in providing an inventory. This will not be the first time that work begun in the OECD has been put to use in GATT. But however outstanding the OECD inventory, it will not in itself suffice for GATT purposes or for the broad agenda that must be addressed in many places in coming years. For one thing, the initial OECD inventory is limited in scope to only those impediments faced in OECD member countries. On the other hand, the OECD exercise need not necessarily be limited to trade impediments, as a GATT exercise is likely to be—it can also consider investment barriers so that its findings may have broader implications. In any case, in considering how the work in the OECD and GATT might be used, by far the most promising possibilities might best be termed the *code approaches.*

The Code Approaches

To the extent that efforts in the services area follow the pattern of existing institutional arrangements and procedures, institutional frictions will be reduced and the likelihood of success will be enhanced. Thus the most successful strategy would be to tie as many issues as possible to tried and trusted approaches. The nontariff barrier codes negotiated in the multilateral trade negotiations were predicated on the proposition that it is impossible to deal with all potential nontariff governmental measures or policies that may impede trade but that it is possible to establish certain principles and procedures to ensure fair treatment for those who are affected by such actions. Numerous variations of this general proposition are possible for services.

Extension of Multilateral Trade Negotiation Nontariff Codes

One option is to explore extending to services the coverage of the codes negotiated in the multilateral trade negotiations. Since the earlier discussion of GATT dealt with this possibility at length, there is no need to dwell on it here except to suggest that the process does not have to be dealt with exclusively in GATT. There is ample precedent for this attitude. The government procurement code adopted in the multilateral trade negotiations had its roots in the OECD. For many years the OECD painstakingly developed and nurtured such a concept, and it was only transferred to GATT after the launching of the Tokyo Round. Certainly a similar process could be undertaken to extend the procurement code more comprehensively to services through carrying out the preparatory research and analysis in the OECD Trade Committee.

Although the procurement code seems the most logical one to tackle—both for historic reasons and because, of all the GATT codes, the most progress has already been made in applying it to services—the groundwork for other codes such as subsidies could also be undertaken in the OECD. For example, the Gentlemen's Agreement on Export Credits represents a long-standing OECD effort in the subsidies area. It can be argued cogently that not only are export credits in themselves service transactions, but related issues involving the export of services and export credits need to be addressed. In short, a preliminary consensus among developed countries on these kinds of issues could be worked out in the OECD, with the actual negotiations taking place in GATT.

Improving Existing OECD Codes Affecting Services

Code of Liberalization of Current Invisible Transactions. The OECD invisible operations code established a wide range of commitments that relate to services commerce and a procedural framework for dealing with problem areas. Its weaknesses were discussed earlier in this study. Much of the code has nothing to do with services trade; long lists of reservations are maintained by member governments; many service activities are not covered by the code, and even those that are have problem areas the code does not cover; low priority has been given to the work of the Committee for Invisible Transactions in recent years; and legally binding obligations are not imposed by the code upon member governments.

Of greatest preoccupation is the intransigence and apathy of governments vis-à-vis the rules already accepted. It seems certain that the service problems pinpointed in the survey under way in the Trade Committee will include many of the reservations and derogations presently maintained by member countries. This should give fresh impetus to reconsidering them and may generate a new-found interest in both the code and the work of the committee. Refocusing attention on these continuing restrictions is the first step needed to revitalize the code. Such activity would best be conducted with a view receptive to considering whether modifications are necessary to encourage broader adherence.

Certain other problems likely to arise may best be dealt with in the context of the invisible operations code. This may require redefinitions and modifications of the code. For example, as noted when the code was described in Chapter 6, for all practical purposes it only affects tangentially such basic service sectors as banking and excludes others altogether such as communications and computers, except when their activities are touched on by such general categories under the code as business activities. A second example relates to the evolution of new kinds of service activities like those associated with technology transfers. Perhaps they, too, should be examined in the context of the code. Another difficult issue concerns the right of establishment. This question has elements transcending both the invisible operations and capital movements codes and remains a controversial unresolved subject. It has a dramatic impact on services commerce because so much of service activity is investment related. Without a government's permission to establish them, many service activities cannot occur. This kind of issue will need to be reconsidered within the framework of both these codes.

Code of Liberalization of Capital Movements. The capital movements code, too, is encumbered by reservations. For example, a number of countries have restrictions that limit the ability of foreign firms to invest in their service sector. These restrictions also are likely to be raised as governments bring to the Trade Committee the problems in services commerce they are most concerned about. Thus a first step in strengthening the code will be to take advantage of a fresh interest in these issues to review the existing reservations to see what progress might be made toward removing them. As in the invisible operations code, such a review would best be conducted with an open mind that welcomes modifications or redefinition, where necessary, to make the code more meaningful.

A second phase of the process that logically follows from the first is to review those service sectors that may have restrictions but that are not covered by the code because they are public monopolies or are covered by other restrictions related to the right of establishment. This will inevitably lead into a discussion of one of the most difficult issues of all: What is the right of establishment? The earlier review of what elements constitute this right concluded that the codes taken together fall far short of conveying it. Yet building a framework to deal with international commerce in services at some point requires grappling with this issue, just as constructing international investment rules covering any economic sector will require the same confrontation. Although this is a highly controversial question, it is strikingly clear that many important borderline cases that fall somewhere between restrictions on inward direct investment (which is covered by the code) and measures involving the right of establishment relate to the service sector (for example, banking, insurance, brokerage, and accounting). A review of the capital movements and invisible operations codes with focus on salient service problems cannot evade this issue.

All such discussions will require interaction with numerous other OECD committees, such as the Committee on International Investment and Multinational Enterprises and specific sectoral committees. But other approaches I have suggested, such as beginning work in the OECD to extend the multilateral trade negotiation codes to services, also will need the advice and consultation of industry-specific ones.

Code on Services or Specific Services Codes

A third approach would be to establish principles or codes of conduct to guide the regulation and operation of services at the international level. These could include both general codes as well as individual codes governing specific service sectors. Clearly, this is not an approach that one could undertake immediately as an alternative to the approaches suggested above. It could only come about in time as an outgrowth of the other exercises and as a resultant conclusion that separate codes need to be constructed for individual sectors or for services as a whole.

As discussed earlier, a code-of-conduct approach has considerable appeal for several reasons. Codes are voluntary, that is, they are based on the establishment of principles to which subscribing governments will try to adhere. Once the code's broad framework is adopted, countries are not so subject to pressure to make concessions, except in a periodic review process where the main weapon used to encourage compliance with the code is suasion.

The other side of the coin, however, is that there is little incentive to comply with the codes unless governments truly are persuaded of the benefits that adherence to them will bring. There is a disadvantage in codes that deal only with services, as contrasted with more comprehensive codes. When both services and goods or other kinds of transactions are dealt with together in a code, a nation might have an incentive to adhere, even though it had little interest in services, because it could see benefits to be gained from other parts of the code. So in theory, it would be best to link codes for services to much wider agreements covering a broad range of international commercial issues. This is one advantage of incorporating services within the relevant GATT codes.

In either kind of code—whether general for services as a sector unto itself or individual in dealing with specific services—the governing principles would be like those described earlier in this chapter. A code on services would establish some general principles, a negotiating framework for establishing mutual obligations, and a procedural framework for the discussion of policy issues relating to commerce in services and the resolution of disputes. Such a code could be approached in two ways: either by developing and adopting general principles guiding governmental treatment of the various elements of international commerce in services or developing the various elements of such a code through first constructing individual specialized codes. Because of its comprehensiveness, the general code would parallel the GATT arrangement for goods trade. It could be limited to trade in services or investment in services, or it might cover both. It would probably include provisions for nondiscriminatory, fair and equitable treatment in services, establish rules on taxation and subsidies and the like, and sanction exceptions to the code's principles for national security or balance-of-payments reasons. Amendments, consultation, disputes, and enforcement procedures would have to be developed. However, probably the strongest rules that could be hoped for initially would be more akin to those governing the invisible operations and capital movements codes of the OECD. Over time, perhaps something with more bite, such as GATT-type arrangements, could be put into place.

It is expecting too much, however, even if the international community were wholeheartedly supportive, to start with a comprehensive code. Instead, a slow process of constructing the elements of this kind of code piece by piece would be a more realistic approach. Individual codes dealing with principles governing specific aspects of commerce in services could be developed separately. For example, in the trade area, government procurement policies in services could be treated in one code, another might cover subsidies. In the investment field, codes governing incentives and disincentives to investment, freedom of establishment, and other matters might be developed. The different problems confronting a financial service such as banking, as contrasted with a professional service or a service like francising, probably would make it necessary to develop subsidiary codes or at least subsections of the general investment code to deal effectively with industry-specific situations.

Another alternative would be to develop codes of conduct for specific service industries—codes that in time might be incorporated in an overall services code. Such codes, addressing themselves to the principles governing trade and/or investment in a specific service sector, would have to deal with the kinds of problems suggested by Brian Griffiths[12] in very precise ways. These include:

The role of government in the particular service industry (for example, defining its role in protecting deposits in banking or in controlling liner conferences in shipping);

Specific measures of liberalization and rules of procedure;

Incentives and disincentives such as subsidies;

Reservation and derogation rules—that is, how exceptions to the code would be applied on a nondiscriminatory basis, with provisions for periodic review, and so on; and

The method of enforcing the measures embodied in the code.

Griffiths gives several examples of how such a code might operate. For example, a banking code would cover the removal of discrimination between national and foreign banks with respect to the conditions of entry, such as minimum capital requirements, liquidity ratios, and restrictions on the maximum rate of interest payable on deposits and charged on loans. It would also cover the precise relationship between foreign banks and domestic banking law, particularly with regard to different techniques of monetary control. (Surprisingly, the goal of equal treatment on occasion actually might place foreign service interests at a disadvantage they would not otherwise encounter. For example, it can be argued that under previous U.S. banking legislation foreign banks enjoyed certain advantages that domestic banks did not benefit from.) A banking code would deal with the extent to which foreign banks should be exempt from cash and liquid asset reserve requirements and the maintenance of capital/deposit ratios because they are branches of larger banks that maintain adequate reserves and capital in their home office. Finally, according to Griffiths, a banking code would also have to address the extent to which monetary authorities should be permitted to impose reserve requirements and discriminate between foreign-owned and domestic-owned deposits.[13]

A truly comprehensive code, however, would have to go beyond the Griffiths approach, which is limited to national versus foreign participation in an economy on a direct or establishment basis, and deal with international banking transactions, that is, trade in banking. This would include the kinds of issues touched on in the invisible operations and capital movements codes.

These comprehensive codes could deal not only with difficult financial services such as banking and insurance but also with other sensitive services, including those that traditionally have been handled exclusively in their own special international forums, such as maritime and air transport. Such an effort does not have to supersede the work of industry-specific forums—rather, it could provide a stimulus for new initiative from a fresh perspective. Or the codes could be developed within these industry-specific forums. Until recently, this would have been considered naive. In fact, anyone who dared tread the mine field of air and shipping regulations was correctly regarded as foolhardy. However, the recent breach in the International Air Transport Association (IATA) of international aviation practices, sparked by the U.S. open-skies initiative of 1978, has proved that determined leadership by a nation with clout can reopen heretofore sacrosanct, highly regulated and protected sectors.

Similarly, the recommendations of the President's Commission for the Review of Antitrust Law and Procedures on Shipping released in early 1979 would, if enacted, lead to a breakdown of the international liner conference system in shipping or at least to U.S. participation in that system. These recommendations would prohibit pooling agreements, dual-rate contracts, and rate-setting agreements and would insist on the right of independent rate action by conference members.

It should be far less difficult to agree on codes governing those service industries that are not so sensitive, such as construction, franchising, and consulting. Tactically, it is no doubt easier to start with less sensitive industries to see if agreement is possible. But such codes would be far less significant in their impact because these services labor under relatively fewer restrictions. In fact, there is no reason to construct a code for each and every service—just as it would be nonsensical to build codes around every manufacturing sector that we find in international commerce. Instead, the kinds of problems confronting less sensitive sectors could probably be addressed within an overall services code, or since they will probably be akin to the international commercial problems confronting most sectors, services or otherwise, within the approaches suggested earlier for the OECD and other institutions. Where exceptions exist and problems unique to one of these industries need to be addressed, it could be dealt with in an ad hoc fashion.

As the code approach progresses, it will be necessary to focus on the new services I have mentioned on several occasions. This will be a difficult task involving, among others, services that have often been provided only by governments, such as communications, and services that are not industry specific, such as management and related services provided by manufacturing concerns to their affiliates or nonaffiliates. The latter go beyond service industries per se and involve questions related to service activities such as royalties and technology contracts. Although these are legitimate service industries issues, they are equally relevant to other industries. The importance of such issues is already perceived; and in time they are likely to be a major focus of international commercial problems. The process suggested above offers a means to begin to deal with them that might facilitate the overall process of working toward their resolution.

How would the work on building such codes actually proceed within the OECD structure itself? As for the industry-specific codes, the fillip for the process might be sparked by the current services work in the Trade Committee. Already the Trade Committee has referred specific sectoral problems and technical questions to existing committees having the competence to deal with industry-specific issues, such as the Insurance Committee. That will be a natural part of the process of building a framework to deal with services, even if it goes no further than that. However, industry-specific committee work, prompted and properly oriented by the Trade Committee, could evolve into an international code-building process. In the case of sectors needing such attention where no appropriate OECD committee exists, one would have to be created on a temporary or permanent basis for the purpose or dealt with within the Trade Committee or the Committee for Invisible Transactions.

As for the other code exercises suggested—where specific but nonsectoral problems like government procurement or subsidies are involved—the center of this kind of activity should remain with the Trade Committee. Although strengthening the invisible operations and capital movement codes would be carried out by the responsible committees, it, too, requires Trade Committee direction, consultation, and oversight. This is emphasized because I am persuaded that direction by the Trade Committee with its broader trade-oriented philosophy is a necessary element for success. Otherwise the exercise will become embroiled in the kind of technical excesses witnessed in the past in the Insurance Committee or will simply be stymied as it has been in the Committee for Invisible Transactions.

Although locating responsibility in the Trade Committee does not guarantee progress, it at least offers some insulation against elements that have frustrated past OECD efforts. It is not simply coincidental that the pressure inside the U.S. government to undertake an initiative within the OECD originated in the Special Trade Representative's Office as opposed to other government agencies intimately involved with the OECD, and it is noteworthy that the United States chose to initiate work on services in the Trade Committee and not in the Committee for Invisible Transactions.

Building a Framework for Services Through the Establishment of New Multilateral Institutions

GATT for Investment

A GATT for Investment is an idea being more frequently discussed. Before examining its relevance to services, I will briefly review the circumstances involving the proposed inclusion of international investment rules in the International Trade Organization (ITO) and then look at some of the shapes this idea has taken in recent years.

Discussions of an international agreement on direct foreign investment occurred in the drafting of the ITO Charter. In response to pressure from U.S. business groups, the U.S. representatives at the Geneva conference in August 1947 proposed the inclusion of an article on investment. Investment provisions were subsequently added, but because of their narrow scope, they were not acceptable to U.S. business. Many business leaders felt they could secure more protection under bilateral agreements.

State Department officials originally opposed the inclusion of foreign investment provisions since they were already having difficulty securing trade provisions acceptable to the U.S. Congress. The negotiation of an investment code, they felt, would be extremely complicated and possibly take several years. U.S. business groups insisted, however, that foreign investment was an important aspect of international commerce in which the United States, as the prime source of capital, played an important role. The business position prevailed in the negotiations.

Article 11 in the Havana Charter of the ITO obligated members not to take unreasonable or unjustifiable action injurious to the international investments of other members. Article 12 obligated members to give reasonable opportunities for investments and adequate security for existing and future investments. It also obligated members to negotiate commercial treaties on request but recognized that members have the right to set up the terms with respect to the ownership of existing and future investments. The charter did require, however, that these terms be "just and reasonable." It also allowed for the discussion of investment issues in the ITO and, at the insistence of any member, in the International Court of Justice.

Although U.S. business groups had advocated the inclusion of investment passages in the ITO Charter, they felt that in the final analysis the provisions that were included did not protect their interests. Their fundamental objections were that the provisions were vague and did not provide any protection against confiscation or discrimination by governments. Ultimately the entire ITO Charter was withdrawn from Congress when it became clear that it would not be ratified. Without U.S. support, the organization was never formed.

In recent years the idea of a GATT for Investment has been revived. In the following pages I sketch the basic concepts some notable experts have proposed during the 1970s. Their ideas cut across a wide spectrum—from an organization to analyze and discuss basic investment issues to the establishment of a new international organization regulating investment.

In 1967 George Ball proposed the creation of a supranational law under which all parents of global firms would be incorporated.[14] This law would include antimonopoly provisions and guarantees against uncompensated expropriation. But the prospects of achieving such an international treaty seem unlikely in the near future.

In 1970 Paul Goldberg and Charles Kindleberger recommended an international treaty similar to the existing GATT.[15] The authors saw problems in the differences that arise when the managerial decisions of a private multinational corporation are seen as detrimental to either the host or home country and in conflict with government policy. They proposed the formation of a General Agreement for the International Corporation. Initially, a preparatory committee would draft the principles and establish the organization to administer the agreement. The organization would deal only with problems related to the multinational corporation and disputes between two or more countries. It would investigate complaints by either countries or companies and make recommendations, with compliance being voluntary. The authors hoped that with a reputation for impartiality and thorough analysis the organization's decisions would be accepted voluntarily.

Seymour Rubin, an attorney who has represented the United States in the United Nations Commission on Transnational Corporations, proposed in 1971 that a very limited organization be established to analyze investment issues objectively and provide a forum for regular discussions.[16] Although recognizing the need for international cooperation on the problems posed by direct foreign investment, he was skeptical of the success of any international agreement. Rubin suggested that at least in its initial stages the proposed organization should be attached to an existing organization that has some concern with investment issues such as the OECD, UNCTAD, or United Nations Industrial Development Organization (UNIDO). On the substantive issues, Rubin proposed studying the nature of international production and its implications for world trade theory and national sovereignty. He also suggested examining the impact of multinational companies on developed and developing countries.

In 1972 J. N. Behrman proposed the formation of an Organization for International Industrial Integration to operate as a mechanism for a sectoral approach to economic integration.[17] The Goldberg-Kindleberger and the Rubin approaches, he stated, were unsatisfactory because they did not recognize that the new game was one of "international co-production," and the inherent problems could best be solved by "focusing sector-by-sector on the needs and objectives of nations in both industry and agriculture." In Behrman's view, the multinational firm, although the source of many problems for governments, does represent a "microcosm" for determining how international production operates.

Behrman's proposed organization is very different from GATT, somewhat resembling the North Atlantic Treaty Organization (NATO) in its coordination of the coproduction of weapons systems. The first steps for Behrman's organization would be the development of a few coproduction projects (obviously nonmilitary), possibly utilizing multinational firms, with the newly created organization having the responsibility for generating and operating the programs agreed upon by the members. Behrman ultimately saw this organization as assuming the responsibility for drafting guidelines governing the use of international corporations in coproduction projects. This differs dramatically from the preceding views in that firms are not just regulated but integrated into the production scheme determined by participating countries through multilateral agreements.

C. Fred Bergsten, assistant secretary for international affairs of the U.S. Treasury in the Carter administration, is coauthor with Thomas Horst and Theodore Moran of a book entitled *American Multinationals and American*

Interests, which outlined a proposed GATT for Investment.[18] In Bergsten's view, a new institution to deal with direct foreign investment would have a greater potential for success if it was a functionally independent organization dealing only with investment, rather than being part of a multipurpose organization. Furthermore, existing organizations, such as GATT and the International Monetary Fund (IMF), that deal with investment as a by-product of their primary concerns, would be hard to redirect to the objective at hand. Coordination with existing organizations would also be difficult, and given their divergent membership, none of them would be comprehensive enough to make a GATT for Investment feasible.

Organizational issues aside, Bergsten suggested that the organization parallel the development of GATT by beginning with a cease-fire agreement on incentives, disincentives, and performance requirements for direct investment. He noted that GATT first sought to halt the escalation of trade barriers and only in its second stage undertook the job of reducing them. In following this approach, the first step for the proposed organization would be a study of existing government policies toward direct foreign investment as well as the collection of data on multinational enterprises.

Bergsten pointed out several areas where international agreements are much needed. The coordination of taxation policy between home and host countries is one major area. In his view, a requirement for multinational firms to make public the data on their activities in all countries, together with the surveillance of transfer pricing by the organization, would alleviate much of the dispute over the allocation of income for tax purposes among countries where the firms operate. Other areas he suggested for multilateral government agreements include antitrust policy and performance criteria for firms.

Bergsten described "safeguard mechanisms" as the central feature of the direct foreign investment agreements. Such safeguards would prohibit all subsidies to induce investment by either home or host country, as well as prohibit barriers to foreign direct investment. Member countries that inhibited the flow of direct foreign investment would be subject to retaliation or compensation payments to injured countries.

Restriction of direct foreign investment by a member, in Bergsten's view, would only be allowed if it met an injury test (that is, if the investment is harmful to national security or the balance of payments), is an infant industry, or causes market disruption. Such exceptions have been criticized as rendering the agreements useless; but in his view this would not be the case, as member countries would have to justify such restrictions. Bergsten does not indicate what constitutes proof that an investment meets the injury test or who decides if the proof is in fact reasonable. Agreements on specific requirements of a proof of injury are at the very core of an effective agreement, and this is the issue that would be hardest to negotiate with a large number of countries.

In an unpublished article written for the Committee for Economic Development, Raymond Vernon envisioned not one but several international organizations to deal with the issues of direct foreign investment.[19] Vernon felt that a single organization cannot handle such a complex area, and agreements based on "overreaching ideological conceptions" are unrealistic at this time. For Vernon the only initiatives with a chance of success are those that are narrowly functional and address particular problems that are recognized as treatable by like-minded nations.

Vernon outlined several such areas that are conducive to international collaboration. Taxation of the international income of multinational enterprises is high on the list. The current proliferation of bilateral treaties in this area indicates that multilateral agreements could possibly be reached in the near future. Issues of market structure and performance (competition, monopoly, and efficiency) are also ripe for international agreements. Other issues for international coordination include aids to industry (import restrictions and export subsidies), problems of corporate disclosure (knowledge of the worldwide operations of firms), worker participation, and joint ventures, although, in Vernon's view, these latter issues are probably not ready for agreements in the near future. The best that can be hoped for are discussion, mutual education, and complaints raised through discussion in appropriate organizations.

Clearly, conceptualization on how to regulate international investment has evolved dramatically since the battle over the ITO. The latter had the rather limited objective of setting reasonable standards to encourage investment, whereas the ideas propounded today seek to regulate the multinational corporation, an entity that while already in existence during the ITO debate had neither the recognition nor importance it does today.

Services in a GATT for Investment. In any such scheme investments in services presumably would be as integral a part as nonservice investments. Incentives and disincentives to investment, restrictions, aid to industry, taxation policy, corporate disclosure, antitrust policy, and the various other elements that have been suggested as integral parts of a GATT for Investment generally are as relevant for service investments as for nonservice investments. Naturally, there are some aspects of international investment that have different implications when applied to services.

One issue, for example, is transfer pricing. To date, this controversial issue, whereby firms are charged with selling products to affiliates at variance with fair market value for tax avoidance purposes, has not centered on services to the same extent as it has on manufacturing. If taxation were included in the proposed regime, distinctions would probably have to be drawn for some services since, for example, financial services are often taxed differently from manufacturing. But probably there would also be the same differences among nonservice sectors as well. Further, there would unquestionably be selected sectors where governments would exclude or at least limit the authority of the regime.

As a general principle, however, there are no outstanding differences between international investment in services and investment in manufacturing, extractive, or agricultural industries that call for substantive distinctions in the handling of their international activities. Thus there should not be as much of a temptation to exclude service investments from a GATT for Investment scheme as there was to eliminate services trade from GATT itself.

Of the various schemes described above, those suggested by Bergsten and Vernon make the most sense. Although the end result should be something along the lines of the Bergsten proposal, Vernon's piecemeal approach of negotiating international agreements within limited areas that are politically acceptable seems a much more likely avenue for creating a GATT for Investment. Thus, strengthening and expanding the basic concepts that were laid down in the OECD agreement on international investment adopted in 1976 and merging them with the best ideas that emerge from discussions going on in other international forums could point the way to founding this new mechanism, which, over the long run, could establish principles, rules, and procedures governing service investments.

Clearly, this is not an idea that will materialize full-blown overnight, although it is now bandied about more frequently in international circles. There are encouraging signs, such as the proposed mini-GATT Round of negotiations to deal exclusively with tax questions. From a services perspective some of the investment-related ideas suggested earlier could play a contributory role in building the framework for a GATT for Investment.

One can make a persuasive case that there is greater urgency in devising international investment rules in the service sector than in other sectors, or that there should be. For one thing, the majority of service sector income originates from direct investment. For another, most of the major industries in the sector that operate internationally are highly regulated, and in many cases participation in these sectors is reserved to nationals or exclusively for the public sector. So the development of a regime governing international investment can be viewed only in a positive light as a step toward constructing principles to guide service commerce.

General Agreement on Services

If a GATT for Investment is only in the incubation stage, a GATT for Services is at an even remoter stage. Conceivably, it could evolve in several ways: out of efforts to integrate services into GATT or into a new GATT for Investment and a resultant conclusion that services as a whole, or at least the trading or investment aspect, would best be treated separately; from efforts, such as that suggested above for the OECD, whereby the process of coming to grips with service problems would lead to a consensus that a specialized framework is needed to deal with them; or because of a multifaceted services effort, both bilaterally and multilaterally, that leads to such continuous frustration and failure that a consensus develops for creating a General Agreement on Services.

Whether a general agreement would address itself to trade in services, investment in services, or both is a question that is best resolved according to the progress made beforehand. Limiting it to a mechanism governing only invest-ment or trade makes sense only if that particular kind of service activity differs substantially from other kinds of trade or investment and if it alone is not being dealt with in another multilateral institution. I have consistently argued that this distinction is basically false. For purposes of this exposition and in terms of my preference, if there is to be a General Agreement on Services, it should be one that regulates both trade and investment in services. In other words, it should regulate services as an economic activity unto itself and seek to address the kinds of issues indicated in our discussion of the inclusion of services in GATT, the OECD, and a GATT for Investment.

Let me clarify, however, what is meant by *services* in this context. Brian Griffiths has suggested that one way to remove constraints on invisible trade would be the adoption of a General Code on Invisibles and Capital Movements. Griffiths envisions such a code as including, inter alia, banking, insurance, com-modity trading, royalties, brokerage, tourism, civil aviation, shipping, and direct and portfolio investment. He is not talking about *services* in the same sense that it has been used throughout this study but, rather, is addressing himself to invis-ibles in general and is significantly broadening the existing OECD codes in terms of both industry coverage and substances.

The concept I am suggesting here, however, is a General Agreement on Services themselves and, perhaps eventually, the services provided by nonservice industries as well. Other issues, such as those concerned with technology trans-fer, might someday be included; but all invisibles transactions and nonservice direct investment itself would not.

The primary advantage of a General Agreement on Services would be that negotiations dealing with international trade and investment in services would be centered exclusively in one forum. The process of establishing such an insti-tution would in itself serve an educational purpose that over time could signifi-cantly improve the climate for liberalization. The major disadvantage of such a mechanism is that it might divert action from other institutions where progress is already being made in liberalizing services. It would most certainly delay the entire process of coming to grips with services unless it evolved out of already existing institutions.

The tone of this discussion reveals my firm conviction that centering such activity in any one approach or institution would be counterproductive—in fact, it would retard the process.

Other Possible Approaches

For lack of a cohesive generic classification, I have lumped together alter-native means for establishing a service framework other than through existing or yet-to-be-created multilateral institutions. They include bilateral mechanisms, regional cooperation, sectoral approaches, and combinations of some or all of the above. But as I suggested at the beginning of this review of how a program dealing with services might develop, they should not be considered as alternatives but rather as part of the overall process. In fact, often they will precede or at least run parallel with the process ongoing in the multilateral institutions. The end result of many of these approaches should be to encourage a broader multilateral approach.

Unilateral and Bilateral Approaches

Efforts to deal with services on a bilateral basis run the gamut from negotiating comprehensive agreements to discussions on problems confronting an individual service sector. But as our earlier review of previous bilateral efforts concluded, this approach has had only a minimal impact. Nevertheless, it does offer some possibilities. One is the inclusion of services in general bilateral commercial agreements. If this cannot be done specifically, they should be included by implication in the accompanying protocol arrangements or in the background discussions where the general terms governing such issues as nondiscrimination and national treatment are considered.

Another approach would be to deal with specific service sectors on a bilateral basis. One avenue might be the negotiation of bilateral agreements governing a specific service sector analogous to the more general Friendship, Commerce, and Navigation (FCN) bilateral agreements or the bilateral agreements governing trade in particular commodities.

Past experience suggests that the most effective approach—although again one having limited impact—is for governments to respond forcefully to discrimination by other governments against a particular service sector activity. If the United States, for example, feels that a nation is discriminating against the U.S. construction industry, it might initiate an effort to remove the constraints and buttress this action with the appropriate means available to it. This could involve a spectrum of approaches: seeking to conclude a bilateral agreement, retaliating or threatening to do so, or filing a complaint before an international institution if an appropriate one exists.

The success of such an initiative depends on the importance of the particular issue to both governments and on their willingness to negotiate a settlement. Traditionally, nations have tended to defend aggressively the international interests of their goods-producing and commodity industries, but only recently has any attention been given to services. This new-found interest is often centered on protecting national service sectors at home—not on removing restrictions overseas.

This book began with the general observation that the services sector has failed to organize itself as a viable political force. This explains why examples of strong government action being taken on behalf of a particular sector are so isolated. In competition with the interests of other sectors, services have invariably come out second-best. This will be a recurring pattern until their emerging economic importance is translated into political clout.

The primary reason for the failure of retaliatory efforts, when they occur, is the absence of effective leverage that might persuade a discriminating government to rescind its restrictions. As a general principle, many governments have a strong preference for avoiding retaliation altogether. They question its effectiveness and argue that if retaliatory restrictions must be imposed, they should be imposed in the same industry or at least in the same general sector. This requires the countries involved each to have important international interests in the same sector, which is seldom the case in the service sector, especially when developing countries are involved. In the U.S. Trade Act of 1974, the retaliatory provisions are not limited in this way: in responding to discrimination against a U.S. service industry, the president can retaliate against any economic activity, service or otherwise.

Although most government officials probably would shiver at the thought that it might become common practice to retaliate against trade and investment restrictions across industry sectors, its use by a major international trading country like the United States would gradually weaken the hesitation to take such steps. Speaking strictly in isolation from other policy considerations, and recognizing some of the inherent dangers of this approach, it would probably be a very effective way to erase impediments imposed by one or a limited number of countries.

If such incidents occur with increasing frequency, they are likely to encourage even those nations most hesitant to address services in a multilateral framework to reconsider their positions. In other words, a proliferation of bilateral service trade and investment disputes will be a spur to the kind of consensus building that makes the approaches suggested for GATT and the OECD more than a pipe dream.

Retaliation is perhaps the most viable means to deal with restrictions in the service sector levied by those countries that do not participate in the established international institutions or abide by the normal international commercial rules of the Western economic system. This refers primarily to the socialist countries, especially those that do not participate in GATT, the most important being the Soviet Union. Such action often offers the only means for relief from restraints imposed by such nations.

Implicit in this discussion is the recognition of a fine definitional line between what might be termed a *bilateral* as contrasted with a *unilateral* effort, with the latter being a recourse available only to those nations with such clout in a particular sector (and often in many sectors) that the actions they take singly affect international commerce in a sector. A recent example is the U.S. decision to liberalize rate setting of trans-Atlantic air traffic. As the opportunities as well as the liabilities of such action by great powers are few and far between, this step will be taken judiciously.

The bilateral approach must be weighed in terms of what it contributes to the establishment of an accepted framework within which to conduct service commerce. The implications for forceful unilateral action were suggested above. The inclusion of services in general bilateral commercial agreements also is a positive step toward establishing a legitimate basis for rules governing services. Any action that reinforces the concept that international commercial principles are as applicable to service transactions as to other kinds of transactions can only be encouraged. And the inclusion of services in one such agreement will encourage their inclusion in another.

Similarly, if bilateral sectoral service agreements are concluded, that, too, leave this responsibility entirely in governmental hands. Even if the United States and other governments were so committed to establishing international agreements on services that private sector initiative were unnecessary, this alone would not be sufficient to ensure progress. The private sector must continue to play the specific sectors. In fact, such agreements could even become a basis for the multilaterization of a bilateral understanding. On the other hand, restrictive agreements that restrain commerce in a service would have to be viewed negatively. In short, both the inclusion of specific services or services in general in bilateral agreements as well as the negotiation of bilateral service sector agreements themselves offer the opportunity to build a multilateral framework.

Regional Approaches

The sterling example of regional cooperation that has produced significant liberalization in services has occurred in the EEC. The most significant progress is that which has been realized in providing freedom of establishment (investment) across EEC members' borders for one major financial service—insurance—and launching the process to establish a similar arrangement for banking. Work is well along to provide freedom of service (trade) in insurance and eventually will be undertaken for banking. Further, the equivalent principle has been accepted and implemented for several professional services such as medicine. While the rules established to govern certain service sectors in the EEC put counterpart service interests outside it at a disadvantage in competing with EEC service sector industries, nevertheless, the results are positive on the whole. Furthermore, the EEC has in several instances provided the means to grant non-EEC services the same benefits as those in the EEC through bilateral agreements between it and third countries.

This contrasts sharply with the attitude prevailing in other regional bodies, which can be characterized not only as imposing restrictive prohibitions against services from outside the region but also as failing to provide liberalized commerce for services originating within the region. The exceptions, like the Association of Southeast Asian Nations (ASEAN), where the member nations are developing a regional service sector approach on shipping, are rare. Yet this is probably the most that can be expected since the other regional blocs are primarily composed of developing countries. Perhaps, over the long run, these sporadic spurts toward liberalizing service commerce, combined with a tendency to imitate the EEC, will encourage the development of more internationally oriented rules on services in these regional groupings.

As to the EEC, over time the goal should be to encourage the negotiation of bilateral arrangements with third countries so as to include as many nations and service sectors as possible as well as to negotiate similar bilateral arrangements with other regional blocs themselves. This could lead to the establishment of the equivalent of a code of conduct for one or more sectors. Eventually such arrangements even might begin to look like a General Agreement on Services if the bilateral arrangements cover not only freedom of establishment (investment) but freedom of services (trade) as well.

A proposal for this type of agreement in insurance has been suggested by Robert Carter and Gerald Dickinson in a study published by the Trade Policy Research Centre.[20] Their goal is to establish an internationally accepted solvency agreement similar to the agreement on the operation of non-life insurance firms within the EEC. The proposed agreement would allow firms from all subscribing countries to freely establish themselves in other countries that adhere to it.

The EEC experiment is unique. It should be viewed as a practical laboratory, a testing ground that will be invaluable and instructive in designing and implementing a services regime. In the long term, the EEC agreements can only enhance the establishment of broader international understandings on services. They prove that formidable problems complicated by technical disputes are surmountable. The long process that was necessary to reach this point in the EEC offers invaluable experience for other such efforts. For example, if the OECD begins to grapple with the right of establishment or trade in services, the EEC experience will be of immeasurable value.

CONCLUSION

The establishment of accepted principles to govern international commerce in services is an evolutionary process that has already begun in a small way. Though most of the steps taken in this direction are recent, the momentum is gaining with surprising rapidity if considered from the perspective of the time frame normally required to establish a consensus to undertake fundamental changes in the international economic system. From the time I first became interested in this subject when the U.S. Trade Act of 1974 was adopted, and especially during the past two years, the awareness of policy makers toward services has improved dramatically. The best evidence of this development is the decision by the U.S. government—and the initial reluctant acquiescence of other major countries—to introduce service issues into the work of two major international economic institutions: the GATT and the OECD. Though it can be argued with some justification that the last-minute U.S. initiative in GATT was nothing but a belated response to congressional and industry pressure, nevertheless, it did occur. I have suggested on several occasions that response to pressure groups, after all, is a major determinant in the formulation of policy. The OECD initiative, however, was an independent executive branch initiative, sparked primarily by the failure to achieve much for services in the multilateral trade negotiations. It was not an alternative suggested or even particularly encouraged by industry or Congress.

The case should not be overstated: the results have been minimal and there is a wide chasm between forcing policy maker recognition of services and the emergence of policy consensus. Further, the process that has begun is almost wholly limited to the United States. But this is not unimportant since U.S. leadership has been necessary for most other international initiatives in the past 40 years.

An earlier draft of this chapter suggested a process of building a framework for international services commerce that was basically a shotgun approach. In other words, I envisioned pursuit of the process in numerous institutions and by a mix of the various alternative approaches suggested throughout this chapter. Ironically, with certain qualifications, this is not far off the mark from the way things have developed. The process that seems to be getting under way is compatible with my view on the only feasible means to accomplish this task.

The most efficacious means to foster acceptance of international principles governing services commerce is through the integration of service issues into continuing international commercial discussions and negotiations. The objective should be to make them an integral part of the major international institutions concerned with commerce. Substantively and sequentially, this means services discussions should go along the same track as the work program of nonservices. Trade issues in services should therefore be addressed in the multilateral forums, and they should precede investment questions. This is precisely what is happening in the two major international organizations where work on services is under way. The work in GATT theoretically can deal only with trade matters because of the nature of the institution. The new initiative in the OECD Trade Committee is initially limited in theory to studying impediments to international trade in services. As it proceeds, however, the nature of the impediments uncovered will of necessity involve investment issues in the process.

So the process has at least begun. Keeping it on track is the challenge. This will require decisive leadership, which, I am convinced, must come from the United States initially and for a long time to come. But it would be a mistake to leave this responsibility entirely in governmental hands. Even if the U.S. and other governments were so committed to establishing international agreements on services that private sector initiative were unnecessary, this alone would not be sufficient to ensure progress. The private sector must continue to play the same kind of active role that provided the impetus to launch the initiatives now under way.

However, it would be a mistake to assume there is unanimity or consensus among service industries. The perspective of the service sector in the United

States, where most of the activity has occurred, illustrates the diverse views of various service industries. A few services have been at the forefront of the initiative to introduce services into international commercial discussions. Others have been opposed to the process, and some have not been involved at all. Some believe that only by having services treated as a group will there be sufficient clout to achieve much. Others who already have established political power see this initiative as weakening their impact and perhaps as forcing liberalization of cartelized arrangements. But within these sectors themselves there is also a division of opinion.

In recent years an understanding of sorts has begun to take shape among service interests. The general consensus is that although it is desirable for service industries to come together as a group to lobby the U.S. government to consider their concerns, governmental action should not necessarily always be taken on behalf of services as a group. In some cases, action on behalf of a wide spectrum of service industries might be appropriate. In other instances unilateral action on behalf of a service—be it in multilateral institutions encompassing a broad range of issues, in industry-specific forums, or in country-to-country discussions—may be necessary.

Whatever the approach, only service industries themselves can force their respective governments—and thereby ultimately international institutions—to deal with these issues. Those concerned should remain alert for opportunities to do so. For example, earlier I discussed the need to test the applicability to services of the new GATT codes on government procurement and subsidies. Testing these codes will require service sectors with grievances to press their governments to bring their cases before the respective GATT consultative committees established to administer the codes.

In the United States, a forceful means for eliciting attention is through utilization of the redress offered by the unfair trade provisions of the Trade Act of 1974. Filing complaints under the act forces the U.S. government and the country against which the complaint is levied to focus on the problem. Such actions have potential spillover effects that could broaden their impact. For example, as stated earlier, the pressures resulting from such cases encourage governments to seek less contentious remedies, such as those that might be found through multilateralizing issues in international organizations such as GATT and the OECD.

In an earlier chapter, I noted the failure of policy making to consider services in much of its analysis and the resultant fallout in policy decisions and implementation. Services industries should search out every occasion to point up these shortcomings. In the U.S. context some of the issues being debated in Washington offer opportunities that should not be missed. One is the tug-of-war over reorganization of the U.S. foreign economic policy apparatus. Whatever the long-term outcome of this struggle, it offers the chance to dramatize the lack of policy attention to relevant service issues. For example, if the reorganization debate offers opportunities to illustrate how services are omitted from the policy process, this will help create a recognition that goes beyond the United States and could have international implications.

The debate over where to house the administration of the subsidies/countervailing duty mechanism in government offered service industries an opportunity to point out that relevant U.S. legislation does not include services, and, therefore, a remedy for subsidies affecting U.S. services is unavailable. The debate over export promotion mechanisms such as the U.S. Domestic International Sales Corporation (DISC), a tax incentive to U.S. exporters, offered the opportunity to point out that, with but a few exceptions, services are excluded from the benefits of such legislation. Both are issues that ultimately need to be dealt with at an international level.

A final illustration of where those with the most at stake in this dialogue, service industries, themselves, can take the initiative to place services on international agendas is found in the bilateral and multilateral dialogues carried on in nongovernmental organizations. This includes prominent private sector institutions such as the International Chamber of Commerce, as well as bilateral business and economic councils established among various national and regional groupings. The U.S. business community, for example, has established bilateral groups with the EEC, Japan, Canada, ASEAN, and various other nations and regional blocs. In recent years, service issues have been mooted in these groups, and in several instances working subgroups on services have been established.

Even given the persistence of concerned private and public sectors alike, at some point and probably on more than one occasion, highly visible and dramatic international attention will be necessary to mobilize action. This will be appropriate only after much of the groundwork has been prepared through an improvement in the knowledge, data, and general understanding of services. What will be required long term is something equivalent to a Tokyo Round on services.

What I have in mind in the relative short term is something like the Rey Group on Trade and Related Problems, that is, the establishment, but with much fanfare, of a high-level expert group on services. If convoked at the proper time and with proper orchestration, its impact could be dramatic. The OECD is an appropriate institution to house such an initiative. Not only is there precedence in the OECD, but it is especially appropriate because of the growing cooperation among OECD members in recent years in coordinating their policies. Such a high-level group, drawing upon the findings of the OECD Trade Committee and other institutional work, would have the mandate of determining what problems exist in services, devising a system to encourage negotiation, and suggesting steps to ensure adherence to agreements resulting from negotiation.

The establishment of such a group under OECD auspices again raises the issue as to the place of the developing countries in the various approaches. Throughout this discussion, both the considerable impediments to services commerce imposed by these nations and the seeming lack of incentive for joining in the process of establishing principles to govern services commerce have been noted. It would be mistaken, however, to assume that this statement applies universally to all developing nations. Some already have vigorous sectors of service sector activity successfully competing in international markets.

A strategy dilemma that merits careful appraisal is when and how to involve developing nations in this process. Some would argue that their early involvement will only retard the process. Besides, the institutions where the early work will be done are dominated by industrial nations, and in the case of the OECD, it is exclusively an industrial nation club. My instinct is to favor their involvement fairly early in the process. This will help discourage a hardening of their willingness to participate by being brought in after the fact. This means their inclusion in most phases—be it in the establishment of a high-level expert group to consider services or in the consultative committees that will administer and develop the applicability of the new GATT codes for services. Clearly, however, this involvement must be carefully managed. Special treatment will have to be considered for many developing nations, as I suggested when I described proposed principles to govern services commerce. But across-the-board preferential consideration should not be expected. Instead, individual nations should be examined in light of their particular situation in each aspect of services commerce. The long-term goal should be their compliance with the rules established. Achievement of this will require frequent reexamination of exceptions granted to the general principles established.

This concluding chapter on what regimes governing international commerce in services would look like has considered various approaches to achieving this end. Ironically, though many economic sectors argue their uniqueness in order to secure special treatment, those favoring liberalizing services commerce are forced to argue the similarity of services with the rest of international commerce to make their case. This concept should be repeated one last time. The one overriding principle that can be derived from the discussion is that services are not residuals or freaks on the international economic scene that must be dealt with in a way uniquely different from other kinds of commerce. Such argumentation is a canard put forth by those who either do not understand international services activities or do not want to. The slogans that have clouded our understanding of services, both domestically and in the international economy, should no longer prevent an objective and dispassionate involvement in the issues arising from the emergence of a global service economy.

NOTES

1. Wassily Leontief et al., *The Future of the World Economy*, A United Nations Study (New York: Oxford University Press, 1977).

2. Organization for Economic Cooperation and Development (hereafter OECD), *Trade in Services (Notes by the Secretariat)*, Trade Committee of the OECD (Paris: OECD, March 22, 1979), p. TC(79)5.

3. OECD, *Guidelines Governing the Protection of Privacy and Transborder Data Flows of Personal Data* (Paris: OECD, 1980), p. C(80)58(Final) Annex.

4. U.S., Congress, House, General Agreement on Tariffs and Trade (hereafter GATT),

Multilateral Trade Negotiations, Group "Non-Tariff Measures," Subgroup "Government Procurement," House Document 96153, Part I, 96th Cong., 1st sess. (Washington, D.C.: Government Printing Office, April 11, 1979), MTN/NTM, W/211/Rev. 2.

5. GATT, Multilateral Trade Negotiations, Group "Non-Tariff Measures," Subgroup "Customs Matters," "Agreement on Interpretation and Application of Articles VI, XVI, and XXIII of the General Agreement on Tariffs and Trade" (Geneva: GATT, 1979), MTN/NTM/W/236; pp. 37, 38.

6. U.S., Department of Commerce, *U.S. Service Industries in World Markets*, 902-720 (Washington, D.C.: Government Printing Office, 1976).

7. Brian Griffiths, *Invisible Barriers to Invisible Trade* (London: Macmillan Press, 1975), pp. 87-90.

8. Ambassador Alonzo McDonald, "The Tokyo Round: Launching a New Economic Consensus" (Address given by the Deputy Special Representative for Trade Negotiations and chief of the U.S. Delegation to the Tokyo Round, to the Foreign Affairs Club, London, February 2, 1978).

9. U.S., International Communications Agency interview, *Askew on U.S. Trade Policy* (United States International Communications Agency, Interview, 1980).

10. "Brock Urges Service Industries to Export," press release of the Office of the United States Trade Representative, Executive Office of the President, Washington, D.C., April 20, 1981, p. 2.

11. The Contracting Parties to the GATT, 1969, *General Agreement on Tariffs and Trade, Basic Instruments and Selected Documents*, vol. 4 (Geneva: GATT, March 1969), preamble, p. 1.

12. Griffiths, *Invisible Barriers to Invisible Trade*, p. 95.

13. Ibid., p. 98.

14. George Ball, "Cosmocorp: The Importance of Being Stateless," *Columbia Journal of World Business*, November-December 1967, pp. 25-30.

15. Paul Goldberg and Charles Kindleberger, "Toward a GATT for Investment: A Proposal for Supervision of the International Corporation," *Law and Policy in International Business* 2 (1970): 295-325.

16. Seymour Rubin, "Multinational Enterprise and National Sovereignty: A Skeptic's Analysis," *Law and Policy in International Business* 3 (1971): 1-41.

17. J. N. Behrman, "Sharing International Production through the Multinational Enterprise and Sectoral Integration," *Law and Policy in International Business* 4 (1972): 1-37.

18. C. Fred Bergsten, Thomas O. Horst, and Theodore H. Moran, *American Multinationals and American Interests* (Washington, D.C.: Brookings Institution, 1978).

19. Raymond Vernon, "Interdependence: Its Implications for the Industrial Policies of the United States" (Article prepared for the Committee for Economic Development, Washington, D.C., 1978).

20. Robert L. Carter and Gerard M. Dickinson, *Barriers to Trade in Insurance*, Thames Essay no. 19 (London: Trade Policy Research Centre, 1979).

BIBLIOGRAPHIC APPENDIX

STUDIES ON INTERNATIONAL SERVICES

It would be misleading to imply that until now no examinations of the international aspects of services have been undertaken. The U.S. Trade Act of 1974, as previously discussed, provided authority to seek liberalization of services. The inclusion of such provisions in the act clearly was not based on anything but the most simplistic understanding of services and their international implications. The Department of Commerce study *U.S. Service Industries in World Markets* was an effort to understand U.S. services in international commerce so as to respond to this mandate.

This study is unquestionably the most comprehensive look ever taken at a nation's international service sector—its characteristics, significance, problems, and the mechanisms to address these problems. The study concluded that the U.S. international service sector was more important now than previously recognized and would probably be even more so in the future. It suggested a broad set of governmental initiatives to redress overseas barriers that inhibit U.S. service sector expansion. Although none of the remedies suggested is startling or particularly innovative, one is rather surprised considering the supposed prejudice of the study's authors. This is the proposal that service industry issues, where appropriate, should be introduced in trade negotiations.

Other organizations have also begun to look at services. The United Nations Commission on Transnational Corporations in 1978 began a series of studies on the activities of multinational corporations in services such as banking, advertising, and insurance and, more recently, began to examine data transmission questions. The United Nations Conference on Trade and Development (UNCTAD) has over the past 13 years examined service industries such as insurance, shipping, and tourism and issued innumerable reports and recommendations on these subjects. For the most part, the studies have not been well grounded empirically and have focused on what developing countries can do to develop these sectors in their national markets.

The London-based Trade Policy Research Centre has approached the service industry issues from a broader, longer range international policy perspective. The center has suggested it is necessary for governments to broaden their international economic conceptualizations and move into those matters falling somewhere "between the international trading system and the international monetary system." By this, it refers to services or invisibles in the broadest sense, including not only services themselves—such as financial, transport, and insurance services—but international investment as well. In this category, the center focuses on the capital flows relating to investment, including interest, dividends, profits, and royalties. The core concern of the center's studies is in understanding the complex relationships of commercial and monetary policies linked together. At the beginning of the 1980s, numerous other institutions began to consider this subject. The International Chamber of Commerce established a Services Committee to address the subject. It commissioned a foreign senior U.K. trade official, Sidney Golt, to work in the field, and he is drawing upon the Trade Policy Research Centre for much of its resource work. The German Marshall Fund of the United States and the Rockefeller Foundation jointly sponsored two services research conferences in conjunction with the Trade Policy Research Center, one on each side of the Atlantic; they, joined with other institutions, are expected to fund a series of research projects arising out of these conferences. A Ditchley Foundation Conference was held in May 1980, a Bologgia meeting in March 1981, and the Council on Foreign Relations established a Discussion Group on Services during 1980/81.

LITERATURE ON DEFINITION OF *SERVICES*

In reviewing the literature on services, one finds that early writers seem to have had no major problems with defining *services*. Colin Clark, in his classic study *The Conditions of Economic Progress*, said "service industries" naturally group themselves into "building and construction; transport and communications; commerce and finance; professional services; public administration and defense; and personal services." He cautioned that only for national accounting purposes was it necessary to distinguish between services supplied directly to the final purchaser and those that are used to assist in production, such as the transportation of goods, wholesale trading, and the services of accountants.

However, as more attention has been given to services, recognition of definitional difficulties have become more commonplace. More than 20 years ago George J. Stigler wrote, "There exists no authoritative consensus on either the boundaries or the classification of service industries." Victor R. Fuchs, perhaps currently the leading expert on service industries, noted that later studies have given us no reason to challenge Stigler's conclusion since some include transportation, communications, and public utilities in the service sector while others exclude these industries; others include transportation and communications but exclude public utilities.

Fuchs further observed that even within the work of a single author there is variation. For example, Simon Kuznets included transportation, communications, and public utilities in his early service sector work but excluded them in his later work. Gur Ofer did likewise in his look at services in the Soviet Union. In his own book, Fuchs defines *services* as including wholesale and retail trade, finance, insurance, real estate, general government (including the military in most instances), and the services "traditionally so designated," including professional, personal, business, and repair services, but excludes what he calls the "service subsector," that is, "government, households and institutions and real estate." Thus while noting the difficulties in definition, Fuchs compounds the confusion.

Yves Sabolo (with J. Gaude and R. Wery), in his excellent study for the International Labour Office, suggests an intriguing definitional approach. He distinguishes between service and nonservice sectors according to their role in production. He does this by dividing economic activities into primary and nonprimary categories as follows:

Primary sector: agriculture, stock raising, and fisheries; and

Nonprimary sectors: activities involving an intensive use of capital and skills—mining, modern industry, water, light, and transport; activities involving little use of capital and skills—construction, handicraft industries, trade, and personal services; and activities involving heavy use of skills—banking, insurance, finance, government services, community services, and business services.

Sabolo concludes, however, that this system is not well suited to his study because each of the three nonprimary sectors defined by use of capital and skills includes service industries. That in itself says a lot about the problems associated with definitions of *services*: they cut across a wide spectrum of economic functions, employing varying degrees of capital and technology. This is in striking contrast to the commonly accepted mythology about services.

Sabolo finally resorts to what he calls the classic division into three sectors of economic activity—primary, secondary (manufacturing), and tertiary (service), including in the latter: commerce; transport, storage, and communications; financing, insurance, real estate, and business services; community, social, and personal services; and activities "not adequately defined." This so-called classic definition is used by the United Nations in its International Standard Industrial Classification of all Economic Activities.

Some of the characteristics of service industries that have attracted attention are the following: they tend to be labor intensive; they tend to have a more-than-average proportion of self-employed workers; they employ a more-than-average proportion of female and part-time labor; there are often difficulties in defining a physical measure of output; and conventional methods of measurement may give a distorted view of the value of services.

Clearly, we are without a universally accepted theoretical framework for either defining or classifying *services*. There are two basic approaches. The most common is based on the commonality of the end product, that is, something intangible. If the firm does not produce a physical product, it is a service industry, and if it does produce a physical product, it is a manufacturing, extractive, or agricultural firm. This concept is usually linked to the idea that services, being intangible, cannot be stored or shipped as goods can. (Unfortunately, this concept implies—and indeed has left in the minds of many—that services cannot be traded in international commerce.) A corollary to this definitional approach is that in many services, as contrasted with other economic activities, the output and the production processes are intimately linked; in fact, they are inseparable or one and the same. A further definitional criterion of a service that follows from the above is the degree to which the particular activity is distant from, or close to, the consumer. Being close to the ultimate consumer implies a service because the production process, the product, and its consumption are closely linked. Thus services generally have a relatively short life-span because they must be produced when and where they are consumed. Presumably, this makes them difficult to import or export.

The second approach is to classify services as a residual sector. This is often applied to a miscellaneous collection of industries that clearly are not in agriculture, mining, or manufacturing. In other words, it is a negative classification based on what does not fit into other categories. Clearly, this is only a classification and not a true definition.

There are obvious problems associated with these approaches. For example, retail trade is usually classified as a service, yet it deals with physical products. The same can be said of construction in that the final result is a tangible. The idea of storage generally holds up, if motion pictures are excluded, but it does not add much clarity to the issue. Can an insurance policy be stored or is insurance simply the protection involved? Similarly, the short time span of services is questionable in many instances. The following are but a few examples of many having a long life-span—insurance services (especially life insurance), banking services (such as mortgage loans), and leasing services.

The idea of a residual sector is troublesome, primarily because of the difficulty of distinguishing between major sectors. For example, are utilities a service or manufacturing industry? Similarly, aspects of construction and publishing include both services and manufacturing. Alfred Marshall alluded to this problem as early as 1929 when he noted that virtually all industries produce services because "man cannot create material things."

Further, some of the classic characteristics of services, such as closeness to the consumer, labor intensiveness, low capital requirement, short time span, and low technology, may be becoming less and less appropriate as the service sector grows more complex.

One, thus, is ultimately forced to conclude that service industries encompass an extremely heterogeneous grouping of economic sectors with different production processes, customers, supplies, and market channels and thus often have little in common other than that their principal outputs are for the most part intangible. After ploughing through enough theoretical considerations such as these, one can easily understand why anyone examining services would ultimately choose to define *services* by selecting those definitions that best fit his purposes. I, like Fuchs and many others, ultimately was forced into accepting a classification-of-services approach without too much regard to definitions (although implicitly definitional considerations go into the classification process).

One may ask, What is the purpose of an examination of definitional difficulties, especially if no meaningful conclusions can be reached as to how *services* should be defined? Primarily, it is intended to provide an appreciation of, and a defense for, some of the problems that have arisen in this book.

THE TRADITIONAL THEORY OF SERVICE SECTOR DEVELOPMENT RECONSIDERED

As Chapter 4 indicates, developing countries are captive to the traditional theories of economic development. These theories were for the most part developed by industrial country economists, based on their interpretation of how the industrial world developed. Services fit in this body of thought as a tertiary industry that evolves into importance after nations have gone through two earlier stages of development—agricultural followed by industrialization. This generally accepted theory is seldom challenged or submitted to meaningful scrutiny. At best, it may be reluctantly admitted that there is a gap in economic thought in that there is no real understanding of service industries themselves. Colin Clark in his book *The Conditions of Economic Progress* stated it very well when he said, "The economics of tertiary industry remain to be written. Many as yet feel uncomfortable about even admitting their existence."

Although it is beyond the scope of this study to examine the economics of tertiary or service industries or to challenge accepted dogma about economic development, I will raise some basic issues deserving further research and thinking.

Those who would reexamine classical thinking about services are easily deterred, be it by their own prejudices, modalities of the time, or practical difficulties. Classical economists like Adam Smith believed that only the primary and secondary industries were productive and others were in some sense parasitic (a view also identified with Marxist thinking on services). This view is encouraged by the fact that much tertiary production tends to be nonprofit, while classic economic analysis has tended to focus on market activities. Also economic analysis has concentrated most heavily on production, more often associated with goods, not distribution, which is itself a service. Thus it is not surprising that the tertiary section is often characterized as residual, that is, that which does not fit into the "more important" sectors. Another reason why services are ignored is the difficulty of obtaining service data, aggravated by the fact that many services operate on a small scale. Further, it is difficult to measure service output; yet output and productivity are one of the fields that economists favor.

The classical explanation of the tertiary sector, the Fisher-Clark theory, while popularly accepted, is often misinterpreted. The heart of the hypothesis is that nations evolve into tertiary or service societies because of increases in per capita income. So as individual incomes rise, more of this income is spent on services than goods. This perceives a causal relationship between income levels and the development of services. Thus the expectation is that richer societies will become service societies.

Although this is really all that Fisher and Clark said, over the years the theory has been generalized to the point that economies are seen as evolving through three basic stages of economic development, almost like natural or inevitable economic evolution. In the third stage societies become service oriented because of the high level of development, complexity, urbanization, and sophistication. But although such societies tend to be richer, higher per capita incomes per se (witness some oil-producing countries)—in the absence of other ingredients—will not automatically develop service economies.

The theory is empirical only to the extent that the research is based on the economic development of developed countries. There has been little research on the validity of the theory in today's developing countries. And it should not be forgotten that empirical data are sorely lacking to justify the interpretations of how developed countries became developed. It could be argued that an examination of today's developing countries, where there are admittedly distressing gaps in data, would still surpass the historical evidence available on economic development in general and on services specifically. Below is a brief review of the evidence available in selected developing countries to see if the development of their service sectors is compatible with the classical view.

In Chapter 2 a surprising amount of evidence was accumulated to indicate that in many developing countries service sector activities are much more important than anticipated. Some studies, most dramatically that done by Wassily Leontief for the United Nations, foresaw services playing an increasingly important role. Yves Sabolo, in a 1975 published study for the International Labour Organization entitled *The Service Industries*, traces service industry development in selected developing countries back to the beginning of this century. In the countries he studied—Argentina, Brazil, Chile, Egypt, India, Japan, Mexico, the Philippines, Portugal, Spain, Sri Lanka, and Turkey—all except Portugal had at the beginning of the century (1900-10) a larger proportion of the labor force— 20 percent on the average—absorbed by the tertiary sector than the secondary sector. Sabolo continues his study up to 1960-70 and finds that in all the above countries except India the proportion of service sector employment as compared with other sectors has remained almost constant while the share of employment of the primary sector has declined. The service sector has absorbed most of the labor influx coming from the primary or agricultural sectors to the secondary and tertiary sectors.

Kuznets examined the association between product per capita and the share of services in gross domestic product (GDP) with the assumption that as product per capita goes up, the importance of services in terms of GDP grows. He found that only certain services—transport, real estate, and financial services— had a positive association. A 1960 study by H. B. Chenery entitled *Patterns of Industrial Growth*, using 51 different countries, reached the same conclusion. The Organization for Economic Cooperation and Development (OECD) study *Service Activities in Developing Countries* found a higher percentage of services in developing countries having low per capita incomes. In general, the study found high percentages of output and employment related to services in developing countries. In Argentina, for example, in the capital city of Buenos Aires service output accounts for over 60 percent of total production; it accounts for 45 percent for the country as a whole.

M. A. Katouzian has perhaps shed the most light in explaining the importance of services in countries in differing developmental stages through a sophisticated amplification of the classic Fisher-Clark thesis. He does this by disaggregating the service sector into subdivisions, which gives a better understanding of the sector and demonstrates that different divisions of the sector will develop at different times and in different phases of economic development. He categorizes these kinds of services as follows. First are the "new services," which are highly related to the growth of per capita incomes and the amount of per capita leisure time. They include education, consumption of modern medical services, entertainment, and travel. Second are the "complementary services," which he describes as those responsive to the process of industrialization. These expand in response to demands created by goods production. Examples are banking, finance, transportation, and wholesale and retail trade. In category three are the "old services," which flourished before industrialization and whose importance and contribution have declined continuously ever since. Examples are domestic services, street services, and personal services. Katouzian, too, notes that the share of services in many underdeveloped countries is already quite large in terms of labor force and national production.

From the above analysis we can conclude that there are numerous countries in various stages of development in which services play an important role. Therefore, the Fisher-Clark thesis is subject to challenge since services often play an important role even when there have not been substantial increases in per capita income. Various observers offer their own explanations as to why services may play a major role even at low levels of income and in developing societies. And we can come up with a few of our own. For example, E. J. Stigler in his 1956 study entitled *Trends in Employment in the Service Industries* cited urbanization, specialization, technological change, income distribution, and the population-age structure as important factors. The OECD study on developing country service activities ruled out per capita GNP as being determinative and instead emphasized urbanization, labor productivity, and industrial expansion.

While various authors cite urbanization as a primary reason explaining the importance of services in developing countries, their interpretations differ. Sabolo explained it as a result of rural migration to urban areas with migrants entering tertiary industries, both because the lack of other industries leaves few alternatives and because the supply of people creates the need for services. By using a logarithmic regression analysis he established a strong correlation between the growth of the service sector and increased urbanization and population growth. However, he observed a residual function with some service sector growth occurring even without changes in the other two factors. Sabolo discovered a "critical threshold" for both population and income levels necessary to spur expansion of the service sector. For better or worse, he saw population growth and urbanization as worldwide trends; so dramatic expansion of the service sector is to be expected in developing countries reaching the critical thresholds.

The OECD study suggested that linkages between service growth and urbanization may occur because many persons in urban areas can afford services owing to relatively high income; also rapid urban growth increases the need for social services like education and health. Whatever the explanation, the study drew a definite correlation between urbanization and growth in output and employment in the service sector.

The most significant observation to be made here is that urbanization alone, in the absence of industrialization, can have a major impact on service development. There has been a tendency to equate urbanization with industrialization, which gives credence to the classical theory of economic development by associating service sector growth with industrialization. However, as Latin America and other developing areas illustrate, there have been mass migrations to the cities with industrialization often lagging far behind.

Industrialization in itself frequently is mentioned as an important factor influencing tertiary employment. W. Galanson in an article entitled "Economic Development and the Sectoral Expansion of Employment" concluded that the growth of manufacturing could be a very dynamic factor in the generation of new employment in the service sector of developing countries. Using regression models he found a substantial multiplier effect in tertiary industries from a given increase in the number of workers in manufacturing.

Perhaps the most accepted explanation for growth in service sector employment is the lack of productivity in services. Victor Fuchs's reputation was established by outstanding research in this field. He argues persuasively that the main explanation for the rapid increase in service employment is a lower increase in output per worker in the service sector compared with agriculture or industry. However, Fuchs's analysis is based entirely on the U.S. economy during the 40-year period beginning in 1929. Thus its universal applicability is subject to question.

One similarity between the Fuchs study of the U.S. economy and studies on other economies is that whereas services tend to start off at relatively high levels of productivity, over time this productivity tends to decline, especially in industrial countries. This supports Fuchs's view that the shift to services in the United States has been in employment terms, not in output.

Sabolo refutes this thesis, at least as applied to developing nations. Using United Nations statistics to support his case, he argues that there have been rapid productivity increases in developing country service industries and equivalent productivity increases among secondary and tertiary industries. He does admit some declines in service output over time in developing countries, which is compatible with Fuchs's work on the U.S. economy.

Interesting noneconomic explanations for the growth of services are given by Katouzian. He argues that in many developing countries the role of the state is much more substantial than it was in the West prior to industrialization. This leads to highly bureaucratic institutions that compel governments to be the primary provider of services. It produces large military and governmental establishments, whose employees all are classified in the service sector. Even in countries where the state does not play such a substantial role, governments will assume responsibility for directing accelerated economic development and general welfare. This expanded involvement of government encourages an increase in service production and employment.

A second reason Katouzian offers to explain service growth is the existence of disguised unemployment in services, brought about by lack of alternative employment, misguided government policies, and the like. Also, in selected developing countries such as Iran and Lebanon, he asserts that the middle classes have traditionally been involved more in wholesale and retail trade than production. This tradition, buoyed by the demand for new services, encourages these classes to involve themselves in import trade to meet the rising demand for more products and services, so that this sector of the economy becomes even more important. Another reason for service growth results from what Katouzian calls the learning effect, meaning that certain activities in industrial countries, such as modern clinical services and general hygiene, set an example for imitation in the developing world. This same demonstration effect also leads those of higher incomes to imitate the more sophisticated services of the industrial world such as use of leisure time.

Finally, Katouzian cites a more internationally related (except for the learning effect) reason for service sector development—the principle of comparative advantage. He argues that the general rise in the volume of British invisible trade in the nineteenth century in shipping, banking, finance, and insurance was mainly due to comparative advantage and that there are analogous examples found in many developing countries today. In tourism development, he argues that countries in the Mediterranean and Pacific, for example, have a comparative advantage in their resources of natural beauty and low labor cost.

All of these explanations are probably accurate at one time or another. To me, the most persuasive explanation for the surprising importance of services in many developing countries is the goal orientation of developing countries. Today in a developing country, either demand by the populace or leadership consciousness exercises a strong pressure to supply services—services that historically would seem to be associated with higher levels of income and more advanced development. This is reinforced by the demonstration effect imported from abroad, which will further influence local attitudes.

FRAMEWORK OF IMPEDIMENTS FOR USE IN COMPILATION OF IMPEDIMENTS TO TRADE IN SERVICES

1. *Legal establishment*
   —denial of access to market by prohibition upon the importation of a service from outside the country of reference;
   —denial of access to market by prohibitions upon establishment of local operations by a foreign service firm;
   —prohibition upon foreign investment in a particular service industry;

- limitations on foreign equity or on the amount of foreign capital allowed for initial establishment; minority holding requirement applies to foreign investors in a service industry; and
- restrictions upon or procedural impediments to the formal process of setting up of a permitted business operation (incorporating a subsidiary, and so on), including discrimination, procedural delay, and so on.

2. *Local purchasing requirements*
- restrictions on importation or access to equipment needed in the operation of a service enterprise;
- requirement that land and equipment be leased rather than purchased by foreign-controlled companies;
- requirement that limits user's choice of service firms—obligatory or forced use of national firms for service procurement; and
- requirement that a portion of a service transaction be placed with or through a local private firm or government facility.

3. *Marketing and selling*
- prohibition or restriction upon the marketing level of sales of a service by a foreign firm;
- requirements that local sales organizations be used by foreign firms;
- restrictions on contractual freedom prices and charges, or exclusivity rights;
- selling below cost by government-owned service companies in local or other international markets; and
- interference with advertising or other communication processes related to a service business.

4. *Access to public sector markets*
- government procurement procedures that effectively limit government contract access to local firms;
- absence of detailed government procurement rules and procedures; and
- failure to enforce existing rules governing procurement.

5. *Personnel*
- discriminatory requirements—employment bans or quotas based upon nationality, race, and religion;
- difficulty in obtaining visas, residency permits, or work permits;
- discriminatory wage controls; and
- limitations upon movement of personnel; unreasonable barriers to movement of personal property.

6. *Foreign government regulatory procedures*
- failure to extend national treatment to foreign service industry operations;
- problems in gaining access to local officials, regulations, courts, and so on to file disputes or resolve problems, or the existence of biased procedures once access has been obtained;

—absence of easily attainable information on local government policies and procedures;
—discrimination or delays in the allocation of government-controlled resources or government facilities necessary to a services operation;
—discrimination or unreasonable requests for contracts, forms, and so on; and
—use of technical regulations, standards, certification systems, or related procedures to discriminate against foreign service firms.

BIBLIOGRAPHY

BOOKS

Bergsten, C. Fred, Thomas O. Horst, and Theodore H. Moran. *American Multinationals and American Interest.* Washington, D.C.: Brookings Institution, 1978.

Blades, Derek W., Derek D. Johnston, and Witold Marczewski. *Service Activities in Developing Countries.* Paris: Development Centre of the Organization for Economic Cooperation and Development, 1974.

Clark, Colin. *The Conditions of Economic Progress.* 3rd ed. New York: St. Martin's Press, 1957.

Gersuny, Carl. *The Service Society.* Morristown, N.J.: Schenkman, 1973.

Griffiths, Brian. *Invisible Barriers to Invisible Trade.* London: Macmillan Press, 1975.

Heilbroner, Robert. *The Making of Economic Society.* Englewood Cliffs, N.J.: Prentice-Hall, 1975.

International Labour Office. *Year Book of Labour Statistics.* Geneva: ILO, 1976.

Lengellé, Maurice. *The Growing Importance of the Service Sector in Member Countries.* Paris: Organization for Economic Cooperation and Development, 1966.

Leontief, Wassily, et al. *The Future of the World Economy.* A United Nations Study. New York: Oxford University Press, 1977.

Lewis, Russell. *The Service Society.* London: Longman House, 1973.

Ofer, Gur. *The Service Industries in a Developing Economy—Israel as a Case Study.* New York: Praeger, 1967.

——. *The Service Sector in Soviet Economic Growth.* Cambridge, Mass.: Harvard University Press, 1973.

Organization for Economic Cooperation and Development. *Policy Perspectives for International Trade and Economic Relations.* Report by the High Level Group on Trade and Related Problems to the Secretary General of the Organization for Economic Cooperation and Development. Paris: OECD, September 1972.

225

Pryor, Frederic L. *Public Expenditures in Communist and Capitalist Nations.* Homewood, Ill.: Richard D. Irwin, 1968.

Sabolo, Yves, J. Gaude, and R. Wery. *The Service Industries.* Geneva: International Labour Office, 1975.

World Bank. *World Tables 1976.* Paris, Baltimore, and London: Johns Hopkins University Press, 1976.

JOURNALS AND PERIODICALS

Azar, V., and I. Pletnikova. "On the Question of the Classification and Full Assessment of Services in Personal Consumption." *Problems of Economics* 18 (May 1975): 87–105.

Ball, George. "Cosmocorp: The Importance of Being Stateless." *Columbia Journal of World Business*, November-December 1967, pp. 25–30.

Behrman, J. N. "Sharing International Production through the Multinational Enterprise and Sectorial Integration." *Law and Policy in International Business* 4 (1972): 1–37.

Bhalla, A. S. "The Role of Services in Employment Expansion." *International Labour Review* 101 (May 1970): 519–39.

Boeker, Paul H. "A Code for Multinationals." *Wall Street Journal*, May 28, 1976.

Corbet, Hugh. "Prospect of Negotiations on Barriers to International Trade in Services." *Pacific Community* 8 (April 1977): 454–69.

Denison, Edward F. "The Shift to Services and the Rate of Productivity Change." *Survey of Current Business* 53 (October 1973): 20–35.

Diebold, William, Jr. "The End of the ITO." *Essays in International Finance* (Princeton University), no. 16, October 1952, pp. 1–37.

"The Disaster in Productivity." *Fortune*, December 1974, p. 24.

English, Edward H. "The Service Sector: U.S. and Canadian." *Conference Board Record* 10 (June 1973): 59–61.

Fabricant, Solomon. "Productivity in the Tertiary Sector." *National Bureau Report Supplement*, no. 10, August 1972, pp. 1–10.

Ghali, Moheb A. "Tourism and Economic Growth: An Empirical Study." *Economic Development and Cultural Change* 24 (April 1976): 527–38.

Goldberg, Paul, and Charles Kindleberger. "Toward a GATT for Investment: A Proposal for Supervision of the International Corporation." *Law and Policy in International Business* 2 (1970): 295–325.

"Guidelines for the Tenth Five-Year Plan." *Current Digest of the Soviet Press* 28, nos. 15, 16, 17 (May 12, 19, and 26, 1976): 13–17; 14–22; 11–19, 28.

Harris, Louis. "Seeking and Resisting Change." *Conference Board Record*, May 1970, pp. 14–18.

Joskow, Paul L. "Cartels, Competition and Regulation in the Property-Liability Insurance Industry." *Bell Journal of Economics* 4 (Autumn 1973): 375–427.

Katouzian, M. A. "The Development of the Service Sector: A New Approach." *Oxford Economic Papers*, New Series 22 (November 1970): 362–82.

Komarov, V. "The Services Sphere and Its Structure." *Problems of Economics* 16 (July 1973): 3–21.

Linden, Fabian. "The Consumer's View of Value Received, 1974." *Conference Board Record* 11 (November 1974): 48–53.

Magdoff, Harry, and David Weintraub. "The Service Industries in Relation to Employment Trends." *Econometrica* 8 (October 1940): 289–311.

"Making the Community a 'Common Market.'" *European Community Background Information*, no. 7 (March 26, 1973), pp. 1–2.

"Manufacturers Move into the Services." *Industry Week*, April 8, 1974, pp. 25–34.

Merigo, Eduardo, and Stephen Potter. "Invisibles in the 1960's." *OECD Economic Outlook*, July 1970.

Nikolayev, D. "Transport's Role in Promoting the USSR Foreign Economic Relations." *Foreign Trade* (Moscow: USSR Ministry of Foreign Trade) (1977): 7–14.

Ofer, Gur. "Industrial Structure, Urbanization, and the Growth Strategy of Socialist Countries." *Quarterly Journal of Economics* 90 (May 1976): 219–44.

"Poland: Private Sector Initiatives." *East-West Markets*, January 10, 1977, p. 3.

"Project LINK: Linking National Economics Models." *Challenge*, November-December 1976, pp. 25–29.

"Resolution on RSFSR Consumer Services." *Current Digest of the Soviet Press* 29 (March 2, 1977): 9–10.

Rubin, Seymour. "Multinational Enterprise and National Sovereignty: A Skeptic's Analysis." *Law and Policy in International Business* 3 (1971): 1–41.

Rutgaizer, V. "Methodological Problems in Assessing the Population's Need for Services." *Problems of Economics* 16 (September 1973): 41–59.

Shelp, Ronald K. "The Proliferation of Foreign Insurance Laws: Reform or Regression?" *Law and Policy in International Business* 8 (1976): 701–35.

Szabadi, B. "Relationship between the Level of Economic Development and the Services." *Acta Oeconomica* 15 (1975): 343–64.

"The U.S. Lead in Service Exports Is Under Siege." *Business Week*, September 15, 1980, p. 701.

Vernon, Raymond. "International Investment and International Trade in the Product Cycle." *Quarterly Journal of Economics* 80 (May 1966): 191–207.

Wolff, Alan William. "The U.S. Mandate for Trade Negotiations." *Virginia Journal of International Law* 16 (Spring 1976): 52–53.

PAMPHLETS

Alton, Thad P., et al. *Economic Growth in Eastern Europe 1965-1976*. Occasional Paper no. 51. Occasional Papers of the Research Project on National Income in East Central Europe. New York: L. W. International Financial Research, 1977.

Carter, Robert L., and Gerard M. Dickinson. *Barriers to Trade in Insurance*. Thames Essay no. 19. London: Trade Policy Research Centre, 1979.

Committee on Invisible Exports. *World Invisible Trade*. London: Committee on Invisible Exports, August 1975.

———. *World Invisible Trade*. London: Committee on Invisible Exports, August 1977.

———. *World Invisible Trade*. London: Committee on Invisible Exports, August 1980.

Fuchs, Victor R. *The Growing Importance of the Service Industries*. National Bureau of Economic Research. Occasional Paper no. 96. New York: Columbia University Press, 1965.

————. *Productivity Trends in the Goods and Service Sectors, 1929–61: A Preliminary Survey*. National Bureau of Economic Research. Occasional Paper no. 89. New York: Columbia University Press, 1964.

————. *The Service Economy*. National Bureau of Economic Research. General Series no. 87. New York: Columbia University Press, 1968.

Fuchs, Victor R., and Jean Alexander Wilburn. *Productivity Differences within the Service Sector*. National Bureau of Economic Research. Occasional Paper no. 89. New York: Columbia University Press, 1967.

PUBLIC DOCUMENTS

Commission of the European Communities. "Commission Pushes Forward Discussion on Mutual Recognition of Professional Qualification." *Information* (P-15), March 1974.

————. "Draft for a First Council Directive on Life Assurance." *Information* (P-73), December 1973.

————. "First Council Directive of 12 December 1977 on the Coordination of Laws, Regulations and Administrative Provisions Relating to the Taking-Up and Pursuit of the Business of Credit Institutions." *Official Journal of the European Communities* (77/780/EEC), no. L 322/30 (December 17, 1977).

————. "First Council Directive on the Coordination of Laws, Regulations and Administrative Provisions Relating to the Taking-Up and Pursuit of the Business of Direct Insurance Other Than Life Assurance." *Official Journal of the European Communities*, no. 185 (July 18, 1967).

————. "Freedom of Lawyers to Provide Services." *Information* (P-23), March 1977.

————. "Free Movement of Doctors Inside the EEC." *Information* (137-76), November 1976.

————. "Proposals for a First Council Directive on the Coordination of Laws, Regulations and Administrative Provisions Relating to the Taking-Up and Pursuit of the Business of Direct Life Assurance." *Official Journal of the European Communities*, no. C140 (November 13, 1974).

————. "Van Binsbergen Ruling." *Information* (81/75), December 1974.

Organization for Economic Cooperation and Development. *Code of Liberalization of Capital Movements*, January 1976.

——. *Code of Liberalization of Current Invisible Operations*, January 1975.

——. *National Accounts of OECD Countries, 1961–1972*. Paris: OECD, 1974.

——. *National Accounts of OECD Countries, 1961–1978*. Paris: OECD, 1980.

——. *OECD Economic Outlook*. Occasional Studies, July 1970, 12/70/01/1.

Organization for Economic Cooperation and Development, Social Affairs Division, Manpower and Social Affairs Directorate. *Manpower Problems in the Service Sector*. Papers for a Trade Union Seminar. Supplement to the Report. Paris: OECD, 1966.

United Nations. *Report of the Drafting Committee of the Preparatory Committee of the United Nations Conference on Trade and Employment* (E/PC/T/34/Rev. 1). Lake Success, N.Y., January 20–February 25, 1947.

——. *Report of the First Session of the Preparatory Committee of the United Nations Conference on Trade and Employment* (E/PC/T/33). London, October 1946.

——. *Report of the Second Session of the Preparatory Committee of the United Nations Conference on Trade and Employment* (E/PC/T/35/139). Geneva, August 1947.

——. *United Nations National Accounts Statistics 1975–Centrally Planned Economies and Hungary in particular.*

United Nations, Centre on Transnational Corporations. *Transnational Reinsurance Operations* (Technical Paper ST/CTC/15). New York, 1980.

United Nations, Conference on Trade and Development (UNCTAD). *Establishment or Expansion of Merchant Marines in Developing Countries*. Report of the UNCTAD Secretariat, pars. 229, 261. New York, 1968.

——. Various studies, reports of expert groups, and meetings of the UNCTAD plenary, the Trade and Development Board, and the Committee on Invisibles and Financing Related to Trade.

United Nations, Department of Economic and Social Affairs. *The Impact of Multinational Corporations on Development and on International Relations* (E/5500.Rev. 1 ST/ESA/6), 1974.

United Nations, Office of Public Information, United Nations Press Section. *Second Session of Commission on Transnational Corporations*, Lima, Peru, March 1–12, 1976 (Press Release TNC/10) March 16, 1976, p. 4.

——. *Second Session of Commission on Transnational Corporations*, United Nations (Press Release TNC/10), March 16, 1976.

U.S. *International Economic Report of the President Together with Annual Report of the Council on International Economic Policy* (4115-00055). Washington, D.C.: Government Printing Office, 1974.

U.S., Central Intelligence Agency. *Research Aid, USSR: Hard Currency Trade and Payments, 1977-78* (ER 77-10035 U), March 1977.

U.S., Congress. *The Trade Agreements Act of 1979, Subsidies Code, Government Procurement Code, Import Licensing Code* (Section 11 contained in Public Law 96-39). Approved by 95th Cong., Subcommittee on Trade, House of Representatives Ways and Means Committee, Senate Subcommittee on International Trade of the Finance Committee, 96th Cong., 1st sess., House Document no. 96-153, June 1979.

——. *Trade Reform Act of 1974*, 93rd Cong., 1st sess., January 1975.

U.S., Congress, House. *Membership and Participation by the United States in the International Trade Organization: Hearings before the Committee on Foreign Affairs*, 81st Cong., 2d sess., March 12–April 19, 1950, pp. 201-2.

U.S., Congress, Joint Economic Committee. *Allocation of Resources in the Soviet Union and China—1976, Hearings before the Subcommittee on Priorities and Economy in Government*, 94th Cong., 2d sess., 1976.

——. *Allocation of Resources in the Soviet Union and China—1977, Hearings before the Subcommittee on Priorities and Economy in Government*, 95th Cong., 2d sess., 1977.

——. *East European Economics, Post Helsinki*, 95th Cong., 1st sess., 1977.

——. *Economic Developments in Countries of Eastern Europe*, 91st Cong., 2d sess., 1970.

——. *Reorientation and Commercial Relations of the Economies of Eastern Europe*, 93rd Cong., 2d sess., August 1974.

——. *Soviet Economic Problems and Prospects*, 95th Cong., 1st sess., 1977.

——. *Soviet Economy in a New Perspective: A Compendium of Papers*, 94th Cong., 2d sess., October 14, 1976.

U.S., Congress, Senate, Committee on Finance. *First Session on Trade Agreements System and Proposed International Trade Organization Charter, Part 1 and Part 2*, 80th Cong., 1st sess., March and April, 1947.

U.S., Congressional Research Service. *U.S. International Service Trade*, prepared by David D. Driscoll, August 21, 1980.

U.S., Department of Commerce. *Foreign Direct Investment in the United States.* Report of the Secretary of Commerce to the Congress, vol. 1, April 1976.

U.S., Department of Commerce, Bureau of the Census. *The Soviet Statistical System: Labor Force Recordkeeping and Reporting,* International Population Statistics Reports (Series P-90, no. 12), 1960.

———. *The Soviet Statistical System: Labor Force Recordkeeping and Reporting since 1957,* International Population Statistics Reports (Series P-90, no. 17), 1962.

U.S., Department of Commerce, Bureau of the Census, Foreign Demographic Analysis Division. *Comparison of U.S. and USSR Employment in Industry: 1939-1958,* prepared by Murray S. Weitzman. International Population Statistics Reports (Series P-95, no. 60), January 1963.

———. *The Labor Force of Czechoslovakia,* prepared by James Ypsilantis. International Population Statistics Reports (Series P-90, no. 13), 1960.

U.S., Department of Commerce, Domestic and International Business Administration. *Service Industries Trends and Prospects,* August 1975.

U.S., Department of Commerce, National Technical Information Service. *Study of Service Industries and Their Relation to Domestic and International Trade, Part I: A,B,C. An Overview of Service Industries, Domestic Service Sector Profiles, Importance of Service Sectors in the U.S. Balance of Payments* (PB-263 095). *Part II. The Impact of Non-Tariff Trade Barriers on U.S. Service Industries in Competitive International Markets* (PB-263 096). *Part III. International Consideration of Service Industry Problems* (PB-263 097), prepared for Bureau of Domestic Commerce by Wolf and Company, October 14, 1976.

U.S., Department of Commerce, Office of the Assistant Secretary for Policy. *U.S. Service Industries in World Markets: Current Problems and Future Policy Development.* Washington, D.C.: Government Printing Office, December 1976.

U.S., Department of Labor, Bureau of Labor Statistics. *U.S. Workers and Their Jobs: The Changing Picture* (Bulletin 1919). Washington, D.C.: Government Printing Office, 1976.

U.S., Department of State. *Havana Charter for an International Trade Organization, March 24, 1948* (Publication 3206, Commercial Policy Series 114), September 1948.

UNPUBLISHED MATERIAL

Aronson, Jonathan. "Industrial Structure, Surplus Capacity, and the International Monetary System: The Role of the Service Sector in the World Economy." Paper presented at the annual meetings of the American Political Science Association, Washington, D.C., August 28-30, 1980.

Committee on Invisible Exports, Economic Advisory Group. "Productivity and Efficiency in Service Industries with Special Reference to Financial Services: Concepts and Methods of Measurement." Report commissioned for private use by Economic Advisory Group. London, September 1972.

The Conference Board. "Toward a Trillion-Dollar Consumer Market." Report on a Consumer Research Conference held March 21, 1972. New York, 1973.

Hymer, Stephen. "The International Operations of National Firms: A Study of Direct Investment." Ph.D. dissertation, Massachusetts Institute of Technology, 1960.

Juhl, Paulgeorg. "Prospects for Foreign Direct Investment in Developing Countries." Preliminary Draft prepared for the International Kiel Symposium on a New International Economic Order, Kiel, Institute of World Economics, December 8-9, 1976.

Krommenacker, R. J. "The Liberalization of Invisible Trade and the Inclusion of Services in GATT Negotiations: The Case of Transport Insurance." Article prepared for GATT, Geneva, Switzerland, November 10, 1976.

Lutz, Ernst, and Andre Sapir. "Trade in Non-Factor Services: Past Trends and Current Issues." Background Paper prepared for the World Development Report, Washington, D.C., 1980.

Madden, Carl H. "Tomorrow's People: What Will They Be Like?" Remarks to the American Management Association's Annual Personnel Conference, Chicago, February 4, 1976.

Peno, Joseph N., Bernard Wasow, Nancy Truitt, John Stephenson, and Ronald K. Shelp. "The Role of Service Technology in Economic Development." Study being prepared under the auspices of the Fund for Multinational Management Education, New York, forthcoming.

Trade Policy Research Centre. Various studies on International Trade and Investment in Services, Trade Policy Research Centre, London, anticipated publication 1981.

U.S. Chamber of Commerce, International Insurance Advisory Council. "Background Memorandum: Trade Negotiations and the U.S. Insurance Industry." Washington, D.C., September 1974.

Vaitsos, Constantine V. "Employment Problems and Transnational Enterprises in Developing Countries: Distortions and Inequality." Paper given under the auspices of Carnegie Center for Transnational Studies at Aspen, Colorado, July 1976.

Vernon, Raymond. "Interdependence: Its Implications for the Industrial Policies of the United States." Article prepared for the Committee for Economic Development, Washington, D.C., 1978.

Wasow, Bernard, and Raymond Hill. "Public Sector Involvement in the Insurance Industry: The Implication for Economic Development." Study prepared for the Center for Applied Economics, New York University, New York, 1980.

INDEX

accounting, 11; innovations in, 90; international markets, 84; regulation of, 102; socialist countries, 41–43; statistics, 61, 65

advertising: international markets, 85; investment restrictions on, 78; regulation of, 103

affiliates: dynamism, 73; investment in, 83; product cycle theory, 92; statistics, 64

Africa, 115

aggregation (of data), 62

Agreement of Cartagena (1968), 113

agriculture, 77

AIMU, *see* American Institute of Marine Underwriters

air transport, *see* aviation; transportation

American Committee for Emergency Trade, 76

American Federation of Labor and Congress of Industrial Organizations (AFL-CIO), 76

American Home Assurance Company, 159

American Institute of Marine Underwriters (AIMU), 159

Andean Pact, 113–14, 120, 168

APESC, *see* Asia-Pacific Economic and Social Commission

architecture, 146

Argentina: insurance, 91, 179; service exports, 40; treaties, 156, 157, 158

ASEAN, *see* Association of Southeast Asian Nations

Asian Reinsurance Company, 115

Asia-Pacific Economic and Social Commission (APESC), 115

Association of Southeast Asian Nations (ASEAN), 115, 207, 211

Australia, 23

Austria: employment in services, 22; GDP in services, 23; service earnings, 32

aviation: cartels in, 86; liberalization framework, 206; regulation of, 109, 117–18; *see also* transportation

balance of payments: GATT and, 183; insurance regulation, 116; invisibles in, 25; liberalization, 152, 168; policy, 76; regulation, 122; service sector and, 12, 13; shortcomings of, 60

Ball, George, 199

banking: codes, 196; developing countries, 81; innovations in, 90; international markets, 83–84; liberalization, 143–44; oligopoly theory, 96; regulation 101–102, 114, 119, 122; service economy and, 7; socialist countries, 58; statistics, 64

Behrman, J. N., 200

Belgium, 23

Bergsten, C. Fred, 200, 201, 203

bilateral agreements, 205–207, 208; taxation, 201–202; *see also* treaties; *entries under names of agreements and treaties*

Bolivia, 113, 156

Brazil, 40, 82

Britain, *see* United Kingdom

Brock, Bill, 187

brokerage, 84, 90

Brussels Commission, 143

Bulgaria, 49

business cycles, 6, 76

Business Week, 20, 74

cabotage laws, 110, 122, 180; *see also* shipping; transportation

CACM, *see* Central American Common Market

Canada, 211; computer services, 106; GDP in services, 23; international/domestic correlation, 33; treaties, 159

capital: liberalization, 129; service economy, 7, 23

capital formation, 39

capitalist class, 1

Caribbean Common Market (CARECOM), 114–15

Carter, Jimmy, 154, 159, 200

Carter, Robert, 208

Central American Common Market (CACM), 114

environment: regulation, 124; service sector and, 6

European Economic Community (EEC), 211; computer regulation, 106; liberalization, 127, 133, 135, 153, 160, 171, 172, 173, 186, 207–208; policy, 120; treaties, 157

exports: developing nations, 39, 77, 78; development and, 82; policy, 76; product cycle theory, 89–90; statistics, 63–64; U.S. services, 18, 20; *see also* imports; markets (international)

export trading companies, 74

expropriation, *see* nationalization

FCN treaties, *see* Treaties of Friendship, Commerce, and Navigation

Federal Republic of Germany, *see* Germany (FR)

Federal Reserve Board (U.S.), 190

films, *see* motion pictures

financial services, 171

Fisher, 218, 220

Ford administration, 154

foreign exchange: developing nations, 77, 78; protectionism, 151; socialist countries, 58, 59, 78; U.S., 76

foreign trade, *see* markets (international)

foreign trading organizations (FTOs), 58

France: employment in services, 22; GDP in services, 23; liberalization, 151; U.S. treaties with, 155, 157

franchising, 74, 108

FTOs, *see* foreign trading organizations

Fuchs, Victor R., 215, 217, 221

Galanson, W., 221

GATT, *see* General Agreement on Tariffs and Trade (GATT)

Gaude, J., 216

General Agreement on Tariffs and Trade (GATT), 174, 208, 209, 210, 212; bilateral negotiations under, 182–83; investment recommendations, 198–203; liberalization, 127, 148–54, 160; liberalization framework, 167–68, 172, 177–78, 189–91; negotiations framework, 184–88; nontariff measure codes, 178–82; possibilities for, 191–208; reform, 184; regulation justification, 122; safeguards, 183–84

Geneva Conference (1947), 198

Gentlemen's Agreement on Export Credits, 192

Germany (FR): GDP in services, 23; international/domestic correlation, 32–33; liberalization, 151; service economy of, 21, 22; U.S. treaties with, 155

Germany (GDR), 45

Goldberg, Paul, 199

Golt, Sidney, 215

government, 3–4, 7, 8; *see also* policy; public administration

Greece, 32, 33, 40

Griffiths, Brian, 130, 185, 196, 204

gross domestic fixed capital formation (GDFCF), 37

gross domestic product (GDP): developed countries, 22; developing countries, 37–38; service economies, 68

gross national product (GNP): developed countries, 22; developing countries, 37–38; employment in services contrasted, 22–23; socialist countries, 45–55; U.S., 16–17, 21

growth (economic), 6, 82

Guatemala, 158–59

Hamilton, Alexander, 121

Havana Charter, 199

Havana Conference (1948), 149

health services, 106–107, 115

Hill, Raymond, 88

Horst, Thomas, 200

hotel and motel services, 103–104; *see also* tourism

Hungary, 79; employment in services, 45; service economy in, 55–56; treaties, 160

IACA, *see* International Air Carriers Association (IACA)

IATA, *see* International Air Transport Association (IATA)

ICAO, *see* International Civil Aviation Organization (ICAO)

IMCO, *see* International Maritime Consultant Organization (IMCO)

IMF, *see* International Monetary Fund (IMF)

immigration, 7

import licensing procedures, 181–82

imports: developing countries, 40; service economies, 4, 71, 72; U.S. services, 19, 20; *see also* exports; markets (international)

income, 219–20

238

Peru, 113, 120
Poland, 51, 58
policy, 75-79; comparative advantage
theory and, 86; developed countries,
75-77; developing countries, 77-78;
international regulation and, 119-21;
socialist countries, 78-79
Portugal, 22, 33
press, 146-47
pricing, 76
procurement codes, 192
product cycle theory, 89-92
production, 10, 11
productivity, 75
profession, 166; liberalization, 144-46;
regulation of, 102; *see also entries
under names of professions*
protectionism, 6, 88, 151
public administration: developing countries, 38; socialist countries, 45;
Soviet Union, 55; *see also* government;
policy
Public Systems Organization (Westinghouse), 73-74

ransom insurance, 91
rate control (insurance), 142
regional approaches, 207-208
regional regulations, 113-15, 120
regulation, 99-126; comparative advantage
theory and, 86, 87; developing nations,
124; insurance, 189-90; international
organization of, 115-19; investment,
111-13; investment-related services,
101-104; justifications for, 121-24,
166; liberalization, 169, 187; policy,
76; regional, 113-15, 120; services, 99-
100; service sector vs. manufacturing
sector, 125; theory and, 99; trade-and-
investment-related services, 104-108;
trade-related services, 109-11; transportation, 99
reinsurance: international markets, 84;
liberalization, 131, 132; regulation,
114, 115, 116, 119; *see also* insurance
research and development, 7
retaliation, 206
Reyners case, 136, 139, 145
risk management, 94
Rockefeller Foundation, 215
Romania: construction, 58; employment
in services, 45; GNP in services, 51;
service economy in, 56; treaties, 160

Rubin, Seymour, 200

Sabolo, Yves, 216, 219, 221
Saudi Arabia, 40
self-employment, 147
Senegal, 39
service sector and economies: bilateral
liberalization, 155-60; categorization
of, 11-12, 48, 100; comparative
advantage theory, 85-87; definitions,
2-3, 10-13, 65, 100, 216-17; developed countries, 13-33, 82; developing
countries, 5-6, 33-41, 81-82; development and, 13, 80-83, 218-22; government and, 3-4, 7, 8 (*see also* policy);
growth of, 8, 73-74; implications of,
6-9, 13; industrial economy and, 3, 77,
166, 220-21; infant industry theory,
88-89; innovation in, 90-91; international projections, 68-73; international trade and, 4-6, 25-33, 59, 83-
85; labor unions and, 1, 3, 6-7; OECD
and, 21-23; oligopoly theory, 95-97;
policy challenges in, 75-79; political
power and, 1, 2; product cycle theory
and, 89-92; productivity of, 75; protectionism, 6, 88, 151; regulation, 99-
126 (*see also* regulation); socialist
countries, 41-59 (*see also* socialist
countries); statistics, 59, 60-65; technology transfer theory, 93-95; theory
and, 80; U.S., 13-21
shipping: cartels in, 86; developing countries, 81; innovation in, 90; insurance,
87; international markets, 84; national
security, 166; regulation of, 109-11,
114, 115, 117, 122; subsidies, 180;
treaties, 158-59; *see also* transportation
Singapore, 40-41
Smith, Adam, 218
socialist countries, 6, 13; banking, 58;
construction, 58; consumption, 55, 56;
GNP, 45-55; insurance, 58; international service economy and, 57-59;
investment, 55; labor force, 42, 43-45,
46-47; liberalization, 206; national
accounting in, 41-43, 61; nonsocialist
countries contrasted, 55-56; policy in,
78-79; service economies, 41-59, 60;
*see also entries under names of socialist
countries*

South Pacific Bureau of Economic Cooperation (SPBEC), 115
Soviet Union, 215; accounting 41; banking, 58; construction, 58; consumption, 54; employment in services, 43; GNP in services, 48; liberalization, 206; management services, 59; service economy in, 55, 56, 57; U.S. Trade Act of 1974 and, 159
Spain, 22, 23, 32, 33, 40
SPBEC, *see* South Pacific Bureau for Economic Cooperation (SPBEC)
Specific Services Codes, 194-98
Stalin, Joseph, 48
Standard Industrial Classification (SIC) system, 11
standardization, 89-90
standards agreement, 181
statistics, 38; improvement recommendations, 64-65; international comparisons, 23; international markets, 25, 32; problems in, 59, 60-65
Stigler, E. J., 220
Stigler, George J., 215
Strauss, Robert, 186
subsidies, 110, 180-81
Sweden, 22, 23, 139
Switzerland, 22, 139, 148

Taiwan, 183
Task Force on Services and the Multilateral Trade Negotiations (U.S.), 65
taxation, 81, 201-202
technology transfer, 77, 78; computers, 106; regulation, 105; service economy and, 7, 73-74; theory, 89, 93-95
terrorism, 91
theory, 80-98; comparative advantage, 85-87; development, 218-22; infant industry theory, 88-89; oligopoly theory of international investment, 95-97; product cycle theory, 89-92; regulation and, 99; technology transfer and, 93-95
Third World, *see* developing countries
Tokyo Round, 113, 152, 153-54, 160, 167, 173, 174, 177, 178, 185, 211; balance of payments, 183; bilateral agreements, 182-83; difficulties in, 185-86; reform, 184; standards agreement, 181; subsidies, 180-81
tourism: developing countries, 40, 78, 81; impact of, 33; international markets,

85; liberalization framework, 171; Soviet Union, 57, 58
trade, *see* markets (domestic); markets (international)
Trade Act of 1974 (U.S.), 127, 153-54, 158-60, 182, 188, 206, 208, 210, 214
trade-and-investment-related services regulation, 104-108
Trade Policy Research Centre (U.K.), 214, 215
trade-related services regulation, 109-11
transborder data flow (TDF), 119, 175, 190
transfer pricing, 202
transnationals, *see* multinationals
transportation, 20, 21; cartels in, 86; developing countries, 40, 78, 81; insurance for, 84; liberalization framework, 170-71; regulation, 99, 109-11, 116, 117-18, 122; service sector definition, 11; socialist countries, 41; Soviet Union, 57-58; statistics, 32; *see also* aviation; shipping
treaties: investment, 199; liberalization, 155-58, 205
Treaties of Amity and Economic Relations, 155
Treaties of Friendship, Commerce, and Navigation (FCN), 155, 156, 205
Treaty of Rome (1956), 136, 140, 141, 145, 147
Turkey, 40
Turnham, David, 33

UNCTAD, *see* United Nations Conference on Trade and Development (UNCTAD)
UNDP, *see* United Nations Development Program
unemployment, 7, 75, 76; *see also* employment; labor force
unilateral approaches, 205-207
unions, *see* labor unions
United Kingdom: computer services, 106; financial services, 87; GDP in services, 23; international/domestic correlation, 32; invisible trade share of, 24; treaties, 157; U.S. treaties with, 155, 156
United Nations, 68, 71, 216; communications regulation, 105; statistics, 65; technology transfer, 94
United Nations Commission on Transnational Corporations, 65, 118-19, 200, 214

United Nations Conference on Trade and Development (UNCTAD), 65, 119, 121, 200, 214; liberalization, 152; regulation by, 115–18; subsidies definition, 110

United Nations Conference on Trade and Employment, 148

United Nations Development Program (UNDP), 116

United Nations Economic and Social Commission for Asia and the Pacific, 115

United Nations Economic and Social Council (ECOSOC), 150

United Nations Economic Commission for Latin America, 11

United Nations Industrial Development Organization (UNIDO), 200

United Nations System of National Accounts, 41, 61; *see also* accounting

United States: cabotage laws, 122; codes, 197, 198; developed countries compared, 25; employment in services, 14–16; financial services, 87; GATT and, 185, 188; GNP in services, 16–17, 21; government procurement code, 178, 179; international markets, 17–21, 40, 83; ITO, 199; liberalization, 151, 153–54, 173, 190, 206, 210–11; OECD and, 32, 174–75, 176; policies, 75; service economy in, 13–21, 23; statistics, 62–64; Trade Act of 1974 (*see main entry*); treaty liberalization, 155–58

U.S. Bureau of Labor Statistics, 15
U.S. Chamber of Commerce, 76, 185
U.S. Department of Commerce, 20, 25, 76, 83, 100, 111, 113, 190, 214
U.S. Department of Labor, 76
U.S. Department of State, 112, 190, 199
U.S. Department of the Treasury, 190, 200
U.S. National Commission on Productivity, 76
urbanization, 81, 220–21
utilities, 171

van Binsbergen case, 136, 139, 145
Venezuela, 113; divestment, 120; investment by, 40
Vernon, Raymond, 89, 90, 201–202, 203

wages: Soviet Union, 43; *see also* income
Warta Insurance and Reinsurance Company, Ltd., 58
Wasow, Bernard, 88
Wery, R., 216
Westinghouse, 73–74
Wilcox, Clair, 149
working class, 1

Yugoslavia, 32, 40

Zaire, 39

ABOUT THE AUTHOR

RONALD KENT SHELP is a leading authority on services in the world economy. He is chairman of the International Service Industry Committee of the U.S. Chamber of Commerce and the government-appointed Industry Sector Advisory Committee on Services. He has served as a member of the U.S. government delegation to various international organizations and has served as a consultant to the Organization for Economic Cooperation and Development and other groups. Mr. Shelp, a frequent witness before Congressional committees, is Vice-President of International Relations of the American International Group, a major New York-based multinational service company. Previously, he managed two international trade associations, served as an assistant to a U.S. Senator and as a journalist.

Shelp has written extensively on a wide variety of subjects concerned with international affairs. His recent publications include contributions to two books, *The Politics of Raw Materials* and *Reference Manual on Doing Business in Latin America*, and to a four-volume study on technology transfer.

Shelp holds an undergraduate degree from the University of Georgia and a graduate degree from the Johns Hopkins University School of Advanced International Studies.

SECRET OF THE SPOTTED SHELL

Westminster Press Books by
PHYLLIS A. WHITNEY

The Mystery of the Gulls
Mystery of the Black Diamonds
Mystery on the Isle of Skye
Mystery of the Green Cat
Secret of the Samurai Sword
Mystery of the Haunted Pool
Secret of the Tiger's Eye
Mystery of the Golden Horn
Mystery of the Hidden Hand
Secret of the Emerald Star
Mystery of the Angry Idol
Secret of the Spotted Shell

SECRET OF THE SPOTTED SHELL

PHYLLIS A. WHITNEY

ILLUSTRATED BY
JOHN MECRAY

THE WESTMINSTER PRESS

PHILADELPHIA

LIBRARY OF CONGRESS CATALOG CARD NO. AC 67-10016

PUBLISHED BY THE WESTMINSTER PRESS®
PHILADELPHIA, PENNSYLVANIA

PRINTED IN THE UNITED STATES OF AMERICA

Contents

1

Ominous Arrival

No one had come to meet her plane that afternoon at the airport in St. Thomas. Wendy
Williams stood in the square box of an airport
building, clearly in view, looking very neat and
proper in her pleated navy blue skirt and white
blouse, with a navy beret pinned to her short, dark
hair. But Wendy's blue eyes, fringed with thick
lashes, looked more than a little worried.

Perhaps it had been foolish to hope that someone
was waiting for her eagerly — someone who was
really her family, although the relationship was
only that of distant cousin. She blinked her eyes
rapidly when she thought of how much she had
begun to count on a home. Not just someone else's
home, where her father paid for her to stay, but a
real home here in the Virgin Islands with Gordon
and Marion Cole. Now it seemed likely that they
had forgotten all about her — or perhaps they had
changed their minds.

She had half expected a change two months ago,
when Stuart Cole had been drowned in that terrible
boating accident. Yet the plans for Wendy's coming
had not been changed at that time, and though a

deep sadness had been evident in Cousin Gordon's words, he had written her a kind, welcoming letter. Marion Cole had not written, and Cousin Gordon had explained that his wife was upset to the point of illness over their son's death. He felt that Wendy's coming might help to cheer her, give her something to live for again.

In the airport someone spoke near at hand: "Hasn't your family come to meet you?"

The voice of the stewardess was kind. Miss Betty Mears had looked out for her ever since Wendy had boarded the plane in New York. Miss Mears had been a stewardess on the big jet, and then had flown as a passenger when they had changed to a smaller plane out of San Juan. Her home was in St. Thomas and she would stay here for a day or two.

"I — I haven't seen anyone who looks right," Wendy told her, trying to hold back the tremor that came into her voice.

Miss Mears was pretty and blond, with brown eyes that never seemed impatient. "Well, don't worry," she said. "There's probably been some delay. I won't go off and leave you. As a matter of fact, I'll be staying at a place very near you, and if necessary you can come along with me. Suppose I phone your family at Villa Mimosa and see what I can find out. Stay here with your suitcase and I'll be right back."

The suitcase was brand-new airplane luggage, bought with money Cousin Gordon had sent. It was gray and streamlined, and it held new clothes her father had bought her. She stared at the suitcase for a moment and then sat down on it because her knees felt as shaky as her voice had sounded. Things couldn't go wrong now—oh, they couldn't! But she mustn't worry about that. She must distract herself somehow.

She closed her eyes tightly and thought of her father. Her mother had died twelve years ago, a little while after Wendy was born, and she couldn't remember her at all. But she remembered her wonderful, brave, dashing father very well indeed. Whenever he was in town he came to see her no matter where she was staying. Big as she was getting to be, he still tossed her in the air and called her "Honeybun!" in that funny way of his, practically overwhelming her with his warmth and love. He always hated to leave her, yet she understood about his leaving. Her father was a "boomer." That was what they called the men who went where great bridges of steel were being built. Since he was an expert, his work took him all over the world. He was in Portugal now, working on a bridge across the Tagus River in Lisbon.

He wasn't much good at writing letters, but he sent postcards now and then with lovely colored pictures of the places where he was working. Of course such work meant that he could not stay home with his daughter, no matter how much he loved her and wanted to be with her. Thus other people's homes had to be the answer. For Wendy, they had not always been a very good answer.

It had been wonderful when relatives on her mother's side—whom she had lost track of com-pletely—found out by accident where she was and got in touch with her, invited her to come and stay with them in St. Thomas. Pop had been happy about this, too. Especially since she could no longer stay with the Parks family.

But she dared not think about the Parkses, or she might start to cry right out in public—and she wouldn't be caught being a crybaby for anything. She made an angry face to keep from showing how she felt, and glowered around the airport building.

A thin, rather small man with a balding head stood nearby, watching her. For a moment she wondered doubtfully if he might be Gordon Cole, come to meet her after all, but then she recognized him as another passenger who had boarded the plane in New York, and made the same change to a smaller aircraft in Puerto Rico. When he saw that she was looking at him, he smiled and the brown moustache on his upper lip curled upward a little at the corners. He took a step nearer to Wendy and she stared at him with suspicion, remembering all the times she had been told, "Never talk to strangers. Call an adult to do the talking if anyone asks you questions." Wendy looked around the big echoing room. One side of it opened to planes and runways. Through another wide opening she could see a lineup of taxis, and passengers getting their luggage aboard, making ready to be driven off to their destinations. Miss Mears was nowhere in sight. There was no adult to summon.

"I heard our stewardess mention Villa Mimosa," he said. "An old friend of mine lives there—Gordon Cole. As a matter of fact, I'm to stay at a small hotel not far from his house. If you're taking a cab in that

ARRIVES
ST. THOMAS 3 3 5

FLIGHT 4 0
LEAVES
ST. THOMAS 3 4 5
ARRIVES
SAN JUAN 4 2 7

direction, perhaps I can give you a lift."

"I don't know where I'm going," Wendy said and looked again in the direction of the telephone booths. If he knew Cousin Gordon, it might be all right to talk to him — except that she didn't want to. She was too worried about herself.

Miss Mears came hurrying back across the big room and Wendy could see that she was no longer smiling. Her brown eyes were grave and worried, and Wendy's heart thumped in sudden alarm. Something really was wrong. Maybe the Coles had changed their minds after all and . . .

"Come along, dear," the stewardess said. "There's been a little slipup in plans. I'm going to Mears Manor, my brother's hotel on Mimosa Hill. I can get you that far. They'll send for you from the Villa later."

At least she wasn't to be put right aboard the next plane back to the States, Wendy thought, and stood up, grasping her suitcase by its smooth gray plastic handle.

At once the man who had spoken to her stepped forward. "Excuse me — I'm going to stay at Mears Manor. Do let me give you both a lift in my cab. My name is Helgerson — Manvil Helgerson."

Miss Mears regarded him gravely for a moment and then nodded. "Thank you. In that case we might as well all go together."

Mr. Helgerson's mouth formed a stiff little smile. "I don't know anyone in the Virgin Islands except Gordon Cole, so I thought this might be a way to start getting acquainted."

Miss Mears thanked him, still grave, and let him take her small bag and Wendy's suitcase. The three walked toward the taxi, beside which Mr. Helgerson had left his own bags. When the suitcases had been stored in the trunk and the three passengers were seated, the cab started on its way.

Outside the shade of the airport, the August sun was hot and all the colors seemed brighter than they were at home—blue sky and even bluer water, green and red and yellow shrubbery, scarlet and purple flowers, all swept in upon Wendy's senses in an intense wave of color. She felt the brilliant flare with a shock of surprise, yet she could not really think about it, or savor it now.

"Was something wrong that they didn't come to meet me?" she asked.

Miss Mears reached out to cover Wendy's hand with her own, and the very gesture was somehow frightening—as though trouble lay ahead and she was being offered sympathy, even before she knew what was wrong.

"There's been so much trouble in that family lately," Miss Mears said. "You know about Stuart's death, of course. I talked to the maid just now, and Mr. and Mrs. Guthrie are bringing their daughter Marion back from the hospital today. The maid was supposed to send a taxi for you, but she was upset, and I'm afraid she got her directions mixed."

Wendy accepted this in silence. It sounded more worrisome than ever. Paul and Elinor Guthrie were Marion Cole's father and mother. In fact, they owned Villa Mimosa, where Marion and Gordon lived. Cousin Gordon was an airline pilot, but she had expected him to be home at this time. Out of four people, you'd think one could come to meet her at the airport. She was sure there was more to this than Miss Mears had told her.

For the rest of the way Wendy sat in silence, trying to listen to Mr. Helgerson as he talked to the stewardess about why he had come to visit the Virgin Islands.

"I'd like to settle here and bring my family down," he was saying. "Gordon has been after me to make the change for a long while. But I wanted to come here first and look things over, get a few ideas of what it might be like to stay in the islands. That's why I'm spending a couple of weeks of my vacation here — at Mears Manor."

"What is your line of work?" Miss Mears asked politely when he came to a pause.

If Wendy had not been watching the small movements of Mr. Helgerson's moustache, she might not have been aware of his slight hesitation. His tongue came out and touched his upper lip and he said — with just that whisker's breadth of a pause — "I work for an oil company. But I expect to retire before long, and it's possible that St. Thomas is the answer to what I want to do. We'll see."

The way he said, "We'll see," sounded as though he dared St. Thomas to show him.

The taxi had turned onto a wide waterfront street, following the curve of the drive around the harbor. Wendy sat up to look out of the windows, her attention caught in spite of herself. She had grown up in New York and she was accustomed to tall buildings and cement pavements. Now and then she had visited suburban towns, but she had never seen a place like this before — an island that lay so brightly in the sun, with all that water and a few smaller islands on one side, a tall spine of green hill running along on the other. The air felt hot, but there was a breeze and she was not uncomfortable. On ahead, a hill that stood alone lifted its peaked top against the blue sky, occupying an arm of land that seemed to curl around the entrance to the harbor.

Miss Mears noted her interest. "That's Flag Hill. And on our left running up the hillside is the town of Charlotte Amalie—the only town on St. Thomas. It's not large, but it's very old—named for a Danish queen when Denmark owned the islands. Mostly, however, we speak of St. Thomas and don't bother with the longer name of the town."

The cab turned off the waterfront and ran briefly through a checkerboard arrangement of narrow streets, and buildings no more than two stories high, before it started up a steep hill. Here the road curved back and forth to lessen the grade as it climbed, and came at length to a dead end, where the hillside pitched away steeply, and there was no more road. On the right-hand side, set lower on the hill, stood a long one-story building with several cottages clustered about it. A grilled iron gateway cut through a hibiscus hedge and opened upon steps running down to the cottages and main building below. Arched above the gate was a sign that read: MEARS MANOR.

While Mr. Helgerson was paying the driver, Miss Mears went to the iron gateway and rang a bell. At once a tall, vigorous-looking red-haired boy, perhaps thirteen and nearly a year older than Wendy, came out from the lower level of the hotel, and ran along the walk between two cottages, hurrying upward in their direction.

"Hello, Mark," Miss Mears said as he reached

the gate. "Can you give us a hand with these bags?"

The boy said, "Hi, Aunt Betty," and bestowed a cheerful grin upon Mr. Helgerson and Wendy as he reached for the bags. A moment later he was loping ahead of them down the steps, with the stewardess following and Wendy close on her heels. Mr. Helgerson wound up the small procession.

A flagstone path cut between two cottages, ending before a few wide steps leading to the front door of the hotel. Inside, there was a small lobby area floored with dark-red tiles and graced by an inviting settee. On the right a sitting room section opened up, with woven straw rugs scattered across the floor and bright-cushioned cane furniture set about. Through sliding glass doors beyond, Wendy glimpsed a veranda that overlooked the hillside, where several people sat in deck chairs. To the left a narrow corridor led to the guest rooms, which were apparently all on one floor.

Mark Mears set down the bags near the hotel desk, and went around behind it. "Mom will be here in a minute," he told Mr. Helgerson, and pushed a large journal toward him. "Would you like to register?"

Then he turned a friendly look in Wendy's direction and she smiled in response. This boy seemed like someone who might be fun to know. Usually she got along fine with boys because she enjoyed their games and she wasn't too fussy about getting dirty or being rough. When she had stayed with the Parkses, Jimmy had taught her to throw and catch a ball as well as any boy, and he had let her play on his team sometimes. If Mark lived near where she would be . . .

Miss Mears was smiling at her nephew and now she pushed Wendy forward. "Wendy, this is my nephew, Mark. Mark, this is Wendy Williams, who has come to stay at Villa Mimosa."

Wendy was watching Mark and she saw the change in his face, the way the smile disappeared from his mouth and his gray eyes seemed to turn suddenly cool, as though he regarded her with some mysterious resentment, now that he knew her name. The change was startling, a little frightening.

"Hello," he said grudgingly and turned back to Mr. Helgerson at once. "Your room is ready, sir. I can show it to you if you like."

The guest raised eyebrows that seemed to repeat the shallow curve of his moustache. "Room? You mean cottage, don't you? It was a cottage I reserved."

Mark threw his aunt a look of entreaty and she stepped toward the desk. "Here comes my sister-in-law," she said. "I'm sure she will take care of you."

Wendy withdrew her own puzzled gaze from Mark's face and glanced down the corridor. Two women were approaching the desk. One—undoubtedly Mark's mother—was a slightly plump, cheerful-looking woman, so short that her head came just above her companion's shoulder. The second woman was tall, generously built without being fat, and she had the proudest, most graceful carriage Wendy had ever seen. She was not young, but she held her head erect, so that her white hair looked like the crown of a queen. Her skin was the color of coffee into which a little milk had been poured, and her features gave an effect of great dignity and beauty. In contrast to Mrs. Mears's yellow print, she wore a simple light-blue dress, and she moved with an air of being calmly assured and gracious. Wendy had never seen anyone like her before, and she found herself staring.

When it was evident that there was some controversy at the desk, the second woman stepped aside, though she continued to watch with bright, interested brown eyes that seemed to miss nothing.

Mrs. Mears threw Wendy a quick look of greeting and touched her shoulder lightly before she gave her attention to the desk. Pityingly? Wendy thought, always quick to be sensitive. Then Mrs. Mears spoke to Mr. Helgerson, apologizing because a cottage would not be immediately available, due to the fact that a family who had expected to vacate one had stayed on for an extra day. After all, she pointed out, Mr. Helgerson had not been promised a cottage definitely—but only if one was available.

When the man began to argue rather fussily, the stewardess drew Wendy aside and led her toward the tall, fine-looking woman with the dark skin and white hair.

"Mrs. Castillo, this is Wendy Williams, from New York."

The woman held out a warmly welcoming hand and Wendy put her own into it shyly. "Welcome to St. Thomas," Mrs. Castillo said gently, as though she understood that Wendy had not been welcomed as she had expected to be.

At the desk Mr. Helgerson had subsided and apparently agreed to be put into a regular bedroom for today. Mark picked up his bag and started

toward the corridor, striding past Wendy with a
dark look that just grazed the top of her head and
did not meet her eyes. What was the matter with
him? she wondered, feeling more puzzled by the
moment, and just a little resentful.

Mr. Helgerson started after the boy, and then
stopped beside a glass display case in the lobby,
where a number of large seashells had been placed
on view. As he paused, a man who looked a little
like Mark, though his hair was black instead of red,
came in from the veranda and stopped to watch. He
was fairly young, but somewhat heavily built.

"Ah," said Mr. Helgerson, reading a sign. "So
these shells were lent by Gordon Cole? I've heard
of Gordon's collection. A fine one, I understand.
I must have a look at it soon."

The second man had drawn near. "I'm Bob
Eagan," he said, "Mrs. Mears's nephew. Are you
interested in shells?"

Mr. Helgerson looked testy again. "Then you're
the owner of this hotel?"

Bob Eagan shook Mr. Helgerson's hand. "No—
I'm only helping out while I'm on vacation and
my aunt's husband is away in the States. I heard
you mention the Cole collection, but I'm afraid you
won't be able to look at it for a while. Maybe you
haven't heard—"

It was the stewardess, Betty Mears, who interrupted his words. "Wait, Bob!" He looked at her
in surprise and she moved nearer to speak to him
in a low voice. "It's the child—she doesn't know
yet. She wasn't met at the airport and—"

The words were hardly more than a whisper, but

Wendy heard the first of them clearly before Miss Mears dropped her voice still more and the rest was lost. There was a moment's silence in the lobby, before Mr. Helgerson threw Wendy a quick look, cleared his throat briskly, and started off in Mark's wake. Wendy's gaze sped swiftly from one to another of the faces, which all seemed to be turned her way. Bob Eagan looked uncomfortable, Mrs. Mears sympathetic and sorry, Betty as though she was not far from tears. Only Mrs. Castillo remained calm and serene.

Oddly enough it was she who rescued Wendy. "Would you like to come to my house for a while?" she asked cheerfully. "I have a granddaughter who has been looking forward to your arrival. Anita is just your age. She's out on an errand now, but she will be home soon."

"Do you suppose you could explain to the child?" Mrs. Mears asked, sounding concerned.

Mrs. Castillo regarded Wendy kindly. "I will explain. I think she will be able to face whatever difficulties must be faced. There is always an answer to be found, if one is patient." Mrs. Castillo smiled at the others and moved toward the door.

"Mark will bring your bag," she said to Wendy, and then turned to Mrs. Mears. "When they phone from Villa Mimosa, you can tell them the child is with me."

Mrs. Castillo went through the door with an air which meant that she expected to be followed. Wendy almost ran in her wish not to lose sight of this new friend. Not even the plane stewardess had given her so great a sense of being with someone safe as did this woman with the dark, smooth skin, and the fine eyes that could flash with spirit and occasional command. What she had said had sounded ominous, but her manner was reassuring.

The two followed the flagstone path, climbed steps to the gate and went through it to the dead-end road. Across the way a steep flight of stone steps ran directly upward, seeming to climb forever up Mimosa Hill. It looked as though there might be nearly a hundred steps. On each side on the way up, several small houses rose from among the pink-blossomed mimosa trees that gave the hill its name. At the very top, across a higher curve of road, stood a far larger house rising from grounds filled with tropical growth.

Mrs. Castillo paused a little way up the steps. "That is Villa Mimosa directly above us. My own house is the second one on the right. We will be happy to have you visit us."

She did not speak again, but left the steps at the beginning of a path that led to a house set along the steep incline of the hillside. Wendy did not follow at once, but stood staring up at the rather grand house which rose high above the top steps. Villa Mimosa! When she had first read the name in letters from the Coles she had loved the romantic sound of it. Now it was merely a place that did not want her.

"Have they changed their minds about me?" she asked. "Those people who live up there?"

"I don't think that's the case at all," Mrs. Castillo said. "Come along with me and we'll talk about what has happened."

2

Tragedy at Villa Mimosa

Mrs. Castillo's house was larger than it looked from the street of steps. It was a stone house, built long ago, with the parlor on the second floor reached by a narrow stairway inside. After the out-door brilliance, Wendy blinked in the dusk of the big shuttered room trying to make out the old-fashioned pieces of mahogany furniture, heavily carved and handsome, but to her eyes very strange. In this room it was cool and shaded and she could understand why the sun was shut out.

One chair in particular caught her attention. It was not mahogany, but a woven chair, with a base like a swirled cane stool. Its back rose in an enormous fan that opened like the tail of a peacock Wendy had once seen in a zoo.

Mrs. Castillo noted her interest. "That is a fan chair from Hong Kong. There are not many of them in St. Thomas. You may sit there, if you like."

She felt rather important, Wendy found, sitting in such a chair—almost like an honored guest. She sat up very straight, a hand on each sloping side, her navy blue skirt pulled neatly over her knees, her feet in white socks and brown loafers, crossed at the ankles. She was trying to be ladylike, for once, trying to make a good impression.

"Will you tell me now, please," she said, and her voice came out sounding small and timid in the big dim room.

Mrs. Castillo sat in a wooden rocker, moving gently back and forth, and as she spoke, her words seemed to match the soft, comforting movement of the rocking chair.

"You know, of course, that the Coles lost their son—their only child—nearly two months ago?"

Wendy nodded. There was a tightness in her throat, a feeling of fear and dread of what was to come.

"You would have been something of a sister to Stuart if he had lived. When the accident happened, Captain Cole took a leave of absence from his work as a pilot for a commercial airline and flew home to be with his wife. Marion went to pieces and was ill for several weeks. Before she was fully recovered, Gordon had to return to his work. He has been back home only once since then."

Wendy knew most of this and she waited, still fearful.

"Captain Cole's regular route took him out to Saigon, Singapore, Hong Kong, and the Philippines. But on his last flight he left the plane in Saigon and went by helicopter flight into the interior of Vietnam."

Mrs. Castillo paused and her eyes were kind as she watched Wendy.

"Two days ago," she went on, "word came that his helicopter had been shot down and he was lost in the jungle. A search is being made, but there is very little hope. The Vietnamese pilot found his way back alone, and didn't know what had happened to Gordon. Marion had to be told, and this time she collapsed completely. Her father and mother—Paul and Elinor Guthrie—took her to the hospital. When she grew worse there, it was decided that she would be better off at home. Mrs. Guthrie has difficulty walking, and isn't very strong so all this has been hard for her too. Today the Guthries went to the hospital to bring their daughter home. This had to be done at the time when your plane was due at the airport, and they left instructions for the maid to arrange for a taxi to go after you. The girl was excited and perhaps confused about the time. But the Guthries will be home soon and they will send for you."

Wendy sat very still in the big fan chair. Her hands were clasped tightly together now, and she felt the rattan of the chair scratching under her knees.

The words Mrs. Castillo had spoken seemed to be stirring around inside her without making very much sense. It couldn't be that two such awful things could happen so close together in one family, and that because of these tragedies in which she had played no part, she might have no place to go.

"I think it was Cousin Gordon who most wanted me to come," she said bleakly. "After Stuart died, Cousin Marion didn't write to me anymore."

"She couldn't write because she was too ill. She's much worse because of this new shock. Nevertheless Captain Cole wanted you here. You must remember that and try to help Marion."

"Help her?" Wendy asked in surprise. "How can I help anyone?"

Mrs. Castillo rocked evenly in her chair, and in the dim light her face looked beautiful, with its white mound of hair drawn gracefully back from an unwrinkled forehead. Her eyes seemed as dusky as the room and as lost in gloom, but the bright, re-assuring note was still in her voice when she spoke.

"The strong must always help the weak," she said, brisk and confident.

The strong? Wendy thought wonderingly. What Mrs. Castillo was saying meant that she believed Marion was weak — which left the word "strong" to refer to Wendy Williams.

An unfamiliar glow seemed to begin inside Wendy and flow through her as the meaning of the word penetrated. This rather grand old lady, of whom she was slightly in awe, had looked at her and had seen that she was strong. Sometimes Wendy recognized this strength in herself, but mostly it faded into an uncertainty for which she substituted quick, un-thinking action.

Once Mrs. Parks had told her that she was often strong in the wrong way — hurling herself into things, fighting and snatching, when other ways would have been better. But no one had ever looked at her with confidence and said such a thing as a compliment.

"I believe you have the strength to stand up to whatever you have to face," Mrs. Castillo went on. "You and I are alike in that. I've had to meet a great many difficulties in my life and stand up to them with whatever courage I could manage. So far, I have never met anything I could not find the strength to live through. It seems to me I can recognize the same quality in you. Even though you're very young, I think you have already been tested a few times. You won't need to be afraid when you grow up—the way Marion Cole is afraid. She is to be pitied, and you must find out how to help her."

While Wendy was thinking solemnly about Mrs. Castillo's words, a girl walked into the room and stood looking around in surprise.

"Grandmother? Oh—you have company?"

"Come join us," Mrs. Castillo said, and then to Wendy, "This is Anita Bergquist, my granddaughter. Anita, this is Wendy Williams."

Anita crossed the room with quick eagerness and held out her hand. She was a pretty girl, with wavy, dark brown hair which she wore drawn back in a long ponytail. Self-consciously Wendy took her hand in a limp shake. She was not used to shaking hands with other children.

As she studied Anita, she found herself putting on the unsmiling face with which she usually greeted strangers. You could never tell about new people. Strangers could change quickly, when you least expected it—the way that boy, Mark, had changed as soon as he knew who she was. It was safer to move with caution.

Anita, however, did not look unfriendly or frightening. Her skin was several shades lighter than her grandmother's, more olive than brown, and she had her grandmother's lively brown eyes that looked at the world with curiosity and interest. There was mischief in them too, as though Anita might be a tease.

The total of Wendy's study seemed to add up to someone who could possibly be a friend. Then she remembered Fran Parks, the best friend she had ever had, and she stiffened herself against Anita. She never wanted to go through anything like that again. It would be better to have no friends at all than to be hurt so badly.

Anita did not seem to notice her resistance. " I'm glad you've come," she said cheerfully. "Let's go outside, where it's brighter. This is such a gloomy old room."

Mrs. Castillo smiled. "My granddaughter is a typical island child. She wants to flood everything with light and color. But go out on the veranda, if you like, both of you, while I fix you something to drink."

Wendy followed Anita onto the shady side of the veranda, and then forgot her for a moment as the wide panorama of the view struck her eyes full force. Thanks to Mrs. Castillo, she felt a little calmer now, just a shade less worried, and thus she could stand at the railing and look down the steeply pitched hillside toward the lower town, the harbor, the islands, and really see them, enjoy them for the first time.

The veranda was almost like the deck of a ship, riding high over the empty hillside, with nothing but a weedy growth of grass and a huge expanse of stone, almost as big as a city block, pitching straight down the hill below the house. She knew the reason for that patch of rock. She had seen several like it on the drive from the airport. Betty Mears had explained that they were called catchments and their purpose was to collect the water that poured down the stone on those rare occasions when it rained, sending it into deep cisterns set underground at the foot of the great rock slides.

But it was the distant view that held Wendy in a spell such as she had never felt before. The clustered houses of the town were mostly white, with a few pastel shades thrown in. Their roofs were all colors, bright and sparkling in the sun. Among them were the green of trees and shrubbery, the gay patches of yellow and red and pink and purple that were flowers. And always there was the intense blue of the water, with green islands floating upon it, and the white line of the waterfront curling around toward Flag Hill. Halfway to the hill rose a lower mound on which stood the buildings of a hotel, with a gray column of stone set among them — like the tower of a castle. She had seen pictures of that and she recognized it.

"That's Bluebeard's Castle, isn't it?" Wendy cried.

Anita was happy to play guide. She explained that though the tower was very old, it hadn't really been a pirate's castle, but was called that because Bluebeard, and also Edward Teach who was called Blackbeard, and even Captain Kidd, had once put their ships into this harbor.

"There was a governor at the time who even encouraged the pirates," Anita said. "But later, law and order came in, and when pirates were caught they were hanged. A famous pirate ship was burned right out there in the harbor. She was called *La Trompeuse,* and before her burning she caused a great deal of trouble in the islands. In fact, a pirate from that ship is supposed to have escaped and come to hide on this very hill the night the ship burned. Sometimes on moonlit nights his ghost goes roaring and clanking around up here."

This Wendy could hardly believe, though she enjoyed the story.

"Clanking?" she said.

Anita's pert face was alight with mischief. "They put leg irons on them, you know, and threw them into prison. So naturally the ghosts clank."

Living far away in New York, Wendy had never known about any of this. She supposed there must be interesting stories concerning almost every place in the world and she had a sudden feeling of knowing very little about anything. Since the feeling left her a little lost and uncomfortable, she turned her back abruptly upon the harbor and the view.

"Do you know Mark Mears?" she asked.

"Of course," Anita said, "but I don't play with him much because I like girls better and he's awfully big and rough."

Yes — Anita would be likely to think that. Wendy looked down from her greater height and considered Anita a gentle little thing — though there was that look of mischief to reckon with. Probably Anita would never stand up to a boy like Mark. But just let Mark Mears start pushing Wendy Williams around, and he'd get a surprise, all right!

"I've been feeling sorry for Mark," Anita said surprisingly. "Stuart Cole was his best friend. Mark was out with him on that same trip the time Stuart drowned. I suppose Mark blames himself for not being able to save his friend — though nobody else thinks it was his fault."

This, however, was not Wendy's main concern. "Mark didn't like me," she said. And added at once, "I didn't like him either." Perhaps that might not have been true if Mark had been nicer to her, as she had to admit to herself in all honesty.

Anita nodded, but she said nothing more about Mark, and an awkward silence fell upon the two girls. Wendy sensed a hint of criticism from Anita, and she began to bristle inwardly in response.

It was fortunate that Mrs. Castillo came out on the veranda with two icy glasses of a drink made from lemons and limes.

"Mark is here with your bag," she said to Wendy. "Mr. Guthrie has phoned from Villa Mimosa and they'd like you to come up there when it's convenient. So finish your drink and you can be on your way."

In sudden anxiety Wendy felt a need to cling to the safety of the Castillo house, and especially to Mrs. Castillo, who had said she was brave, and had made her feel a little braver by saying so. She sipped her drink as slowly as she could, but eventually it was gone.

"Come now," Mrs. Castillo said to her. "Mark and I will walk up the hill with you and introduce you to your new family."

When Anita would have spoken, a question in her eyes, Mrs. Castillo shook her head. "There mustn't be too many of us. You'll see Wendy again—soon, I hope. So tell her good-by for now."

Anita did not look quite so friendly as she had in the beginning, Wendy thought when they exchanged good-bys. Only that wasn't too important because Mrs. Castillo had spoken a word that made Wendy's spine stiffen again—the word "family." She had almost forgotten. The Guthries and Coles, however distant their connection, were related to her. Marion had written her about that feeling of family in the beginning when they had found out where she was and that she was in need of someone to take care of her. Wendy still had that first wonderful, warm letter that Marion Cole had written — before she lost her son.

With Mark carrying Wendy's bag, the three started up the steps, Mrs. Castillo going first, and Wendy and Mark behind. The red-haired boy scarcely glanced at Wendy, and he did not speak on the way up.

Never in her life had Wendy climbed so many steps and she felt a little breathless before she reached the top. Mrs. Castillo was accustomed to hills and steps and she climbed easily, without getting out of breath. Mark went up like a strong young goat, passing them, so that he reached the top first.

On either hand, thick shrubbery crowded the edge of the steps, with walks cutting through to the houses on each side. The sun beat down warmly on their heads, though it was now growing late in the afternoon. Slowly they neared the Villa Mimosa, and Wendy kept her eyes upon it anxiously as she climbed.

It was a square, two-storied structure of pale yellow stone, with numerous white-shuttered windows all around, and a white roof that sloped gently upward on four sides to a slight point at the center. Both upstairs and down, wide galleries ran across the front, framed by a series of lacy ironwork arches painted white and supported by slender white columns. The beauty and dignity of the Villa was far from reassuring to Wendy. It looked like a place

where very rich people would live, and Wendy knew
nothing at all about rich people. For all its difference
from what she was accustomed to, she had not felt
uncomfortable in the Castillo house. But this house
looked altogether too grand and remote from her
experience, like a house that would disdain to notice
anyone so unimportant as Wendy Williams.

They reached the road at last, and Mrs. Castillo
paused for a moment's rest. This was not a dead-end
turn. The road curved past the Villa and round its
grounds, to climb on up the hill. Where it curved
above the pitch of the hill, there was a rough stone
wall upon which sat a bald-headed man with a brown
moustache, apparently studying the Villa Mimosa
with great concentration. From a leather strap
around his neck hung what looked like a bulky
camera case. Wendy recognized the rather dis-
agreeable Manvil Helgerson, who had come to the
hotel with them from the plane. Since Gordon Cole
was a friend of his, she wondered why he was sitting
there on the wall, instead of going up to the house.

As Mrs. Castillo crossed the road to where an
iron gate stretched between two stone posts guard-
ing a driveway, the man on the wall got up and
strolled toward them. Apparently he had recognized
Wendy, for he smiled at her in that way which
twitched the small moustache at the corners of his
mouth.

"Good afternoon," he said politely to Mrs.
Castillo, and nodded at Mark. Then he spoke
directly to Wendy. "Have you heard anything
further about Gordon Cole?" he asked.

How could there have been time? Wendy won-

dered as she shook her head.

"I've been very much disturbed by the news," he went on. "I hope everything will be all right in the long run."

"So do we," said Mrs. Castillo with quiet dignity. She too undoubtedly remembered Mr. Helgerson's behavior at the hotel and had not been favorably impressed.

With a little nod that seemed to dismiss any further questioning, she led the way to the gate and waited for Mark to open it and let them in. A driveway of crushed shell curved uphill around a stretch of green lawn, interrupted here and there by flower beds and brightly colored shrubbery. Near the house grew several pink-blossoming mimosa trees. Above rose the slim white columns of iron lacework that fronted the house. The front door was lost in the shadow of a wide stone arch.

As they followed the drive, Wendy paused halfway up and looked back toward the road. Mr. Helgerson was sitting on the wall again, but now she saw that what she had taken for a camera case really held binoculars, through which he was staring in their direction. He must have seen her watching him, for he put down the glasses and waved carelessly. It still seemed odd to Wendy that he should be studying the Villa Mimosa and their approach to it with such interest.

The rest of the climb through neat, well-kept grounds did not reassure Wendy in her growing feeling about the house. It was clear that the people who lived here must employ servants to keep everything looking so well. Indeed, as they neared the door, a yard man came from behind a clump of shrubbery, carrying a rake. He did not look like a native of the islands but as if he might be Chinese. And, she recalled, there had been earlier talk of a maid. Of course the Parks family had a cleaning woman come in once a week to help Mrs. Parks with the housework, but that had been Wendy's only experience with hired help. This place looked as though it might have servants who lived here and did everything. The very idea made Wendy feel increasingly uneasy. How would she know what was right to do and say in a place like this?

Someone inside must have noted their approach, for just as they reached the arched gallery that was set a step or two up from the drive, a man came through the inner door and crossed terra-cotta tiles to greet them.

He held out his hand to Mrs. Castillo and greeted Mark with a smile. Mrs. Castillo drew Wendy gently forward, presenting her to Mr. Guthrie, and for the first time in her life Wendy looked up into the face of someone other than her father who was related to her. Wendy's reaction was not the one of recognition and affection she had dreamed it would be. Instead, she had a feeling of fright, of despair, of knowing that she was anything but brave. Until this moment the magic word "family" had always sustained her. It was as if the word itself could erase all strangeness and make her feel at once loved and comforted and completely at ease. Now she found that this imagining was far from true.

She looked up fearfully into the face of a tall, handsome man with hair that was thick and dark, except at the graying temples, whose gray eyes seemed remote with pain—and she knew him only for a stranger. His skin was tanned as if he was accustomed to an outdoor life, and he wore slacks and a sport shirt so well cut that they seemed to Wendy to give him a well-dressed, expensive look. At no time did her father—even when he was off the bridge and dressed for town—ever manage to look like this. Paul Guthrie belonged to a different world from hers.

He held out his hand gravely and she could do nothing else but put her own into it.

"I'm sorry about this afternoon," he said. "The fault was mine. I should have made better arrangements, but my wife was almost in a state of collapse herself and we had to get Marion home from the hospital. I hope you'll forgive us."

Wendy looked at him, swallowing hard, feeling horribly self-conscious and unable to think of anything to say to this tall, distinguished-looking man.

He seemed to sense her fright, even though he probably did not understand it, and he smiled at her —a sad, kind smile—before he let go her hand and invited them all inside.

Mrs. Castillo shook her head. "Not just now, thank you. Mark and I will run along and leave you to get acquainted with Wendy. At least this mix-up enabled us to meet her sooner than we expected."

Still Mark did not look at Wendy but set down her bag with a thump and stood aside to wait until someone told him what to do with it.

"Thank you, Mark," Mr. Guthrie said. "I'll take the bag now. And thanks to you both for bringing Wendy up here."

Mrs. Castillo paused a moment before turning away. "Marion? How is she?"

Mr. Guthrie shook his head and the sadness in his eyes deepened. "We're worried about her. I'm afraid she has given up completely. It's dreadful to stand by and find ourselves helpless to do anything."

"Healing will take time," Mrs. Castillo said. "Perhaps Wendy's coming here will help."

Mr. Guthrie nodded. "I hope so. Though I'm afraid it's not going to be very cheerful or interesting for a young person to stay in this house just now."

"Wendy will do fine," said Mrs. Castillo with confidence, and touched Wendy's shoulder lightly. "If there are moments when she doesn't know what to do, you can always let her look through Gordon's shell collection. That's a fascinating experience for anyone. And she must come and visit Anita soon."

At mention of the shell collection, Mr. Guthrie looked faintly worried. "Well — I don't know. Thank you again for your help. Come in, Wendy, and meet your Aunt Elinor."

Mrs. Castillo and Mark set off down the drive and Wendy found herself feeling even more alone than she had at the airport. Up to this point she had looked forward to meeting her family. Now she knew the truth. These people were only more strangers, and they could not possibly want her here at this time. She followed Mr. Guthrie into the house, but she was far from sure that she would "do all right," as Mrs. Castillo had said. Just before she stepped through the door, she turned her head quickly, entreatingly, to look back at her new friend. But Anita's grandmother was already far down the drive with the unfriendly red-haired boy at her side.

3

Inside the Villa

THE MAIN room of the Villa Mimosa was like a
long, very wide hall, running through from front
to rear. The outside galleries kept the sun from
streaming into this room, and it was cool and comfortable, though not so shuttered as Mrs. Castillo's
living room. At first glance the room seemed overwhelming to Wendy. It was so big and so elegant.
That was the right word, she felt, though until now
she had come across it only in storybooks.

The parquet floor was glossy with polish, and the
furniture that occupied the vast space looked like
something out of a magazine picture. It was not the
furniture for an any-old-place where people lived
together in homey comfort. Lamp shades were
creamy-white parchment, and lovely paintings
glowed upon the walls. Far overhead was the highest of ceilings, almost like those she had seen in
museums in New York. It was gleaming white, with
plaster ornamentation at the corners, and in the
center rosette hung a great chandelier, dripping and
twinkling with crystal. All this seemed unreal to
Wendy. It was too grand, like something out of a
movie.

Tongue-tied and growing more uncomfortable by the moment, she moved in the direction Mr. Guthrie's hand gently propelled her. As she walked down the room, an alarming thought swept over her. In her mind was a sudden vision of her father whooping his way into this room, setting the crystal of the chandelier to shrilling with the very timbre of his voice, laughing out loud, so that all the paintings on the walls would shiver at the sound. He was always so full of life and used to being out of doors, that houses seldom silenced him. Her skin prickled at the thought of his coming into this room in his usual way.

Because she hated any criticism of her father, she scowled fiercely at Mr. Guthrie, who had made none and who looked a little surprised. He led her toward a woman lying on a sofa in a shadowy part of the room, her head propped against cushions, and a handkerchief held to her mouth. Wendy saw a single metal crutch on the floor nearby.

"Elinor dear," Mr. Guthrie said, "I want you to meet our young Wendy."

The woman on the sofa choked with an emotion she could not control and put out her other hand. Wendy could see little of her face because of the handkerchief held across her mouth, but Elinor Guthrie's eyes were red and swollen from weeping, and the thin wisps of gray hair around her forehead looked damp and untidy. Wendy touched the hand that reached toward her, and withdrew from it at once because the fingers felt unpleasantly hot and seemed to quiver as they touched her.

"We've decided," Mr. Guthrie spoke to Wendy,

overlooking the lack of welcome on his wife's part, "that even though your relationship to us is that of a cousin several times removed, we had better simplify matters by having you call me Uncle Paul and my wife Aunt Elinor. Then you can address Marion as Cousin—and Gordon too, when he comes home. Will that suit you?"

Nothing suited her. All Wendy longed for was to escape from this awe-inspiring house, from the weeping woman on the couch, and even from the tall, dignified man who was trying so hard to be kind. But escape where? to what?

"Take her up to Marion!" The woman on the couch found her voice, though it trembled. "Take her upstairs and see if it will do any good."

Uncle Paul hesitated, looking uncertainly down at his wife. "I'm not sure—" he began, "perhaps we'd best not move too quickly."

Impatience marked Elinor Guthrie's answer. "What is there to lose? Anything that might bring Marion to life must be tried. She can't go on like this. I can't go on like this!"

"You're right, of course," Uncle Paul said. "But I was thinking of Wendy. Perhaps this is rushing things a bit—when the child has been brought so suddenly into a strange place, into a situation she never expected." He turned to Wendy, still grave and courteous, as though she were grown up. "What would you prefer?"

Wendy found herself looking desperately about the room as if for an answer. One of the pictures on the wall was of a snow scene in the woods—of brown trees, a small brown house, and golden winter

sunshine falling along a rutted, icy road. She let her
eyes rest on the strange contrast the picture offered
to the hot, bright, tropical scene outdoors. At least
a picture of snow looked familiar and she let her
gaze focus on it, let it soothe and calm her a little.

Finally—because Uncle Paul was waiting—she
said grudgingly, "I don't care." Marion was just
another stranger. Gordon—who had seemed ready
to love and accept her—was gone. The one friendly
letter Marion had written was now as though it had
never been.

Mr. Guthrie led the way toward a staircase that
rose at the back of the room. Wendy came with him,
and he spoke again in his gentle, rather formal way.

"I suppose we're more used to boys than girls in
this house," he said as they started up the graceful,
curving staircase.

Wendy knew he must be thinking of his grandson,
Stuart, who would never go running up these steps
again.

Upstairs everything in the long hallway, except
the polished floor, was painted white and had a cool,
spotlessly clean look. Outside a door that was partly
ajar, Uncle Paul paused.

"Don't expect too much at first," he said to
Wendy. "I have a feeling that this is something we
must go into gradually. Remember that Marion has
endured two dreadful shocks in a short space of time
and she isn't herself. At the moment I think she's
trying not to feel anything."

Wendy would have liked to hold back, but the
door to Marion's room stood open before her. Uncle
Paul's hand was on her shoulder, with a light pres-

sure once more exerted. He spoke over her head to someone in the room — a nurse, apparently.

"May we come in, Miss Smith?"

A brown-skinned young woman came to the door, nodded gravely, and then stepped aside.

The bedroom, Wendy saw, was large and airy, with white shutters half closed against the sun. Cotton draperies in a green bamboo pattern hung beside windows and glass doors, and the furniture was all of some pale-colored wood. Twin beds stood with their heads against one pale green wall, and one of them was made up and empty. In the other lay a woman with short, curly blond hair and a face that might have been young and pretty — had it not so much resembled a colorless mask. Her eyes were closed and they did not open until Uncle Paul spoke to her.

"Marion dear, I've brought Wendy to see you."

When her eyes opened, Wendy saw that they were a deep, violet-blue, but blank and without any feeling in them. There were no pink traces of constant weeping here, no swollen eyelids. The violet gaze regarded her for a moment and then shifted to the ceiling. The woman did not speak, and it was clear that she had no greeting, no word of welcome to offer Wendy. It was as if she did not see her, or accept her presence in the room.

Uncle Paul sighed, but when he spoke there was a note of reproof in his voice.

"Gordon wanted her to come, Marion — you must remember that. Even after what happened to — to Stuart, Gordon felt that it was right for Wendy to come, that you both had something to give her, and

that she had something to give you. It's time now
to remember this."

The woman on the bed closed her eyes again and
the words she spoke were so faint Wendy could
hardly catch them.

"I don't want to remember. I don't want to remember — anything."

"Come, my dear," Uncle Paul said gently to
Wendy. "We'll try again another time. That's all
we can do — keep trying."

But Wendy did not want to try anymore. Her
situation only seemed to be getting worse.

"Perhaps you'd like to see your room," Uncle
Paul was saying as he led the way along the hall.
"I think you'll like it. Marion gave a great deal of
thought to getting it ready for you because you're
our first daughter in this house."

She could feel his kindness reaching out toward
her, but she rejected and resisted it. His being sorry
for her wasn't going to help one bit.

Uncle Paul stepped ahead of Wendy to open a
door at one side of the hall. "Here you are," he said.

The room welcomed her.

She had not expected that anything could get past
her guard at the moment, but this room reached out
to her and told her it was hers. It wasn't a girly-girly
room, all frills and furbelows of the sort she disliked,
and she suddenly recalled the questions both Marion
and Gordon had asked of her in their letters, learning about the things she liked to do, her interests.

It was a room filled with the warm golden yellow
of the Virgin Islands sun and the green of growing
things. That was because she had written them

about a suburban house she had once visited in the spring. There had been no gray city streets and she could be outdoors all the time. In this room they had prepared for her, daffodils grew on the walls, so that it would always be spring. Even the green bedspread had a pile like thick green grass.

The furniture was maple, with a no-nonsense shelf, instead of a fussy dressing table, and a neat oblong of mirror hung above it. There was a big green chair filled with small pillows, a lamp ready beside it; a long-legged, growing girl could curl up in that chair in any position she liked and read comfortably to her heart's content. There were shelves with books — whole rows of books. It was the books, more than anything else, that held her attention and welcomed her. She had told them how much she liked to read. In spite of everything, her heart lifted a little.

"I hope you'll be happy here," Uncle Paul said.

He truly wanted her to be happy and the thought brought tears to her eyes. To hide her feelings she stood in the middle of the floor and stared at the circular straw rug that was woven into a design like fine lace.

He thought she was interested in the rug and explained it to her. "The natives of the island of Dominica weave those rugs," he said. "We like them because they're cool and decorative. Marion picked that one for your room."

Wendy nodded and said nothing because there was nothing to say. The room welcomed her, but Cousin Marion had not.

Uncle Paul glanced at his watch, "It's not long

till dinner time. I see your bag has been brought in. Suppose I leave you to unpack and get freshened up. There's a bathroom just across the hall. Do you know about our water shortage in St. Thomas? We never have enough water, so we have to be careful not to leave taps running, or waste water in any way."

Again Wendy nodded and waited for him to leave.

"Come down when you hear the gong," he said. "I'll be looking for you."

He went out and closed the door softly behind him. Wendy drew a long, deep breath and relaxed a little. Slowly she moved about the room, examining everything, letting each piece of furniture speak to her. Things were safer than people. Things stayed the same and never let you down the way people did.

When she knew everything that the room had to tell her, she knelt on the floor beside her suitcase, and opened it to unpack. As she hung her things away in the big closet, where they took up very little room, she pretended to herself that she was the daughter of a wealthy family and was coming home from school for summer vacation. Of course loving parents were waiting for her downstairs and she must unpack quickly so that she could join them. Soon the telephone would begin to ring because all her old friends would be calling her up to tell her how glad they were she was home, and making plans, making dates for swimming and boating — all the lovely things there were to do in these islands.

Once she paused beside the bookcase to draw out a volume, and reality swept back These were new books, not long-treasured old ones. Someone had taken the trouble to choose them for her, to fill most of the space on the shelves with books about all sorts of things—travel and baseball and science fiction. As she bent to read titles, she saw stories that were old favorites, which she would love reading again, and stories more recently published, waiting to beckon her into exciting new worlds.

Examining the books reminded her of how recently she had begun to love reading. When she had been sent to the Parkses' house, she hadn't cared about books because she couldn't read very well. But Mrs. Parks was a teacher and she set to work helping Wendy to enjoy reading. Since everyone read in the Parks household, it wasn't long before Wendy picked up the habit—and now books had become an important part of her life. Books could be counted on.

More than anything else, the books on these shelves told her of the love and welcome that had gone into making this room ready for her. Surely these feelings couldn't have vanished because Gordon Cole was lost in some Vietnamese jungle, and because Marion lay across the hall not wanting to live.

Yet they could—they had.

She put the last book back and turned away, knowing that she had been making believe. There was no family, no old friends. This room was hers only on loan—for how long, she couldn't tell. If Marion no longer wanted her here, she probably could not stay. No matter how kind Uncle Paul might be, he could not take care of her if his wife and daughter did not want her here.

Resentful again, she looked into the mirror at her own face. Her eyes were as blue as Pop's and they flashed the way his could at times. She drew a comb through her short, dark hair with sharp tugs and then crossed the hall to the bathroom to clean up.

A gong sounded just as she finished and she went doubtfully toward the stairs. The nurse was carrying a tray to Cousin Marion's room — soup and crackers and a glass of milk. She smiled at Wendy as she went past, but Wendy could not smile back.

The staircase curved in a way that drew the eye pleasingly. There was a polished mahogany rail and beneath it the same sort of lacy ironwork she had seen in those arches across the front of the house. The steps turned in polished wedges around the curve and then straightened to carry her directly down into the big main hall.

As she descended, Wendy saw that Aunt Elinor no longer lay upon the sofa. Only Uncle Paul stood waiting for her near the foot of the stairs. He had put on a white jacket for dinner and looked very handsome with his tall figure and distinguished-looking, graying hair. When she reached the last step he made her a slight bow and she sensed that he was anxious about her, even if no one else was.

"I hope you will do me the honor to dine with me tonight, Miss Williams," he said. "The rest of the family has forsaken me, and I don't like dining alone."

His gray eyes had an unexpected twinkle in them and she knew he was making a little joke. She had not thought he could unbend like this, but her face still wore the stiff, angry look she had seen in the mirror, and she did not know how to change it. She could not feel like smiling or playing silly games. He seemed not to notice her expression, as he led her into the dining room, behaving as though she was indeed an honored guest. Just as the bedroom upstairs had welcomed her at once, this room quickly awed her. It was big and high-ceilinged and grand. The walls were paneled in polished wood; the table was the longest she had ever seen. There were place mats of pale beige linen, instead of a tablecloth, and the table was set with beautiful silver and glassware. Again there were handsome paintings on the walls, some of them with their own little lights shining above, like paintings in a museum.

"This is a big table for the two of us," he said, "but I see that Rachel has put us cozily together at one end. Suppose you sit in this chair on my right, and I'll take my usual place."

He drew out one of the high-backed chairs and she slipped onto the rush seat and let him push her into place at the table. At least she knew about watching others at a table when she was uncertain about what to do. Mrs. Parks had taught her that.

They ate in a pleasant glow of candlelight, and it was a little like dining in a storybook castle. In the center of the table and on the buffet, white candles burned, their flames steady and tall because they were shielded by great cylinders of glass — hurricane globes, Uncle Paul said. The soft light touched the bars of gray at his temples, and softened the lines of sadness in his face.

Wendy found that she was terribly hungry. The

jellied consommé and salted crackers were deli-
cious, and not even the elegant room and complicated service could dampen her appetite. Now that
she was safely seated at the table, she ate through
the entire meal with considerable relish. At least
she could stop worrying about everything else
while she was hungry. All the concerns and inner
resentments, all the fears, ceased for a little while.
She simply put them off until later and enjoyed the
island fish and puffy little potatoes, the crisp salad
— made with lettuce and tomatoes that had to be
brought from Puerto Rico and Florida, Uncle Paul
told her, because St. Thomas was too dry for the
growing of vegetables. At the end there was lemon
sherbet and cookies for dessert, and when she was
done with the meal, Wendy found that she felt much
better than she had before eating.

She could even smile at Uncle Paul and listen to
his stories without feeling resentful. She knew that
he had tried very hard to keep her entertained all
through the meal and had asked her questions that
got her to talking a little. By the time she left the table,
Wendy felt almost comfortable for the first time in
this house, and when something interesting caught
her eye, she found she could ask questions herself.

In one corner stood a huge, very old, ironbound
chest, its rounded lid closed with a big iron padlock.
It looked battered and rather out of place in a dining
room.

"What's that?" Wendy asked.

Uncle Paul took pleasure in showing it to her.
"This is a real pirate chest, brought up from the
sea and dating back to the days when pirates roamed

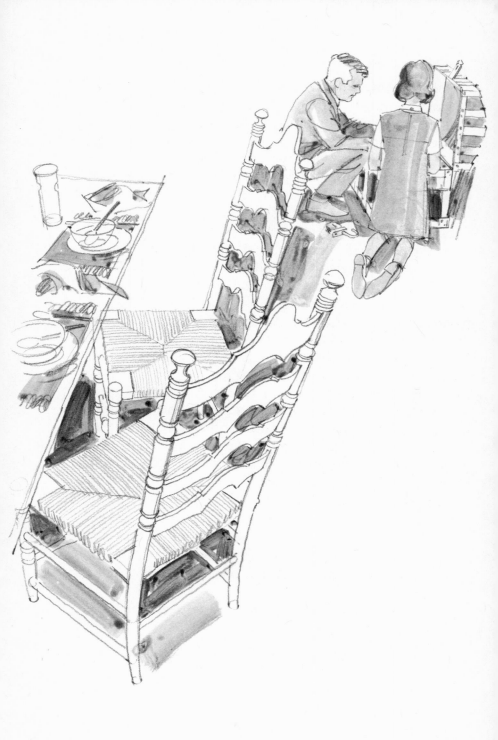

these waters. I've had it partly rebuilt, because sea-water disintegrates everything. But it's still the real thing. Look what I have inside."

He removed the padlock and opened the creaking cover. One by one he drew out articles of fine clothing—a great plumed hat, a green doublet, leather boots with deep turned-over cuffs, a dark red velvet cape with a golden buckle. And last of all, a murderous-looking sword with a handle guard and curving blade.

"This is a cutlass," he said. "The machetes of the Caribbean are based on these old swords that came into the area aboard sailing ships hundreds of years ago. These clothes are supposed to have belonged to a pirate who was hanged on the gallows on Frenchman's Hill."

Wendy stared, fascinated, though slightly disbelieving. She had read *Treasure Island* and she didn't think pirates had dressed like this.

Uncle Paul seemed to read her doubtful expression. "Not all pirates went around wearing a black patch over one eye and looking like ruffians. Many were renegade gentlemen, and they liked to dress like gentlemen when they came ashore. They say there was an elegant house on this very hill where pirates were welcomed and entertained. Legend has it that when there's a gibbous moon, you can hear them roistering and laughing and—"

"Clanking," Wendy put in.

Uncle Paul smiled. "Somebody's been telling you about the leg irons."

"Anita told me," Wendy said.

Uncle Paul put the cutlass back in the chest and

closed the lid. The pirate garments he laid on a chair.

"I promised to lend these to Mrs. Mears," he said. "There's to be a fancy-dress party at the hotel and she wants to borrow them to copy for her nephew, Bob Eagan, to wear. He's an interesting fellow, by the way. His company sends him all over the world to find unusual articles to import to Caribbean stores, and he can tell some pretty exciting stories."

Though Wendy was listening with interest, she suddenly surprised herself with a wide yawn.

Uncle Paul smiled in sympathy. "You've had a long day. Perhaps this is one night when you might like to go to bed early."

She had to agree. Her eyes were growing heavy in spite of herself. Uncle Paul walked with her to the foot of the stairs and held out his hand gravely. He made no attempt to joke now.

"It's always possible for tomorrow to be better," he said. "So don't worry—just hope. We want very much to make you feel welcome here, Wendy, even though we can't tell what the future holds. Maybe you can help us, and then everything may improve."

She knew what he meant, but she could not feel entirely comforted. There was no telling whether she could remain here or not—because who was to look after her properly if she did stay? How she was to help that, she didn't know. She said good night solemnly, and climbed the stairs to her room.

The quick dusk of the tropics had fallen while they had been eating dinner at the candlelit table, and her room was dark when she opened the door and stepped inside. She turned on no lights. All her fear and uncertainty, all the strangeness of this house, had come sweeping back. She did not undress and get ready for the night, but simply went to the bed and flung herself across it. From the open French doors that led to the gallery outside her room there came a loud humming of night insects, and a touch of cooling breeze from the sea.

She lay quietly on the bed and wept without making a sound. Long ago she had learned how to cry without letting anyone know. Because if other children knew, they laughed at you; and if grown-ups knew, they came rushing in with silly questions and scoldings, beseeching you to cheer up and tell them what was the matter. She didn't want to cheer up or explain anything to anybody. She simply wanted to be alone with all her troubles and doubts so that she might cry herself out.

Practically in the middle of a choking sob she fell sound asleep and knew nothing more of her surroundings until she felt a hand gently shaking her awake. She sat up with a start and found that a lamp had been lighted in her room and a woman in a white uniform was shaking her by the shoulder. It was the young nurse with the warm brown eyes and gentle smile — Miss Smith from Cousin Marion's room.

"It is better not to sleep in your clothes," she said softly, "so I must wake you up. Otherwise in the morning you will be uncomfortable. But now, since you are dressed, will you please come to Mrs. Cole's room? She wishes to speak with you."

Mrs. Cole? That was Cousin Marion. Wendy rolled herself off the bed. She could not have been asleep very long. Standing in the middle of the circular straw rug, she stretched widely and shook herself awake. Her face felt odd and she knew it was stiff with dried tears — but she could not worry about that. If Cousin Marion was asking for her, that must mean something. Something good. It must mean that Marion was feeling better and wasn't in the unfriendly, indifferent state she had been in earlier.

Miss Smith sensed the hope that flooded through Wendy, and shook her head. "Please — she is the same. But she wants something of you. I don't know what it is, but you must come quickly."

Wendy ran ahead of her toward Cousin Marion's door. Then, suddenly hesitant, she waited for Miss Smith to open it, to push her gently inside. She heard the door close behind her, heard Miss Smith go off down the hall. For the first time Wendy was alone with Cousin Marion.

4

The Cone-shaped Shell

A SINGLE LAMP burned on a bed table. In its radiance Marion Cole lay against the pillow, her face pale and expressionless, her eyes closed. Though a cool breeze blew in from the gallery door, the tendrils of fair hair around her forehead looked damp with perspiration.

Wendy went to stand at the foot of the bed, studying her doubtfully. Marion must have heard Wendy come in, yet she did not open her eyes, or make a sound. On the foot of the bed lay a palm-leaf fan that the nurse must have been using, and Wendy gestured toward it.

"Would you like me to fan you?" she asked.

The violet-blue eyes opened and really looked at her for the first time. Not in any friendly, affectionate, welcoming way, but as if the woman on the bed was trying to learn something by staring. When her question came, it was whispered in a voice so low that Wendy had to lean toward her to hear it.

"Can I trust you?" Marion Cole asked.

It was a startling question under such circumstances, and Wendy had no idea what it meant. Nevertheless she sensed that this was not the time to challenge, or to ask a question of her own.

"I—I think so," she said.

Cousin Marion raised herself weakly against her pillows. "That's a better answer than an outright promise. I want you to do something for me—but without telling anyone else about it."

Wendy listened uncomfortably. She had no idea whether she should do what Cousin Marion wanted or not, so she simply waited to see what more was to come.

Marion must have sensed her hesitation, for she made an attempt to explain. "If I ask Mother, she'll be upset and frightened—and I've already upset her enough. If I ask Father, he'll laugh at the whole idea. I'm afraid the nurse or any of the servants would talk. So I've been lying here thinking of you. Will you help me?"

Thus appealed to, Wendy could do nothing else. After all, her whole future might depend on whether or not she could please Marion Cole.

"I'll try," she said.

"Come closer then," Cousin Marion whispered, and when Wendy came around the end of the bed, she reached out and clasped her hand in tight, warm fingers. "Has Father shown you Gordon's shell collection yet?"

Wendy shook her head. She did not like being grasped so frantically, but she did not dare to pull away.

"The shells are kept in a little room downstairs, just off the main hall. It's the first room at the back, on the right-hand side near the stairs. There's a light switch inside the door, but close the door before you turn it on. Then no one will see the light. Do you understand what I'm telling you?"

"Y—yes," Wendy faltered.

The voice of the woman on the bed grew stronger as she continued. "You're to go straight down the room to the end. You'll see that there are shelves all around, with the shell collection set out on display. At the very end of the room there's a corner row of shelves. Count three up from the bottom. On the third shelf, right in the corner, is a big conch shell—rather spiny and ugly. If you reach behind it, you'll find a smaller, cone-shaped shell. It's cream-colored, with dark brown markings on it that look almost like lettering. That's the shell I want. Bring it to me here."

The hot, tight fingers let go of Wendy's hand and the woman lay back on her pillow, looking pale and exhausted.

Still uncertain, Wendy went to the door. Just as she reached it, Marion spoke to her softly across the room.

"Tell the nurse I'd like some lemonade. Ask her to make it fresh in the kitchen. That will keep her busy while you bring back the shell. Mother's in her room and Father will be outside for his evening stroll. Don't let anyone see the shell. Do you understand?"

"I understand," Wendy said and stepped into the hall.

At once Miss Smith rose from a chair where she had been waiting and came toward her. Before she could ask questions, Wendy delivered the message about the lemonade, and the nurse hurried downstairs to the kitchen without any objection.

Quietly Wendy stole after her. The long main room glowed with lamplight, but it was empty now. Wendy slipped behind the curve of the stairs and found a door at the back of the house. The knob turned easily at her touch and she stepped into the hot darkness of a closed room. Nervously her hand sought the wall switch beside the door and at her touch the small room sprang into life, clearly lighted by a frosted ceiling fixture overhead. Wendy stood very still looking about her, and for the first time since dinner something of her discouragement and uncertainty fell away and she tingled with unexpected excitement. After all, it was rather fun to be sent on a secret mission by Marion Cole. If she could do exactly what her cousin wanted, this might be the beginning of a friendship between them. Besides—the errand seemed mysterious, and this was a mysterious room and therefore intriguing.

It was furnished with a leather-topped desk and a few chairs, but mainly it was a room of shelves with shells set upon them, as Marion had said. Wendy would have liked to linger, looking at one strange seashell after another, but she must move quickly before Miss Smith came back with the lemonade.

As she went down the room she glanced hastily around at shells of every shape and size and color. The room was like an underwater chamber, where wriggling fish might come swimming past at any moment.

There were windows, and although they were closed, she wondered if someone might see the light shining out upon the garden and come to find out what she was up to. What would she say? Hurrying, she found the corner row of shelves. She did not need to count three shelves up because the big conch shell was clearly in view. It was an odd-looking shell with spidery legs sticking out from its lower edge. One of them pricked her hand as she reached past it and closed her fingers upon the smaller, cone-shaped shell Marion had sent her for. It was a heavy shell for its size — a little too large for her hand to close around it completely. As she drew it out, she noted the dark brown markings set all around in even rows, like lettering on a piece of paper.

It must be the right shell, and she clasped it tightly and ran back toward the door. As she was about to open it, she heard voices and quickly turned out the light. She opened the door cautiously and peered out. From where she stood she could see down the long main room through wide doors to the gallery out in front. There two men sat in cane chairs talking quietly, clearly visible in the light from the house. One of them was Uncle Paul, the other Mr. Helgerson from the hotel. Apparently he had decided to come up here to talk to Gordon's father-in-law.

Both men sat turned away from her, and Wendy hurried up the stairs without being seen. From the direction of the kitchen she could hear the tinkling of ice, so she was still ahead of Miss Smith.

She had left Marion's door open a crack and she slipped through quickly and closed it behind her. Then she went to the bed and held out the spotted shell without speaking. Marion was waiting for her,

and she lifted her hand to take the shell. A quick look seemed to tell her that it was the right one, and she shoved it out of sight beneath her pillow and closed her eyes.

Once more at a loss, Wendy stood watching her. If she had expected some friendly response, a few words of thanks, she was disappointed. It was as if, now that she had the shell, Cousin Marion had forgotten all about her. Nevertheless, looking down at the white suffering of the face on the pillow, Wendy could not feel as resentful as she had before. For the first time a faint stirring of pity moved her. Here was someone who had even worse trouble than she had — someone whose inner hurting must be very hard to bear.

The woman on the bed spoke suddenly without opening her eyes. "Thank you for helping me. But don't tell anyone. When you go, will you turn on the dressing-table lamp and switch off the one by the bed? It shines in my eyes."

Silently Wendy sped to the dressing table and reached her hand toward the lamp switch. As she did so, she noticed a photograph in a silver frame resting on the glass top of the dressing table and she bent to see it better. It was the picture of a man, a woman, and a boy. The man wore a pilot's uniform and he had an arm about the woman, a hand on the shoulder of the boy. This, Wendy knew, must be Cousin Gordon, who had written her such friendly letters. The woman was the pretty, gay Marion of a happier time, and the boy, of course, was Stuart, who might have been like a brother to Wendy Williams if he had lived.

The family looked happy together and it was a family she might have belonged to. Wendy swallowed hard past the lump in her throat, turned on the dressing-table lamp, and hurried to switch off the one on the bed table. Marion said nothing more and Wendy reached the door just as Miss Smith returned with the lemonade. The nurse's dark eyes questioned her, but Wendy slipped quickly away. She did not want to be asked any questions she could not answer.

Back in her own room she got ready for bed, taking off her clothes and putting on her pajamas. Then she went to the gallery door and stepped outside into the warm, buzzing night. What an uproar the insects made, and how bright the moon was, coming up over the island. Her door opened on the side of the house, and the gallery, shimmering in silver light, invited her to explore. Walking softly in her straw slippers, she went around a corner to the front where the broad veranda stretched behind its arches of lacy white ironwork. She stepped to the rail and looked down upon the shadowy garden, and as she did so, the two men left the gallery beneath and came out on the driveway. There Mr. Helgerson shook hands with Uncle Paul and started toward the hotel.

Wendy watched until he was out of sight on the long flight of steps that ran down the hill. There was something strange about that man, she thought. Somehow he did not act quite like other people. That was it—he acted as though he were acting. Why didn't he behave in a natural way? Why had he seemed so interested in the Villa Mimosa? And what had been his business here with Uncle Paul?

Well, it wasn't her affair.

She put her hands upon the cool iron railing and stood looking out over the gold and navy blue of the nighttime scene. In New York the sky was often a murky yellow and it was hard to see the stars, but this sky was a very dark blue and there were millions of bright, close stars. Far below them the lighted windows of the town seemed to float against the sea. Following the crescent of the dark harbor, lights made a necklace of bright beads and there were airplane beacons on the highest hills. A separate concentration of lights clustered where Bluebeard's Castle stood on its mound. Thinking of the name made her remember pirates and Uncle Paul's words.

What, she wondered, was a gibbous moon? Somehow the word had a spooky sound. She looked warily at the area lost in shadow below the villa and wondered if anyone had really seen that roistering, clanking figure of a pirate in recent years. When she looked out across the curve of harbor where the shape of Flag Hill rose black against the dark blue sky, she could imagine how it must have been out there on the night that pirate ship, *La Trompeuse,* had burned to the water. She shivered pleasantly and took a deep breath of the flower-sweetened air. Somehow she liked this place, pirates and all—liked it increasingly. It would be lovely to stay here—if only it weren't for people! Unfriendly people who didn't know what to do about Wendy Williams.

Abruptly she turned from the glittering scene, unable to bear its beauty any longer, and fled back along the gallery and around the corner of the house to her own room. There she knelt before her suit-case and searched the remainder of its contents for two things. The first was a small framed snapshot tucked into a side pocket of the case. She drew it out and sat there on the floor studying it while the lump in her throat grew larger by the moment.

The man in the snapshot was large and rather burly. He wore a heavy khaki shirt and trousers, and the rounded "hardhat" of his trade sat squarely upon his head. Behind him rose the massive steel girders of a bridge. The jaunty smile she knew so well seemed to tease her, and his heavy, bristling eyebrows rose in that high curve that marked them whenever he smiled broadly.

Resolutely Wendy carried the small picture to her dressing shelf and set it there, just as the large picture was set on Cousin Marion's dressing table. It wasn't, she reminded herself for the thousandth time, as though she was really an orphan. Pop cared about what happened to her. He worried about her a lot. He had told her so. He sent her postcards whenever he could and he sent money for her clothes, and presents at odd, unexpected times. When he was with her he often talked about the education he wanted her to have — a better education than his own. When he had worked on the Ver-razano-Narrows Bridge out in New York harbor, he had come to see her several times and he had been concerned because it might be necessary for her to leave the Parkses. When the invitation from her mother's relatives had come up, he had been pleased and had given his permission by telegram. Later he had written her one of the few long letters he had ever sent and she had treasured it. In it he said that perhaps someday he would visit her in St. Thomas. Remembering her reactions when she had arrived at Villa Mimosa today, she felt a little uneasy about that. Still — he probably wouldn't come, and she might not be here, anyway. She wasn't one to worry ahead of time.

There was something else she had left in her suitcase, tucked beneath an old sweater. She pulled out a squashy, plush koala bear and sat for a while holding it tightly. Long ago she had given Pookie up as a toy to sleep with, but now she wanted him with her. Pop had sent him to her when she was small and he was bridge-building in Australia. The little bear had been with her practically all her life.

Someone knocked on the door and Wendy started up guiltily, dropping Pookie back into the suitcase. The voice was Miss Smith's.

"I've brought you a glass of milk and some cookies," she said. "Your uncle sent them up to you. He wants to know if there's anything you need."

Wendy ran to the door and took the plate with the glass on it and thanked the nurse. When she carried it back to her bed and sat there drinking the milk, she felt a little better. They hadn't forgotten her completely. Someone had thought of her comfort. Later, when she turned off the light and got under the sheet, she pushed the pillow away and rested her head on Pookie without shame. The two of them belonged to each other. Together they had gone through all the changes that had beset Wendy in her life. Besides, he made a very good pillow. He had been punched and squashed and even chewed on for so long that he fitted right into the curve of her cheek and shoulder.

She fell asleep easily and soundly, and without any more tears.

5

Marion

THE NEXT morning Wendy slept late and no one disturbed her. Somehow Pookie was under the bed when she got up and she put him somewhat shamefacedly back in her suitcase and closed the lid. She was glad he could remain a secret.

As she washed and dressed, she remembered what Uncle Paul had said last night: "Tomorrow can always be better." Everything did seem better about this bright, sunny morning. The very daffodils on her walls had a cheerful look. When she was ready she went downstairs and the maid, Rachel, directed her to a little room where she could breakfast alone at a small table without feeling overpowered by the grandness of the big dining room.

As she ate she began to consider seriously all that had happened to her since her arrival. While it had been happening, there had been very little time to think. Particularly she wondered about the strange errand Cousin Marion had sent her on last night, and the secrecy for which she had asked. Why—with all the trouble that beset her—had Marion Cole been concerned about a shell? It must have been a very important matter for her to rouse herself and send Wendy to get the shell for her, and then to insist that she tell no one what she had done. Wendy wished there was someone she could ask about this, but she had promised Cousin Marion to say nothing.

She had finished her scrambled eggs and bacon when Uncle Paul looked in to ask how she had slept. She tried to be pleasanter than she had managed to be yesterday, and he seemed pleased with her response. Perhaps if she behaved nicely, if she was quiet and gave no one any trouble, they would let her stay here and wait for Marion to get better. Certainly Cousin Marion could not be wholly against her after asking a favor of her last night.

Wendy went into the main room with Uncle Paul just as Mark Mears came across the gallery to the front door, and Uncle Paul invited him in. His hair looked redder than ever in the morning sun. He wasn't a handsome boy, and the gloomy, worried expression he wore did not help his appearance. He addressed himself at once to Uncle Paul, with only a faintly resentful look for Wendy — which she ignored. There was no reason to be nice to Mark, when he so clearly did not mean to be nice to her.

His mother had sent him to see if there was anything useful he could do for Uncle Paul. But when it seemed that there was nothing, he had a request of his own to make, and he made it awkwardly, with a sidelong glance of warning at Wendy, as if he feared she might laugh at him.

"Mom said it would be all right to ask. Do you suppose, Mr. Guthrie — that is, do you think —" he broke off and then started over in a rush. "Could I have something to keep that belonged to Stuart?"

Uncle Paul nodded kindly. "I'm sure you can, Mark. But let me check into the matter first. If you can stay around for a little while, I'll let you know. Something must be done soon about Stuart's things."

Mark nodded silently and twisted his big hands behind his back. He looked upset and sad, Wendy thought, and she felt a little sorry for him, in spite of her resentment.

When Uncle Paul went upstairs to talk to his wife and daughter, Mark wandered toward the rear of the room, and Wendy, not anxious to be alone with him, stepped outside onto the gallery. The view by day from this hillside was even more beautiful than by night—but after she had stared at the bright blue waters for a while, and watched the big white cruise ships that were docked across the harbor at the foot of Flag Hill, she got tired of a scene where nothing seemed to be happening and went back inside. Mark had disappeared, and down the length of the room the shell collection seemed to beckon to her. Last night she'd had no chance to look at the individual shells. Since she had nothing else to do, perhaps this would be a good time.

The door of the little room stood ajar and she opened it with caution and stepped inside—only to find that someone was there ahead of her. Mark Mears stood before one of the shelves, in the act of either taking down or putting back a shell. Wendy would have thought nothing of the fact, but when Mark heard her he paused with one hand in the air and glanced around with a start that made him look as guilty as a little boy caught with one hand in the cooky jar. Wendy's gaze sped to the shell nearest his hand and she saw in surprise that it resembled the cone she had taken to Marion's room last night.

Really curious now, she walked over to Mark. "What sort of shell is that?" she asked bluntly.

He scowled at her. "What shell? This room is full of shells."

"The one you were looking at," she said. "This one."

Since he wasn't going to admit anything, she reached past him to the shelf and brought down the shell. The moment she had it in her hand she knew it could not be the one she had taken upstairs last night. This shell felt lighter and smaller. It was hardly more than two inches long—a little more than half as long as the other shell, and it was not nearly so heavy and bulky. Yet, when she looked at it, there seemed a similarity. This too was a cream-colored shell but with reddish-brown markings around it in even rows, reminding her of letters across a page. Like the other, it was perfectly cone-shaped, but the nose of this shell rose to a decided point out of a swirl of ridges around the top. She seemed to remember that the nose of the other shell had been flat.

Mark was staring at her angrily, but he seemed a little worried too, as if concerned because she had caught him in this room looking at this particular shell.

"What sort of shell is this?" she repeated.

After a slight hesitation, he answered her. "It's just a common old Caribbean cone shell. There are

lots of them like that. *Conus spurious atlanticus* is
its name. But we just call them alphabet cones."

Now that he had found his voice, he seemed to
feel that words might cover up his uneasiness, and
he reached out to take the shell from her hand, explaining as he did so.

"See those ridges running down the outside?
There's a big one here going all the way, and
another, deeper one there."

"Like cracks?" Wendy said.

"They're not cracks. Sometimes ridges like this
are growth marks. They mean the shell animal didn't
get the proper food for a while and stopped growing.
But this mark is worse than that. This fellow looks
as though he'd had a real fight, so that he grew up
with his shell scarred like that for life."

This was interesting, Wendy thought, and she
wished Mark would go on talking to her. Apparently
he knew a lot about shells—and this was a new
world she had never thought about before.

But now he was silent again, looking at the shell,
seeming to study it, almost as if he did not want to
put it back on the shelf. Before he could decide what
to do with it, Uncle Paul came to the door and
looked in, a little surprised to find them there.

"You can come along if you like," he told Mark.
"My wife thinks it will be fine if you pick out something of Stuart's that you'd like to keep. Marion has
consented too. Though she may not be able to talk
to you, Mark. She isn't feeling well, so don't be
concerned if she doesn't speak to you."

Mark hesitated, not going at once to the door.
"Could—could I ask you something else, Mr.

Guthrie? It's fine if I can have something that belonged to Stuart. But I – I wondered – " He seemed to speak against a choke in his throat, and for a moment he could not go on.

Uncle Paul waited, not hurrying him.

"I wondered," Mark said at last, "if I could have something that belonged to Gordon too. He – he was a good friend to me, sometimes almost as much as Stuart was."

"I think that can be arranged," Uncle Paul said gravely, "though you know we haven't given him up as lost yet. Have you anything special in mind?"

Mark held out his hand with the shell upon it. "This shell is what I'd like to have."

Uncle Paul took the alphabet cone and looked at it thoughtfully, as if trying to make a decision. Then he shook his head in regret.

"If you had picked anything but a shell, I might agree. But I'm afraid I can't let you have anything in this room. I would have to consult Marion, since she knows Gordon's collection almost as well as he did. Some of these shells are probably valuable. Anyway, we mustn't behave as though he is lost for good. We're still hoping that Gordon has got away safely into the jungle, Mark. Perhaps one of these days he'll be home, and you can ask him for that shell yourself."

Mark did not look at all convinced. He put the shell reluctantly back on the shelf and turned away.

Uncle Paul remembered Wendy. "You may come too, if you like," he said.

Wendy threw a last look at the alphabet shell, memorizing the place where Mark had put it, before she followed the other two upstairs.

At the door of Marion's room Aunt Elinor waited for them, leaning on the aluminum crutch that braced one arm and offered a firm grasp for her hand. She looked very small and frail as she stood there, and her eyes were still red from weeping. It was clear that most of her concern was for her daughter, lying on the bed in the room behind.

"She's no better." Aunt Elinor shook her head unhappily at her husband. "She won't interest herself in anything. Come in, children. Go and speak to her, Mark — you were Stuart's friend."

The nurse was busily opening the shutters wide to the bright morning, but the outdoor brilliance seemed to stop at the windows and the gallery door. It did not reach the bed or touch the woman who lay there staring at the ceiling, her face pale and drawn.

At Aunt Elinor's insistence, Mark approached the bed, while Wendy waited near the door beside Uncle Paul.

"Hi, Mrs. Cole," he said hesitantly.

Marion Cole moaned softly and closed her eyes. It was as if she could not bear to look at Stuart's best friend — who was still alive — while Stuart was gone.

Aunt Elinor propelled herself awkwardly to the door of an adjoining room and beckoned to Mark with a finger. Barely able to conceal his own emotion, the red-haired boy went into the next room.

"Come," said Uncle Paul to Wendy. "I'd like you to see Stuart's room, since you never had a chance to know him. He was a fine grandson, a fine boy."

Wendy had an increasing feeling that she wanted only to run away from all this unhappiness and from the place where Marion Cole lay shutting herself away from life, shutting out those who loved her. Cousin Marion did not seem aware that her mother and father were suffering too, and that even young Mark missed his friend sorely. She behaved as though what she felt was the only thing of any importance in the world. Yet last night, she had pulled herself together and been perfectly able to talk to Wendy, and send her on an errand. There was something very strange about all this. Strange and disturbing.

When they had stepped into the bedroom next to Marion's, Uncle Paul closed the door so that their voices could not be heard by his daughter. Aunt Elinor gestured sadly to Mark and he went to a cabinet where Stuart had stored his favorite possessions. Clearly Mark had been in this room a good many times and he knew where to look. It must hurt him to be here now, Wendy thought, as she gazed around.

This was the room of a boy who liked boats and ships and the sea. Small sailing vessels decorated the cotton draperies and there were fixtures of brass and a bunk for a bed, as though this was the cabin of a ship. Stuart had loved boats and a boat had betrayed him. But he had evidently liked other sports too, and now Mark was looking through football and baseball gear. Wendy could see that his face was working as though he had a hard time holding back the tears.

Uncle Paul rested his hand lightly on Wendy's

shoulder and spoke so only she could hear. "Perhaps you've come here at a time when we need you most. Perhaps my daughter needs you more than she knows."

Wendy flashed a surprised look at him, but before she could speak he went on.

"If you can make friends with her in the slightest way, it may help. She needs something outside herself to think about, even to worry about. If you can catch her attention, interest her — you may be the one to help your cousin most. She's been as listless as this ever since Stuart died. Not even Gordon could do very much for her. And now that he is lost, she has given up completely."

Except when it came to worrying about a shell, Wendy thought. What a strange thing that was!

In the center of Stuart's room Aunt Elinor stood leaning on her single crutch, blinking her reddened eyes against tears that were all too ready to come. She looked at Wendy and shook her head mournfully.

"It's so dreadful — so tragic! Our young grandson was looking forward to your coming, dear. He was an only child and he always wanted another child in the family. It was wonderful for him to know that a sister was coming here to live."

Across the room Mark dropped a baseball bat on the floor and leaned over angrily to pick it up. "That's not true!" he said rudely.

"Why, Mark!" Aunt Elinor cried.

Mark was angry because he was trying hard to keep back the tears, Wendy thought in sudden understanding. She knew about that sort of anger, and she could not blame him. Aunt Elinor shouldn't make everything worse at a time like this. In some ways she was like Marion — not really helping.

"Stuart never wanted a sister," Mark went on, his voice rough and choked. "He wanted a brother. His mother and dad were going to adopt another boy close to Stu's age, maybe a little younger. And then *she* came along!" He gave Wendy a dark look. "After that, Stu knew he'd have to do with a sister, whether he liked it or not. Now she's here and he isn't!"

"Mark!" said Uncle Paul, and Wendy had never heard his voice so cold and stern.

Mark turned his back, not apologizing, but stirring roughly through a drawer of Stuart's things.

"It wasn't quite like that," Uncle Paul said to Wendy. "You'll have to forgive Mark, because he's feeling pretty bad right now."

Wendy nodded and said nothing. The answer had come to her. She understood why Mark had begun to look at her with resentment as soon as he found out who she was. In his eyes she was a substitute whom nobody really wanted. It wasn't so much that he disliked Wendy Williams. Mark was hurt because Stuart was gone and he couldn't feel happy with anyone who might take his friend's place.

"I don't know what we're going to do!" Aunt Elinor wailed. "I don't know how we're going to manage!"

Uncle Paul put a comforting hand on Wendy's shoulder, but she did not feel comforted. Everything was growing clear, and she had a feeling that Mark would never forgive her for something she could not help.

Making his choice abruptly, Mark turned to face
Uncle Paul. "I'd like to have this—if it's O.K. with
you." He held up an old catcher's mitt, greasy and
worn, obviously a favorite of Stuart's.

"That's fine," Uncle Paul said, understanding.

Aunt Elinor shook her head, not understanding
at all why Mark would pick such a dirty old thing.
But what she thought didn't matter because Mark
had in his possession something that Stuart had used
and loved. Wendy could tell by the look on his face
how he felt as he held up the glove.

Uncle Paul gave him an affectionate thump on
the shoulder and let him out by way of the hall door,
so he needn't go back through Marion's room. When
he had gone, Aunt Elinor returned to her daughter.

For a moment longer Wendy stood looking about
Stuart's room trying to understand, to believe. It
still seemed strange and incomprehensible that the
boy who had occupied this room would never walk
into it again—that she would never see him, never
know him. Whether he had wanted a sister or not
no longer mattered. Or at least it mattered only to
Mark. And perhaps to Wendy Williams.

"Come along," Uncle Paul said, and led Wendy
back to Marion's room where he went to stand beside his daughter's bed. "Suppose we leave Wendy
here with you for a little while, so you two can get
acquainted. Perhaps Wendy can offer you a good
shoulder to lean on when you want to get up and
move around."

Marion spoke faintly, her eyes closed. "I'm not
going to get up. Go away, please, Dad. Just leave
me alone."

Wendy found herself suddenly making her own

angry face again. Somehow she had allied herself
on the side of Uncle Paul. Perhaps he was feeling
all that had happened more deeply than anyone else,
but in spite of that he was trying—really trying!—to
help the others. And no one was giving him a
chance. Mark was rude. Aunt Elinor was a weepy
sponge. And Cousin Marion had shut herself up
with her own unhappiness, not wanting to understand that other people could hurt too. Maybe there
was a way in which Cousin Marion could be startled
back to life. A plan for action began to stir in
Wendy's mind.

Even though she felt nervous and uncertain about
what she meant to do, she put on a bold manner as
she stepped to the foot of Marion's bed. Sometimes
it helped her own courage to bluff a little.

"Could I stay a little while?" she asked. "I'd like
to talk to Cousin Marion."

Uncle Paul looked surprised, but rather pleased.
He hushed his wife when she would have objected,
and got Aunt Elinor and himself quickly out of the
room. Marion behaved as though she had not heard
Wendy's words. She simply lay there with her eyes
closed as if she had gone far off into some place in
her own mind where she could shut out the world
and ignore it.

Wendy had visited people in hospitals a few times.
She knew that you did not lean on a patient's bed, or
jiggle it. Now she leaned hard on Marion's bed,
making it jiggle.

Her cousin's eyes flew open. "Don't do that—it
hurts my head," she said plaintively.

Wendy took a deep breath and tried her plan.

"I'll bet you don't have that shell anymore," she said.

This time Marion Cole stared at Wendy. "What makes you say that?"

"Because I think I saw it downstairs with the other shells," Wendy said. "Or one just like it."

"There isn't one just like it." Marion turned on her side to reach under her pillow and draw out the shell. "You see? Of course I have it." Her voice was weak, but there was more life in it than before.

"What kind of shell is it?" Wendy asked. Now that she had Cousin Marion's attention, she meant to see if she could hold it, for a few minutes at least.

As though the shell was too heavy for her to hold, Marion let her hand fall to her chest, so that the cone rested on her frilly nightdress. "It's a lettered cone from the Pacific. What difference does that make?"

"I just wondered if you had the right shell. I mean the shell you really wanted me to bring you. There's another one down there with brown spots running around it that looks a little like that one. Mark says it's an alphabet cone."

Marion had lost interest. On her chest the cone shell moved gently up and down with the rhythm of her breathing.

"Are you going to sleep with it under your pillow all the time?" Wendy asked. "Won't someone take it away when your bed is made?"

"I won't leave it there," Marion said. "I'll find a place to put it. Did you tell anyone about it?"

"Of course I didn't," said Wendy indignantly.

"Then you're the only one who knows. So you

can help me find a place to hide it."

Cousin Marion took other people too much for granted, Wendy thought, beginning to feel stubborn and uncooperative. If she could not think of others, then why should anyone else feel like helping her?

"Why should I help you hide it?" she asked, looking as stubborn as she felt.

Marion's lagging attention focused on Wendy. "What do you mean by that?"

"You wanted me to come to Villa Mimosa," Wendy said bluntly. "You and Cousin Gordon. Now that I'm here, you've changed your mind. So what are you going to do about me?"

"I don't want to do anything about you," Marion wailed. "I don't want to do anything about anything. All I've cared about in my life is gone and I never want to care about anything again!"

Without warning she burst into tears, while Wendy stood at the foot of the bed watching her, not feeling very sympathetic or kind, but just waiting for her to stop. Marion lay on her back and wept with great sobs that nearly choked her, while tears ran back from her eyes, dampening her pillow. After a few minutes, when no one came to soothe and calm her, and Wendy continued to watch with impersonal interest, Marion stopped crying with a last choking gasp and looked as angrily at Wendy as Wendy looked at her.

"Go away!" she cried. "Don't stand there staring at me! Just go away!"

"You told me you wanted me to hide the shell for you," Wendy said calmly. "If I do, will you tell me about it?"

"I don't need your help. I'll do it myself!"

With an effort, Marion pushed herself to a sitting position and thrust her legs over the side of the bed. There she swayed dizzily for a moment before she fell back on her pillow.

"I can't get up," she moaned. "I get dizzy. If I try to walk across the floor, I'll fall."

Wendy watched her with continued interest. There was nothing apathetic about Marion Cole at the moment. She was thoroughly aroused, upset and angry. The shell had fallen into the bedclothes and she searched for it frantically, found it, and held it out to Wendy.

"You've got to help me! There's a philodendron growing in a red pot over on that table by the window. Put the shell in the pot. Bury it in the earth so no one will know it's there. Hurry, hurry! I just can't endure any more. Someone will come in and I don't want to explain."

Wendy took the shell and looked at it curiously. It was definitely bigger and heavier than the shell that had interested Mark in the collection downstairs. Yet it resembled the other shell in several ways. The lettered rows on this shell were a darker brown, but the cream color and the general shape were the same.

"Do hurry and put it in the flowerpot!" Marion cried.

"Why?" Wendy asked.

For the first time Marion made a real attempt to pull herself together and speak more quietly. "If you'll hide the shell, I'll tell you."

The philodendron was a large, healthy plant. Its

glossy green leaves hung all around the big red pot and there was room in the damp earth to dig a hole large enough to bury the shell. When the earth had been patted smoothly over it, Wendy dusted the dirt from her fingers and came back to the bed.

Marion was watching her despairingly. "So you're the girl we brought home in order to give Stuart a sister?" she said, and her voice sounded stronger, more exasperated. "But you're not the sort of girl we expected. We hoped for a daughter who would be loving and gentle, and not so — so rough."

The words hurt more than Wendy would have thought possible. For that very reason she had to be defiant. She stuck out her lower lip again and scowled.

"You've stopped crying," she said crossly. "And you're talking to me. You wouldn't even talk to me before!"

"Oh!" Marion cried, her exasperation rising. "Oh, but you're a dreadful child!"

Wendy had begun to feel rather pleased over hurting someone who had hurt her.

"I'll go away, as soon as you tell me about the shell," she said.

Outside the sheet, Marion's fingers clasped each other nervously. When her words came, Wendy had to lean toward her to hear.

"All right — I'll tell you. Gordon was involved in something very serious. Perhaps something dangerous that has to do with that shell. I don't know what it was. That's all I know. Now will you go away and leave me alone?"

Unexpectedly Wendy's heart misgave her and she

felt suddenly sorry for this thin woman with the damp blond hair and tear-veiled violet eyes. She was troubled by an unexpected wish to help her in some way, do something for her. All she had done so far was to upset her, and it was too late now to try a gentler way.

As she moved dejectedly toward the door, Marion's voice stopped her. "You mustn't tell anyone about this — you mustn't!"

"I won't," said Wendy gruffly. "You can trust me."

From across the room the two looked at each other for a moment. Then Wendy turned the knob of the door. Behind her, Marion said something that sounded like, "I really believe I can." But Wendy wasn't sure as she went out into the hall and met the nurse coming toward her. She escaped from the woman quickly and went downstairs and out to the garden.

All she knew at the moment was that she felt terribly ashamed, and more than ever like crying. But she wouldn't cry. She was Wendy Williams, the daughter of a boomer, and boomers never cried. Sometimes they died in terrible falls from great heights of steel, but Wendy was very sure they never cried. She had a father of whom she was proud. She had a tradition to live up to. It didn't matter in the least if Marion Cole wanted some other kind of daughter. Wendy herself would have preferred a different sort of mother.

6

More About the Shell

BEFORE WENDY had much time for brooding by
herself that morning, Uncle Paul found her in
the garden staring at the brilliant and unfamiliar red
blossoms of the hibiscus.

"I am going downtown on an errand," he said.
"Will you come with me, Wendy? I'd like to have
your company, and you need a change from the
house."

Wendy was eager to go, yet uneasy as well. She
was afraid of questions that might bring out what
had happened when she had been left with Marion
this morning. She felt increasingly uncomfortable
about how she had spoken to her cousin. It was true
that she had managed to jar Cousin Marion out of
her apathetic state, but she had behaved badly to
accomplish that. As a result, she felt thoroughly
mixed up, resentful toward Marion and distrustful
of herself. This was a state of mind that she could
not possibly explain to anyone—let alone understand.

It was a relief to get into Uncle Paul's car and
drive down the steep hill into town. The Villa
Mimosa, she discovered, was only about halfway

up the steep spine of hills that made a ridge along the back of St. Thomas. As they drove down, she could look up at the high green ridge, where a few houses showed far up the hill. Overhead, in the dazzling blue of the sky were the usual puffs of cloud that seemed to sail endlessly over St. Thomas, and their lazy progress added to the peaceful scene, helping to quiet her tormenting thoughts.

As the car descended, the varicolored houses crowded all around, many of them set in small gardens abounding in flowers and shrubbery. Even the bushes had leaves streaked with yellow and red, almost like the flowers themselves.

In a few minutes they were in the main part of Charlotte Amalie. Uncle Paul found a parking place and they left the car to walk down the narrow Main Street that the Danes had once called Dronningens Gade — pronounced Gah-da, Uncle Paul said — which translated into "Queen Street." It was a street of fascinating shops — dress shops, curio shops, a shop of African wood carvings, shops where jewelry was sold. There were shops for almost everything imaginable. Tourists, it seemed, spent a good deal of time buying things in St. Thomas.

Although the most popular time of the year to visit the Virgin Islands was in the winter, when Americans loved to come here to escape the cold, there were still a great many tourists on the streets in the summer as well. Wendy found that she could recognize visitors by the odd clothes they wore — wild prints, outlandish straw hats, and every variety of shorts and trousers possible. The people who

lived here, as Uncle Paul pointed out, dressed more
quietly, and island women didn't go downtown
wearing shorts.

After Uncle Paul had stopped at a bank and gone
to the post office, he suggested that they have lunch
in town. Wendy agreed with pleasure. She was
beginning to feel more comfortable now. Uncle
Paul had asked no difficult questions, nor had he
brought up any worrisome subjects. When he led
the way into a maze of side alleys that ran from
Main Street to the waterfront, she found herself
caught by a sense of the very old, a feeling of long
ago.

The stone buildings that lined these alleys were
now occupied by shops and offices, but once they
had been the warehouses and slave markets of the
old town. In the days when St. Thomas had been
the first entry port to the Caribbean, all ships had
stopped here and it had been a busy, colorful place.
The very stones of the warehouses had been brought
here as ballast, filling the holds of ships before they
took on their West Indian cargoes and sailed for
home.

Uncle Paul led the way through modern arches
of pink stucco and into a long alley where palm
fronds met overhead, rustling in a breeze that blew
through from the waterfront. Here a few small tables
had been set out upon the brick walk and it was possible to sit outdoors and order something to eat and
drink.

Uncle Paul had thought this place might appeal
to her, and Wendy discovered that it was fun to sit
outside where she could watch people walking back

and forth, cutting through from Main Street to the waterfront.

As they waited for their order, Uncle Paul told her a little about the Virgin Islands—how they had been discovered by Columbus and occupied by various nations, including Denmark. In between their discovery and 1917, when the United States had purchased the islands from the Danes, they had changed hands a good many times. Now St. Thomas, St. John, and St. Croix were American islands, while Tortola and several others of the Virgin Islands were British-owned.

Wendy listened contentedly enough, since there was nothing dangerous about any of this talk. Once their order came, however, Uncle Paul spoiled everything. Just when she had relaxed and felt sure he would not bring up any unpleasant topics, he asked her about the time she had spent with her cousin.

"How did you manage with Marion?" he wanted to know.

Wendy stared gloomily at the sandwich on her plate. She simply could not tell him everything.

"I upset her. I said the wrong things," she admitted.

Uncle Paul nodded. "Perhaps Marion needs to be upset. It's hard to be unkind when I know how much she has to face, but sooner or later she must face it, accept it. She won't recover until she does."

"Other people are suffering too," Wendy said, feeling stubborn again.

Uncle Paul reached across the table and touched her hand. "I wish you could have seen Marion before the accident to Stuart. She was a warm, kind, happy person. Perhaps she will be like that again if we are patient. What did you talk about?"

This was the question she could not answer and Wendy filled her mouth with sandwich and chewed for a while in silence. Then she shrugged vaguely and asked a question of her own.

"Was Cousin Gordon's work very dangerous?"

"As an air pilot? No more dangerous, I suppose, than driving a bus. He was a very good pilot, I think, and he always loved to fly. He enjoyed that Orient hop—out to Saigon and Singapore, to Hong Kong and the Philippines. He used to bring back shells for his collection from all over the world."

The word "shell" made Wendy wince. "How did he come to be lost in Vietnam?"

"He went into jungle territory to look for a friend," Uncle Paul said. "He had received a message that was a cry for help. It came in the form of a seashell brought to him by a South Vietnamese who had escaped from his captors. The man did not speak English, but he had been told to give the shell to Gordon Cole at the airport, and to repeat the one word, '*Hurry*.' As soon as he could arrange it, Gordon got a leave of absence and went by helicopter from Saigon to a village in the jungle. That much of his plan we know."

"He must have cared a lot about his friend," Wendy said.

"They were as close as brothers. Gordon was born here, you know, just as Marion was. He and this friend, David Stockton, and Mark's cousin, Bob Eagan, as well as our Marion, all grew up together right here in St. Thomas."

"But why was a shell sent to Cousin Gordon?" Wendy asked.

"I believe Gordon had once given this particular shell to Dave as a good luck souvenir. And when it was brought to him by the Vietnamese with a message to hurry, he knew it came as an identifying token from his friend. Dave was out there as a war correspondent, and he had disappeared, so when the shell was brought to Gordon between flights in Saigon, he knew the general area in which Dave must be, and he decided to try to get him out."

"What happened to the shell?" Wendy asked cautiously.

"Gordon brought it home first. He couldn't go into the jungle as quickly as he wanted to. He had to tell Marion what he meant to do. I believe he left the shell here in his collection before he went back to look for Dave. Then his helicopter was shot down—and that's the end of what we know."

Uncle Paul sat silent and sad, no longer wanting to talk.

How strange about the shell, Wendy thought. If it had served its purpose in identifying his friend to Gordon, why had Marion been anxious to hide it? And why had Mark Mears been interested in another cone shell that resembled the one Marion had asked for? But she could not question Uncle Paul about these things, much as she might have liked to.

Before they finished eating, someone stopped beside their table and Wendy looked up to see Bob Eagan, Mrs. Mears's nephew. He thanked Uncle Paul for sending down the pirate clothes which Mrs. Mears would copy for him to wear at the fancy-dress party.

"How do you think I'll look as a pirate?" he asked Wendy jauntily.

She had a feeling that a real pirate would probably have been a lot thinner than Mr. Eagan, but at least he had a mane of thick black hair and a certain dashing manner.

Wendy found nothing to say, and at Uncle Paul's invitation, Bob sat down in the extra chair at their table.

"I suppose there's been no further news about Gordon?" he asked.

Uncle Paul shook his head. There was a look of concern on Bob's face and his fingers drummed absently on the table.

"I don't think I ever told you about the time Gordon and Dave and I met in Hong Kong some months ago," he said. "It was quite a reunion. Dave was in town on an assignment for his paper, and Gordon was en route to the Philippines and Japan. I was there picking up what bargains I could from Hong Kong merchants for sale in the Caribbean. We all ran into each other at the Peninsula Hotel and got together for dinner."

Uncle Paul listened, nodding, and Wendy watched Bob Eagan curiously. He seemed worried about something, as if he wanted to broach some special subject, but could not quite get around to it. As she watched, he picked up a saltshaker and set it down, then absently picked it up again.

"Gordon had a lot of Chinese friends in Hong Kong, didn't he?" he said at last. "What with the Chinese border being so close to Kowloon—just across the harbor from Hong Kong Island—the whole area must be a pretty good listening post for word coming out of China."

"I suspect it is," Uncle Paul agreed, looking puzzled.

Bob Eagan picked up the saltshaker again. "Maybe it's a listening post both ways," he said.

Uncle Paul stared at the man as if the tone of his voice had suddenly alerted him. "What are you getting at?"

The younger man hesitated for a moment as though he wanted to add something more. Then he shrugged. "Nothing much," he said, and rose abruptly from the table. He thanked Uncle Paul again for the loan of the pirate clothes, and said to Wendy, "Betty wanted me to tell you good-by for her, since she's gone back to her plane today. She took quite a liking to you, you know, while you were in her care. She'll be interested to hear how everything works out for you."

That was something Wendy was interested in hearing herself. But it was pleasant to know that the stewardess, at least, had liked her.

Bob Eagan said good-by somewhat hurriedly after that, and took himself off like a man with troublesome problems on his mind.

Uncle Paul stared after him in bewilderment. "I wonder what's worrying that young man. I had the feeling that he was about to say something more — and then thought better of it."

Wendy had felt the same thing. Bob Eagan certainly had more on his mind than the words he had spoken.

"At least Bob has settled down a bit in recent

years," Uncle Paul mused, half to himself. "If you can call a job that has him running all over the world settling down. I can remember when he used to worry his aunt by getting into scrapes of one sort and another. So this is a welcome change. At least he has stepped in to help Mrs. Mears at the hotel while Mark's father is away in the States. Since he knew both Dave and Gordon well, I think what has happened has hit him hard. Well—enough of that. If you've finished your sandwich, Wendy, I'd like to show you more of our town."

Wendy swallowed the last of her glass of milk, took the final bite of sandwich, and when Uncle Paul had paid the charge, they followed Palm Passage through to the waterfront.

Just above the surface of the harbor, so that the water seemed to lap at their very feet, ran a wide cement sidewalk. As they followed its curve toward the rise of Flag Hill, Wendy saw that several small sailboats were drawn up to the edge of the stone walk, their wares spread out upon it. There were great stalks of green bananas, sacks of oranges, baskets of vegetables, and all sorts of barrels and boxes of food, each piece being bargained for by St. Thomas women. Once as Wendy passed, a man raised a huge conch shell to his lips, startling her with a blast that could be heard all over town. That, Uncle Paul explained, was to let housewives know that a catch of fresh fish had just come in on the waterfront.

By the time they returned to where the car was parked, Wendy felt much better than when she had left the house. Her senses were a little dizzied by

the warm brilliance that assailed her on every hand
—from the flower gardens and brightly painted
houses, from all the colors of sea and islands and
sky. She had never been in such a lovely place
before, and when worrisome shadows rose at the
back of her thoughts to remind her of drab city
streets, of concrete and steel, of murky, gasoline-
tainted air, she shivered in the warm sunshine. She
did not want to go back to that—ever. It was
beautiful here, and she wanted to stay—if only it
could belong to her with certainty, and for good.

All the way up the hill the question that worried
her most hovered on her lips, but she did not blurt
it out until they were inside the gracious main room
at Villa Mimosa. Even then she might have held it
back if she had known that Aunt Elinor was just out
of sight in the nearby dining room. But she did not
know, and the words came out in a rush as she faced
her uncle.

"What will happen to me now? Will I stay here,
or will I be sent away? If Cousin Marion doesn't
want me, and Cousin Gordon never comes back—"

Uncle Paul put his hand on Wendy's shoulder
gently, silencing her outburst. Beyond him, she saw
Aunt Elinor standing at the dining room door, and
she knew that her aunt had heard her words.

Aunt Elinor came slowly toward them, her expression as anxious as ever, her eyes worried as
they rested on Wendy.

"That will depend on Marion," she said. "What
did you do this morning that disturbed her so badly,
Wendy? When I went in to see her she was dreadfully upset."

Wendy stared at the polished parquet floor, unable to look at Aunt Elinor, not daring to meet Uncle Paul's eyes. To her relief, her uncle came to her aid.

"Perhaps it's good for Marion to be brought out of her self-absorption. Perhaps if Wendy can do that for her, it's a step in the right direction."

Aunt Elinor lowered herself into a chair. "How can you say such a thing, Paul? I won't have my daughter aggravated and disturbed. If she doesn't take to Wendy, we can't keep the child here indefinitely. It's only fair to be honest about that. You and I are too old to go back to the responsibility of child-raising now."

Wendy hated it when grown-ups talked about her as though she wasn't present, or as if she could not understand what was being said. She scowled determinedly to hide the feeling of fright and despair that was rising again to make her heart thump and tighten her throat.

Uncle Paul did not try to stem his wife's words. He seemed to understand how upset she was, how unable to contain herself. He simply held out a hand to Wendy.

"Come sit down here for a moment," he said. "There's something we must talk about — something you must understand."

Anxiously Wendy sat on the edge of a chair and waited to hear the worst. Aunt Elinor sniffed and dabbed at her eyes, but she listened too, with a wary look at her husband, as though she feared he might commit them to something she would not like. Already Aunt Elinor wanted her gone — Wendy was sure of that.

"First of all," Uncle Paul said, "you must understand and believe, Wendy dear, that you belong to our family, and that we are now responsible for you. We wouldn't have it any other way. It was only by chance that we found out where you were, since we had lost track of your branch of the family long ago. You are related to us on your mother's side, and you're the only one left of that family connection. We don't mean to lose sight of you again. The best arrangement would be for Marion to rouse herself and accept the responsibility she and Gordon took upon themselves in bringing you here. But if she is unable to do this, and we can't keep you with us, we will surely find a good school in the States where you can be happily settled."

She knew he meant to reassure her, but she was not reassured. A school would never be like her own family.

"If you don't want me here, my father will find a place for me," she said proudly. "Pop always looks after me."

"I'm sure he does," Uncle Paul said. "But it must be difficult when he has to be away most of the time, and—"

Sensing what might be criticism of her father, Wendy's eyes flashed. "He can't help that! He would stay with me if he could. He's told me so!"

Aunt Elinor seemed to hear the temper behind Wendy's words without paying much attention to their meaning. She took the handkerchief from her eyes and regarded Wendy in disapproval.

"You see, Paul? She's not a grateful child. It's as Marion told me just now—she's not the sort of little girl we expected."

Uncle Paul gave his wife a reproving glance. "Little girls don't come made to order," he said. "They come the way they are. When there are rough edges, then it's our responsibility to help smooth them over. But we have to start with what is there. It seems to me that in Wendy's case, there's a good deal of real value to begin with."

When he spoke about worth, she felt like squirming. She was not at all sure that she was worth very much when you added everything up.

Aunt Elinor had flushed. "I'm only thinking of Marion," she said. "I have to think of Marion first." She struggled to her feet, and Uncle Paul went quickly to help her.

"I am thinking of Marion too," he said.

His wife drew herself away from him as soon as she could stand, and moved toward the stairs, clearly indignant with both Uncle Paul and Wendy.

Was this all her fault? Wendy wondered miserably. It was all too much — too awful.

Perhaps her aunt thought a little better of matters by the time she reached the stairs, for she turned to look at Wendy, and when she spoke her voice was more kindly.

"I'm sorry, child — I have a message for you, and I forgot to tell you. Mrs. Castillo phoned a little while ago and invited you to come and visit Anita this afternoon. I'm sure it will be all right — if you want to go."

Wendy said nothing, and her aunt sighed and turned away to mount the stairs.

"Do you like Anita?" Uncle Paul asked.

Wendy nodded vaguely. She was beginning to feel

the way Marion did. She could not really care about anything outside of her own problems. Everything else became indistinct and remote because of the fear for her own future that gripped her. In the face of that fear, it didn't make any difference whether she liked Anita or not, or whether she visited her or not.

"I'd like to tell you something about the Castillos and the Bergquists," Uncle Paul went on, speaking casually. "I don't think you've known anyone like them before."

Wendy had no interest in what he might tell her, no interest in anything except the knot of dreadful worry that was tightening inside her. But Uncle Paul would not let her go. He challenged her with a direct question.

"Have you ever known anyone like Mrs. Castillo and her granddaughter?"

The question could not be ignored. Wendy answered indifferently.

"I knew some Negro girls in schools I've gone to."

"Did you like them?"

Wendy shrugged. "Some of them I liked, and some I didn't."

"Good!" said Uncle Paul, and she looked at him, startled.

"Good that I didn't like some of them?"

He smiled. "Good that you judge people on their own merits. Just as they have to judge you on *your* merits. That is, on how you behave, on whether or not you are likable."

At the moment, Wendy thought, she didn't care

about being likable. But Uncle Paul had tried to be kind, and she had the feeling that he liked her a little anyway, so she listened as he went on.

"We don't use the word Negro very much in our islands," he said. "Perhaps that's because the name has come to mean a dark-skinned person and we like to think of ourselves as being color-blind. What anyone's skin color is doesn't matter here. The people whose families have lived here for a long time—like the Bergquists and the Castillos—are native Virgin Islanders. They call those of us who have come down here from the United States 'continentals.' We have to remember that we are the outsiders, and we have to earn the respect of those who already live here, before we can expect them to accept us. Tell me, Wendy, do you know what your own racial heritage is?"

She jumped a little at the sudden question. Fortunately, she did know.

"Sure—Pop has told me lots of times. I'm Irish and English and Scotch. And some Polish, and—I guess other things too."

Uncle Paul nodded. "It's the same with Anita's family—it's a mixture. She is probably descended from Spaniards and Puerto Ricans and the Danish and the English, and—most interesting of all—from the men and women who were stolen from Africa and brought here as slaves hundreds of years ago. Though they didn't remain slaves in St. Thomas as long as they did in some parts of the Caribbean. Here they were made freedmen early and they became the professional people—the shopkeepers, the lawyers, the doctors, and all the rest, that their descendants are today. You have only to look at Mrs. Castillo to know that she is a woman who has never had to live with prejudice. It is kind of her to take an interest in you, Wendy, and to want her granddaughter to be friends with you. I know I can count on you to be equally thoughtful toward her and toward Anita."

Wendy fixed her eyes upon her uncle's face, studying his expression which was half stern, half kind, looking into deeply set gray eyes that regarded her as no one else had ever done. He was treating her, she thought wonderingly, almost as if she was a grown-up like himself. As if she was someone he could trust. A feeling of warm affection for him swept through her, erasing the anger and the hurt, wiping the scowl from her forehead.

"I won't let you down," she promised earnestly.

He smiled at her and stood up, drawing her to her feet. "You couldn't say anything I'd like better, Wendy. It's exactly what I hoped you'd say. Run along now and have a good visit with Anita. I think you'll find her a friend worth having."

As she ran down the drive toward the big gate, Wendy knew that she had not felt as happy as this since she had come here. Nothing had changed, really. The problems that remained were still frightening and unsolved, but at least Uncle Paul was on her side and she could trust him. For this little while she could feel happy. She could look forward to seeing Anita.

7

Wendy Throws a Ball

WENDY CROSSED the road and started down the long flight of steps that led past the house where Anita lived. The steps in themselves were interesting. She had never before known anyone who lived on steps instead of on a street, but with all these steep hills she could see that steps were necessary in some places.

Anita was waiting at her gate and she waved when she saw Wendy coming toward her. Today Anita's long ponytail had vanished. Instead, her hair was wound in a pat on top of her head, with curly tendrils escaping around her ears and forehead. She looked more grown-up than she had yesterday, but her smile was warm and her lively brown eyes seemed to light with pleasure as Wendy reached the gate.

"I'm glad you've come to our neighborhood," Anita said. "There aren't any girls my age around here. Grandmother's waiting, so come on in. My mother and father want to meet you, too, sometime. But Mother is a secretary at a bank downtown, and Dad works in the governor's office. Except at night when he drives a taxi."

She was leading the way into the house, and she must have noted Wendy's look of surprise, for she smiled. "Most Virgin Islanders don't earn a great deal, so they take on extra jobs. Taxi-driving is sort of special—lots of men do it in their spare time."

"My father works at building bridges," Wendy said.

Mrs. Castillo looked up from her embroidery as the two girls stepped into the cool parlor. "Good afternoon, Wendy, How interesting that your father builds bridges. Where is he working now?"

Thus urged, it was easy enough for Wendy to pick up her acquaintance with Anita and Mrs. Castillo. She told them about Pop being in Lisbon working on a new bridge that was being built across the Tagus River. She even warmed to a description of what her father had told her it was like—working high up, walking on steel beams that hung above nothing but air and the water far below. She explained that bridge builders were called boomers because so often boomtowns grew up in the vicinity of a new bridge.

Seldom had Wendy had a more interested audience, and it was gratifying to feel that she brought something new to Mrs. Castillo and Anita, just as they did to her. For a little while the underlying worries had quieted and she could ignore them.

When they had talked for a while, Anita took her outdoors—not to the steps this time, but behind the house to where the steep hillside pitched away, and they could look up at the veranda that projected out into space. The veranda was a little like a bridge itself, except that it didn't go anywhere. They stood for a time near the top of the catchment — that great spill of rock which would be used to collect water whenever it rained.

As Wendy looked around, once more drinking in the heat of the sun on her face and the clean dazzle of air, of which she could never get enough, a flash of light uphill caught her eye. Looking upward toward the same wall where she had seen him once before, she spied Mr. Helgerson, his binoculars to his eyes as he stared out in the direction of the harbor. A flash of sunlight on his glasses had attracted Wendy's attention.

"What do you suppose he's looking at?" she asked Anita.

The other girl shrugged. "Visitors always look."

"But he's not focusing on the town, or on Flag Hill, or even on the waterfront," Wendy said. "It seems as though he's staring at something far out on the water. What's out there to see?"

Anita gazed toward the opening to the harbor, where the Caribbean turned dark blue beyond the arms of land formed by Flag Hill and Hassel Island.

"There are some little islands out there, and some rocks. And of course there are ships belonging to the United States Navy." She pointed. "You don't need glasses to see them."

Wendy followed the direction of Anita's pointing finger. Low and gray, riding upon the water, were several American destroyers.

"Why are they there?" Wendy asked.

"We've had navy ships in Virgin Islands waters ever since the trouble with Cuba began," Anita said. "Cuba isn't far away, and I suppose the ships

are on guard here so they can get to any trouble
spot quickly if they're needed."

Wendy looked with new interest at the man with
the binoculars. Some of the books she had read
recently—mysteries and spy stories—were fresh
in her mind.

"Maybe he's a spy," she said.

Anita laughed aloud in delight. "That would be
exciting! Nothing much ever happens in St. Thomas.
It isn't like the old days. But I don't suppose he's
really a spy."

"I don't suppose so," Wendy said regretfully. She
did not care much for Mr. Helgerson, but there was
no real reason to think that a person who happened
to look through binoculars at United States destroyers was a spy. If she had a pair of binoculars,
she would look at the ships herself. Once she had
seen such ships at close hand in the harbor of New
York, when Pop was working on the Verrazano-
Narrows Bridge, and had taken her for a ride on
the Staten Island ferry.

By now the girls had seen enough of the view, so
Anita led the way along a narrow path that edged
the hill and they followed it until they reached the
dead-end street that ran past Mears Manor.

Here they found that Mark was in the roadway,
playing catch with his cousin, Bob.

"Let's watch," Wendy said, and since Anita was
willing, they sat upon a stone wall, where a big
flamboyant tree shaded them with its wide umbrella-
like top. The tree was scarlet with flaming blossoms,
and now and then Wendy looked up into its branches
in wonder. She had never seen trees that looked

like the flamboyants of St. Thomas.

Anita called out "Hi" to Mark, but Wendy said nothing, knowing very well how the red-haired boy felt about her.

Nevertheless, as she sat on the wall watching the play, she began to grow interested and her fingers almost tingled to feel that ball. She longed to get into the game, even though she knew Mark would never ask her.

"I wish I could play too," she said wistfully to Anita.

For an instant the other girl looked surprised. Then her eyes began to dance with the mischief Wendy had seen in them before.

"Why don't you watch for your chance?" she said. "Maybe you can surprise Mark."

Maybe she could, Wendy thought, and began to watch the back-and-forth movement of the ball with new interest.

Bob Eagan wasn't the best catcher in the world. Being overweight, he had begun to puff by the time the chance Wendy waited for came her way. The ball escaped his mitt and bounced directly toward her. She jumped off the wall and caught it up swiftly. Then, without hesitating, she ran out into the road, ready to throw a long pitch to Mark. He saw that she was about to bypass Bob, who was puffing down the road toward her, and he shouted a warning.

"Hey, watch out! Don't let that ball go down the hill!"

Wendy paid no attention. The ball felt right in her hand, and her arm came back with sure control as she put her best into the throw. With a smack that must have stung, the ball went straight into Mark's mitt and he stood staring at it for a moment in astonishment.

Bob Eagan laughed. "There you are, Mark! You've found yourself somebody to play with. I'm not in training to play ball these days."

He tossed his mitt to Wendy and she put it on eagerly, without waiting for Mark's permission. Then she cast an apologetic look at Anita. "Do you care if I play for a while?"

Anita's eyes were still adance and she seemed pleased that Wendy had shown Mark what she could do. "Go ahead," she told Wendy. "Show him how good you are."

Mark was hardly enthusiastic. "Oh, come on!" he shouted as Bob headed toward the wall to sit beside Anita. "That was only a fluke. Girls are no good for playing catch."

"Try me!" Wendy challenged. She flexed her knees and held out her glove.

Mark tried her, resentfully. He gave her a straight pitch that would have gone zinging over the plate if there had been one, but Wendy was ready and the ball made a satisfying plop right into her glove. When she threw it back to Mark as surely as she had thrown the first one, he reluctantly stopped objecting and set himself to playing the game.

Back and forth went the ball, and Wendy's heady confidence in herself began to grow. She knew she was every bit as good as Mark at this, and maybe a little better. She tried a few tricky throws that Jimmy Parks had taught her, and had the pleasure of seeing Mark miss the catch once or twice—even though her aim was sound. When Mark, put on his mettle, tried throwing the ball in a high toss way up into the air, Wendy was able to gauge its fall and be right under it with her mitt when it came down.

It was her own self-confidence that betrayed her in the end. She was so pleased with herself, so sure, that her arm went suddenly wild and the ball streaked past Mark's ear, hurtling down the hill at a great rate, flying in the direction of the hotel. There was a sudden loud crash of glass — followed by a stunned silence.

Wendy stood staring in dismay in the direction of the crash. No outcry came from anyone at the hotel. Its buildings dreamed quietly in the sun, with most of the guests out for the afternoon. Apparently no one nearby had heard the sound. It was Mark Mears who recovered first and waved a disgusted hand at Wendy.

"I told you not to let it go down the hill. Now Mom's going to be mad. She'll tell me I can't play out here anymore — and it'll be all your fault."

Wendy scowled, but she knew the fault really was hers. She felt a little frightened.

Bob Eagan got up from the wall where he was sitting beside Anita. "Hey — stop that!" he told Mark. "It could have been your fault just as easily as Wendy's. Everybody misses sometimes. I'll go see what's broken and find out about putting in new glass."

He gave Wendy a reassuring look that made her feel guiltier than ever, and started toward the gate to the hotel. Before he reached it, however, an angry voice stopped him. Wendy swung around and saw

Mr. Helgerson coming down the long flight of steps from the hill above. He was clearly indignant, and waved his binoculars at them as he came.

"That's my window you've broken!" he shouted. "You kids have no business playing ball so near the cottages. Which one of you did this?"

For a moment no one said anything, though Anita came to slip an encouraging hand though the crook of Wendy's arm. The last thing Wendy wanted was trouble—and Mr. Helgerson's bad temper spelled very real trouble. Nevertheless, the fault was hers and she had to take the blame.

"I did it," she said firmly and went to stand directly in front of him as he descended the steps. He looked so furious that she didn't dare meet his eyes, so she scowled at his binoculars instead.

"Don't worry," Bob Eagan told him. "I'll take care of the matter right away. Wendy didn't mean any harm."

Mr. Helgerson paid no attention to his words. He was studying Wendy with sudden interest, as if he had just recognized her. "Oh, yes—you're the child who's staying up at the Villa, aren't you? Well—that makes it very simple. Suppose you come along with me and we'll talk to Mr. Guthrie about this right now."

He put a hand on Wendy's shoulder and turned her toward the steps. She would have liked to wriggle free and run away from him, as she knew she could, easily. But she did not quite dare. The very grasp of his fingers told her how serious was his intent, and she suspected that if she ran away, everything might be made that much worse.

No one else seemed to know what to do. Anita was watching in alarm now, all the mischief gone from her eyes. Bob Eagan looked annoyed and impatient, and even Mark seemed more sympathetic toward Wendy. Mr. Helgerson's bad temper had somehow pulled them all together to side against him. But if the man recognized this, he did not care.

"Come along," he said, and drew Wendy up the steps.

Bob Eagan hurried after them. "In that case, I'll come along," he said. "Perhaps Wendy will need a witness for the defense."

They had started the climb, but at Bob's words, Mr. Helgerson turned to look down at him severely. "I would prefer to handle this myself," he said.

Bob stood his ground. "Just the same, I'll come along," he repeated.

"Then maybe I'd better come too," Mark offered, with a sheepish look at Wendy.

Bob shook his head. "You go see about that glass. Wendy doesn't need an army escort."

They started up the steps, and Wendy moved slowly, dragging back as much as she dared with Mr. Helgerson's hand on her shoulder. Something brushed her arm gently, sympathetically, and she glanced around to see Anita beside her.

"I'll tell my grandmother," she said. "Don't worry. You haven't done anything very terrible." She ran off toward her own gate, pausing to wave a reassuring hand at Wendy before she disappeared inside.

Wendy could only march upward, clumping at Mr. Helgerson's side, feeling a little desperate. It wasn't that a broken window was the end of the world for most kids. But it might be for her. The one thing she didn't want was to cause serious trouble that would make Uncle Paul decide he could not keep her here any longer. There were already enough counts against her because of the way Aunt Elinor felt and because of her upsetting Cousin Marion. Mr. Helgerson's unreasonable anger might make everything that much worse.

Bob Eagan had fallen behind a little, puffing as he mounted the steps, so that Wendy and Mr. Helgerson climbed alone. The pressure on Wendy's shoulder had lessened and she looked up to see that Mr. Helgerson was studying her without any trace of his recent anger or indignation. His moustache twitched a little at the corners the way it did when he managed to smile.

"I'm sorry this is necessary," he said surprisingly. "Just bear with me, and I think everything will turn out all right in the end."

Wendy would hardly have been more astonished if one of the steps under her feet had spoken to her. This was the last thing she would have expected from Mr. Helgerson, and even as she stared up at him to see if she had heard aright, he spoke to her more testily.

"Will you run away if I let go of you? I'd like to put my binoculars away."

"I won't run," Wendy told him. "I'm not afraid."

Her claim was not altogether true, she admitted to herself, but Mr. Helgerson could not know or understand how uncertain and confused she was. It seemed hard to believe that a little while ago she

had come running down these steps for her visit
with Anita, feeling buoyant and happy. She had
known that the happy feeling could not last, but
she hadn't expected it to evaporate so quickly.

Beside her as he climbed the steps, Mr. Helgerson
busied himself with fussy movements, putting his
glasses back into their case, fastening down the
flap. The glasses reminded her of something, and
she asked a question, quickly forgetting to be
cautious.

"Why were you looking at those destroyers out
in the harbor?" she asked.

He turned his head sharply to stare at her, and
the shallow crescents of his eyebrows went up in
surprise. "What do you mean? Why shouldn't I
look at whatever is out there in the harbor?"

It was true that there seemed no good reason why
he shouldn't look at anything he pleased with his
glasses. Why she felt uneasy, she wasn't sure, so
she kept still.

He went on. "I've been aboard quite a number
of destroyers. I know a good deal about them and
such ships interest me. They're a sort of hobby of
mine."

Wendy had nothing more to say. She hurried her
climbing, leaving the two men behind as she went
upward on long, young legs. She was still ahead of
the other two by the time she reached the gateway.
Villa Mimosa rose above her, pale yellow, and glowing in the sunlight. She ran ahead up the driveway,
and through the front door of the house.

"Uncle Paul!" Wendy called. "Uncle Paul,
where are you?"

At once he came to the door of the little room he used for a study. "What is it, Wendy? What has happened?"

She blurted out her story, meaning to tell him before Mr. Helgerson could mix everything up. "I was playing ball with Mark Mears just now, and —and I missed—and the ball went through a window down at the hotel. Mr. Helgerson says—" but she was able to get no farther, for Mr. Helgerson and Bob Eagan had come up the steps to the front door, and Uncle Paul was already inviting them in.

"I'm sorry to hear there's been an accident," he said to Bob. "Not too serious, I hope. Suppose you let me foot the bill for the glass."

Mr. Helgerson looked as though the force had been taken out of the complaint he had intended to make. In fact, by now, he did not seem especially disturbed, and Wendy wondered why he had bothered to come up here at all.

"The point," he said mildly enough, "is to keep this young lady out of the range of windows hereafter. From where she was, that must have been quite a pitch."

"I'm sure Wendy will know better next time," Uncle Paul said, and invited the two men to sit down.

The crisis seemed to be over, yet Wendy could not feel entirely relieved. There had been a report of her actions to Uncle Paul, and it could only add to his uneasy feeling about her.

Bob Eagan started to say that he would get back to the hotel and mend the window, but when Mr. Helgerson made no move to leave, Bob decided to remain too, and both men sat down.

"I know it's too soon to go into this," Mr. Helgerson continued, sounding almost friendly, "but I'd like to touch again on the subject I brought up when I came to see you yesterday — the matter of disposing of Gordon's shell collection. In case it should become advisable, that is."

Wendy had been about to slip away, feeling that it would be better if all three forgot about her for the moment, but now she paused to listen, leaning on the back of a chair.

Uncle Paul stiffened a little at Mr. Helgerson's words. "I believe I mentioned last night that this matter is not in my hands."

"I know, and I wouldn't trouble you," Mr. Helgerson went on, "except that I won't be here too long this trip, and I'd like to put in a bid for some of those shells while I'm here. If it's at all possible to see the collection during my stay in St. Thomas, I would greatly appreciate —"

"That would be up to Marion." Uncle Paul broke in. "She's the one who knows all about the collection. She used to help Gordon when he went diving and dredging for shells, and she helped with the cleaning and preserving of them as well. But I certainly don't want to bother her with such matters now."

Mr. Helgerson looked crestfallen, and he turned a little testy. Watching him, Wendy had the sudden feeling that her breaking of a window had merely given this man a chance to get inside the Villa Mimosa again so he could talk to Uncle Paul. It wasn't the window he cared about. His indignation was an act he had put on for this one purpose, and if this was true, she disliked him all the more, Wendy decided. He really was as snoopy as a spy!

Bob Eagan listened as they talked, though he made no comment. When Uncle Paul stood firm, Mr. Helgerson excused himself regretfully and said he would get back to his room and see if the broken glass had done any damage. Bob did not go with him, and as soon as Mr. Helgerson was out of sight he expressed his disapproval.

"I don't like that fellow," he told Uncle Paul. "I don't think he knows anything about shells. He's a fussy busybody who wants to pretend he's an expert on everything."

Wendy spoke without meaning to. "That's the way he is about destroyers," she said.

Bob Eagan turned quickly in her direction. "This Helgerson is interested in *destroyers?*"

Wendy wriggled uncomfortably. "Well," she said, "he was looking at those ships in the harbor through his glasses a little while ago, and when I asked him why, he said destroyers were a sort of hobby of his."

Bob looked thoughtful, but he said no more about Mr. Helgerson. "Concerning Gordon's collection," he went on to Uncle Paul, "if you should need any assistance in appraising those shells and Marion isn't up to it, I'd be glad to help. I know a bit about the subject myself and I can at least point out what may be of value in the collection. Gordon showed it to me a few times, you know. And he lent my aunt some shells for an exhibit at the hotel."

"Thank you," Uncle Paul said politely, "but I hope the selling of this collection is a good while off.

In any case, I'll leave the matter to Marion. Certainly I know very little about it myself."

Bob Eagan seemed to understand, but Wendy thought he looked worried about more than the breaking of a window.

While Uncle Paul walked to the door with him, Wendy stayed behind, turning over in her mind a sudden new thought that had come to her. This time, however, she would not rush into anything. It was an idea that had grown out of Mr. Helgerson's remark about buying some of Gordon's shells. Perhaps there was a way in which Marion might be startled awake again, and coaxed into an interest in what was going on. First, though, Wendy meant to think over her budding plan carefully. There must be no mistakes this time.

8

A Scrap of Paper

THERE WAS no chance to take action for the rest of that day. Marion did not want to be disturbed, Aunt Elinor said, and Wendy was not to go to her room without permission. Nothing more was said about the broken window, and Uncle Paul did not mention the matter to his wife.

After dinner that night Wendy was given an unexpected opportunity to see Gordon's shell collection herself. When she seemed to have nothing to do, Uncle Paul took her into the small room where the shells were set out upon the shelves, and showed her around.

While he had disclaimed much knowledge of the collection to Mr. Helgerson and Bob Eagan, he nevertheless seemed to know a good deal about the names and various species of shells. He introduced Wendy to glossy cowries, strangely ridged whelks, spiked augurs, and a rare spiraled wentle-trap. He showed her flat limpets that had lived in shallow warm water when they were alive, and West Indian top shells that made wonderful chowder. He showed her a scorpion conch — the big shell, on the corner shelf, which had pricked her fingers with its spines when she had come here to get the cone shell for Cousin Marion.

One thing at least she was able to make sure of — the small alphabet cone that had so interested Mark was still in its place on the shelf where he had left it, and she was able to take it down and look at it carefully without Uncle Paul's guessing the reason for her interest.

The world of shells was fascinating, and she found that it was pleasant to wander about the room, handling any shell she pleased. The only things that returned to worry her here were the memory of Mr. Helgerson's curious interest in Gordon's collection and her knowledge of the shell that was hidden away upstairs in Marion's bedroom. If other people were trying so hard to get in and look over this collection, it might be just as well that the lettered cone had been removed from its place among the others. Clearly that shell, out of all of these, meant something of importance to someone. If she could find out why it was important, perhaps she would then know something about Mr. Helgerson that would be worth telling Uncle Paul. If she could be of service in some way, perhaps she would be found useful and would be invited to stay.

In the meantime, there was still her plan concerning Marion. She tingled in anticipation when she thought about that, though nothing at all could be done now. She had to wait till the next day.

On the following morning Uncle Paul announced at breakfast that he was taking Aunt Elinor for some tests at the hospital. The nurse would not be in until later in the day and it would be a great help if Wendy would sit in Marion's room and keep her company, get her anything she wished. Aunt Elinor did not care much for the idea and seemed to think Wendy's presence would be disturbing. Marion herself, however, had agreed to have Wendy there.

So it was that when Uncle Paul and Aunt Elinor were ready to leave, Wendy was taken to Marion's room. Her cousin had breakfasted and then gone back to sleep, and Wendy, with a book to read, sat in a chair beside a window, making scarcely a sound.

When she heard the car start outside on the driveway, she tiptoed onto the gallery to watch it go through the gate. After Charlie Wong, the yard man, had closed the gate, and the car had disappeared around the curve of the hill, Wendy returned to Marion's room and stood for a moment or two listening to the soft breathing of the woman in the bed. Asleep, something of the strain and the blankness that seemed to alternate in her cousin's face was wiped away. She looked prettier and younger than when she was awake, her lashes long on her cheeks, and her lips parted softly with the puffing of her breath. If only she could be as attractive when she was awake!

But Wendy knew she had no time to waste, and she left the side of the bed and hurried toward the huge philodendron on its table near a window. Trailing green tendrils hung thickly over the edge of the pot, and it was like parting long green locks of hair to open them and thrust her hands inside. At once she found the irregular place in the earth where the shell was buried and she dug into it with her fingers. The earth was loosely packed and the shell came free at once, sprinkling a little dirt on the carpet as Wendy pulled it out.

With her back to Marion, she turned the shell around in her fingers, studying it. She even raised it to her nose and sniffed the odd, fishy smell — a smell of the ocean — that still clung to the shell's interior folds. It was very different from the alphabet cone downstairs. A single growth mark ridged its surface crookedly, but this shell had never been seriously scarred. It had no pointed spire of a nose like the cone Mark was interested in, but ended in flat white whorls that circled its top. Over the rest of its surface dark brown dots ran in orderly rows, some of them shaped like blurred letters of the alphabet.

When she tried to see into the interior, Wendy found that creamy-white folds curled in at the shell's base. Not even her little finger could be pressed into the narrow opening, but when she held the shell toward the light and tried to peer inside, it seemed that the edge of some obstruction showed deep within. It did not look like a stone, or a bit of broken shell — but rather like grayish paper.

Her heart began to beat a little faster as she hurried to Marion's dressing table and stood looking around its surface. First she tried an orangewood stick, poking it into the shell, attempting to get hold of the bit of paper. The stick had a tendency to thrust the paper deeper into the little cave inside the shell and she put it aside. Next she picked up a curved pair of tweezers with thin points and a scissors-like handle. Working carefully, she managed to pinch the scrap of paper between the

tweezer tips, and pull it gently from the shell. It seemed to be a tiny wedge of folded newspaper, but before she could unroll it and examine her find, a voice spoke from the bed.

"What are you doing?" Marion demanded.

Acting on pure impulse, without stopping to think, Wendy let the scrap of paper drop to the floor and turned to face Marion with the shell in her hands.

There was a moment of silence while Marion stared at her from the bed and Wendy tried to recover her voice.

"I was just looking at the shell you told me to hide," she said as soon as she could speak.

Marion's cheeks had flushed to a brighter color, perhaps from sleep, perhaps because of her annoyance with Wendy. When she spoke, her voice sounded stronger than before.

"Well, don't look at it! Put it back in that pot and cover it up at once!"

Wendy did not move. She stood where she was, still turning the shell curiously in her hands.

"I was just wondering," she said.

"Wondering what? You're such a maddening child! Why can't you let my things alone?"

"I'm still wondering whether you have the right shell," Wendy said. She was used to being called maddening, and she didn't especially mind. If Marion was wide awake now, the plan that was growing at the back of Wendy's mind might work all the more easily.

"Suppose you tell me what you're talking about," her cousin said and pushed herself up on one elbow, the better to see Wendy's face.

Cautiously Wendy came closer to the bed. "It's only that a lot of people seem to be interested in this shell," she said, and waited to see the effect of her words upon Marion.

Her cousin's attention seemed focused on her now. "Go on," Marion said. "Tell me what you mean."

"There's another shell," Wendy told her, "a smaller one, in the collection downstairs. It's a little like this one. Mark was looking at it and said it was an alphabet cone from the Atlantic Ocean, and that there are lots of them around the Caribbean. I don't know why he should care about it in the first place."

Marion lay back on the pillow and her lashes fluttered down to hide her eyes. "The cone you're holding belongs to the same shell family, but this one is called a Conus litteratus. It's what is known as a Pacific lettered cone. It probably came from waters off the Philippine Islands, and I think it's a more interesting shell than Mark's alphabet cone."

Wendy studied her cousin for a moment. Marion seemed to be making an effort to talk — as if she wanted to draw attention away from what was really important about this shell.

Wendy took a deep breath and plunged into her news. "Mr. Helgerson wants to buy some of the shells in Cousin Gordon's collection," she announced. "He's being awfully persistent about it."

"And who is Mr. Helgerson?" Marion did not open her eyes.

"He's staying at Mears Manor and he says he knows Cousin Gordon. He has been coming up here to talk to Uncle Paul about seeing the shell collection, but so far Uncle Paul hasn't let him look at it. He told Mr. Helgerson that if anything is done about those shells, it will be up to you."

At first Marion had seemed interested, but now she fell into apathy again. The news that Wendy had thought might wake her up and really startle her seemed of no importance after all. It was as if the small effort she had made had used up all her strength and she had none left.

"It doesn't matter," she said wearily. "Nothing matters. Put the shell back in the flowerpot and don't touch it again."

The deep hole in the earth was waiting. Wendy thrust the shell into it and patted dirt over the top. There was room in the pot to hide the shell, but it was rather a tight fit. With the long green tendrils and heart-shaped leaves of the philodendron plant hanging down all around, nothing of the hiding place was visible.

Wendy felt very much disappointed. Marion had not responded as she had hoped she would to the news of Mr. Helgerson's odd interest in the shell collection. Yet she was not as disappointed as she might have been had there not been something else pulling her attention. There was still to be considered the scrap of paper that lay on the floor. If she picked it up and carried it to Marion now, her cousin might be even more annoyed with her for prying it out of the shell. Nevertheless, Wendy knew she had to see what that bit of paper meant.

Standing at the dressing table, idly picking up articles on its top, she managed to drop a hairbrush on the floor, and when she bent to pick it up, she retrieved the small scrap of paper. With it concealed in her closed hand, she turned back to the bed.

"Do you care if I go to get a drink of water?" she asked.

Cousin Marion shook her head indifferently, and Wendy hurried out of the room. Instead of getting a drink, she slipped into her own room and closed the door. Then, very carefully, because the folded paper did not seem very strong, she spread it open in her hands and studied it in bewilderment.

At first she had thought the paper might be wrapped about some object, but that wasn't the case. It was simply a rough scrap of newspaper apparently torn from a corner. Someone had punctured it with holes—as if a pencil had been poked through it in a number of places so that it looked like an uneven piece of Swiss cheese.

Strangest of all, however, were the curious printed markings on the paper in between the holes. There were no words, as she knew printed words, but only vertical rows of queer characters that meant nothing to her—probably Chinese characters. This bit of paper must have been torn from a Chinese newspaper and tucked secretly into the cone shell. At the moment it seemed that no one here knew of the paper's existence except herself.

She folded the scrap carefully and thrust it deep into the pocket of her skirt. Then she hurried to Marion's room. She must find a way to put the paper back inside the shell until such time as she could tell someone about it. Not Marion, since her cousin was already annoyed by her interest in the shell.

Cousin Marion was waiting for her when she returned to the room and seemed a little restless now.

"Can I get you anything?" Wendy asked.

Marion shook her head without answering, and Wendy found herself watching her cousin with a growing sense of impatience. Staying in bed and giving up would never do her any good. This way she was no use to herself, or to anyone else—but how in the world could she be made to see that?

"Why don't they put a bed on the veranda for you?" Wendy asked abruptly. "Why don't they put you outside in the sun?"

Marion stared at her. "Why should I be out there?"

Wendy tried to put her vague feeling into words. "Because out there everything is warm and—and alive and growing. Maybe the sun and all the bright colors would start you growing too."

Something almost like a smile touched one corner of Marion's mouth and then disappeared. "What a strange child you are, with such strange notions. But I don't want to grow. I don't want life to touch me—ever again. I don't want to do anything or be anything. I just want to lie here in the shadows and be nothing."

Wendy stepped closer to the bed, staring openly at the pale face as it turned against the pillow. The brief flush of indignation was gone from Marion's cheeks, and with her eyes closed, her face looked lifeless. This was something Wendy could not understand. No matter what awful things might happen to Wendy Williams, she knew she would stand up and fight. She wouldn't give up and try to be nothing, as Marion was doing. As long as a person kept moving from one moment to the next, from one hour to the next, day after day, it was always possible for things to improve. That was what Uncle Paul had meant. But sometimes it was necessary to help things along a bit, to give them a push now and then.

Without opening her eyes, Marion spoke. "At least you don't fuss over me. You don't poke at me and pity me. You worry me in other ways, but sometimes I think I'd rather have you here than my mother. All Mother does these days is wring her hands and cry. I'm past crying. Gordon isn't coming back, and I know it. And Stuart is gone. So all I want is to be numb without any feeling. Why should I feel, when there's nothing left to care about?"

Wendy wanted to say, "There's me," but she knew that would mean nothing to her cousin.

"Uncle Paul won't believe that Cousin Gordon isn't coming back," Wendy said. "He thinks you all have to keep hoping and waiting. I guess all sorts of things can happen out in those jungles. Why should you give up when you don't know what has happened to him? Maybe he'll need you when he comes back—and where will you be if you're too sick even to get out of bed and walk across a room?"

There was no telling whether Marion heard her. She had turned on her side, as if to shut out the sound of Wendy's voice, and her eyes were squeezed tightly shut.

Once more Wendy sat near the window with her

book and tried to read. But the philodendron plant was nearby and her fingers itched to get at the shell and return the paper to its hiding place. Somehow she managed to sit quietly for a while, turning a page of her book from time to time, though she had no idea of what was printed there. Now and then she stole a look at the woman in the bed, but Cousin Marion seemed to be sleeping again.

When she had waited until she could bear it no longer, Wendy put down her book and reached toward the plant.

"Don't touch it!" Marion said at once. "If you ever take that shell out again, I'll ask them to keep you out of my room for good!"

The very tone of her voice rubbed Wendy the wrong way and suddenly she was past caring whether she upset Marion or not. She stood up and went boldly over to the plant, turning her back on Marion. She could hear her cousin struggling to get up from the bed, but Wendy knew the paper had to be returned to the shell, and she paid no attention. It didn't matter anymore if she was forbidden to come to Marion's room. Her own hopes were fast dying out, and she was scowling as she lifted the long strands of leafy growth. But before she could succeed in her purpose, the door opened and Miss Smith walked in.

At once Marion began to talk excitedly, telling the nurse to put Wendy out of the room immediately, telling her she was not to return, and that she wanted to talk to her father and mother about the child as soon as they got back from the hospital. Marion's entire mood had changed, and there was no more talk of preferring Wendy's presence to her mother's.

There was a flurry of excitement as Miss Smith drew Wendy away from the plant and hurried her gently, but firmly, from the room. Out in the hall she shook her head sadly at Wendy and then returned to Marion, closing the door behind her. Wendy stamped away to her room and took Pookie out of his hiding place in her suitcase. After that she sat down at the neat desk that had been prepared for her in this room, and drew out a sheet of paper and a ball-point pen. Pookie, sitting with his back against the daffodils on the wall, watched as Wendy began to write.

For some little while she wrote furiously, earnestly, pouring out words to her father in Portugal. She told him exactly what the situation was at Villa Mimosa, and how everything had gone wrong, so that she wasn't wanted here. About how everyone hated her and wished her gone, and how she wanted to be gone. She told him all this in spite of the fact that the island was so beautiful and she might have loved it here—if it wasn't for a family that wasn't really a loving family at all.

Only once before had she ever written a despairing letter to her father. That time she had managed to get into some unpleasant trouble with the family with whom she was staying. Later she had realized that the fault had been mainly her own, but her father had been worried enough to leave his job and come flying home to see her. That was when he had arranged to move her in with old friends of her mother's—the Parkses. And he had stayed a while to take her all around New York. They had rowed in Central Park, gone to live television shows, and even to a musical stage show — the only one she had ever seen.

Afterward she had lived several years with the Parks family — until Mr. Parks had an accident that put him in the hospital. He might not be able to work for a long while, and Mrs. Parks had to get a job and leave Fran and Jimmy in a sister's care. Much as they had loved Wendy, she wasn't a real part of their family and she understood that they couldn't look after her anymore. It was lucky that the invitation from the Virgin Islands had developed around that time. For Wendy, it had appeared to save everything.

Only it hadn't — it hadn't!

For a moment, sitting there staring at her letter, Wendy felt angrier at Pop than at anyone else. Why couldn't he be like the fathers of other girls? Maybe he deserved to be upset by a letter like this. Maybe he would come and take her away. Perhaps he would tell off this make-believe family that regarded her only as a nuisance.

Once more an uncomfortable picture flashed through her mind of Pop in that beautiful room downstairs, his bridge shoes rough on the polished floors, his voice sounding loudly through the quiet, and she wriggled uneasily. She wasn't sure what Uncle Paul would do about an angry Pop. But she might as well find out. She signed her letter with an indignant scrawl, folded it, and thrust it into an airmail envelope. She had a fifteen-cent stamp — the airmail to Lisbon — and she pasted it on and pressed it down with her fist.

Pookie seemed to be watching her in mild surprise from fixed and beady eyes. She scowled and pushed him off onto the floor.

"I'm going to mail that letter!" she told him. "I really am!"

Voices sounded from downstairs and Wendy went to the door and held it open, listening. Uncle Paul had brought Aunt Elinor home. As she heard them coming upstairs, she closed the door softly and stood with her ear against the panel.

She knew they went into Marion's room, but after that the voices were hushed by closed doors and she could hear nothing of what was being said. There was more moving about in the hallway and on the stairs, and suddenly a knock on the panel right beside her ear made Wendy jump back, startled. After waiting a moment, she opened the door.

The little maid, Rachel, was there. "Come to me, please," she said in her odd island way. Wendy, knowing that she meant "come with me," followed her toward the stairs. Her heart was thumping again, and she fixed her scowl firmly in place because she knew trouble lay ahead. She had been left with Marion, and she had upset her badly. Neither Aunt Elinor nor Uncle Paul would be pleased about that.

All the way downstairs Wendy told herself she didn't care, but in her heart she knew that she had begun to care a great deal, and in spite of the letter to her father, she did not really want to leave Villa Mimosa. What she wanted was a hopeless dream that seemed to move farther from her all the time — the old dream of a loving family, from which she would never be sent away.

In the big cool room, with the hillside breeze blowing through, Aunt Elinor sat on one of the sofas, with Mrs. Mears, Mark's mother, beside her. Uncle Paul was pacing restlessly around the room, and when Rachel brought Wendy down the stairs, he came toward her gravely.

"Mrs. Mears has an invitation for you," he said. "Don't frown so, my dear."

His kindness was almost worse than if he had been angry with her, and she had a feeling that it was best to keep right on scowling—because if she didn't scowl, she might cry.

Aunt Elinor, however, had none of her husband's reluctance to speak out in front of Mrs. Mears. The moment she saw Wendy, she burst into words.

"What have you done that has upset Marion again? Our poor darling was almost in hysterics when I went upstairs. How could you treat your cousin so, when she's suffering and ill? I didn't want to leave you with her in the first place—and I was right."

"Don't, Elinor," Uncle Paul said gently. "Now you're upsetting yourself, and the doctor says you must take things more calmly if you're to preserve your own health."

Aunt Elinor went right on, as though he had not spoken. "Wendy broke a window yesterday, too! There's no end to the trouble she seems to cause. She evidently doesn't know how to behave."

"Wendy knows perfectly well how to behave," Uncle Paul said. "Sometimes even the best of us get ourselves pointed in the wrong direction and then we don't know how to shift gears and turn around."

Aunt Elinor gasped and stared at him.

Wendy swallowed hard upon the tears that wanted to come. Not even Uncle Paul understood all that was wrong. He didn't know about the shell, and that scrap of paper in her pocket, or about the secret Cousin Marion was trying to keep—a secret that somehow concerned Gordon.

Mrs. Mears had caught her breath and she smiled at Wendy. "The broken window is already mended, and it doesn't matter anyway. With a boy in the family and young visitors often staying at the hotel, such accidents aren't unusual. Mark seems impressed by Wendy's skill with a ball, and I've thought she might come down and stay with us for a week or two. Perhaps that would help you up here until Marion feels better. I have an extra room now, so if Wendy would like to visit us, we'd be happy to have her."

Aunt Elinor fairly snapped up the suggestion. "That would be wonderful! I'm sure it would be better for Wendy, too. And it would give us more time to decide what must be done on a permanent basis."

"It's up to Wendy," Uncle Paul decided. "If she'd like to visit you, that's fine. But I don't want her to feel she is being sent away."

In spite of her gloom, a rush of feeling rose up in Wendy—a feeling of affection for Uncle Paul. It so surprised her, coming at this moment, that she forgot to frown and gave him a lopsided smile instead. Perhaps a visit with Mrs. Mears would be a good idea, after all.

"You needn't decide right away," Mark's mother

went on. "In the meantime I'd like to invite you to the beach with us this afternoon—if you care to come, Wendy. I've already phoned Mrs. Castillo to ask Anita, so she will be there, as well as Mark and his friends."

Feeling only a little better, Wendy spoke hesitantly, not very graciously. "I guess I'll go to the beach," she said, and the matter was settled.

When Mrs. Mears had gone, Aunt Elinor went upstairs to lie down, and Uncle Paul came out upon the lower gallery, where Wendy had gone to sit in a cane chair, soaking up the sunlight, of which she could never get enough.

"Would you like to tell me what has gone wrong between you and Marion?" he asked. "There's something here I don't understand. Marion isn't specific about anything you've done, but she is upset and she doesn't want you in her room."

Wendy jumped up at once. She had nothing to tell him. She would have liked to tell the whole story of the shell, but she had promised Marion that she could be trusted, and the secret wasn't hers to give away. There was nothing to do but shake her head at Uncle Paul's question and escape from his company as quickly as she could.

He did not try to keep her, and she ran upstairs to her room. There she took the scrap of paper from her pocket and examined it once more. For a few moments she stood thinking, while her fingers played idly with the paper, rolling it up, smoothing it out again. It rolled up easily into a cone shape that was about the size of the shell—as if it might have been intended as a cover in which to wrap the lettered cone. But since it had been tucked inside the shell, rather than used as a cover, the fact had no meaning.

Finally she hid the paper beneath the sealed air-mail letter on her dressing-table shelf. Later she would see how she felt about mailing the letter to her father, and she would see if any notions had come to her concerning the bit of paper with its Chinese characters and strange perforations.

Having postponed all unpleasant thoughts for the moment, she got out the bathing suit with its halter top and ruffled blue pants — one of the gifts she had found in a drawer in this room. In spite of everything, her spirits had begun to rise. At least she had the afternoon to look forward to — and Anita to see again. What was more, Mark didn't seem to be mad about her breaking that window with a wild throw and apparently he hadn't objected to his mother's suggestion that Wendy come to the hotel for a visit.

Nevertheless — if the choice had been left up to her — she would not accept that invitation right now. Something deep inside seemed to warn her that her real problems were here in this house, and until she had solved them, she would not be happy anywhere else.

9

Fight on the Beach

NEVER BEFORE had Wendy visited such a lovely spot. The few times when she had gone to beaches in New York the sand could hardly be seen for all the people who lay upon it. Swimming pools at school and at the Y were apt to be crowded with other children, and they resounded with shrieks and loud splashing. She would always remember those echoing swimming pool sounds, the bright green, artificial color of the water, and even the smell of chlorine.

Here where a yellow-white crescent of sand curved around the indentation of the bay, there were only a few sunbathers and swimmers. The little bay lay shimmering in its own natural blue under a sunny blue sky, with liquid green lace of lighter water edging the shallows where small islands rose from the sea. Everything smelled fresh and clean and fragrant — smelled of the sea and the flowery land.

A stillness lay upon everything. There was a sense of empty spaces where no one crowded her elbow — a sense that was forever absent in the city. There was no rushing here, and she found herself surrendering to the spell, ceasing the struggle within herself for a little while.

She left the others—even Anita—and went to sit cross-legged on damp sand at the water's edge, soaking up the quiet and the peace, watching gentle waves sweep up to the beach and then recede, over and over again. When she turned her head landward she could see the thick tropical growth massed upon the hillsides all around, with palm trees and banana plants waving green fronds in the light breeze. Close to the edge of the beach grew the sea grape trees, their thin grayish-white trunks slanting out toward the water. They were not very tall trees, but their big heart-shaped leaves offered shade for anyone who wanted to get out of the sun.

Anita seemed to sense Wendy's need for solitude and she stood a little apart in her red bathing suit, letting the ripples break over her bare feet, watching Mark and his friends swimming and ducking and splashing. After a while she waded into the water and then looked back, beckoning to Wendy.

Only then did Wendy jump up and run into water that did not shock with cold like the water she was used to—water that seemed to buoy up her body as she began to swim. Swimming lazily beside Anita, parallel to the beach, she could watch what was happening there.

Mark and his two friends were playing noisily with a big beach ball. Mrs. Mears in a bathing suit and Mrs. Castillo in a loose blue dress were busy setting out a picnic supper, while Mr. Helgerson lay on the sand watching them, watching everything. He was the one unpleasant surprise that had happened to this outing. At the last minute, when he had heard that Mrs. Mears was taking them to the beach in her station wagon, he had invited himself along, and there had been no way for her to say "no," though Wendy suspected that Mark's mother might have liked to refuse him. At least he had said nothing about the broken window and he didn't seem to be fussing as much as usual. He had left his binoculars at the hotel and was not snooping on anyone today.

The most pleasant surprise had been the coming of Mrs. Castillo, who had decided to accompany Anita, in response to Mrs. Mears's invitation. Wendy still felt drawn in a special way to Anita's beautiful, dignified grandmother. She had a feeling of knowing where she stood with Mrs. Castillo. Wendy sensed a kindness and a wise understanding in her, yet she also had a feeling of certain lines being drawn that one would never dare to step over. Because Mrs. Castillo had evident respect for herself, she could also respect other people and treat them generously, Wendy felt, knowing very well that she would never dare to behave with her as she might sometimes behave with others. Not because Mrs. Castillo would do anything drastic if she did, but just because she would not want to lose her respect by behaving badly.

When the two girls tired of swimming, they splashed in through shallow waters and raced each other along the sand, laughing and breathless. When they slowed to a walk, Wendy began to notice the flotsam that drifted in at the edge of the water — shells and bits of wood and seaweed. Once she bent to pick up a few battered shells and found among them a perfect little cowrie — brownish-yellow in color and about an inch long. She had never before found a perfect shell of her own, and she had the feeling that it would be a good luck piece for her from now on. It would remind her of this peaceful time here on a St. Thomas beach, when all her problems had been thrust behind her, and she had stopped fighting the world to enjoy Anita's friendly company.

When they had explored the beach long enough, they sat on towels in the sun, building damp mounds of sand over their legs, then making earthquakes with their knees that cracked the coverings. Wendy set the small cowrie on a mound of its own, where it would not be lost, and talked for a while to Anita.

Oddly enough, what she talked about was wintertime and snow. These were things she knew about and Anita didn't. New York could be cold and blustery during the winter months, but it could take on a sort of magic as well. Wendy told about the last Christmas she had spent with the Parks family, about a trip they had taken to Radio City, and a walk down Fifth Avenue, with all the shop-windows gleaming with the colors of Christmas and the snow falling softly all around. Sometimes the sound of a choir was broadcast over the Avenue to add carols to the holiday feeling. Anita listened to her with shining eyes and prompted Wendy with questions at the right time. Both girls were lost in a winter fantasy, hardly aware of the sun on their heads, or the burning heat of the sand, until a boy came down the beach toward them and stopped beside Wendy.

"Hey," Mark said to Wendy, "can I talk to you for a minute?"

She glanced up at him uncertainly. She could never tell about Mark's mood, and she had no idea how he felt about her now. His red hair was wet from the sea and beginning to curl up in little tufts as the sun dried it. His gray eyes were solemn and watchful. Their look flicked in Anita's direction, and she needed no further hint.

"I'll go help your mother and my grandmother," Anita said to Mark, and ran up the beach toward the grown-ups. Mark's two friends must have been told to stay behind, for they were playing together in the water.

Wendy would have liked Anita to remain with her. She did not want to be left alone with Mark. Whatever he might say to her would probably plunge her back into trouble, and she wanted to cling to this new feeling of a peaceful place where no impossible problems intruded.

Without invitation, Mark dropped down beside her and wriggled his toes into the sand. Wendy reached for the cowrie before he could bury it and held it tightly in her fingers, as if to remind herself that there was still such a thing as good luck.

"It's a shell I want to talk to you about," Mark said. "That shell with the alphabet markings back in Gordon's collection."

Wendy wriggled on her towel and said nothing, tossing the cowrie back and forth from hand to hand.

"Will you get that shell for me?" Mark asked abruptly.

For a moment Wendy stared at him in astonishment. Then she said, "Why?" sounding as blunt and abrupt as Mark.

He ran an impatient hand through his hair, leaving

it streaked with a powdering of sand. "Because it's important—that's why!"

Wendy had no intention of telling him that he was chasing after the wrong shell, but she had to know more. "Important because it's the shell Cousin Gordon's friend sent out of the jungle when he was asking for help—asking Gordon to hurry?"

"That's right." Mark seemed surprised that she knew about the shell. "Gordon told us about it when he came home the last time. He was planning to go back and search for Dave. But afterward he started to worry about the shell."

"Worry about it?" Wendy repeated.

"On the way back to Saigon, a notion struck him that he hadn't thought of before," Mark went on. "He began to think there might be some message connected with the shell that he hadn't understood. When Gordon and his friend David Stockton, and Marion, and my cousin Bob were all kids here in St. Thomas, they got interested in codes and ciphers. They used to send secret messages to one another. So Gordon began to think there might be a message of some sort connected with the shell that he hadn't stumbled onto. In the beginning he thought sending it was only to identify Dave—since Gordon would recognize the shell when it was brought to him. Then he got the idea that it might mean something more and he wrote Bob a letter about it, just before he went into the jungle aboard the helicopter. He told Bob the shell might contain dangerous information and he didn't want it to fall into the wrong hands. He asked Bob to go to Marion and have her show it to him and see what the two of them could make of it. In the meantime Gordon would see if he could find Dave and bring him home."

"If that's the case, why doesn't Bob go to Marion and ask her?" Wendy said.

Mark snorted in disgust. "As if anybody would let him! They've got Marion packed in cotton wool, haven't they? Besides, Bob doesn't think Marion ought to be upset about this now."

She was already upset, Wendy thought. Marion knew something too and she was anxious to hide that shell from everyone. It was all very confusing and bewildering. She remembered how worried Bob Eagan had seemed when he had met Uncle Paul and herself downtown, and how he had seemed on the verge of saying more than he had. Now she knew what had been worrying him. But there was still something that puzzled her.

"How do you know which shell Gordon meant?" Wendy asked.

"Because he described it in his letter. He didn't give its name, since Bob doesn't know a whole lot about shells. He said it was a creamy-white cone shell with brown markings all over it like letters of the alphabet. So of course that's the alphabet cone."

But it wasn't, Wendy thought. She stared at Mark, the cowrie suddenly quiet in her fingers. It was easy to see how the mistake had come about. Both cone shells had brown spots on them that looked liked letters. Something else Mark had said puzzled her more, and she put her bewilderment into words.

"I thought Bob knew a lot about shells. I heard him offer to help Uncle Paul with the shell collection if he wanted to sell it. He said he knew some of the rare shells Gordon had collected."

Mark threw her a disgusted look. "Bob was trying to get a look at the collection so he could find that alphabet cone. I almost had it that one time—and then you walked in and spoiled everything."

Wendy continued to regard him thoughtfully. "Why doesn't Bob just go to Uncle Paul and tell him the truth? Uncle Paul would probably let him have the shell right away."

A look so unhappy, so nearly despairing, came over Mark's face that Wendy was startled. "He can't do that," Mark said. "Something awful might happen. Something might come out that nobody must know about. Something dangerous. I shouldn't be telling you this much, but I thought maybe you'd help me."

Marion too had used the word "danger"—but what could it mean? Wendy wondered. Danger to whom? and from whom?

She shook her head in answer to Mark's words. The only way she could help him was to take the shell out of its hiding place in the flowerpot in Marion's room—and *that* she had no intention of doing. All she could do now was to pretend indifference.

"I guess you'll have to wait till Gordon comes home," she said and got to her feet, to stand on the towel, looking down at Mark.

He returned her look with more disliking than ever. "Maybe Gordon isn't going to come home."

There was something strange about the way he put it—as though he did not mean that Gordon was lost or dead in the jungles of Vietnam, but as if he intended something else, something frightening. She asked no more questions. Suddenly all she wanted was to get away from Mark and back to the quiet friendliness of Anita's company. She wanted to hear nothing more about this matter of the shell — nothing more at all.

But before she could step off the towel and pick it up, Mark rolled onto his knees and snatched at one corner of it, giving it a sharp tug. Wendy's feet went flying from under her and she fell on the sand with a thud that shook her to her very teeth. The fall not only shocked her — it made her furious. Already Mark was dashing toward the other two boys, waving the towel tauntingly as he ran.

Wendy went after him like something shot from a catapult. She was light and quick, and her long legs covered space in a hurry. It took no more than a moment to catch up with him, and when she was close enough she launched herself into the air in a flying tackle, landing with her arms around his legs, bringing him down even more suddenly than he had thrown her with the towel. At once the two were locked in combat, rolling over and over in the sand, punching at each other, with Wendy trying to pull Mark's hair and trying to scratch him as well.

It took Mr. Helgerson's best efforts to pull the two of them apart. He grasped an arm of each, shaking them none too gently.

"Cut it out, Mark!" Mr. Helgerson said. "You can't fight a girl."

Mark glared across the intervening space at Wendy. "I wasn't fighting her — she was fighting me!"

Somewhere nearby, Mark's friends snickered and he made a growling sound at Wendy.

Mrs. Mears had run across the sand to join Mr. Helgerson. "Now stop this, both of you," she said. "I don't want to hear anything about who is to blame or who started what. You've both behaved disgracefully. We're nearly ready to eat, so go wash off the sand and come back here behaving yourselves. Don't you touch each other again, do you hear?"

In spite of Mr. Helgerson, Wendy had felt pretty good until Mrs. Mears spoke. She had shown Mark that he couldn't get away with playing such a trick on Wendy Williams. She had shown him that she was just as good at most things as he was. And she had made his friends laugh at him. But now, with Mrs. Mears regarding her in anger and regret, everything swept back: all the trouble she was in — all the uncertain future. Now Mrs. Mears would not want her to visit at the hotel if she had to be taken away from Villa Mimosa — so even that loophole was gone. Something made her glance in the direction of Mrs. Castillo. Anita's grandmother did not seem to be watching. In her blue dress she knelt before the picnic things, her hands busy, her attention apparently on what she was doing. Yet Wendy had a feeling that she had seen everything and a wave of angry shame swept through her.

She turned her back on Mark and his mother and marched down the beach, her head high, her cheeks warm with a despairing kind of anger. When she reached the water and began splashing herself to rinse off the sand with which she was plastered, she heard Mark doing the same thing nearby, but she did not look at him until he spoke.

"If you go telling anybody what I told you just now, I'll fix you good," he said in a low voice.

She did not trouble to answer him. There wasn't anyone she wanted to tell, but she wouldn't give him the satisfaction of a promise. When the sand was off, she remembered the cowrie shell and went slowly along the beach where she and Mark had rolled, until something small and light-colored showed against the sand. At least she hadn't lost her own shell. Without speaking to Mark again, or so much as looking in his direction, she picked it up and went back to where the picnic supper had been spread out on a checkered cloth. When she dropped into a place beside Anita, the other girl moved close to her, whispering so no one else could hear. "I saw what happened. I'm sorry."

Wendy could not trust herself to speak. She was still furiously angry, but at least she had shown Mark up before his friends. As the other two boys came over to where the food was set out, they looked at each other and grinned. Wendy suspected that Mark would be in for teasing sooner or later, and that would not make him like her any better. But what did it matter? Nothing mattered very much. Not a cowrie shell or anything else could bring good luck to Wendy Williams.

On sudden impulse she held out the shell to Anita. "Here—it's for you. I don't want it anymore."

Anita accepted the shell doubtfully. "I'll keep it for you," she said. "When you feel better I'll give it back."

Wendy had a feeling that she was never going to feel better. For once she wasn't even hungry. The good food Mrs. Mears had provided seemed to stick in her throat and she could not swallow. Now and then she cast an angry look in Mark's direction, but he paid no attention to her, and all three boys were eating with a healthy appetite. She could not look in Mrs. Castillo's direction at all.

Once Anita bent toward Wendy and spoke softly. "It's no use trying to think up ways to get even. I used to do that when I was mad at someone. But Grandmother says the only way to stop trouble is to stop. You can't go on stirring things up."

Wendy gave her a dark look. "How can you stop when somebody else won't stop? You'd better talk to Mark about that."

"Should I?" Anita asked.

Wendy made a face. "As if he would listen! But I think I know how to fix him."

After all, she had not promised that she wouldn't talk to anyone about the things Mark had told her, the hints he had dropped. Perhaps it would be a good idea to go to someone about all this and tell what Mark was up to. Maybe that would show Mark he had better not play tricks on a girl like Wendy Williams.

The beach was on the opposite side of the island over the ridge from Charlotte Amalie. From the town one could see the sunrise, but this was the sunset side. There were enough puffy clouds floating overhead so that a clear, rosy glow lay upon sky and water and land. Even the green hills behind the beach were touched with rose, and the pink air had a shimmer to it that was magical.

At any other time Wendy might have responded to the beauty that lay all around her. Now she knew only that these things would soon be taken away from her, and that her days in these islands were numbered.

Anita finished her drippy hot dog and wiped her fingers on a paper napkin. "What good does it do to scowl so much?" she asked. "How can anyone like you when you scowl?"

"What do I care?" Wendy snapped.

Anita looked a little hurt, and after that she had nothing more to say. When the time came to clean up after the picnic, Wendy could not bring herself to help. She slipped away from the others and went to sit some distance off on the sand, staring obstinately at the sea and the rosy sky, but not really seeing either one.

"May I sit beside you?" asked a calm voice, and Wendy looked up in dismay to see that Mrs. Castillo had come along the beach and was standing near her. She could not bear to talk to Anita's grandmother now. If there was one thing she regretted most about what had happened, it was having Mrs. Castillo witness the whole horrible affair. But she had witnessed it, and as a result Wendy could only feel angry with her too.

Without waiting for Wendy to agree, Mrs. Castillo sat down on the sand, arranging the full skirt of her dress gracefully about her.

"I know you're feeling terribly upset," she said. "And of course you don't like any of us at this moment. You think Mark is the most dreadful boy you've ever met, and somehow you're blaming all of us for what happened."

This was true, and Wendy listened in astonishment. The words had been spoken calmly, without criticism or blame. Mrs. Castillo had simply stated facts that were obviously so. Wendy nodded fiercely and said nothing.

There was a little silence, during which Mrs. Castillo began to build a chunky castle in the sand. Her small graceful hand plumped and patted the mound, built it up, forming a tower and a wall all around. She worked quickly and purposefully — as though there might be a reason behind her actions. Though why she should sit there silently building a sand castle at this particular time, Wendy wasn't sure. Undoubtedly a scolding of some sort was yet to come, and Wendy was braced for it.

"The worst thing of all," Mrs. Castillo said at last, pressing the battlements into shape, "is being secretly ashamed and disliking ourselves. Everyone does this once in a while, you know. It's painful, but human beings have emotions and sometimes they get away from us."

Wendy scowled and stared at the castle, but she was feeling more and more surprised.

"Sometimes we have to permit ourselves unpleasant thoughts about people, until we can stop being angry," Mrs. Castillo said. "Perhaps it helps a little when we realize that other people can have such thoughts too — even toward those they love. Thoughts can be permitted because they can change and improve, and they needn't do us any harm. About actions, we have to be more careful. What we *do,* we must be responsible for. But enough of that. There — what do you think of my castle?"

Wendy merely grunted.

"Smash it up good and hard," said Mrs. Castillo and rose to her feet. "Break it to bits for me, will you?"

While Wendy looked after her openmouthed, Anita's grandmother walked back to join the others. Dusk was beginning to fall as the pink faded from the sky, and the "no-see-'ems" bugs had begun to bite. Wendy slapped furiously at one arm, looking toward the place where everyone was busily getting ready to leave. No one was paying the slightest attention to her.

With a fury that surprised her, she fell upon the castle. She smashed into it with her hands and pounded it with her fists. She stood up and kicked at it with one foot at a time, and then jumped into the wreckage with both feet at once. When the castle had been strewn all over the beach, flattened beyond recognition — completely destroyed, Wendy stood looking down at it aware of a strange sense of calm and relief. All the wild, tingling anger was gone, and her resentment with it, though she was still ashamed. When Mrs. Mears called her name, she hated to go back to the others. At least the sand castle had served its purpose and she understood what Mrs. Castillo had intended. She was not angry with Mark anymore.

On the drive home, Mrs. Mears put Wendy between herself and Mr. Helgerson in the front seat of the station wagon, and let the other children sit in the back. Thus wedged between two adults — undoubtedly to keep her out of trouble — Wendy was silent, thinking her own thoughts, not listening to the casual talk that went on over her head. Though she was no longer angry, she could not undo the serious damage her actions had caused.

When Mrs. Mears dropped her off at the gateway to Villa Mimosa, she managed to say thank you for the outing. Mrs. Mears still sounded annoyed as she answered, so that Wendy knew she probably would not be asked again — not to any more outings, or to visit at the hotel. Anita leaned out of the car window at the last minute and told her good-by, but there seemed to be no way to retrace her steps right now and go back to the earlier friendship between herself and the island girl.

The evening was already dark by the time Wendy started up the drive to the Villa. A blaze of bright stars had come out in the sky and a lopsided moon was rising from the direction of Tortola. The scented air was sweet with jasmine and the lights of the house burned warmly as if to welcome her. But how could she be welcome anywhere when she had behaved so badly?

Uncle Paul was sitting outside in his favorite chair on the gallery. As she came up the steps he spoke to her pleasantly, asking if she had enjoyed herself. Wendy said, "I guess so," in a subdued tone, and started for the door of the house.

Her uncle spoke to her cheerfully. "I've some good news for you. Marion decided to sit up in a chair tonight, and she ate a good dinner for the first time in a long while. Fighting with you seems to have given her an appetite. Maybe some stirring up is what she has needed."

Wendy had nothing to say. Soon Uncle Paul

wouldn't speak in this light, joking way about fighting.

She was glad not to meet Aunt Elinor on the way upstairs. Her bathing suit had dried under her short beach coat while she was eating supper, but she was eager to get out of it and brush herself free of scratchy sand. The door to Marion's room remained closed, and she went past it softly and hurried into her own room.

When she had turned on a lamp she went to the dressing-table shelf and looked at her face in the mirror. She looked as awful as she felt, and that realization made her feel even worse.

Then her gaze fell on an empty space on the shelf and she saw that the letter to her father was gone. Someone must have seen that it was stamped and ready to mail and had sent it off. That was fine with her. She was glad that she had written it. She wanted to get away from Villa Mimosa and the island of St. Thomas as quickly as she possibly could.

When she was out of her bathing suit and had put on a pair of shorts and a blouse, she felt restless and unable to settle down with a book. There were times when even a good story could not help the unhappy, aching feeling inside her. After a while she went out on the upper gallery and wandered toward the front of the house. A patch of light from Marion's room fell upon a portion of the gallery, but here in the shadow Wendy could not be seen.

Moving softly in her sneakers, she went to a place where bougainvillea clung to the lacy iron trim of white arches, its purple blossoms black by the light of a gibbous moon. She knew what "gibbous" meant—she had looked it up. It meant being hump-backed, or having a protrusion like a hump. That was how the moon looked now—when it was be-tween the half-moon and the full. Under such a moon the pirate ghost was supposed to walk on this very hill, but that knowledge did not frighten Wendy. Even if she had believed in ghosts, it was too early in the evening for clanking spirits to wander abroad. Midnight was the witching hour, and midnight was a long way off.

Below the railing the garden looked shadowy and inviting—a place in which to hide from everyone, even from herself. In a moment Wendy was over the rail, the toe of one sneaker searching for the open work of a pillar that ran to the ground. Her hands reached through bougainvillea to grasp for support and found plenty of finger holds in the wrought iron. It was easy enough to climb to the ground.

In his chair on the lower gallery, Uncle Paul did not look toward Wendy as she stole softly across a patch of open lawn, seeking the shadow of bushes, crouching as she ran.

When she reached a crescent of yellow shrubbery, white now under the moon, she knelt to catch her breath and looked all around: up at the lighted win-dows of the house, toward Marion's room, toward the place where Uncle Paul sat—then away to the lower part of the garden and the gate that meant freedom. What she sought to escape from she did not know, but the urge to run was upon her, forcing her into action.

Making another dash across open spaces, she

reached the hibiscus hedge and knelt in its shelter, waiting to see if anyone had noticed. But house and garden were quiet, and there were bushes between Uncle Paul and herself. Just as she rose to make her next dash, something strange caught her eye.

Hidden from the house by a growth of shrubbery, but fully visible in the moonlight from Wendy's vantage point, stood something that was not a bush. For an instant she blinked her eyes in disbelief and then stared more intently. She was used to shadows and moonlight by now, and she could see the figure clearly. It wore a cloak and a plumed hat and boots with wide turned-over cuffs—the garments that might have been worn by a renegade gentleman turned buccaneer.

Midnight or no, the pirate of Mimosa Hill was abroad.

Wendy glanced at the lopsided moon—that gibbous moon by which the pirate was said to haunt the hill, and unreasoning terror seized her. She did not wait to hear the clanking sound his leg irons might make when he moved. She turned her back on the dreadful sight and fled wildly toward the gate.

Someone had closed it, but she climbed to its top and dropped to the shell drive beyond. As she landed she slipped, and fell to one knee. At once she felt the smarting hurt as powdered shell cut into the skin. Nevertheless, she was up at once, running along the paved road.

She had no idea where she was going, but she wanted to get away from this ghostly haunting of the Villa Mimosa.

10

The Pirate of Mimosa Hill

WENDY FOLLOWED the pavement as far as the place where it took the next zigzag in a turn uphill. There she left it for a path that curved down the hill. Overhead, the gibbous moon seemed very bright, and for a space there were no trees or brush to throw eerie shadows. Only the straggly guinea grass of the hillside stretched away beneath her feet.

She guessed that this was the upper end of the path that wound downward below Anita's house and came out eventually near the wall where she and Anita had sat beside the dead-end street watching Mark play catch with Bob Eagan. Her heart still thumped, but her first senseless terror was fading as her own down-to-earth good sense asserted itself.

The figure she had seen in the garden of the Villa had been no pirate's ghost, but someone human wearing pirate clothes. Perhaps those very clothes which Uncle Paul had lent Mrs. Mears so she could make a similar costume for Bob Eagan to wear to the hotel party.

She wished that she had not been in such a hurry to run away. But it was too late now. If she returned, the figure would surely be gone. It was likely that he had seen her scooting across the grass, though he could not know for sure whether she had seen him.

The downward path grew steep and her knee was smarting badly. Once she bent to dust away stinging particles of shell and felt a wetness on the skin that meant the scrape must be bleeding. She hadn't a handkerchief to wipe it with, but no matter. This wasn't the first time she had skinned a knee. Limping. a little to favor that leg, she went on down the path until it leveled out above the stone catchment which pitched its enormous expanse down the hill. Here she found an outcropping of rock and perched herself on its flat top where she could look out over the scene.

Except for a nearby orchestra of insects, everything wore an early-evening quiet. From here she was able to see almost as far as she could see from the upper gallery of the Villa. Between here and where Flag Hill rose black against a starry sky, the little houses of the town descended toward the water, their windows small boxes of light. A breeze stirred across the Caribbean, ruffling treetops, touching Wendy's face. For a time she stared at the necklace of lights worn by the waterfront, and then looked up at the sky—up at all those millions of close stars overhead. What was going on up there? Was there some being like herself on some faraway planet who looked up at the earth in *her* sky and thought it only a twinkling star? The thought made her feel very small and unimportant.

Yet when she looked away from that great dark-blue arch of the sky and considered what lay at her feet, the feeling was reversed and she became important again. The steep precipice of the catchment gave her a dizzy sense of height, a feeling that she was somehow in command of the world. Pop had told her about sometimes having such a feeling when he stood on the high steel girders of a bridge with nothing but air and space around him.

Thinking of Pop made her remember the letter she had written him, and she worried, knowing that by now it was on its way to him. While writing it, she had thought only about herself. Now she thought of her father. It wasn't right to worry him over what he could not help. It would be even worse if she pulled him away from his job and brought him flying across the Atlantic to comfort her. What could he do, anyway? Sometimes she was stupid—dreadfully stupid.

The words Mrs. Castillo had spoken returned to her mind and she thought about them soberly. Angry thoughts did no one any harm, and they might make a person feel better. Everyone had them sometimes. But when you put your thoughts into reckless action, then you could be in real trouble. When you felt angry, it was better to smash up a sand castle. That was action when you needed action, and it did no one any harm.

Now, sitting here on this quiet hillside, she did not hate anyone. All the wild anger had seeped away, leaving behind it a sad tranquillity—a grieving for the unpleasant girl she so often turned into. How many times had people told her that she was inconsiderate, undisciplined, destructive? Yet she did not really want to be any of those things. She would much prefer to be cheerful and smiling, kind and sympathetic like Anita Bergquist. The problem was how to achieve that when she had to live with Wendy Williams.

Her scraped knee had begun to sting and she blew on it to stop the smarting. As she did so a rustling sound on the hillside above made her jump and look around, just as a small brown animal darted across the path at her feet and lost itself in the grass of the hillside. She knew it was probably a mongoose and she waited to see what had startled it into flight. Almost at once she heard the sound of footsteps thudding rapidly down the path in her direction. Before the figure came around a bush into sight, she guessed what she would see, but this time she was not the least bit frightened.

She sat as still as the rock on which she perched, and the boy in pirate garb did not know she was there as he came along the path. He walked awkwardly in his cuffed boots, his cape flapping, and he held something small and white in his hands. Just as he passed her, Wendy jumped up and caught at the floating folds of the cape.

"Mark!" she cried. "Wait a minute, Mark!"

The boy whirled around in alarm, and Wendy saw that what he held in his hands was a shell. A shell that he had undoubtedly taken from Uncle Paul's collection. As usual, she acted on impulse and made a dive for the shell, trying to snatch it from his grasp. Mark did not let go, and for a moment they struggled together for its possession. Then the small shining thing slipped from their hands and went flying into the air, while both Wendy and Mark stood watching

in dismay. It made a wide arc outward and plummeted down the hillside toward the catchment. Wendy held her breath, hoping it would fall short, but the shell struck the stone, bounced out into space, and went down the steep rock slide striking with shattering force here and there on the way before it bounced out of sight at the bottom.

Wendy fully expected Mark to turn on her in anger. Oddly enough he did not. He stood quietly beside her, waiting until the sound of the shell's fall died away. Then he sighed almost as if in relief.

"Maybe it's a good thing," he said. "Now it's gone for good and it can't hurt anybody—unless someone finds it down there."

"That was the alphabet shell from the collection, wasn't it?" Wendy asked.

He nodded, seeming as surprised by her own lack of anger as she had been with his. "Yes. I went in the back door when nobody was looking and got it. If anybody saw me, I hoped they'd think it was the ghost and stay away."

It was on the tip of Wendy's tongue to say, "That was the wrong shell," but she managed to hold back the words.

"How could a shell hurt anyone?" she asked.

Mark looked unhappy. "Maybe it could hurt Gordon. Or anyway, his reputation. Maybe it could hurt Marion. And your aunt and uncle."

"But how? Why?" Wendy persisted.

Mark began to take off the pirate clothes. He made no attempt to answer her until he had folded everything into a neat pile, with the hat on top. Then he stood there in jeans and pullover shirt, his head bare. The moonlight washed all color from his bright hair, wiped away the tan of his skin and made him look pale.

He gave Wendy a long, measuring look. "This afternoon I was sore because you wouldn't help me. That towel was handy, so I gave it a jerk."

"I know." Wendy felt a little surprised at the calm sound of her own voice. "I was mad too. Afterward I was sorry, but I didn't know how to stop what I'd started."

"I suppose you'll tell your uncle?" Mark said. "About what I've done—about the shell and all?"

Wendy shook her head. There was no need to tell. The shell that had gone down the catchment had no value, no importance, and now, at least, Mark would stop trying to get hold of it. That way the shell in Marion's room would be safe.

"It's better if the shell is lost," he repeated.

She was still curious. "Can't you tell me why?"

"Not all of it. But you might as well know a little —so you'll keep still about what has happened. You know about Dave Stockton—the friend Gordon went out to Vietnam to find. Well, they think Dave went over to the other side."

Wendy knew the right word from having read so many spy stories. "You mean he was a defector?" she asked in astonishment.

"I guess so. The worst of it was that he was trying to use Gordon. Gordon wrote Bob a letter and said he had a feeling something dangerous was going on and the shell might hold the clue to a lot of things. The minute he got back to Saigon that last time, he tried to follow up his hunch about the shell. He got hold of the man who'd brought it to him from Dave and talked to him through an interpreter. The fellow didn't know much but he said enough to convince Gordon that more of a message than was evident might be concealed in that shell. So he wanted Bob to get the shell quickly, to keep it from falling into the wrong hands before Gordon could get home. He said not to talk to anyone but Marion. I told you some of this before. There isn't much left to tell."

Mark gathered up the heap of pirate clothes, shaking his head over them ruefully.

"My disguise didn't help much," he said. "How could I guess that you'd be doing some pretty odd things yourself tonight? What are you out here for, anyway?"

"I—I'm not sure," Wendy faltered. "I was just trying to figure things out, I guess."

She was half afraid that Mark would laugh at so feeble an excuse, but he was not thinking of her or her problems. His mind was still on the shell and the letter Gordon had written to Bob Eagan. In the bright moonlight Wendy could see the crease above his eyes as he drew his brows together in a frown. Mark was trying hard to figure things out, just as she was.

"The trouble is that Bob doesn't think Gordon was telling the whole truth in his letter," he went on.

"What do you mean?"

A note of dejection crept into Mark's voice. "What if Gordon isn't dead? What if he isn't lost in the jungle, or trying to rescue Dave? What if he went to—to *join* Dave?"

Wendy stared at Mark in horror. "But that's awful! Why would you think such a thing?"

"Bob says something was going on one time when he ran into Dave and Gordon out in Hong Kong. Something they didn't want him to know. He thinks Dave was scared of being caught and had to do a disappearing act."

Wendy recalled the time when she had been downtown with Uncle Paul, and Bob Eagan had stopped to talk to them. She'd had the feeling that something was worrying him, that he had wanted to tell Uncle Paul about it, and had held back. Now she could see why.

"But what would anything Dave did have to do with Cousin Gordon?" she asked Mark.

"I don't know. Bob has some reason for thinking Gordon might have been caught in this too — so that it was better for him to follow Dave. All that talk about protecting the shell might have been to protect Dave — and Gordon."

Wendy felt a little sick. She had never met Cousin Gordon, but she remembered the letters he had written her, remembered his generous offer of a home, even after his son had died and Marion had gone to pieces. Even then he had not wanted to let her down. It seemed dreadful to think such ugly things about him.

"Do you really believe this about Cousin Gordon?" she asked Mark. In the moonlight she could see the way his face twisted in pain, as if he fought against his own feelings. "Gordon was a swell person. I wanted to grow up and be a flier too, just like him. Bob knows how I feel, and he hated to tell me this. He's upset about it himself because he thinks a lot of Gordon. That's why I'm glad the shell is smashed and gone for good. It might have told too much. Maybe it's better if we never know for sure. Better for Marion and the Guthries and all Gordon's friends."

Wendy said nothing more, but her thoughts were busy, and more troubled than ever. Mark's confidence in the destruction of the shell was misplaced, because there was still the real shell — the shell that might tell too much. Gordon had sent a message to Marion too, though apparently he hadn't told her all he had told Bob Eagan. He had only warned of some vague danger and asked her to keep the shell safe until he got home. By telling two people, he must have felt that one of them would get possession of the shell and keep it out of sight. He had not guessed the sort of confusion that might result.

From the direction of the Villa a voice began to call her name and she recognized Aunt Elinor's plaintive tones: "Wendy? Wendy — where are you? Wendy, Wendy!"

"I've got to go back," Wendy said. She was glad of an excuse to get away before Mark tried to exact a firmer promise of silence from her. She waved a hand at him and ran up the path, wincing a little as her knee began to smart when she moved it.

Uncle Paul stood at the gate she had climbed over a little while before and she ran along the pavement toward him, out of breath from hurrying.

"Here I am!" she called.

He waited gravely, opening the gate for her as she came near. Not until she started up the driveway beside him did he speak.

"I know how good it feels to be off alone on a moonlit night," he said. "But after this, suppose you let us know where you're going. It worries your aunt to have you leave the grounds after dark. Will you think about that next time?"

"I'm sorry," Wendy said, and found she actually was. She had not thought they would worry about her, though when she heard Aunt Elinor calling, she had expected a scolding. Instead, Uncle Paul had tried to understand how she really felt.

Not until they reached the house did he tell her what had happened to set everyone searching for her.

"Your Cousin Marion has been asking for you," he said. "She refuses to go to bed until you come to her room. We all think this is a good sign, so do hurry upstairs and see her."

Wendy wasn't sure that it was a good sign. Marion had been far from pleased with her earlier in the day, and she might have good reason to be further displeased with her now. For this reason Wendy did not hurry on the stairs, but climbed slowly, arriving with reluctance at Marion's room. The door stood open and the nurse was there waiting for her. Miss Smith spoke over her shoulder to her charge when Wendy came into sight at the head of the stairs.

"Here she is, Mrs. Cole."

She stepped aside to let Wendy into the room, and then closed the door softly and went away, leaving Wendy alone with her cousin.

Marion was apparently feeling a good deal stronger than before. She was sitting up in a chair, dressed in a violet negligee that matched her eyes.

She no longer looked pale and indifferent or without feeling. Something had brought her thoroughly to life and her eyes were a bright, dark violet, her cheeks flushed with ominous color. When Wendy appeared, Marion thrust her hand into the pocket of her negligee and pulled out the lettered cone shell. She held it toward Wendy without smiling.

"There was something hidden in this, wasn't there? Before I put it under my pillow the other night, I could see something inside. Now it's gone. You took it out, didn't you?"

Wendy could only nod mutely.

"Then you'd better get it for me at once!" Marion said, her voice strong and firm. "Whatever you've taken from the shell, go and get it right now."

11

The Alphabet Cone

WENDY DID not try to answer. She opened the door and ran to her room. A moment later she stood before the shelf that served as a dressing table, searching its top frantically.

She had put that bit of newspaper right here, she was sure—yet it was nowhere in sight. She lifted her brush and comb, searched among other articles, moving everything about in a desperate rush. The paper was not there!

Next she dropped to her knees, ignoring the sting of scraped skin, and looked all about the floor, crawling around, hunting beneath each piece of furniture and even under the bed. Perhaps the paper had blown off, been carried across the room. But no amount of searching revealed its presence.

In turn, she pulled open one dresser drawer after another, opened the drawers of her desk—but there was no piece of paper to be seen anywhere.

She remembered very well what she had done with it. When she had come back to her room before the picnic, she had hidden the scrap beneath the letter for her father. Someone had come into the room and taken the letter to mail. So the same person must have picked up the scrap of paper as well.

She ran out of the room and dashed down the back stairs and out to the kitchen, where Rachel sat at a table, having supper with the cook. Wendy almost pounced upon her.

"Did you find the letter in my room, Rachel? Did you mail it?"

The girl nodded. "I put it with letters for the post office when somebody takes. It has gone now."

"But there was a piece of paper under the letter. An old piece of newspaper. What did you do with that?"

Rachel shrugged. "It is for trash — I throw away."

Wendy hung onto the kitchen table. "Where — where? Where did you throw it?"

Rachel's bright dark eyes regarded her in astonishment. "What it is?" she said, using the island transposition of the words.

"It's something awfully important!" Wendy cried. "It's something that belongs to Mrs. Cole. I guess I shouldn't have had it at all, and now she wants it back."

The little maid burst into a stream of words, speaking so quickly that Wendy could only struggle to understand. She had already found that the "calypso talk" so often used in the island was a sort of English, but it had a different accent, often a different arrangement of words. It could pour out in a staccato manner that usually left the newcomer without the slightest understanding of what was being said.

The cook — a plump, smiling woman — reached out and prodded the maid cheerfully. "Talk slow,"

she said, and Rachel quieted. In a moment or two
what had happened became clear. Rachel had
thrown the bit of paper into Wendy's wastebasket.
Then she had carried the basket away to be emptied
with other trash. By this time the yard man had
taken everything away to be disposed of. The paper,
however valuable, was gone for good.

For the second time that evening Wendy felt a
little sick. What had happened was not Rachel's
fault, but hers. The precious scrap of paper should
have been put carefully away so that Wendy would
have it when she wanted it. Although she could
hardly bear the thought of facing Marion and telling
her what had happened, there was nothing else to
do.

She climbed the stairs even more slowly than
before, dragging her feet all the way. Miss Smith
was in the upper hall having a cup of coffee, and she
regarded Wendy with concern.

"You don't look very happy," she said. "Is
something wrong? I hope you won't upset Mrs.
Cole, now that she is feeling better."

"I have to upset her," Wendy said, and went
into the room.

Cousin Marion sat where Wendy had left her, the
lettered shell resting in her lap. "Where is it?" she
demanded at once.

Wendy showed her empty hands. "It's gone.
Rachel thought it was a piece of scrap paper and she
threw it away. The yard man has emptied the trash
and it's gone. There's no way to get it back."

Marion's stared at her for a long moment. Then
she closed her eyes and the flush faded from her

cheeks. "I never had a chance to find out what it meant. I don't even know what message the shell might have contained. The one thing Gordon asked me to take care of! And I've failed."

"I don't think there was any message," Wendy said. "The printing was all in Chinese."

At once Marion opened her eyes. "Did you look at the paper carefully? Can you tell me what it was like?"

Wendy reached for a pad and pencil that lay on the stand beside Marion's bed and sat down to draw a picture of the piece of paper.

"It was about this shape and size," she said. "And there were holes all over it—like a piece of Swiss cheese."

Marion stared at the drawing. "I suppose the paper had weathered and rotted in the shell. Perhaps if there was message, it would have been destroyed anyway."

Wendy wished she could snatch at this hope and excuse herself a little, but she had to tell the truth.

"I don't think the paper was that rotten. I think those holes were punched into it with a pencil or something pointed."

"And you're sure there was no writing—nothing you could read?"

"I'm sure. I looked all over it on both sides, and all the writing was in Chinese characters. I think it was a corner torn from a Chinese newspaper."

Weakly Marion got to her feet. When Wendy tried to help her, she pushed her hand away and faltered across the room to the philodendron plant. There she thrust the shell beneath the flowing tendrils of leaves. She did not trouble to bury it this time, and Wendy knew that the shell itself no longer mattered. It was the scrap of paper that had been important — and that was gone.

"Will you ask Miss Smith to come in," Marion said. "I think I'll get ready for bed."

Wendy did not move. She felt horribly guilty and ashamed over what she had done. If she had not been so curious, all this might have been prevented. She could not even explain to Marion the things Mark had told her, or suggest that the best thing that could happen was for the message of the shell to be lost forever. If it carried any secrets dangerous to Gordon Cole, it was far better they were never read and Marion was better off with the scrap of paper lost. But Wendy could hint at none of this. There was only one feeble thing she could say. As she spoke the two words, she had a discouraging feeling that she was always saying the same thing to someone, though always for different reasons.

"I'm sorry," she murmured.

Marion did not so much as look at her. "Just go away," she said. "Go away before I get really angry."

Wendy ran for the door. There was no use trying to hold back her tears. She wasn't brave and strong like her father. Being a boomer's daughter didn't help when you hurt all over, inside and out.

She ran past Miss Smith and fled toward her room, the tears already spilling. Fortunately, Miss Smith's main concern was for Marion and she did not stop her for questions. But when Wendy pushed open her door, she found she could not be alone after all.

Beside the open French doors, waiting for her, sat Aunt Elinor.

"Did you and Marion have a nice visit?" she asked as Wendy burst into the room.

Without answering, Wendy flung herself stormily upon the green bedspread she had once thought resembled soft grass, and buried her face in the pillow. This time she did not bother to weep quietly. It didn't make any difference now if she cried right out loud. Nothing at all would ever be any better, and nothing really mattered—nothing!

Aunt Elinor propped herself up on her single crutch and came slowly across the room. Wendy felt her aunt's weight on the springs beside her as she sat on the edge of the bed. At once she wriggled as far away as she could and turned her head so that her wet face was hidden. She knew what was coming. Grown-ups always said things like, "Don't cry . . . it can't be that bad . . . you're a big girl now . . ." and she braced herself to resist comfort.

Aunt Elinor spoke in a faint, soft voice. "I'm sorry," she said. "I'm terribly, terribly sorry."

The familiar ring of the words startled Wendy in the middle of a sob and she lay suddenly still, listening in surprise.

"You go right ahead and cry," Aunt Elinor said. "You'll feel better if you let your feelings out. I've been letting mine out. I'm afraid I've been thinking only of Marion, trying to protect Marion, trying to bear some of her suffering along with what I feel myself. That hasn't left any room for you. Your uncle has been trying to make me understand that. My husband has a great deal more good sense

than I have. I am a very silly woman."

With one last choking gulp Wendy's sobbing stopped. A hand reached out to give her a wad of paper tissues, and she wiped her eyes and blew her nose. She had been prepared to weep for hours if anyone told her not to. She had been ready to resist any suggestions Aunt Elinor made. But when Aunt Elinor admitted that she was silly and wrong—and sorry about it, what could Wendy do? She knew so well what it was like to be sorry herself.

"Do you want to tell me?" Aunt Elinor asked gently.

Oddly enough she wanted very much to tell someone. Not about the shell and the details of what had happened with Mark, but about something else.

"I don't know how to stop getting into trouble," Wendy said mournfully. "I don't know how to turn around and go the other way."

Aunt Elinor nodded and Wendy did not resist the gentle touch of a hand upon her shoulder.

"I know how you feel because I'm so often there myself," her aunt said. "I suppose there are people who always know how to do the right thing. But I'm not one of them. Though my intentions are good, even when my wits aren't working very well—I suppose that's why Paul and Marion put up with me."

Wendy looked up into her aunt's face and saw that the lines around her eyes had crinkled upward and her lips were smiling ruefully. Surprisingly, Aunt Elinor was laughing at herself.

Wendy felt completely astonished, and a sudden desire to comfort Aunt Elinor surged up inside her.

"You've had a lot to worry you," she said, sitting up on the bed.

"Yes, I suppose that's true," her aunt agreed. "But sometimes I worry senselessly and I do neither myself nor anyone else any good. Of course I usually feel terrible afterward. Because I know I've been selfish and blind. Still—I'll never be strong and wise like Paul. So what am I to do? Even Marion loses patience with me and sometimes doesn't want me around. But I mustn't start being sorry for myself again. Wendy, come down to the kitchen with me and let's have some milk and crackers and start getting acquainted. If you're willing to try."

Wendy discovered, to her surprise, that what she wanted most at the moment was to help Aunt Elinor to feel better. Words Mrs. Castillo had spoken to her the first time they had met flashed through her mind. About the strong helping those who were weaker. Her words applied now, even though Wendy was young and Aunt Elinor old.

She rolled off the bed and stood up. "I'd like that," she said, and was surprised at how cheerful she sounded.

Cook and Rachel were through in the kitchen and Wendy got out a bottle of milk and a package of crackers. The two sat at the table munching and talking, until Uncle Paul came out to join them.

"I thought you two would get together after a while," he said. "And I'm glad of it, because now there are three of us to figure out what to do about Marion."

In the hour during which they sat talking, nothing much was settled, but Wendy found for the first time that she was no longer an outsider. She was beginning to feel a part of this household and she began to long more than ever to be a permanent part of it.

By the time she went upstairs to bed, she felt a great deal better. She did not take Pookie out of her suitcase, because tonight she did not need him. He was only a stuffed toy, anyway—not a real friend. She felt older and more sensible tonight, and she knew there were better kinds of friendships to be had than the one Pookie offered her. Besides, there was still Marion and her desperate troubles to think about. More than ever, Wendy wanted to make up for what she had done and somehow win Marion's friendship. For the first time she was beginning to realize that a new family could not come ready-made, even if it was related. First it was necessary to win herself a place among the others.

Only one unhappy thought returned to trouble her before she fell asleep. She wished the letter to her father had not been mailed. Pop was like her. He often acted on the first notion that came into his head. It was easy to imagine him rushing impulsively to her aid and roaring around about how he wouldn't have anyone mistreating his daughter. But even this thought was not enough to keep her awake.

The next morning she was up early. Breakfast would not be ready yet and she wandered onto the upper gallery and found that though the sun had recently risen, the day was already warm. There was none of the cool feeling she sometimes experienced early on a summer morning at home. The canyons of New York could hold dampness, and their cold stone resisted warmth until the sun was well up and everything began to steam with humidity. Here it was not like that. Always there was the quick tropical heat of the sun, with all the island colors coming alive at once, and the blue sky overhead empty except for a few puffy clouds.

As she leaned on the rail, she saw movement in the direction of Mears Manor. Mr. Helgerson was up early too. He was climbing the steps toward the upper road, his binoculars slung about his neck as usual. At the beach yesterday he had behaved quite well and had not complained about anything. But she could not forget his continued interest in the shell collection, and in the light of what Mark had told her, she began to wonder if he might really know something that could be harmful to Gordon. Or even whether he was on that "other side" Mark had talked about, so that he had some special, secret reason for trying to get hold of the shell himself.

Anyway, it didn't matter now — whatever the message was, it was lost for good.

Such thoughts made her restless, and she decided to do a little exploring before breakfast. A thought had come to her while she was dressing that might help to make up to Mark for what she had done last night. This time before she went out, she found Rachel and told her where she was going, so no one would worry.

There was no need to climb the gate when she had run down through the garden. Now she could take time to unlatch it properly and close it behind her. By bright morning light, some of her actions of the night before seemed pretty silly. Even her scraped knee seemed an unnecessary accident.

Mr. Helgerson sat on the stone wall where she had seen him that first day, and once more he was looking at the harbor through his binoculars, as if the movements of the destroyers out there continued to interest him. A new ship must have come in yesterday, for there were three ships anchored out there. He did not see Wendy as she passed behind him, hurrying toward the path she had taken last night. She hoped he would not interest himself in her actions.

The path was easier to follow by daylight and she reached the top of the catchment quickly. Here, as she had thought it might, the path branched and and went in two directions. One part of the Y wound below Anita's house in the direction of the dead-end road and the hotel, while a second branch ran to the left, curving down the steep hill beside the stone slide of the catchment.

It seemed a long way to the bottom, but Wendy went down, sometimes scrambling and slipping in the steepest places. The nearest houses were the ones above on the street of steps with more clustering far below where a road wound well beneath the catchment. She did not want to go down there. It was only the bottom of the rocky slide that interested her. When she reached it, however, she saw that bushes rimmed the lower edge and it would be impossible to search the ground below the catchment, as she had thought she might do.

Instead, she climbed onto the lower rim of the catchment itself and found that a gutter ran its entire width, covered by wire mesh to let the water through, but filter out leaves and debris that might be swept down when it rained. A feeling of excitement quickened her movements. What if that alphabet shell had not shattered last night? What if it had not bounced off into the brush, after all, but had been caught in the mesh of this gutter? Her thoughts about finding it and returning it to Mark were not altogether clear. It was just that it might make him feel better toward her to have it in his possession, even though she knew it could contain no secret message, being the wrong shell.

She began to walk along the stone of the catchment, searching the wire mesh. But though occasional clumps of leaves and twigs were cluttered along the trap, no shell came into view. When she glanced upward it was like looking up an enormous, slightly slanting stone wall that must reach a full city block. What a terrible fall anyone would have who ventured too near the top and lost his balance. She shivered and went on with her search.

Then, quite suddenly and unexpectedly, she found it. A gleam of something white in a nest of dead brown leaves caught her eye and she knelt on the stone to fish among them. When she stood up again she held the alphabet cone in her hand. It gave her a sense of triumph to have found it. Perhaps this shell didn't mean anything, but at least it would be an offer of friendship toward Mark—since it had been her fault that he had lost it last night.

She stood for a moment turning the shell about in her fingers, examining it carefully. Its trip down the catchment had done it no good, and it bore the chips and cracks of that tremendous fall. Fortunately both this shell and the one in Marion's room were thick and tough and far from fragile. There were shells in Cousin Gordon's collection that could be crushed to powder in the fingers, but there were some that seemed as hard as a rock. This one was of the latter type.

Just for fun she held it up in the bright sunlight and tried to see into the interior through the place where the folds curled in at one end. A tiny stone was jammed there, but otherwise the shell seemed empty. It had, of course, no message to give anyone.

Before she started back to the Villa, Wendy stood for a moment on the catchment, searching the heights. A troubling thought had come to her, and she found almost at once that she was right. There on his stone wall far above, sat Mr. Helgerson. He was watching her intently through his binoculars. He must have noted her every move in her search for the shell, and with strong glasses he could probably see it in her hands. She had a sudden impulse to hide the shell behind her back, but that would give her away, so she grasped it in one hand and waved the other in a careless greeting to the man with the glasses. At least she had the satisfaction of seeing him put down his binoculars, though he did not return her greeting.

She hurried to the edge of the catchment and jumped down to the path. Uncle Paul breakfasted early at the Villa, and he must be up by now. Wendy was getting used to hills and she returned up the path almost as quickly as she had come down. Once she was on her way along its twists she could no

longer see Mr. Helgerson. But when she reached the
place where the Y branched, she found him waiting
for her. She could not continue in the direction of
the Villa without brushing past him, and when she
started to do so he put out his hand to stop her.

"Do you mind letting me see what you've
found?" he asked.

Even though it was the wrong shell, she did not
want to give it to him. This matter was none of his
business and she found herself disliking him more
than ever.

"It doesn't belong to you," she said, putting on a
bold front.

"Nor, I suspect, does it belong to you," he answered and reached for the shell.

She backed away. "It belongs to Mark! I'm going
to give it to Mark as soon as I find him. And I'm not
going to give it to anyone else!"

They were quite close, facing each other. Wendy
looked up into pale steely eyes set in an unsmiling
face. There was no lift at the corners of that neat
brown moustache now. Always before, in spite of
her spy joke, Wendy had thought of him mainly as a
sort of nuisance — a fussbudgety kind of person who
liked to snoop and complain. Now he was deadly
serious, and suddenly she was afraid.

Step by step she began to back away toward the
upper path. If she could get far enough from him,
she could run, and then he would never catch her.
But she could not lengthen the distance between
them. With every step she took, he followed and
she knew that in a moment he would take the shell
away from her, whether she liked it or not.

12

End of a Shell

PERHAPS IT would be better to give him the shell, Wendy thought. Especially since it did not really matter. Returning it to Mark didn't matter either—except as a gesture of friendship.

"Let me see what you have!" Mr. Helgerson commanded and Wendy gave up, drawing the shell from behind her back.

But before she could place it in the man's hands, someone reached past him and took it from her.

"I'll take charge of this!" Bob Eagan said.

She could have hugged him. So intent had she and Mr. Helgerson been on each other's actions that they had not heard Bob come along the path from the direction of the hotel. Now he stood balancing on the balls of his feet, his eyes alight and watchful of Mr. Helgerson. Bob was younger than the other man, but he was overweight, and not so wiry or quick on his feet as Mr. Helgerson seemed to be. Wendy wondered what he would do if the older man insisted upon having the shell. Antagonism bristled between them and it was clear that they did not like each other.

It was, however, Mr. Helgerson who gave in, using words instead of force.

"This must be a pretty important shell," he said, his malice evident. "When I asked this young lady to let me see it just now, she seemed considerably alarmed. And here you come along, ready to rescue the maiden in distress. What's going on here?"

Bob Eagan was still on guard. "I've been just as puzzled watching you," he told the other man. "It certainly looked as if Wendy might need rescuing, so I dived in to help."

"I only wanted to give the shell back to Mark," Wendy put in, to make sure that Bob understood for whom it was intended.

The younger man nodded carelessly and held the cone up for Mr. Helgerson to see, though Wendy noted that he stayed out of reach lest it be snatched away.

"I don't know what all the excitement's about," Bob said. "This is a common little Caribbean alphabet cone. If Mark wants it, I'll be happy to return it to him."

An odd change seemed to come over Mr. Helgerson. Quite visibly he seemed to relax. "An alphabet cone?" he said. "From the Caribbean?"

"Yes, of course," Bob told him. "What did you think it was?"

Mr. Helgerson looked cross and fussy again. "How should I know? This whole incident seems foolish to me."

Wendy had a feeling that he was putting on an act and she could guess why he had lost interest in the shell. Mr. Helgerson *knew* this was the wrong shell. Though how he could know anything about these shells, or how to identify the right one, she had no idea.

He glanced at his watch in his fussy way. "Must be breakfast time by now. I think I'll get back to the hotel." Without another word he went off along the path that wound behind Anita's house to the street below.

Bob Eagan looked after him speculatively. "I'm beginning to wonder what that fellow is up to," he muttered.

Wendy was no longer interested in the odd Mr. Helgerson. "Will you give the shell to Mark?" she asked Bob. "I—I made him lose it last night, so will you tell him I found it and wanted him to have it?"

"I'll tell him," Bob agreed with a cheerful grin, and turned to follow Mr. Helgerson toward the hotel.

Wendy climbed the path, in a hurry now to get back to the comfortable safety of Villa Mimosa. Thoughts tumbled through her mind as she went up the hill—confused thoughts that were full of questions. What was Mr. Helgerson really up to? How did he happen to know that the alphabet shell was not the message shell, so that he had lost interest as soon as Bob told him the kind of shell it was? If it had been the Philippine Island lettered cone that Bob had taken from Wendy, what might have happened? The two men had seemed ready for trouble, and their mutual disliking was clear.

It was good to get back to the house where bacon and pancakes were ready, and to find herself in the reassuring company of Uncle Paul and Aunt Elinor. For once breakfast was a more cheerful meal. Today Aunt Elinor made an effort to suppress her worry about Marion and the change seemed to please Uncle Paul, so that he was happier too.

As she ate breakfast, Wendy found herself worrying again about the letter. Probably Pop wouldn't pay any attention to it, she tried to tell herself. He didn't come running every time she was upset. And if he didn't come, then there was no need for Uncle Paul or Aunt Elinor to know that she had written such a letter. On the other hand, if he decided to come without warning — since he seldom bothered to write or wire ahead, wouldn't it be safer to prepare them? But how could she? How could she bear to spoil this pleasant new feeling that existed between the three of them? If they knew about the awful things she had put into her letter, they would never feel the same about her, or trust her again. No — it was better to keep quiet, to wait.

After breakfast she walked down the long steps toward Mears Manor, wanting to see Mark and make sure Bob had given him the shell. As she passed Anita's house on the way down, Anita came to the gate and Wendy stopped to talk to her. The other girl wore her hair in the long swishy ponytail that Wendy liked and her smile was once more as friendly as ever.

"What was happening this morning?" Anita asked. "I was out early on the veranda at the back of our house and I saw you climbing around the bottom of the catchment. Then you came up and met Mr. Helgerson on the way back. When Mr. Eagan came along the path, it seemed as though you were all talking about something you must have found on the catchment."

"We were," Wendy admitted. Without giving away what must not be told, she explained about meeting Mark last night and accidentally causing him to drop a shell he was carrying. And about how she had retrieved the shell this morning and given it to Bob Eagan to return to Mark.

Anita swung on the open gate and listened attentively, her brown eyes bright with speculation. Wendy had a feeling that Anita knew very well that something was being held back, but she asked no questions and when Wendy was through, she had only one thing to say.

"I wonder if Mr. Eagan really gave the shell to Mark the way you asked him to?"

Wendy stared at her. "What do you mean?"

"There's something I'd like to check," the other girl said and came through the gate to join Wendy on the steps. "Mr. Eagan didn't go straight back to the hotel after he left you. I couldn't see him all the way along the path because the trees and the house below ours hides part of it. But I could see him when he came out near that wall where we were sitting the other day, and he did something very strange."

Already Anita was leading the way down the steps, and Wendy hurried beside her. "What do you mean — strange?"

"He climbed over the wall," Anita said, "and he began looking for something. Then he knelt down and I couldn't see him anymore, but I could hear a noise like two stones being banged together. What do you think he could have been doing?"

Wendy shook her head, but she had an uneasy feeling that she could guess. If she was right, it would be simple enough to check.

"Show me where you think he climbed the wall," she said as they reached the bottom of the steps.

Anita was no longer exactly sure of the place, so

Wendy climbed over the wall herself and began to walk behind it. The earth was rough with a low weedy growth, but there were some bare spots. At a place where bougainvillaea flung purple blossoms over the wall, Wendy came to a stop, staring at the ground before her. She knew now what Bob Eagan had done.

"This is the place," Wendy said, and Anita climbed the wall to stand beside her.

Bob had found a large flat stone he could use as a base. A second stone—used for a hammer—lay nearby. Upon the flat stone were the crushed remains of the alphabet shell. He had not given it to Mark at all.

Wendy knelt and picked up bits of shell to make sure. Yes, she could recognize the reddish-brown speckling, and the tough crown of the shell with its slightly raised whorls had not been pulverized. The white nose had previously broken off in the fall down the catchment, and she found the cracked place where it should have been. She knew very well why Bob had done this—he was looking for the shell's secret. A secret that did not exist. But she wished he had waited to give it to Mark first.

"Why would he do such a thing?" Anita asked.

Wendy evaded the question. "I meant the shell for Mark—so he wouldn't be angry over what happened last night. He—he was beginning to be nicer to me. I guess we're both sorry over what happened on the beach."

Anita smiled. "I'm glad you've stopped fighting. Maybe you'd better find him and tell him about it. Since I haven't had breakfast yet, I'll go along home. Then you can talk to him by yourself."

They climbed over the wall together, and when Anita had gone Wendy sat on its top watching the gate to Mears Manor, hoping that Mark would come into view. She did not want to go down there just now and meet Bob Eagan. She did not trust him anymore.

The sun was growing hot and she moved over to the shade of a flamboyant tree that hung over the wall. On the wall and on the ground all about, flaming red petals had fallen so that the tree seemed to grow out of a pool of fire.

For a long while she sat dreaming in its glowing shade, not thinking hard about anything—not wanting to think. It was Mark's whistle that called her back from pleasant emptiness.

"You waiting for a bus?" he asked, wandering over to join her.

That was a joke, of course, since no bus came to this dead-end street. At least he wasn't angry with her if he could make a joke.

"Look," she said, and pointed beyond the wall, where shattered bits of shell lay upon a flat rock.

Mark jumped onto the wall beside her and looked over, though his expression did not change.

"Bob didn't give you that shell, did he?" she said. "I found it this morning and I wanted to give it back to you so you could do whatever you wanted with it."

"It doesn't matter," Mark said. "Bob told me about smashing it. He didn't find anything. You know that, too—don't you?"

He was watching her intently now, and she could feel the warmth in her cheeks. When she said noth-

ing, Mark went on, still watching her, though not angrily as he had on the beach yesterday.

"Bob says I got the wrong shell from the collection," he told her. "I guess he must be right. Do you know where the other one is?"

She could not tell him. She did not dare. Vaguely she looked up into the cloud of flaming blossoms over her head and hoped the flush would go out of her cheeks. Maybe she had done a lot of things wrong, but nearly always she told the truth, and when she did not she usually gave herself away.

"We want to help Marion and Mr. and Mrs. Guthrie," Mark said, still not losing his temper. "At least Bob does. What I want is never to have this story about Gordon come out. Because maybe it isn't true, and then nothing but damage will be done if people know about it."

"And if it is true?" Wendy said. She was watching Mark now as intently as he had watched her.

He looked up into the tree as she had done, and avoided meeting her eyes.

"Stuart was my best friend," he said, and was silent.

Wendy understood. Mark could not bear the thought of such dreadful things coming to light about Stuart's father. Besides, if he was gone out of reach, there was nothing to be done.

"I had a best friend once," Wendy said, thinking of Fran Parks. "I still miss her a lot. It hurts when I think about her. But not as much as it did at first."

Mark threw her a surprised look—surprised perhaps that she should understand his own feelings so well. Again he was quiet, but now the silence was not unfriendly. Somehow a common ground had been established between herself and this prickly boy. Perhaps they would not need to be enemies anymore. Because of this Wendy felt more friendly toward him, wanting to offer him something more than she had been able to so far.

"You don't have to worry about the other shell," she said. "It's in a safe place."

At once Mark stiffened. "That means it's not in the collection, doesn't it?"

"I don't want to talk about it," Wendy said. "Can't you just let it alone and not worry about it? No one will find it where it is."

Mark puzzled aloud to himself. "If it's in a really safe place, then I'll bet your cousin Marion has it. Gordon said in that letter to Bob that he'd written her to keep an eye on the shell. So maybe she's trying to do that for him."

Mark was too quick, Wendy thought. She had told him too much. Still, it did not really matter, since whatever secret the shell had contained was gone forever in the lost message. There was no need to feel nervous anymore about the right shell.

Mark jumped down from the wall. "Look," he said, "I just don't believe Gordon would ever do anything wrong. Maybe we ought to have a look at the other shell so we can prove the truth about it. Maybe I was wrong to feel relieved when I thought this one was lost last night."

Wendy shook her head, hating to admit the truth. "It wouldn't do any good. I've already looked at it. There's nothing it can tell you—any more than that alphabet cone could tell you anything."

Clearly, Mark did not believe this. "You probably don't know where to look. How did I get those shells mixed up anyway?"

"They belong to the same shell family," Wendy told him. "But the right one is what they call a Pacific lettered cone. It's bigger, with darker brown spots—though both of them look as if they had writing on them."

"Maybe the right shell does," Mark said. "Have writing on it, I mean."

Again Wendy shook her head. He was wrong about that. Anyway she had talked to him long enough. The shell belonged to Marion, and she had promised she would not tell anyone where it was.

"I've got to go back," she said abruptly. She turned away from Mark, and began climbing the hill of steps.

He did not come after her and she did not look back. She wasn't at all sure how long she could hold out against him, and she had to keep her word to Marion.

When she reached the Villa, she found Uncle Paul turning away from the telephone. He smiled at her as she came in.

"I've given up," he said. "I suppose there's no harm in letting this Helgerson chap have a look at Gordon's collection. It's probably simpler to show him through it and get rid of him. It seems that he wants to buy some of the shells, though of course he can't do that unless Marion gives her consent. Anyway, he's coming up here now."

Wendy heard her Uncle's words with growing dismay. There was something terribly wrong about Mr. Helgerson. More and more she had the feeling that he was not what he pretended to be, and that Uncle Paul should not allow him into the house. She had to tell her uncle this thought.

"I think Mr. Helgerson is up to something. I think — I think maybe he's a — a — "

"An undercover agent, perhaps?" Uncle Paul asked, laughing at her gently.

"Anyway, he's a snoop!" Wendy declared. "Maybe you ought to find out what he's snooping for."

Uncle Paul was still smiling. "Mr. Manvil Helgerson's credentials are perfectly good, Wendy. You'd better not let your imagination get out of hand."

There was nothing more she could say, but a new determination possessed her and she ran upstairs and down the hallway toward Marion's room. Just as she reached it, Aunt Elinor came out and pulled the door shut behind her.

She shook her head uneasily at Wendy. "She's feeling ill again and she wants to be alone. You'd better not go in."

Wendy nodded and went to her own room instead. But her determination did not fade. As soon as she heard her aunt go downstairs, she went out upon the gallery and stole around toward the front of the house where she could see the open French doors to Marion's room. Her cousin lay on the bed, her eyes closed, and when Wendy tiptoed closer, she could see that the nurse was not in the room. Softly she tapped on the glass and Marion opened her eyes.

"Could I talk to you for a minute?" Wendy said.

Marion shook her head listlessly. "I don't want to talk to anyone."

Wendy stepped through the doorway and approached the bed. "I need to talk to you. It's about something important."

A shiver ran through the woman on the bed. "What an exasperating child you are! I don't have the strength to deal with you. How can I want a daughter who can't be kind and considerate?"

Stubbornly Wendy stood beside the bed. "I never wanted a mother like you, either," she said.

The violet eyes flew open and the two stared at each other. Then Marion propped herself up on one elbow.

"I suppose I deserve that. I apologize. Now will you just go away? We'll talk again when I'm feeling stronger. I know you've helped me and I don't want to be ungrateful."

"You'd better get up and do something about what's happening downstairs," Wendy said hotly. "Uncle Paul has just told that awful Mr. Helgerson that he can have a look at Cousin Gordon's shell collection. He wants to buy some of the shells, and I guess he won't let Uncle Paul alone until he lets him in."

Marion dropped back on her pillow. "There's nothing to be found there. I can't stop him—and it doesn't matter."

"What if he's looking for the cone shell? What do you suppose he'll do if he doesn't find it?"

"What can he do?" said Marion without interest.

Somehow Wendy's conviction that all this mattered a great deal, and that something should be done about Mr. Helgerson, was growing stronger by the minute. She played her last card—the one she hated to play.

"Cousin Gordon wrote a letter to Mr. Eagan down at the hotel. He sent it from Saigon before he went into the jungle. Mr. Eagan thinks it means that Dave and Gordon were mixed up in something serious and they had to escape before they were caught."

The words sounded dreadfully harsh said right out loud like that, but at least Marion came wide-awake and sat up in her bed.

"I never heard anything so vicious — and so silly — in my whole life!" she cried. "Gordon is my husband, and Dave is an old friend. Don't you think I know them both? Get the shell from the philodendron pot and bring it to me."

Wendy hurried to the plant. Since Marion had not buried the shell in the earth last time, the sun had fallen on it all morning through openings in the leaves. When Wendy pulled it out, it was as hot to her touch as a shell picked up on a sunny beach. She stared at it in bewilderment.

"It looks different," she said.

It did indeed look different. Where, before, the orderly rows of dots had marched across a white ground, now the white had nearly vanished and the shell looked as though it had broken out in a bad case of measles. Every patch that had been white was marked with tiny brown dots, so that hardly any empty space remained.

Startled, Wendy carried the shell to her cousin and held it out. Marion took it from her hand and examined it carefully. Then she looked up at Wendy.

"I should have known," she said. "I should have guessed."

13

A Case of Brown Spots

Her cousin was silent and Wendy spoke anxiously. "What is it? What have you found?"

Marion gestured. "There's a magnifying glass over there in the drawer of my dressing table. Bring it to me, please."

Wendy ran to the drawer and came back with the glass. Carefully Marion studied the shell through the lens and then handed both shell and glass to Wendy.

"Look at it and tell me what you see."

Wendy held the speckled cone to the light and studied it through the magnifying glass as Marion had done. At once all the measles spots, which had seemed meaningless before, sprang out in their true character. Each tiny brown spot was a letter of the alphabet. Not every letter was clear. Some seemed smudged or faint—but they really were letters. Wendy looked at her cousin in bewilderment.

"I should have known," Marion repeated. "When Dave and Gordon and I were children we were always sending secret messages to one another. We learned that we could make invisible writing using lemon juice, or other plant and fruit juices. Nothing would show until heat was applied — then the writing would come out. This is a very simple and well-known trick, but it might be something Dave could manage out in the jungle when he found a chance to send the shell to Gordon. He probably hoped that Gordon would remember those kids' games we used to play, and really study the shell."

Marion covered her face with her hands, trying to think, trying to figure everything out. When she took down her hands and stared at Wendy, she no longer looked limp and apathetic.

"Of course, in the beginning Gordon thought Dave was asking for help and identifying himself by sending the shell, so he didn't look for any message. That idea came to him later, after he had left the shell here and gone back to Vietnam. That's why he wrote to me about it — to make sure I kept track of the shell until he could have a look at it himself. But before I had time to get it from the collection, he was lost and I didn't think about it again until I got back from the hospital. Now it's too late."

"Why is it too late?" Wendy demanded. "If all the letters are there, can't you read the message?"

"How can I know which ones to pick?" Marion asked. "That's what that scrap of paper would have done — it would have given us a means of deciphering the code."

Wendy's heart seemed to sink to her very toes as she looked blankly at the shell in her hand. She could remember the shape of the paper very well, and how, when she had played with it, it had rolled easily into the shape of a cone — as if the paper were meant as a covering for this very shell. And she remembered the numerous holes punched in the paper.

"The holes would have told you which letters to use—is that it?" she asked unhappily.

"I'm afraid that's true," Marion said.

Wendy turned her back upon her cousin. She set the shell upon the dressing table and put away the magnifying glass. She could hardly have felt much worse. Behind her she heard Marion moving and when she glanced into the mirror she saw she was standing beside her bed.

"Will you get Miss Smith for me, please?" her cousin said. "I'm going to get dressed and go downstairs. It's time I met this Mr. Helgerson and found out what he's after. Or what it is he thinks he knows. I'm going to talk to Rachel, too—about that piece of paper she threw away."

An overwhelming feeling of relief swept over Wendy. For the first time a grown-up was going to take over the burden of this terrible problem that was too much for her. Surely a grown-up could solve it.

Marion saw her eagerness, her bright face, and shook her head. "Don't count on anything. It's just that I have to try something. I can't lie around helplessly in bed where I'm no good to myself or to anyone else. At least you've done that for me, Wendy Williams. Now hurry and get Miss Smith. If there's some terrible rumor going around about Gordon, I must find a way to stop it."

Wendy flew to the door. The nurse was waiting in her usual place in the hall, and Wendy brought her back to Marion's room at once. Then, since no one sent her away, Wendy stayed while Miss Smith helped Marion dress, and when her cousin was ready to go downstairs, Wendy sprang up to offer a sturdy shoulder.

"You can lean on me," she said, eager to help.

Marion smiled weakly and put a hand on Wendy's shoulder. Before they went out of the room, she paused before her dressing table and looked at the framed photograph of herself and Gordon and Stuart. For a long moment she studied the three smiling faces. She did not smile in return, but Wendy saw her brace herself, gathering her courage as she moved toward the door, leaning upon Wendy's shoulder.

On the stairs Miss Smith held her arm on the other side and they all went down together. Wendy welcomed the feeling of Cousin Marion's weight, of the slight hurt of Cousin Marion's grasp upon her shoulder — as if by hurting enough, Wendy Williams could make up for some of the wrong things she had done since coming to this house.

The door to the shell collection stood open and voices could be heard inside. As they approached the room, Aunt Elinor came out and gave a little cry of alarm upon seeing Marion.

"I'm all right," her daughter assured her. "It's time I came back to life. I want to meet Mr. Helgerson."

It was like Uncle Paul to show no astonishment, no distress at the sight of Marion. His daughter kept her hand on Wendy's shoulder as she came into the room, leaving Aunt Elinor and the nurse outside.

Across the room, Mr. Helgerson was looking

pleased with himself as he examined a row of shells on a shelf. As Marion came in, he turned and waited until Uncle Paul introduced him.

"I knew your husband, Mrs. Cole," Mr. Helgerson told her. "I met him several times when he visited the States, and he promised me the chance to see his shell collection. Your father has kindly agreed to show me through it, though I'm sorry it has to be under such sad circumstances."

Marion removed her grasp from Wendy's shoulder long enough to shake hands with Mr. Helgerson.

"Nothing in the collection is for sale," she said stiffly. "And I don't know that we have the right to show anyone through it while Gordon is away."

Good for her! Wendy thought. That was telling Mr. Snoopy off!

Neither Mr. Helgerson nor Uncle Paul seemed disturbed by her words. Wendy saw them exchange a meaningful look, and then her uncle came toward Marion and helped her to a chair.

"Sit down for a moment, my dear. I think there are some questions we both would like to ask Mr. Helgerson. Wendy, we'll see you later. Would you mind closing the door on your way out? And please ask your aunt to see that we aren't disturbed for a little while."

Much as she hated to leave that room when she wanted to know what was going to happen, Wendy had to go. She did as she was told and closed the door behind her. She delivered the message to Aunt Elinor and then ran upstairs to Marion's room, before anyone could tell her not to, and waited for her there. Perhaps Marion would tell her what had happened when she returned.

More than once Wendy picked up the shell from the dressing table and looked at it with and without the magnifying glass. Now that she knew what they were, she could make out the letters without the help of the glass. But no matter how carefully she studied them, the tiny marks that had been traced into the white spaces were only a senseless jumble. Unless she knew which ones to choose, none of them could be made to give a message. Or if she looked at it in another way, she could concoct almost any message she pleased just by forming random words from the assorted letters.

It was easy now to see how it must have been done. Working with his jungle materials, Dave must have first set down the letters of the message he wanted to send. Then he had punched holes in a piece of newspaper torn to the right shape — holes that would fit the letters of the message. After that he had simply filled in all the rest of the space with various letters of the alphabet, hiding the significant ones in the jumble. Only a person who possessed the paper with its punched holes which Dave had tucked inside the shell, could figure out the proper words.

It seemed a long time before Marion returned. When she came, it was Uncle Paul who helped her up the stairs and brought her to her room. The moment the two appeared in the doorway, Wendy's gaze sped from one face to the other and in neither did she find reassurance. Marion looked white and ill again, and Uncle Paul's expression was very grave. He left Marion with Miss Smith, and would have called Wendy to come out of the room. But Marion pleaded for her to stay.

"Wendy is my friend, and I need her now," her cousin said.

The warm smile Uncle Paul gave Wendy was approving, and Wendy once more found it hard to swallow for the emotion that choked her throat. But this time it was an emotion of gratitude and affection—not one of resentment or indignation.

When he had left, Marion refused to go back to bed and sent Miss Smith away, so she and Wendy could be alone.

"I've got to stay up," she said. "I've got to start living again because there are so many things to do. Wendy, I spoke to Rachel downstairs, but what you told me is right—the paper went out in the trash and there's no way to get it back."

She sat down in a chair near the gallery doors, and Wendy brought a footstool close so that she could sit near her, waiting hopefully for whatever she wanted to reveal.

For a time her cousin was silent, as if her thoughts were turning over everything that had been said downstairs, turning the words over and rejecting them. Wendy could tell by the flush in her cheeks, by the bright look in her eyes, that something had been said which Marion could not, would not, accept.

"I won't believe that dreadful man!" she said at last. "I don't care who he claims to be—he couldn't have known Gordon well. He couldn't know him the way I know him. And somehow—somehow I've got to prove him wrong."

"Can I help?" Wendy asked, leaning forward earnestly, her hands clasped about her knees.

Marion reached out and touched her hands. "You're on my side, aren't you, Wendy dear? I've behaved badly toward you, but I have a feeling that you're still on my side—and on Gordon's."

"Oh, I am! I really am!" Wendy said warmly.

Marion closed her eyes and as the flush of anger died away, her cheeks looked paler than ever. She did not seem like a person who was strong enough to fight any sort of battle—if battling was needed.

"Tell me what happened," Wendy said. "I want to help."

"It's much worse, much bigger and more threatening than anything I could have imagined. Some sort of serious sabotage plot has been going on. Cuba is very close, you know, and outsiders are helping Castro. The plot was discovered and stopped by our government, but the men who were acting as go-between here in St. Thomas are still wanted. Otherwise there could be more Caribbean trouble in the future."

A picture returned to Wendy's memory—of Mr. Helgerson watching those destroyers out in the harbor. Ought she to tell Uncle Paul about that? But of course she could not. It was no more than a notion on her part, and nothing like logical proof of someone's wicked intention.

"But what had Cousin Gordon to do with any of this?" she asked.

"That's the part I don't believe!" Marion cried. "Someone thinks his friend Dave was in on this dreadful plan before he went out to Vietnam, and that he left it to Gordon to take over his position when he escaped into the jungle. Afterward, Gordon is supposed to have learned that the game was up and he followed Dave, to save his own skin. At least that's what they suspect. They think that's why Gordon tried to get a message to me by means of that shell, and that's why he warned me of danger, warned me to take care of it. Or anyway, this is what Mr. Helgerson claims."

"How does he come into this?" Wendy demanded.

"I don't know. I don't trust him. I think he's playing some sort of game, so we will turn the shell over to him. He knows there is a shell, and he even knows what kind of shell it is. He asked me right out to give it to him. All I could do was pretend I didn't know what he was talking about."

"What can you do now?"

Marion opened her eyes and looked thoughtfully at Wendy. "We can still try to find out the message of the shell. We can write all the letters down and see if it's possible to make anything of them. And you can go to the library for me. You can try to get some books about ciphers and codes. Perhaps that sort of thing will help us."

"I'll ask Anita to take me to the library this afternoon," Wendy promised. "It's all my fault about that piece of paper."

This was true, and there was nothing Marion could say. She looked exhausted, and Wendy went to call Miss Smith.

That afternoon, right after lunch, Wendy went down to Anita's and explained about the books she wanted from the library — of course without confiding the true reason which concerned Marion.

Anita was willing to help and they walked down the hill together. Always before, Wendy had driven down in a car, now she found that it was much more interesting to walk. Now she could look into some of the fascinating little side streets of Charlotte Amalie and enjoy the beauty and strangeness of the island of St. Thomas.

The library was located near one end of Main Street, housed in a big stone building that had once been a family mansion. Anita led the way through a tunnellike passageway that opened into a large paved courtyard which had been the garden of the mansion. In all the earthy spaces grew flowering tropical trees and shrubbery, but Wendy scarcely had time to look around before she saw Mr. Helgerson there ahead of them. He was busily taking pictures like any harmless tourist, though she could no longer regard him as a mere tourist who was considering the island as a future place to live. She would have ducked past him without speaking, had he not seen her first.

"Hello!" he said. "I've been wanting to talk to you. Perhaps this is a good opportunity."

To talk about the shell? Wendy wondered. To ask what she knew about it—because he had some dark reason for wanting to get hold of it? A reason he had not told Uncle Paul? If that was what he meant, she certainly would not help him.

"I have to do an errand right now," she said hurriedly. "I have to look for a book in the library."

He seemed mildly disappointed. "Oh, well—another time, perhaps. Run along, if you must. Your friend Mark Mears is in the library."

Anita must have been puzzled by the way she darted off across the courtyard toward the steps, but Wendy could not explain. She whispered, "Let's get away from him," and Anita asked no questions.

Quickly they climbed the stone steps that led from the courtyard to a wide veranda above. A spacious wooden staircase inside led to an upper floor, which was occupied by offices. Since the library rooms opened off the veranda, the moment Anita led the way in Wendy saw Mark sitting at a table, completely absorbed in a book that lay open before him. He did not notice them as they came in, and Wendy did not speak to him at once.

First the girls asked for help at the desk and when the librarian had consulted the files and looked through books on a shelf, she told them the one book the library had on ciphers must be out.

Only then did Wendy walk over to where Mark sat, and even before she glanced over his shoulder at the book he was studying, she had a sinking feeling. One look at the page gave her the answer. The book that lay open before Mark was the book on ciphers and codes.

The moment Mark saw the two girls beside him, he moved a paper to cover the pages that so interested him.

"You don't need to hide your book," Anita said, teasing him. "That's the one we're looking for, too."

He regarded them darkly, running a hand over his bright red hair as if he did not know what to say or do.

Wendy asked a direct question. "Why do you want to find out about ciphers right now?"

"Why do you?" he countered.

Each had blocked the other and Wendy had a feeling that Mark would not give up the book easily. She did not want to show too great an interest in it by arguing, but it was very puzzling that he should happen on a book about secret codes at this time.

"Have you been talking to Mr. Helgerson?" she asked.

Mark threw her a disgusted look. "Him!" he said—which was not a very good answer and did not tell her whether or not Mr. Helgerson had tipped him off.

He must have seen the question that remained in Wendy's eyes for he added a few more words. "I wouldn't believe anything that guy says. All he's interested in is making trouble."

"I think so too," Wendy agreed. Perhaps Mark could be trusted to be on Gordon's side. "Cousin Marion wanted me to bring her that book," she admitted.

For a moment Mark sat staring up at her, his expression doubtful, questioning. Then he slid aside the paper that hid the pages and pushed the book toward her.

"You can have it, if you like," he said, and stood up.

Wendy was too surprised to answer, so it was Anita who thanked Mark and quickly picked up the book. But before she could carry it to the desk to be checked out on her card, Mark spoke again.

"Mom says if you two want to have a look at everybody in their costumes on the night of the party, you can come over to the hotel early and she'll fix a place where you can watch. You needn't stay late and I'll walk you home afterward."

"That will be fun," Anita said promptly. "You'll come, won't you, Wendy?"

She supposed she would come and she said so, but her mind was still on more important and troublesome matters than a costume party.

Nevertheless, when Anita and Wendy were on the way home with the book Mark had let them take, Anita's talk about the excitement of the coming party began to stir Wendy's imagination. Anita had been permitted to watch this annual party in other years and she said it was fun to see the characters people chose to be, and how well they acted their parts. Of course, children weren't invited and the party lasted too late for her to see the unmasking — but she always found out the next day who the most interesting characters at the party had really been.

Back at the Villa, Wendy took the book at once to Marion's room, and together they pored over it for the rest of the day. Marion had already made an index of all the letters she could make out on the shell — but when they were lined up on paper, there was no way to make sense of them, any more than when they were studied on the surface of the shell itself. What was worse, the cipher book told them nothing they did not already know. The code which used a perforated paper to spell out a message was described — but since they already knew this was the code that must have been used on the shell, they were not ahead in any way.

"Just the same," Marion said wearily, "I'm not going to let Mr. Helgerson know I have this cone shell. If I can't decipher the letters, then I can't. But I won't put it into his hands to make use of against Gordon, and that's the end of that."

There was no longer any need to keep the shell buried in the philodendron pot, and Marion set it aside on her dressing table and tried to forget about it.

Wendy, however, was not one who gave up easily and during the next few days the problem was seldom out of her mind. She had a strong feeling that it must not be put aside. Others were working against Cousin Gordon and thus against his family. Others who perhaps had unsavory secrets of their own to hide.

This was her family now, Wendy told herself fiercely, and above all else, Cousin Marion must be saved from further hurt.

14

Flight of a Bat

DURING THE next few days nothing much happened—except that Marion's worries and anxieties began to grow to an alarming degree. Even though she had given up the problem of the shell, she fretted and grieved, and could find no satisfactory way to occupy herself. Instead of returning to her former state of apathy—where nothing mattered and she would not think or make any effort to act, she began to move restlessly about the house, without purpose, yet always seeming to look for something.

Once Wendy asked her what she searched for, but all Marion would say was, "An answer—only an answer. Wherever I can find it."

At least it was something that she came downstairs to meals and went outdoors in the garden. In fact, in one way and another, she was truly coming back to life. But living meant pain and Marion had never learned how to live with pain.

Miss Smith was no longer needed, and both Aunt Elinor and Uncle Paul were delighted to see their daughter moving about. Only Wendy continued to worry, and to recognize that danger still lay ahead.

A good deal of the time Wendy followed Marion around. When her cousin wanted to be quiet, Wendy was quiet. When she wanted to talk, Wendy listened, or even talked a little herself. By now she knew a great deal about Stuart and about Cousin Gordon, and Marion knew about the Parks family. It was as if Marion's well-being and Marion's future were bound up so inextricably with Wendy's own, that Wendy breathed as Marion did, and was cheerful when she tried to be cheerful, sad when she was sad.

Uncle Paul did not wholly approve of this. "You're not a little lapdog, Wendy," he told her one day. "You have to live your own life, you know, and be with young people your own age. I don't think it's good to be so constantly with someone who is making her first steps toward recovery from a tragic experience."

Of course Wendy did not stay with Marion every minute. Not even Marion wanted that. One day she went with Anita on the tramway up Flag Hill, riding in a small car that hung suspended from wires. A tremendous view of both sides of the island was possible, as well as a glimpse of distant islands in the seas all around. Even Puerto Rico could be seen on that fine clear day.

They made the trip on the afternoon before the fancy-dress party. Afterward Wendy came home to find Marion resting in a chair in the Villa garden, beneath the pink blossoms of a feathery mimosa tree. Bob Eagan and Mark were with her, sitting on the grass and talking. Wendy had left Anita at her house, and when she came up to the Villa alone she joined the others on the grass.

Marion and Bob were talking about old times when they had been children, and Gordon and Dave had lived not far away. As they talked, the screen door to the house opened and Wendy looked around to see that Uncle Paul and Mr. Helgerson had come out upon the gallery. So he was still around, still persistent about stirring up trouble, Wendy thought uneasily.

Several times Mr. Helgerson glanced at the little group on the lawn, and gradually he managed to edge himself and Uncle Paul closer, though only Wendy seemed aware of the fact. She wanted to whisper, "Look — Mr. Snoopy is busy again!" but no one was paying any attention, and she could not say it aloud with Mr. Helgerson right there listening.

Their own talk had turned to the party tonight and Marion's expression had grown sorrowful. "Last year Gordon and I went together," she said.

Bob nodded. "Yes — I remember. You were dressed as Titania from *A Midsummer Night's Dream* and Gordon came as King Lear. Under all those wild whiskers nobody guessed who he was. Lear was hardly Gordon's sort."

There was a slight edge to Bob's voice, and Wendy had a feeling that he was thinking of the grief the present-day Gordon had brought to his family.

Mark seemed to sense his uncle's unspoken criticism, and he broke in quickly.

"Mom says she hopes the party won't disturb you tonight," he said to Marion.

"I won't let it disturb me," Marion assured him. "I don't want to stay awake to remember last year. The doctor has given me something to help me sleep if I need it—and tonight I will need it very much. I don't think I could bear it otherwise."

There was an awkward silence, and Wendy found herself saying the first thing that came into her mind in order to draw attention away from her cousin's suffering.

"Anita and I are going down to watch for a while. At least we'll be able to recognize you," she said to Bob Eagan. "Since Mark's mother copied those clothes for you to wear, we know you'll be a pirate."

Bob grinned at her and glanced toward the gallery, where Uncle Paul stood with Mr. Helgerson.

"I'm going to fool you," he said. "I've given up my pirate costume to our friend there. Helgerson has nothing suitable to wear, and he wants to come. You wouldn't think gay parties would be his sort of thing. Anyway, I'll probably come done up in a bed sheet like a Halloween ghost. Dressing up isn't all that important to me."

"How can he wear something made for you?" Marion asked. "You're hardly the same size."

"A few tucks and pins will do the trick," Bob said. "After all, the cape will hide a good deal of him."

So Mr. Helgerson would be at the party, Wendy thought in surprise. There was something strange about that, as Bob Eagan said. He didn't seem a party-loving sort of person. Though it was true that he had come with them for the picnic. Perhaps he was lonely away from home and wanted to be in on some of the festivities. At least pirate dress seemed appropriate for him. Wendy could easily imagine him in a pirate's role—but not the swashbuckling, dashing sort of pirate who would wear a plumed hat and velvet cloak. She could picture him better with a black patch over one eye, a slinky moustache, and an even more slinky manner.

The more she considered his coming to the party, the more Wendy's sense of uneasiness increased. It was as if events were somehow gathering beneath the surface, ready to boil. Something seemed to be stirring just out of sight, almost ready to burst into the open.

She found herself watching Mark, half hoping that he had sensed this too, so that she need not feel herself wholly fanciful. But the red-haired boy appeared relaxed, with no shadow of dark thoughts hanging over him.

After sitting out on the lawn for a while, Marion was ready to go early to her room and have Rachel bring her a light supper. When dinner was over, Wendy went upstairs to tell her cousin good night, and found her already asleep. It was a good thing, Wendy thought. Now the music and sound of dancing, the laughing voices, would not come to her from down the hill to remind her of a year ago when she had been a happy wife, with a husband and son to love and cherish.

For a moment or two Wendy stood near the bed, looking down at her cousin and thinking again how young and pretty she looked asleep, with all the pain and worry wiped away. If only Cousin Gordon could return and clear up the mystery, banish the ugly rumors. Wendy glanced toward the framed picture on the dressing table. He had such an open, smiling look about him. It was not the look of a man engaged in dreadful schemes that might hurt his country. Nor could she believe that he was the sort of man who would run away, no matter what happened. Marion and Mark were right to believe in him with all their hearts, and she wanted to believe too. The one to be distrusted was that sneaky Mr. Helgerson who had somehow put himself over with Uncle Paul and was managing to fool him.

Before she turned away, she saw that the spotted shell had been set beside the picture. Its flattened nose pointed toward the bed where Marion lay asleep—as if it stood guard. Wendy could almost feel its spotted eyes watching as if it were saying, "I can give you the answer. Just ask me the right questions and I will tell you the truth."

But there was no way to ask such questions, and Wendy turned and went softly out of the room.

When it was time to leave, Uncle Paul took her down the steps to Anita's house, and then accompanied both girls to the hotel. Mark was to see them home around ten o'clock. The party would still be young, but at least they would be able to watch the fun for a little while.

Mrs. Mears had fixed a sort of box seat for them on stools behind the lobby desk. All the furniture had been set back against the walls, with the lobby opening into the sitting room, so that guests could move about freely. Local guests from the island were coming as well as those from the hotel, and quite a crowd was expected. Here, behind the desk, Wendy and Anita would be out from underfoot.

At any other time Wendy would have been excited since she had never before been present at a grown-up fancy dress party. Tonight, however, her uneasiness seemed to increase and she kept a watchful eye out for Mr. Helgerson's appearance. Once she had located him, she did not mean to take her eyes off him for the length of time she was here.

Anita's dark brown eyes were alight with excitement, and when guests began to appear, she leaned toward Wendy to whisper teasing comments. "Look at Cinderella there! You'd never guess that she likes to run a catamaran about the harbor in all sorts of weather. And look at fat Falstaff just coming in. He owns a grocery store and probably eats a lot of his own goods."

Wendy looked and smiled — and waited for the pirate to appear. Unfortunately, several pirates came in at the same time, and before the party was long under way there were six buccaneers swaggering around the lobby, flirting with the ladies, twirling false moustaches, or hiding their faces behind domino masks and false beards.

To her dismay, Wendy found that she could not even recognize the right pirate clothes. She had seen the copied articles Mrs. Mears had made only by moonlight the night when she had caught Mark on the hillside. She had not paid much attention to them then. When Mark had taken them off and folded them into a pile, she had not looked at them closely. There had been a plumed hat, she knew. But three of the pirates out there in the lobby wore plumed hats — one with a skull and crossbones pasted on the turned-up brim, so there would be no mistaking his calling. Wendy enlisted Anita's help but neither girl could pick Mr. Helgerson from among the others, or guess how he would act once he was in fancy dress.

"Everyone changes," Anita whispered. "Dressing up gives you a chance to pretend you're somebody else. Maybe somebody you wouldn't dare be in real life."

There was a three-piece band for the dancing, and a calypso singer as well, and as the evening wore on, Wendy found that all the colors and sounds, the music and the movement of feet on a bare floor were combining to make her sleepy. Once or twice she nodded toward the desk, and had to pull herself upright to try and stay awake. Mark was helping his mother, and he brought them glasses of fruit juice poured over ice, and that helped a little to wake her up. But by nine thirty Wendy was dozing again, with Anita prodding her occasionally, so she wouldn't fall off the stool.

The thing that brought her suddenly wide awake with a new idea rushing through her mind, came in a completely unexpected way. One of the costumed guests with a long, thin, droopy moustache came up to talk cheerfully to the two girls. He was dressed as a Chinese mandarin of bygone days, and wore a long brocaded satin coat, a skull cap with a jade button on top, and a false pigtail that hung down his back in the old-fashioned manner.

"How do you like me?" he said, and only then did Wendy recognize Bob Eagan.

It was not that he had found a costume which startled her awake, but the sort of costume it was. While he explained about a friend not being able to come tonight and thus loaning him the mandarin dress at the last minute, Wendy stared at him, her

thoughts tumbling excitedly. Of course! That scrap
of paper in the shell had been torn from a Chinese
newspaper. *Chinese*. It was not Bob Eagan, but the
Chinese costume that had suddenly caused something in her mind to click. The chance was a slim
one — but it was possible. She could hardly wait till
morning to put her new idea to a test. Unfortunately,
it could not be managed tonight. She had better not
tell Marion her plan ahead of time since it might
not work out, and then her cousin would have
another disappointment to face. Perhaps Wendy
could be up early and try out her idea before Cousin
Marion was even awake.

The party no longer interested her. She smiled
vaguely at Bob, grateful because his borrowed
costume had put her mind to work, but no longer
able to pay much attention to what was going on
about her. She wished she could confide in Anita,
but that would mean telling her the whole story, and
the secret was not hers to reveal.

Fortunately, Anita too was growing tired of
watching, and when Mrs. Mears came to ask if they
would like to go home, both girls were ready. They
slipped away from the bright noisy room, with its
lights and gay costumes, and stepped outdoors into
a cool and windy night. Mark came with them as
they climbed the steps.

The moon was no longer gibbous, but had grown
to a full yellow sphere, swimming in a dark blue sea
speckled with golden stars. The Caribbean wind
rushed through the treetops and flung flower petals
across the steps — petals that would have been
scarlet and yellow by day, but were like black con-

fetti by moonlight. There was a scent of jasmine on the air and a smell of the sea.

Wendy said nothing until Anita had been left at her house. Then as she and Mark went on up the hill together toward the top of the steps, she asked him a question.

"Which pirate tonight was Mr. Helgerson?"

Mark snorted. "Couldn't you tell? He was the one who kept fussing because his hat didn't fit and his cape kept getting caught on things." Wendy had not noticed, but she was glad to know that he had really been at the party. Somehow she'd had the feeling that he might slip away on some wicked mischief of his own, while no one else was watching. It was good to know she was wrong about her imagining that something was building up beneath the surface and getting ready to burst out in some sort of explosion. Nothing at all had happened. Everything was fine. Besides, now she had something unexpected to think about—her plan concerning the scrap of Chinese newspaper.

Mark took her to the front door of the Villa and then hurried back to the party, apparently not at all sleepy. Uncle Paul was waiting and he welcomed a drowsy Wendy and sent her off to bed at once.

Upstairs, Marion's door was ajar and before she went into her own room, Wendy roused herself enough to look inside. Her cousin's even breathing told her she was deeply asleep. The sounds of the party that still drifted up the hill could not touch her now, or make her remember a happier party of a year ago.

Back in her own room, Wendy was glad enough to go right to bed. Since her doors opened on the side

gallery, the party sounds scarcely reached her. She would not have stayed awake anyway. All she wanted was to sleep as soundly as Marion was sleeping, and not waken till morning—when she could put her new idea into action.

Ordinarily this was what she would have done — slept soundly, hardly stirring until it was time to get up the next morning. But during the night, something went wrong. Quite suddenly she came awake with a jerk that brought her sitting up in bed. The room was dark and quiet, undisturbed except by the thudding of her own heart. Outside, the night insects were chirring, and there was a sound of the blowing wind. Everything indoors appeared quiet and serene. Yet it seemed to Wendy that some unfamiliar sound had brought her awake—some sound of warning that had come from within the house.

She slipped from her bed and ran barefoot to the gallery doors. Her pajamas were thin, but the air was not cold, and she needed no covering as she stepped outside. Except for the wind and those busy creatures that made such a tumult at night, everything seemed quiet. She had no idea of the time, but it had to be late, for the moon was far down the sky and the party sounds were over. Still—something was wrong. She knew with all her senses that all was not as it should be.

Softly she moved toward the front of the house where the gallery ran past Marion's room. On bare feet she made no sound on the boards of the gallery as she crept to the corner of the house—and no farther.

Here she could look around the corner cautiously and see the entire front gallery. All lay dark and empty, untouched by moonlight. The shutters of Marion's room stood open, and it was dark inside. Then, unexpectedly, Wendy caught a glimmer of light — a light that moved and turned, and was suddenly cut off. In Marion's room someone moved about with a flashlight.

While Wendy hesitated in alarm, not sure what to do, something terrifying burst from the room. A great flapping bird dashed across the gallery and seemed to fly to the rail at the far corner where the bougainvillaea vine crawled up a fretted iron pillar. As it flapped over the rail, Wendy saw that it was not a bird, but a man — or a boy — wearing a wide cape that floated out like the wingspread of a bat and nearly entangled itself on the balcony rail as he went down.

As Wendy already knew, the gallery pillar offered strong hand- and toeholds and he had no trouble in reaching the ground. While she watched, too surprised to cry out, the figure seemed to fly across the lawn to disappear behind a clump of shrubbery, just as Wendy herself had done one night last week.

It had all taken no more than seconds. Wendy recovered the power of movement and ran along the gallery to Marion's room. Through it she could see that the hall door was still ajar. Some light came from the hall, and Wendy could make out the bed where Marion lay, breathing deeply. Listening for only a moment, she stumbled through the dimly lit room toward the wedge of light from the door. Once out in the hall, she ran to Uncle Paul's room and tapped softly, calling to him.

He came to the door at once, and in spite of her

wish not to disturb Aunt Elinor, her aunt had heard
and she followed him almost immediately. Wendy
would only flutter her hands at them and try to
gulp out words.

"Someone—in Marion's room. In a cape! He got
away. Down the pillar to the garden. If you hurry—"

Uncle Paul waited for no more. He dashed for
the stairs and they heard him go out the front door
below. Aunt Elinor and Wendy stared at each other,
and then her aunt turned in alarm toward Marion's
room.

"She's all right," Wendy whispered. "I went
there first and she's sound asleep."

Aunt Elinor had to see for herself, and Wendy,
waiting near the head of the stairs, saw the light
flash on in her cousin's room as Aunt Elinor moved
about. It flashed off again quickly, and her aunt
joined her, agreeing that everything seemed all
right. Marion was still asleep.

"If it was a burglar, you must have frightened
him," Aunt Elinor said.

Wendy was glad if she had. It must have been
some sound the man had made that had wakened
her—just in time to frighten him away.

Lights came on downstairs, and they looked over
the banister to see Uncle Paul coming toward them,
carrying in his arms a red velvet cloak, and a plumed
hat.

"A masquerader from the party," he told them,
"—though why he would come up here, I don't
know."

Was it Mark again? Wendy puzzled. Could he
have tried the same thing he had done before—

coming up to the Villa in pirate costume? No—she knew very well who must have worn the garments Uncle Paul was carrying.

"Mr. Helgerson wore those things at the party tonight," she called down to him.

Uncle Paul looked up at her as he climbed the stairs. "But there would be no reason for Helgerson to do such a thing. Did you actually see—?"

Wendy shook her head. "I couldn't see who it was—only the clothes."

"Then let's not guess at who would do a thing like this." Uncle Paul sounded stern. "After all there's no reason for Helgerson to sneak into a house he can enter openly by day. What could he want?"

"To look for something in Marion's room," Wendy said. And she believed she knew what. The man would have been looking for the spotted cone shell that he had not found in the collection. She could not explain this to Uncle Paul, however. Not until she had talked to Marion.

"In any case," Uncle Paul said, "it's after three o'clock and we'd better all go back to bed. In the morning we can have a better look around the garden and through Marion's room."

Aunt Elinor was plainly upset, but this time she did not forget Wendy. She reached out to touch her shoulder gently.

"Will you be all right in your room, dear? Are you frightened?"

Wendy said quite firmly that she was not afraid. For the first time Aunt Elinor kissed her good night and Wendy returned to her room and got into bed. She did not feel comfortable there, and in a moment she got up to make some changes. First she closed the gallery doors and opened the hall door. Then, a bit shamefacedly, she got Pookie out of her suitcase and tucked him into the pillow, beside her. After a time the quivering at the pit of her stomach quieted and she fell as soundly asleep as Marion.

She had stayed up very late and spent a busy and exciting night, and there was much to be done tomorrow.

15

Mortal Combat

SOUNDLY AS Wendy slept, some inner clock
sounded its alarm in her mind long before
breakfast time the next morning. Instead of waking
drowsily, reluctant to be up, the feeling that there
was something important she must do roused her
instantly.

As she sat up, all the events of the night swept
back—not only her memory of the figure in the pirate cape who had climbed to the gallery while
Villa Mimosa slept, but also a remembrance of the
party and of Bob Eagan in his costume of a Chinese
mandarin—that costume which had given her an
idea of something to try.

She washed and dressed, brushed her hair out of
her eyes, and was ready. Yet even the few minutes
that were needed for such hurried preparation were
enough to dispel some of last night's enthusiasm.
Wendy had found that it was often like that in the
morning. An idea that seemed wonderful late at
night, was apt to change into something silly in the
clear light of day. This morning she saw her idea for
what it was—one slim chance in a thousand that
anything would come of it. Still—she must try.

No one was astir in the big living area downstairs as she hurried through it and out the front door. The warmth of early morning in St. Thomas always surprised her. The sun was up, heating the air, setting the harbor waters aripple with golden fire. In its shining light the mounds of Flag Hill and Hassel Island floated like green guardians of the bay.

Her sneakers made no sound as she ran across the gallery and down the shallow steps into the garden. As she had expected, Charlie, the man who worked at all the yard jobs around the Villa, was already busy at his weeding. Wendy ran across the grass to where he knelt and stood beside him.

It would not do to ask her question too suddenly and impolitely, and for a little while she watched in silence wondering about him. He was not a young man. His hair was gray, his face leathery with wrinkles. He spoke English in the manner of one who had not been born in this country. Probably Charlie wasn't his real name.

As she stood watching, he looked up at her briefly and smiled, then returned to his work as though he was accustomed to children, so that he did not mind her presence. Maybe Stuart had been his friend.

After a while she asked a question. "Were you born in China?"

Charlie nodded. "Born old China. Born Hankow up Yangtze River."

She considered him thoughtfully. Did he have any family here? she wondered. Had he been lonely coming to a place so far away from his home? Were there other Chinese in the Virgin Islands? Uncle Paul had said there were people here from almost any nation you could mention. But she could not ask him such personal questions, even though the answers interested her. Instead, there was that other big question she must ask. Perhaps she was putting it off because her hope that this man could help was already fading. Nevertheless, she had to plunge.

"One day last week," she said, "Rachel took a piece of paper off the dresser in my room and threw it into my wastebasket. Then she took the basket downstairs and emptied it in with the other trash. I wanted to keep that piece of paper, but by the time I asked her about it, she said you had thrown out all the trash."

Charlie Wong withdrew his hands from the earth and sat back on his heels to look at her. "What paper you mean?"

"It was just an old piece of newspaper," Wendy said. "I think it must have been torn from a Chinese paper."

Charlie dusted the dirt from his hands and reached calmly into a pocket of his work pants. "This is paper you want?" he asked, drawing out the scrap with its Chinese characters and perforations.

It was all Wendy could do not to snatch the scrap joyfully from his hands. Instead, she nodded eagerly. "Yes — that's it." Please — may I have it back?"

He looked almost wistfully at the folded scrap on his palm. "My language," he said. "Chinese writing. When I see in trash, I take. But if you want, I give back."

He held it out to her, and she took it carefully from him. "Thank you — oh, thank you very much! You'll never know how important this piece of paper is to — to all of us."

It seemed that her feet hardly touched the grass

as she ran back to the house. Uncle Paul was in the living room, but she scarcely heard his "Good morning," as she dashed through. Now—now at last, she had the means to read the message of the shell. Now it would have to give up its secret for Marion to read, and she knew it would tell them something important.

Marion's door was closed, and she had to stop long enough to rap. When there was no answer, she opened it and walked in. Her cousin was still asleep and Wendy hurried across the room to the dressing table, reaching toward the place where the shell had stood guard beside the photograph.

A glance told her it was gone. In sudden fear, she looked about the room, but the shell was not in the philodendron pot, not on the bed table beside Marion—in fact, it was nowhere to be seen. She could not look through drawers without Marion's permission, and anyway the sinking feeling inside her warned that a search would do no good. Now she knew that the figure which had climbed to the gallery last night had found what it had come for. The spotted shell was gone. In her hands she held the means for reading its secret—but someone had come here and taken the shell during the night. Someone who had been desperate enough to do so risky a thing. Someone who had known that Marion would be soundly asleep, having taken her doctor's sleeping prescription.

It could not have been Mark—oh, certainly not Mark. Suddenly Wendy remembered Mr. Helgerson standing at the very edge of the lower gallery yesterday afternoon, doing his best to listen to everything the little group on the lawn was saying. She had been aware of his interest, and she had already begun to suspect just how desperate he was. Not desperate to read the message of the shell as were Mark and Bob, who only wanted to save Gordon's name from disgrace — but desperate in his wish to hide the shell so no one would ever know what it really said. No matter what Mr. Helgerson had done to convince Uncle Paul that he was a friend, Wendy knew better. By now he would have gotten rid of the shell and it would be too late to do anything about it.

Frustration and disappointment flooded over her in one great wave. Furious over this trick of fate, angry with herself because she had not foreseen that this might happen, angry with Uncle Paul for trusting Mr. Helgerson so foolishly, Wendy ran back to her own room, still clutching the now useless piece of paper.

She longed to slap out at someone, to hurt someone, to pay someone off. It was as though all the hurts and angry emotions she had felt since she had come to this house surged up together in a sickening wave. She could not stand against such a feeling without doing something violent herself. A memory of smashing up that sand castle and releasing all her feelings of anger by kicking at it and stamping upon it, returned to her mind. There was no sand castle around to smash, but she saw a substitute.

She went over to her bed and picked up the pillow, and then and there she gave it the hardest, most furious thumping it had ever received. She must have pounded it for a good sixty seconds before all her anger drained suddenly away, and she began to feel very foolish indeed. What a good thing that there had been no one around to see. At least she could think more clearly now. Sheer anger would get her nowhere. Not when something useful needed to be done. It was just possible there was still time.

She thrust the scrap of paper into a deep pocket in her skirt, tucking it underneath a handkerchief, so she would not lose it. Then she ran downstairs. Uncle Paul stood beside a table examining the clothes he had picked up in the garden last night.

Wendy paused beside him, finding that she could speak with surprising calm.

"It was Mr. Helgerson who climbed up to Cousin Marion's room last night," she said. "And I know what he took. Uncle Paul, will you come to the hotel with me right away and make him give it up? Perhaps he hasn't got rid of it yet. If he isn't stopped, we'll never know the truth about Cousin Gordon. Please, Uncle Paul!"

Her uncle stared at her in mild astonishment. "Oh, come now, Wendy—you're letting your imagination run away with you again."

Her calm was forsaking her. How could one ever make grown-ups understand these things that seemed perfectly clear?

"Don't you see?" she said urgently. "It was Mr. Helgerson who wore that pirate costume to the party last night. And afterward he came up here to get what he wanted from Cousin Marion's room. We've got to stop him—we've got to! Maybe he'll even get away from the island if we don't hurry."

"Now wait a minute," Uncle Paul said, losing a little of his usual patience. "In the first place these clothes aren't part of the costume Mrs. Mears made. This cloak and hat are the original garments I lent

her, and I must say I don't like the idea of their being carelessly worn, or dropped around outdoors.
So you see — ? "

Wendy did not want to see, and she could not
bear to waste any more precious time. She dared not
even ask for permission, so she said, " I'll be back
soon," over her shoulder and ran out the front door.

The lawn sloped downhill and she ran headlong in
the direction of the gate, startling Charlie Wong as
she went by. Nobody had opened the gate, so she
climbed up and over, dropping to the ground on the
other side. Her feet pounded across the pavement as
she ran in the direction of the steps. Only when she
reached the top step did she pause to keep from
plunging down that dangerously steep descent.

Then, just as she started down more slowly, she
saw a man far below come running up the few steps
from the hotel and hurry through its gate to the road.
It was Mr. Helgerson and he was in more of a rush
than Wendy had ever seen him before. She was too
far away to follow him and she checked her descent
to watch for the direction he might take. As she
stared at the quickly moving figure, she saw him
disappear into the opening of the long path that led
around the hillside, past Anita's house and out
above the catchment.

At once Wendy turned and ran along the higher
street. Her heart was pounding with excitement —
because now she knew how to head off Mr. Helgerson. The moment she reached the street she turned
toward the place where the upper end of the path
started down the hill. Behind her a car pulled up in
front of Villa Mimosa, and someone leaned out to
ask directions. Wendy had no time to be helpful and

polite. She fled toward the path without answering, even though she had the impression that someone back there was calling her name.

In her hurry, she found herself slipping and stumbling, with little regard for her own safety. All she knew was that she had to meet Mr. Helgerson head-on before he reached the Y in the path and made his escape ahead of her down the hill past the catchment. What she would do if they met in headlong collision she hadn't the faintest idea, and she could not stop to make a plan. If he was carrying the cone shell, then perhaps she could snatch it out of his hands before he knew she was there, and run off with it as fast as she could—get it into the hands of some grown-up like Uncle Paul or Bob Eagan. Once the shell was safe and she could match the bit of paper to it, everyone would stop their arguing and would believe in Mr. Helgerson's wickedness.

The sun blazed hot upon her bare head, but she paid no attention, any more than she paid attention to the roots that humped across her path trying to trip her, making her stumble. She could not see very far ahead because of wild hillside growth. Not until she reached the curve above the catchment would she know if she was in time. A big bush grew across the path at the turn and she flung herself around it in desperate haste, caught her foot in the hump of a stubborn root, and went sprawling across the path on her hands and knees. Even in the shock of the fall, she saw with an upsurge of relief that she would not have to fight this battle alone. Someone else had seen Mr. Helgerson and come after him—to stop him where the path swung above the steep slide of the catchment.

For a moment Wendy knelt where she had fallen, paying no attention to stinging hands and knees. She simply knelt there, panting, trying to get her breath, watching the furious struggle that had begun on the path ahead.

Bob Eagan was not going to let Mr. Helgerson get away. The two men were locked together, pummeling and grunting as each thudded blows into the other's body. Mr. Helgerson was not young, but he was thin and wiry. Bob Eagan was younger, but he was heavier and he could not move as fast, so the two were more evenly matched than Wendy liked to see. As they fought, something flew out of one man's hand and struck the path not far from where she knelt. She crawled over and snatched it up. It was the spotted cone shell, and she held on to it in triumph.

Now Bob Eagan was down and Mr. Helgerson was on top of him. As she watched in fright, Wendy realized that both men were rolling dangerously near the edge of the catchment. She jumped to her feet and began to scream warnings at them. In the fury of the struggle they paid no attention to her shouting and she saw that they were only inches away from the edge. Another turn might send them crashing down that immense rock slide in a fall that would kill them both.

Wendy closed her eyes in terror and screamed and screamed until a powerful hand came down upon her shoulder and shook her into silence. She opened her eyes to look up into Pop's bright blue gaze — and knew in astonished relief that the best fighter of them all had come miraculously upon the scene.

16

Secret of the Spotted Shell

WENDY remembered the car stopping on the road above, the voice calling her name. Only there was no time to express surprise or anything else.

"Stop them!" she shouted. "Stop them before they roll down the catchment."

Pop was already in action. She had forgotten how big he was, and how strong. In three quick strides he stood above the fighters, reaching to grab each one, holding them powerfully apart. When the two still struggled to get at each other, Pop gave them a rough shaking.

"Cut it out now!" he yelled. "Cut it out, or I'll pitch the both of you down that hill."

With Pop in command, the struggling ceased and the two men stood panting and glaring at each other, held apart by Pop's big hands.

"Now then," he said, "what's all this about? What do I do with the two of you?"

Wendy jumped about in wild excitement. "He's the bad one!" she shouted to her father, pointing at Mr. Helgerson. "Don't let him go!"

When Pop's hand dropped from Bob Eagan's collar, Bob stepped back angrily. "The little girl is right," he said. "Keep hold of that fellow. The police will want to talk to him."

Mr. Helgerson began to object futilely, still squirming in Pop's grip. "The s—s—seashell!" he sputtered. "Where is the shell?"

The shell, of course, Wendy thought, and stared at it in her hand. It took only a moment to pull the scrap of paper from her pocket. By now it was somewhat the worse for wear, but it curled easily into the shape of a cone, and when she folded it about the shell, it formed an exact cover. Carefully she turned the paper so that the place the edges met coincided with the shell's first fold. At once tiny letters showed up in the punched holes that ran diagonally around the paper.

Vaguely Wendy heard Bob's voice, thanking Pop for coming to the rescue. "If you'll hold onto him," he said, "I'll get to a telephone and call the police," and he started swiftly in the direction of the hotel.

Mr. Helgerson had gone limp, apparently understanding the language of Pop's hand, recognizing the uselessness of words. He stood without further struggle, watching Wendy as she studied the perforations.

At first Wendy began to spell the message out a little at a time, but she quickly found that wasn't necessary. Her eyes read the words easily as they ran around the shell, and as the stunning message they delivered came clear she flung herself upon her father.

"No—no! Let him go. We've caught the wrong one. Oh, Pop—don't let that Bob Eagan get away!"

She had the most wonderful father in the world.

He didn't stop to ask questions, or to reason things out as Uncle Paul would have done. He simply dropped Mr. Helgerson and took off along the path after Bob Eagan. Mr. Helgerson pulled himself together with a wry look at Wendy and followed at a trot. Wendy went after him, a little sick with shock over what the shell had told her.

In front of Mears Manor, Pop caught up with Bob Eagan. "You'd better stay right here," he said, "until we find out what this is all about."

From the corner of her eye Wendy saw Mark coming up the steps from the hotel level, and her heart sank. This would be awful for Mark.

Bob started to object, bluffing a little, yet clearly scared. Mr. Helgerson took a card from his pocket and showed it to Pop. This was a new Mr. Helgerson, his fussy tourist role completely discarded. The fight had left him bruised and disheveled, and one eye was beginning to close, but he was now in charge of the situation.

Pop looked at the card and nodded, but he was always one to be fair, and he wanted an explanation. "Let's get this straight," he told Mr. Helgerson. "What am I holding this fellow for?"

Mark had come close, and he added his voice indignantly to Pop's. "You'd better tell us what Bob has done!"

"I can tell you some of it," Mr. Helgerson agreed, and spoke directly to Bob. "Apparently someone took that pirate cloak and hat belonging to Mr. Guthrie and used them to masquerade in last night after the party was over. Mr. Guthrie phoned me early this morning to tell me so. I suppose you thought you'd be taken for me—is that it, Eagan?"

Bob Eagan admitted nothing. He grimaced unpleasantly and did not speak.

Mr. Helgerson went calmly on. "You went up to the Villa Mimosa knowing Mrs. Cole would be asleep, knowing how to get to her room without waking the house. You found the shell you were looking for in her room and brought it home. You found out what it said and knew that it was dangerous to you, as you'd expected."

This last wasn't so, and Wendy broke in excitedly. "He couldn't read it. Not without this paper to fold around it!" And she held up the perforated scrap.

Mr. Helgerson gave her a surprisingly pleasant smile. "I stand corrected. The result was the same, however, wasn't it, Eagan? You knew that the shell could give you away, so you had to get hold of it. Your mistake was in waiting in the hope that you could read the code yourself and find out what was known, instead of destroying the shell at once—as you destroyed the wrong one, when you had it. After Mr. Guthrie phoned to tell me what had happened at the Villa last night, I knew I had to watch you. So when you went out this morning, I followed. You were about to smash the shell and throw the pieces over the hillside, when I caught up with you."

Wendy listened in dismay. How stupid she had been—leaping to all those wrong notions, and not seeing the real clues that had been under her nose. It had not been Bob chasing Mr. Helgerson this morning, but the other way around. Just about all that Wendy Williams had done in this affair was to take the wrong side and mix everything up hopelessly.

"How can any of this be true?" Mark asked, looking miserable.

"Of course it's not true," Bob Eagan said.

But Bob was still bluffing, and they all knew it.

"You told me to get hold of that shell in order to protect Gordon," Mark accused him. "You told me—"

"It's no use, Mark," Mr. Helgerson broke in. "I'm sorry, my boy. He seems to have told a number of people things that were far from true. It's thanks to the ingenuity and curiosity of young Miss Wendy Williams that we've caught our man. Perhaps she has followed her heart a bit too enthusiastically down the wrong road some of the time, though I can't blame her for disliking the fussy tourist I had to pretend to be. I needed to come into this looking like something other than what I was."

He smiled again at Wendy and went on.

"When that shell with the message, 'Hurry,' was given to Gordon Cole in Saigon while he was there between flights, he consulted with the American authorities at once. Everyone thought that David Stockton was asking for rescue quickly. Efforts were made to get Dave out, but they failed. Gordon brought the shell home to St. Thomas, meaning to go back as soon as he could and look for Dave himself. It wasn't until he was in flight on the way back to Saigon that he began to wonder if there was something more to this shell than he first suspected."

Mr. Helgerson paused and looked around at the varying expressions of his audience. Bob Eagan was wilting by the moment, his cocky manner entirely gone.

"That was when Gordon took several separate

steps," Mr. Helgerson said. "He wrote to his wife to keep an eye on the shell and not let it out of her hands. He also wrote — mistakenly — to an old friend, Bob Eagan, and asked him to talk to Marion and see what they could make of the shell. If they found anything, they were to report to Washington. Of course the letter tipped Eagan off, and after that his one idea was to get hold of that shell and destroy any message it might contain. I think he must have been tipped off by his bosses as well, that Stockton had passed on secret information from North Vietnam by means of the shell."

Mark made a sound of disgust and impatience. "So that's why you kept after me to get the shell for you," he said to Bob. "That's why you sent me to the library for a book about ciphers, so you'd be ready once you had the shell!"

Bob Eagan could not meet Mark's eyes. He looked pale and shaken, his clothes still untidy from the fight, a streak of blood drying on one cheek.

"I'm glad it's over," he said unexpectedly.

Mr. Helgerson seemed to understand. "They had you over a barrel, didn't they — because of that old scrape you were mixed up in out in the Far East? They threatened exposure, I suppose? So you would be disgraced and lose your job. That's how a lot of reluctant agents are recruited. Something a man has done in the past puts him in jeopardy unless he goes along with what is wanted in the present. In other words, blackmail by the enemy. When a man is too weak to stand up to them — " he did not need to finish his words.

Mark turned his back on Bob. "But how would

Dave Stockton—out in Vietnam jungles—find out something that was going to happen in the Virgin Islands?"

"Maybe we'll never know exactly," Mr. Helgerson said. "But there are always worldwide links these days. There are those who move about constantly between Cuba and the mainland of China and North Vietnam. We can guess what might have happened. Maybe somebody who knew that Dave came from the Virgin Islands boasted in his hearing about what was going to happen in the way of sabotage in St. Thomas. Dave knew he had to get word out to someone he trusted, someone who would get the whole thing stopped in time. Maybe that was what the verbal message, 'Hurry,' really meant. Dave must have found a way of sending out a secret message by means of a Vietnamese who was on our side—using a shell that Gordon was sure to recognize."

Wendy burst in again. "That's exactly what he did!" She held out the shell to Mr. Helgerson, with the paper fitted about it.

He took it from her and studied the perforations with the tiny letters under them, nodding as he read.

"Here it is," he said. "He needed only four words: 'Eagan—traitor—danger—plot.' That would have been enough to alert Gordon. Fortunately for us, the sabotage plan was discovered in other ways and stopped. The thing we still needed to know was where the leak was so we could pick up the go-between through whom a lot of undercover business was being managed. When Gordon had his second thoughts about the shell, he alerted the U.S. au-

thorities in Saigon. They got in touch with us and I was sent here to find out what I could. We were already pretty sure that the danger spot existed somewhere close to the Villa Mimosa, so I checked in at Mears Manor. The only difficulty was that I managed to be seriously suspected by a young lady named Wendy Williams."

Wendy stared at the ground, aware that everyone was looking at her. It was Pop who broke the uncomfortable silence.

"I always knew I had a smart kid! She's got more brains than her old man any day! And that reminds me, Wendy—I got your letter and I've come to take you away from this place where they aren't treating you right. Maybe somebody else can take over with Eagan now, and you and me will go up to that big house and get things settled."

Mr. Helgerson threw Wendy a startled look, and then nodded at Pop. "Thanks for the rescue, Mr. Williams. I think you can let go of Eagan. This is an island, and there's no place he can run to."

When Pop let Bob go, Mark gave his uncle a disgusted look and spoke to Wendy. "I'm glad it wasn't Gordon," he said, and for a moment Wendy felt a little better. It was Gordon Cole who had been Mark's hero, far more than Bob had ever been.

But there was no time now to think about that. Pop was already on his way toward the long flight of steps leading up to the Villa and clearly expecting her to follow. She could only hurry after him and cling to one of his big hands, trying to slow him down.

"No, Pop—wait! I wasn't thinking when I wrote

that letter. I feel better about everything now. Pop—
wait!"

It was no use. As she knew very well from past
experience, when her father got a single idea in his
head he was apt to follow through at all costs. It
seemed that she had never gone up those steps so
fast. Pop was used to heights and to climbing. He
went straight up, the way he'd have walked at full
speed along a flat road. Anita came to her gate and
watched in surprise as they went by, and Wendy
could not even wave. One of these days she might
have a lot to tell Anita—but she could not tell her
now.

At the top of the hill the driveway gate stood open
and Pop stalked through it, taking Wendy with him
like the tail of a kite. Up the driveway they marched,
and Wendy's effort to make a brake of herself made
her feel like a puppy hanging onto a roaring lion. By
the time they reached the front door, Pop had
wrought himself up to a state of angry resentment
over injuries done his daughter.

Desperately Wendy thrust herself ahead of him
and pushed open the screen door. If it was possible,
she wanted to get away from her father and warn
Uncle Paul. The moment she was through the door,
however, she saw that the worst was about to happen. All her new family—Uncle Paul, Aunt Elinor,
Marion—were there in the room. Before Wendy
could gulp out a word, the three turned toward her
and she saw that they had been grouped around the
telephone. Surprisingly, their faces were alight with
a joy she had never seen in them before.

Marion moved first. She flew across the room, and

caught Wendy in her arms, hugging her, crying and laughing at the same time.

"We've just had a phone call from Gordon!" she cried. "He's in a hospital in Saigon, but he's all right. Wendy — he's coming home! He went into the jungle and brought Dave out, and they'll both be all right!"

Wendy hugged Marion back, laughing and crying too, almost forgetting about her father. Almost, but not quite. Pop himself saw to that. She heard his voice crashing through this new happiness.

"I'm Wendy's father, and let me tell you right now — "

He got no farther, because at once Uncle Paul crossed the room to shake him vigorously by the hand. To Wendy's astonishment she found that Uncle Paul could speak almost as loudly as her father.

"That's wonderful!" he was shouting. "It's great that you're here! You couldn't have come at a better time. We've just had word that our daughter's husband is alive and well. Come in, come in and meet the rest of Wendy's family."

Somehow Pop found himself shaking hands in bewilderment, first with frail little Aunt Elinor, who was hopping about on her single crutch as Wendy had never seen her do. Then — not shaking hands with Marion — but being hugged by her, much to his further astonishment.

"How lovely to meet Wendy's father!" Marion cried, and went up on tiptoe to kiss his rough cheek.

After all the thumping of backs, the fluttering, and the cries of joy, the excitement died out, and everyone sat down and was remarkably quiet for a few

minutes—perhaps because they needed to catch
their breaths before the next outburst of wonder and
joy. Into this moment of quiet Pop spoke, and though
he now brought his voice down to a reasonable
pitch, he said what he had come to say. Not all the
excitement, or the huggings, or back-thumpings had
switched him from his track. He had been slowed
down for a few minutes, but now he was moving full
speed ahead to crash into his daughter's life.

"Wendy wrote me about not being happy here.
So I've come to take her away. She doesn't need to
stay with anybody who doesn't treat her right and
doesn't want her around."

There was a stunned silence, and Wendy could
meet no one's eyes. All she wanted was for a large
hole to open in the floor at her feet so that she could
disappear into it and never be seen again.

Uncle Paul managed to speak at last, gravely and
a little sadly. "Is this true, Wendy—that you're unhappy here? That you feel we haven't treated you
well?"

Pop gave her no chance to answer. "I've got
Wendy's letter right here. I'll tell you what she wrote
me."

"Wait a moment," said Uncle Paul, and there was
a note in his voice that stopped Pop from reading
that awful letter. "Whatever Wendy may have written," he went on, "the thing that matters is how she
feels now. Do you want to stay here with us, Wendy
—or would you prefer to go away?"

Wendy stared helplessly at her uncle and could
not speak at all. It would be so easy to say, "Please
let me stay. I don't want to be sent away," but she
could not speak the words. It had never been settled

whether or not she was to stay and she did not want to thrust herself upon anyone. She had done a lot of foolish things since she had come here—writing that letter was only one of them—and she had some of her father's pride. She did not want to stay where she wasn't really wanted.

Pop stood up. "There!" he said. "That's your answer. Go pack your things, Wendy, and we'll catch the next plane out of here. I can't take much time off my job, and we've got to move fast."

But however fast he planned to move, Marion moved faster. Before Wendy could take a single miserable step toward the stairs, Marion jumped up and ran to Wendy's father. She looked very small and slight—like something he could have brushed aside with one hand, but she had no fear of him. Her violet eyes were snapping with spirit, and she was very nearly as angry as Pop.

"I never heard anything so ridiculous in all my life!" she cried. "I don't think it's up to Wendy at all. I don't care what sort of letters she writes when she's unhappy. Lots of people—including me!—don't behave well when things are going wrong. But I won't let Wendy out of this house for anything. I want her here. I need a daughter exactly like Wendy, and I hope she'll give me another chance to show her I can be a better sort of mother than I've been up to this time. Even if she *wants* to go—I won't have it!"

Pop seemed to wilt before the attack of this small, furious person. He seemed to shrink helplessly, uncomfortably, and now it was to his daughter that he looked for help.

Wendy found her voice. "Five minutes after I

wrote that letter I—I didn't mean any of it," she faltered. Her voice sounded faint in her ears, but it strengthened as she went on. "I love being here. Everyone has been good to me—and I want to stay. It's not your fault, Pop—you couldn't know how stupid I was being."

For a moment her father's face worked in further bewilderment, as though he struggled with several contrary emotions at the same time. Then Marion held out welcoming arms and Wendy flew into them. Uncle Paul saved the awkward moment for Pop.

"There—that's settled as it should be. And now, surely, Mr. Williams, you can stay with us till an afternoon plane. Wendy hasn't had breakfast yet, so perhaps you'll join her."

After that they all found themselves sitting around the small table in the breakfast room. Pop's plate was heaped with pancakes and sausage, while Uncle Paul talked to him about the days when he had worked his way through college by taking construction jobs in the summertime. He had never worked on anything so big and important as a bridge, he assured Pop, but it was the sort of thing that was good for a young fellow and got his head out of books for a while.

Wendy, for one of the rare times in her life, had no appetite. How could anyone think about food with all this excitement? Thoughts of all these remarkable happenings churned around inside her. So she sat at the table, pretending to nibble, while she watched her family—all her family, including Pop. What nice people they were. It didn't make any difference that Pop worked on a bridge—these were good people and they were being kind to one another. Pop was one of them, and he was kind too.

After breakfast Uncle Paul took Pop out to show him the garden and introduce him to Charlie Wong. Aunt Elinor kissed Wendy on the cheek and went upstairs to rest. Only Marion stayed at the table.

"Someone took the cone shell last night, didn't they?" she said when the others had gone.

Wendy nodded. "I can tell you about it. Everything's all right now. All right for everyone but Bob Eagan. You don't have to worry about Cousin Gordon any more."

"I never did, really," Marion said. "But never mind the shell. Come and help me write a letter to Gordon. I want it to go aboard the next plane."

"I—I'm not very good at letter writing," Wendy said sheepishly.

Marion jumped up and drew her away from the table. "And I'm not very good about a lot of things. I never knew before what courage was all about. I never knew how to fight for my life. Fight in the right way, I mean. Come help me with the letter, Wendy. We need to work at this together, don't we?"

As they walked toward the stairs with their arms linked, a breeze blew its flowery scent through the house, and Wendy took a deep, satisfying breath. The island belonged to her now, and she belonged to the island. After a while, when Marion's letter was written, she would go down the hill to find Anita and she would tell her all the things that had happened this morning. Afterward she would bring Anita up the hill to meet Pop. Not every girl had a father so big, so handsome, so loving as she had. She could hardly wait to show him off to her friend.

Note from the Author

WHEN I ARRIVED on St. Thomas in the Virgin Islands to gather material for new books, one of the first places I visited was the Public Library. It was fun to walk in and find several jackets of my books on display to greet me. A young library page, Joanne Reese, was "loaned" to me for my visit, and we went around the island together several times during my stay. She was especially helpful when it came to giving me a glimpse of what life in the Virgin Islands is like for the children who live there. She told me about her school and about the things she liked to do; her friendly company made my stay very pleasant.

One afternoon I was invited to a party in the Children's Room of the library. There had been a summer reading contest going on, and those who had read the greatest number of books were to receive awards. When the program was over and the prizes had been given, Mrs. Beulah Harrigan, the children's librarian, announced that she had one last award to make. Since prizes had been given to readers, she and the young people thought it would be nice to give a prize to a favorite author as well. I will always remember how pleased and touched I felt when she called me up to accept my prize — and how delighted I was when I unwrapped my appropriate gift. I had been given a little ceramic figure of a boy and a girl poring over a storybook together. Their heads were bent, their faces rapt, as they shared the story they were reading.

That piece still sits on my desk, reminding me of the lovely time I spent in the Virgin Islands, and it is also a reminder for me of young readers who follow my books. When I look at those small, absorbed faces in the china figure, I know I must try to tell a story so well that real readers will pore over the pages of my books in the same way.